BETWEEN THE SHADE AND THE SHADOW

COLEMAN ALEXANDER

THE REALMLESS, LLC

COPYRIGHT

BETWEEN THE SHADE AND THE SHADOW

COLEMAN ALEXANDER

Cover art by Keira Nagali, 99 Designs

❀ Created with Vellum

DEDICATION

To my wife for all the lost mornings

And to my son, who hopefully conforms to his own story

PROLOGUE

SHADOW

Midnight had come and gone and Ahraia still hadn't found a shadow. If she didn't find one soon, she was dead.

Her hair stuck to her face even in the bitter cold and though the sky was clear and overflowing with stars, a fine dusting of snow spun from the treetops with the gusting wind. The branches swayed and shifted. The light of the moons danced dangerously across the ground. But it was a lifeless dance—the woods were desolate. Deserted.

Dead, Ahraia thought. *Like I'm going to be.*

The lightrise was coming.

Cold sweat froze upon her neck and mixed with her rising dread, sending shivers through her spine with every step. She shuddered to think what awaited her if she dared return home to the darkening without a shadow: condemnation to the shadow woods, where the Shad-Mon lurked.

Even dying beneath the blistering light of the Dae-Mon would be better than that.

She tried to push the thought aside, but her hope was fading. Even if she managed to find a shadow, she still had to bond it and bind it and that took time—time that had already slipped past her like the moons through the night sky.

How could I have failed? she thought.

Her mother had never told her what to do if she didn't find a shadow—no one even mentioned it as a possibility. Even the weakest spritelings found *something* to bind. It was as if every shadow in the forest had sensed her and fled.

Her thin boots crunched over the frozen ground. She brushed the frost-tinged strands of hair from her face and blew out a hard breath; the air fogged before her, a portent of her fate to come.

Maybe if I just keep running . . . maybe if I find a dark hollow and hide . . .

She wondered if her mother would send the wards after her. Would they hunt her down? Would they drag her back to Daispar to condemn her? Or would they assume that the light had taken her?

Maybe if I just leave the forest . . .

No. That was impossible. No sprite left the safety of the deep roots and dark hollows. No one risked walking beneath the bright fire in the dead of day.

Ahraia ran on, lost in worry until she noticed the forest ahead was growing brighter—not deadly, like the first hint of the Dae-Mon creeping over the horizon, nor sharp like the flicker of a lightwalker's angry flame. But luminous. Incandescent. Broad and expansive and ominously so. She shivered, her ears standing on end in nervous anticipation.

The Endless Plains.

She squinted. The snow glowed painfully white. The last silhouettes of the forest stood judging her, their eaves crossed disapprovingly. She ducked beneath them, feeling both daring and afraid, flitting from one tree to the next, until at last, she stood under the very last tree, at the edge of the woods.

Her breath caught in her throat.

The Endless Plain stretched before her into nothingness, extending beyond thought or reason as the light of the Bright Moon burned overhead. The night sky was dim and the stars were withdrawn. They seemed shy and fitful in the brilliance of their mother. The Blood Moon rested behind her round face, watchful, as ever.

Ahraia marveled at the great expanse. How could a land be so barren and free? How could it be without cover? She had never stood so near to it—so *dangerously* close. She wondered what it would be like to run across such open lands.

I should be looking for a shadow, she thought.

She shivered, imagining what the unhindered light might feel like on her skin: bright and boundless, painfully sweet and soft. The grasses rose above the thin snow and ruffled in the gusting wind, uncaring of the coming morning. She yearned to feel like that, to run amongst them, to run without a care and laugh with the rolling downs.

The wind danced before her.

Come with me, it seemed to say, tugging at her mind. Her cloak whipped outward, the veins of the eaves-web glimmering indecently, chasing the wind onto the plains.

"That's forbidden," she murmured back. *I have to keep looking.*

She meant to turn away. But her feet didn't move.

Her mind wouldn't let them.

Instead, she stood perfectly still, captivated, as her eyes adjusted to the brilliant landscape. Running beneath the moonlight would mark her. And if she was caught afield when the Dae-Mon rose, discovered by day's light, it would mean death of another sorts. Trapped. Burned. Blistered by the Dae-Mon.

What's worse—dying condemned or dying afire?

Her answer came easily; the wind was calling her. It turned about her and pulled her white hair across her face, tickling at her cheek.

Come with me, it seemed to say. *Run with me.*

She took a step, and then felt her worry wrench her to a stop. *There aren't any shadows out there.*

Come with me, she heard again.

For the first time in her life, Ahraia stepped out of the forest.

The moonlight prickled perilously on her pale skin. She looked down. Her skin wasn't pale—it was gray, ashen. It was gray like the Bright Moon was white, as ashen as the fallen aspen leaf. Her markings emerged on her wrists, revealed as the faintest speckling. Her hair was a mixture of the Bright Moon and her skin: a translucent sheet of silver that shimmered against the stars and played amongst their light. It was bright. She grinned.

And her mother said bright was a bad thing.

She giggled and took another step. She unsquinted her eyes. More light. She laughed. The wind stirred beneath her, pulling at her heart. She took another step, and then another.

And then she began to run, her fear falling about her feet as she let herself race with the wind, unhindered by the dark and tumble of the forest. She laughed and delighted beneath the forbidden light. Nothing else in life compared. She ran like she had never run before, time slipping by until her lungs burned like a brilliant and terrible fire. The moons stared down on her and still Ahraia ran.

When she finally stopped, the forest extended as a distant black line behind. Her hair settled around her in a halo of cold light and she breathed in great, puffing breaths beside a dark pool. The waters formed a rippling reflection of the night above. Ahraia stopped to drink and looked down at her reflection as the wind calmed. The markings on her face and neck showed too now, veins of silver-red seeping across her skin—the markings of the moonlight. She had never seen them so sharply. For a moment, her simmering fear returned.

Unnatural. Unwanted. Unwelcome.

Those were the thoughts her mother would use. No decent sprite would let herself be scarred so plainly. None but the dae-wards who roamed on the fringes of daylight were marked like this.

And none of the other spritelings would run across the Endless Plains, a rebellious part of her thought. She laughed at the audacity of it. She would be dead with the lightrise. Why shouldn't she laugh at her markings? Her mother would never even know.

And then laughter echoed from across the pool, quiet but unmistakable.

A shadow?

Ahraia looked up and there stood a dark shape silhouetted against the white snow of the plains. It stared back at her, smiling.

A flush of excitement ran through her.

A shadow.

How had she not noticed it? Had it been running with her the whole time? Ahraia smiled, aware of how unlikely it was—a shadow, here, where there were no shadows to be found.

Of course you find shadow where there's light, she thought.

She reached out with her mind and discovered she already recognized the shadow. She had felt its presence the very first time she had seen the Endless Plains. This was one of their keepers—and it had been waiting for her. Ahraia smiled.

The shadow smiled back.

Its fur was light like her skin, light but not pale—gray, ashen. It was gray like the night was sometimes black, as ashen as the charcoal of the fire pits, shimmering under the light of the stars. Around its large ears, its coloring was darker, a mixture of its fur and the night.

Ahraia walked silently around the pool, her eyes fixed on the shadow. It stood and watched her, its long tail swishing restlessly in the night. Ahraia paused, her ears quivering. She tried to remember everything she had been told about bonding and binding a shadow, but all she could focus on was how beautiful it was. It stood almost as tall as she, even though it prowled on four legs. Its eyes shone yellow, like her own.

As she neared it, she giggled again, nervously.

She reached out to cast the bond, but found the connection was already formed. How long had it been there? She didn't know, but it was perfect.

She stood before it for a long moment and then reached out with a gray, light-scarred hand to touch its black nose. It was wet and warm and she laughed. The shadow licked at her hands, a warm and rough embrace, the type a shadow makes. Ahraia kissed it on its forehead.

"So you are my shadow?" she asked in a whisper as she ran her fingers through a big clump of fur behind its ears.

The young wolf nuzzled her in silent agreement.

"And I am your shade," Ahraia said.

Ahraia walked with her hand grasped firmly in the fur of her newly-found shadow, hoping it wouldn't slip away. It walked next to her with steady, rolling strides, but doubt was creeping into her wolf's mind as they returned to the safety of the woods.

What will I call you? Ahraia thought, hoping to distract it from its worries, wondering if she had bound it as she should have—a proper binding as her mother called it. They had spent the last hour of the night running after the moons and chasing after the wind. They had dashed light-footed over half-frozen streams, leaping over ice that was far too thin to hold them, while laughing at the thrill of it. They had startled a herd of keress, the great elk of the plains and Ahraia's shadow had howled with glee, causing the beasts to bray and stomp and shake their antlers all the more.

But now the morning approached, and they both were growing wary. The Bright Moon had joined the Dark Moon beneath the horizon, and only the Blood Moon remained just above the hilltops. It was an ominous time to be out.

"Do wolves have names?" Ahraia murmured aloud.

The wolf's thoughts burned like dim flames, ill-conceived beyond instinct. Her shadow's ears tucked back nervously. She was thinking of the plains and the moons and her pack.

We tell stories about the moons, Ahraia conveyed, making her thoughts known to the wolf. *They were wolves once, like you, sisters who roamed the plains. My people tell the story of the Blood Wolf and the Dark Wolf, but my favorite is the story of the Bright Wolf.* Ahraia ran her finger's through her wolf's fur, knowing how unspritish that was to admit. The Blood Moon and Dark Moon were smaller and slower—they didn't burn like the Bright Moon. Her shadow didn't care. Her ears stood straighter; she was listening.

The Bright Wolf was the strongest wolf to ever walk the lands," Ahraia thought to her wolf. "*Losna was her name, and it was known from Everdark to Everlight. But one day, Losna's mother was killed by the Dae-Mon. So bitter and angry was she that she leapt into the sky to chase after the Dae-Mon. Losna became the Bright Moon, the Masah, the great hunter of the night. Now she spends her night ruling over the world and her days chasing the Dae-Mon. That is why the wolves call for her. Because they love her. And they miss her.*

Ahraia let her mind fall into silence. They walked for a time, dodging between slivers of moonlight that fell to the forest floor.

Losna, her shadow thought.

"I will call you Losna." The name rolled off Ahraia's tongue and rumbled in her heart. She nodded, as though it was decided. "It's a good name," she said, running her fingers through her shadow's fur. *You called me, didn't you? It wasn't the wind. It was your thoughts carried on the wind.*

She felt her shadow warm next to her.

But how could you call me if you don't speak?

Ahraia lowered herself deeper into the enchantment, trying to sense what the wolf was feeling.

Wary.

It wasn't so much a word as it was an emotion, imperceptible except as a vague feeling. It was the wolf's state of being. *Losna's state of being*, Ahraia thought, the name tugging their link tighter.

The Dae-Mon lurked just below the horizon and gray light tinged the snowy land. Ahraia's skin burned but she didn't dare hurry—her only concern was keeping Losna tight to her body and mind. She found the tread of a familiar path and they followed it deeper into the woods, the world around them growing steadily brighter, until at last, she saw the tightly laced wall of trees ahead. The Darkening. She breathed out a sigh of relief.

Daispar.

Danger? Losna bristled.

Ahraia flinched. The thought pierced their bond, sudden and raw —nothing like the conveyance she was accustomed to. When sprites like her mother or father made their thoughts known, their conveyance was articulate and clear. This was instinct—less a thought than a bare emotion; it was only Ahraia's own mind that teased it into coherence. Yet the feeling was lucid and pure as the darkest night, fierce and sharp as the winter wind.

Losna sniffed at the air and hesitated, staring at the wall before them.

Home, Ahraia conveyed, reaching inside herself as she tried to conjure the emotion of the dark safety awaiting inside. The darkening was the village–the sprawling tree that formed a massive shelter inside the forest, keeping out the day's light.

Our darkening . . . our den. She breathed out, stilling her fears so that her shadow could feel the reassurance of her emotions.

Losna lowered her head and sniffed before continuing closer, never letting her eyes drift from the trees ahead, where the snow clung in white, half-drawn layers across the deep forest.

Ahraia bound the branches of the darkening's wall in enchantment; they were stiff with cold, frozen and sleepy.

Open, she thought, rousing them, helping them know how they needed to move. The branches shifted, causing snow to tumble to the ground in soft thumps as a narrow closure formed in the side of the darkening.

A pulse of fear emitted from Losna as the wall moved. But it wasn't fear of the dark or the cold: it came from knowing that dark things—creatures of the night—lurked inside. She growled at the pitch-black maw, ready to run. Ahraia dug her fingers into Losna's fur.

It's okay, she thought, tense as though the Dae-Mon had fully risen. *It's safe. Come. I will protect you.*

Relaxing her grip, Ahraia let her mind envelop the feeling of safety. *This is home.* She stepped inside, waiting to see if Losna followed her into the darkness.

She sensed the darkening waiting for her, full of sprites and spritelings, shades and shadows. They surrounded her, their wraith-like eyes showing with night-gleam. The shift of feet and a flutter of wings broke the silence. Her ears turned at a whispered voice and the wicked laughter that followed. After a moment, a thought came out of the perfect dark.

Are you a shade now? Where is your shadow? What happened to your skin? It was her mother's conveyance, the Astra of the darkening.

A hush spread nervously through the others.

Ahraia had forgotten about her markings. She held her breath and waited. The darkening tree above kept all light from penetrating, keeping it night even as the day swelled lethally outside.

Did you fail to bind a shadow? Her mother conveyed, her anger bristled beneath her words. Gavea and Tallin, two shades with imps for shadows, leered at Ahraia.

Losna? I need you, Ahraia conveyed, trembling. She could feel Losna as though they stood beside one another, even with the darkening wall separating them. Her shadow was thinking of fleeing, back to her pack and the plains. Unease grew within the darkening. Her mother's judgment twined with the sickening excitement of what her failure would mean to the others.

The moment stretched on for an eternity.

Please. I'll run with you. I'll keep you safe.

Ahraia could feel Losna's decision solidify around her promise. A shape stalked through the closure: a hulking, wolfish silhouette formed and then Ahraia felt coarse fur and the press of a warm, wet nose. She smiled, her ears batting in relief. Low muttering both spoken and conveyed billowed through the darkening. The branches of the closure intertwined again, closing out all the dawn's creeping light. Her eyes prickled in momentary blindness.

A wolf? Her mother conveyed, her shock rising above the collective disbelief of the rest. *Do you realize what you have done? Do you have any idea?*

Ahraia's eyes adjusted to see Kren, her older sister, staring at Losna with unabashed jubilance. Her own shadow, Flit, was perched proudly on her shoulder. Flit's great owl-eyes beamed at Ahraia. Gavea and Tallin were staring jealously, but a smile spread across Ahraia's mother's face.

"You will bring darkness to the Gelesh," she said aloud. "You will be the Astra one day."

A shiver of triumph and terror erupted in Ahraia's chest. She had never heard her mother's voice before.

1

THE DARKENING

Ahraia's mother knelt before her, a summer breeze rustling the silver-white hairs that had escaped her tarry-vine.

"Do you know the *true* purpose of our shadows?"

Ahraia used Losna to steady herself, clutching tightly to the thick clump of fur at her neck.

To guide us as shades? she conveyed. Her eyes and ears tipped down as tears dripped over her cheeks.

Three years had passed since she returned from binding Losna, and, since that day, she had heard her mother's voice many times—but this would be the last.

Fog swirled from the opposite bank, spilling out over the waters of the Winnowlin and hiding the stars above. Her mother's cheek bled from the Posturant's cut, her mark of defeat.

Her mark of condemnation.

If she was nervous, she didn't show it. Her stark-white eyes were fixed on Ahraia, her ears upright and face a veil of calm. Ahraia's own lip quivered, and she couldn't help as a stricken sob escaped.

Stop that, her mother conveyed. Golden veins darkened across her eyes, like tendrils of clouds crawling across the Bright Moon. *It shows weakness. And you of all shades can't show weakness.*

Ahraia dragged a light-scarred hand across her face and sniffed hard. Losna nuzzled her, her tongue scratching across her wrist.

That's better. Her mother wiped the remaining damp from her cheek, ignoring her own bloodied face.

"The true purpose of a shadow is not to guide the shade—but to make a sprite of her. Our shadows are a measure of us. They choose us as spritelings, when we are weak and naïve, grown of soft roots—and they leave us as sprites, hardened and sharp, cut from stone. But it's what lies *between* that makes us who we are."

Ahraia leaned closer to Losna. They stood across the river from the Shadow Woods, surrounded by the other sprites, shades, and spritelings of Daispar. Kren stood next to her, along with the rest of their nit. Her older sister's fingers crept briefly into her hand, squeezing her for courage.

Her father, Beran, stood next to the new Astra who stared triumphantly at their whole nit, her perfectly pale face twisted into a sneer. Her belly already bore the first signs of a spriteling—her father's new brood. Ahraia's mother either didn't notice or didn't care. She was knelt down in front of Ahraia, as though they were alone in the deep hollows of the forest.

"Between the shade and the shadow lies a bond. Two minds intertwined. Two hearts beating as one. Two creatures who breathe and bleed together. And the stronger the shadow, the stronger the bond—the stronger the bond, the stronger the sprite that emerges."

Ahraia flinched as a tree creaked towards the water, enchanted against its will by a dozen sprites. Its trunk groaned from the strain, settling just above the rushing current, branches and leaves gurgling in the river. Her mother ignored it.

"Wolves have ever been the most revered among us. Like us, they're ruled by the strongest, with no heart for the weak. Losna marks you, as the light marks you. But unlike the light"—her mother paused, took her hands and turned them, so her scars were hidden—"Losna marks you for greatness. She marks the strength within you."

She locked eyes with Ahraia and conveyed the next so softly that no one but Ahraia was privy to her thoughts. Y*ou will be an Astra one day. Perhaps even the Masai of the whole Silh.*

Ahraia's heart fluttered nervously. She sniffed and tried to straighten up, holding her ears a little straighter and her chin a little higher.

"Sister . . ." the Astra said with an edge to her voice. The drain was still poised in her hand, the narrow blade held away tensely, as though the fight might recommence at any moment.

"Since the first nights of the Silh, there have only been a handful of wolf binders." Her mother ran a hand through Losna's fur, but her conveyance played softly beneath her words. *To every Astra across the Silh—to even the Masai—you are a threat. They see you as I see you: a force that will one day rise to condemn any one of them over a similar bridge.*

The fog curled out of the Shadow Woods, engulfing the far end of the bridging tree. Ahraia swallowed nervously. Her mother glanced towards the tree before her gaze slid past the Astra.

You must be wary, she conveyed.

The Astra took a step forward. "Behra . . . it's time."

A tear ran unchecked past Ahraia's cheek. Ahraia's mother reached forward and pressed down on it with her thumb, as though she could squash the emotion from Ahraia.

"Understand this." *The Astrael . . . the Masai, they are no threat to you, not yet anyway. They are but a ripple from a stone that hasn't even been cast yet.* She fixed Ahraia with a hard stare. "The greatest threat to you is you. If you can't send Losna back to the forest when the times comes, then it will be you walking across this bridge."

"Behra," the Astra said, her voice cutting with impatience.

Ahraia's mother stood up, pursing her lips. She nodded once to Ahraia and then turned to Kren. She reached inside of her cloak and removed a dark orb, with a dangerous slit of muted light showing out. The orb was small, fitting just inside her fist, and was in the shape of a seed. She passed it to Kren.

"You're in charge of the nit now," she said, patting the top of Kren's hand once.

Kren nodded bravely, remaining hard-eyed and stoic.

Then their mother leapt up the bank, clambering onto the trunk of the bridging tree. She stood above the sprites and her gaze found Ahraia's father, but he wouldn't meet her eye. Ahraia could only guess what was conveyed, but her father shuddered, and the new Astra watched on with a faltering smile, her hand resting on the curve of her belly.

"Look after my darkening, sister," her mother said. Then she turned and crossed the river. The fog and mist swirled about her as she reached the far bank and leapt to the moss-covered Shadow Woods.

"Unbind the tree!" the Astra called.

The enchantment lifted and the bridge sprang back, spraying water across the forest with a wild rush of leaves. Fog billowed about her mother.

"Don't drink the water. Don't touch the trees. Don't make a noise . . ." Kren whispered over and over.

Then every sprite in the darkening knelt in ritual to drink from the river, Ahraia's father and the Astra among them. The touch of their lips to the water elicited a distant but menacing roar from the heart of the forest.

The Shad-Mon.

Fresh tears streamed down Ahraia's face. Her mother stood on the far bank and met her eyes.

Don't let your shadow cast you into the light, she conveyed. Then she turned and disappeared into the woods.

No! Ahraia thought helplessly.

Losna whined and shifted on her paws. In no time at all, a horrible, guttural roar rose from the woods. Losna howled and Ahraia screamed in despair, but the roar of the Shad-Mon drowned out both, echoing on without escape.

~

Ahraia awoke with a start.

Ringing silence replaced the roar, but her heart pounded in her ears. A deep sense of unease lay over her and a stab of loneliness constricted her throat. It took a moment to realize that the warm fur beneath her head and the gentle breathing beside her was her shadow's.

Losna raised her head, awake. *You dreamt of it again, didn't you?*

Ahraia laid her head back down, comforted by Losna's presence. Yet the memory of her mother's death remained and an unsettling fear still festered in her mind, lingering just beneath the surface.

"It's getting worse," she said. "And if it isn't her, it's me in the Shadow Woods . . ." Her voice came out hoarse and timorous. She shifted to conveyance, uncomfortable with the unwelcome noise. *Creaking trees and drifting fog, and that roar . . .*

A low growl reverberated in the depths of Losna's chest.

It's been ever since you started tending the nit tree . . .

Ahraia sighed. She didn't need a reminder of Kren's departure. The emptiness of their nit stung the air, like the breath of winter's first nights, biting and bitter.

"Someone has to look after the rest of the nit." She sat up and noticed a faint glimmer broke the perfect dark. Beyond their shade tree was her family's nit tree, and beyond that, the darkening. But a hint of light snuck through from the west. Dusk was coming.

She stood up and Losna raised her head from her paws.

"Come on," Ahraia said, "we're late."

Losna rolled to her feet and shook her fur. Ahraia folded back the branches of the shade tree and headed into the nit with her shadow close behind.

"Hayvon! Wake up already," Ahraia hissed, peering into the pure black of her brother's shade tree. The scent of deerskins permeated the interior, keeping back the light that his haphazard folding couldn't.

A figure rolled over and something scampered across the floor of the shade tree. Losna's ears twitched and her eyes gleamed. She pushed up next to Ahraia and sniffed at the dark interior. *Vesta?* she thought, looking for Hayvon's marten. A thin sliver of dull light streaked past her onto the floor of the shade tree.

"Ahraia, is that you?" Hayvon mumbled. "What are you doing up already?"

At the sound of Hayvon's voice, Losna pushed past Ahraia and into the shelter.

"Losna—no. Hey! Get out of here," Ahraia heard, only able to see her shadow's tail wagging in the streak of dimness. "Is it still light out?" Hayvon asked incredulously.

"It's almost night," Ahraia said, lowering the branches back. "Get up. Kren's test starts anytime now."

A sigh escaped from inside the shade tree.

"It's still dusk," Hayvon said, nonplussed.

"So . . .?"

"So you shouldn't be up. *We* shouldn't be up . . . besides, once night falls we're not allowed anywhere near the Makers."

"I know," Ahraia smiled. "That's why we're going to leave *before* nightfall. Come on."

She pushed the branches of his shade tree back to reveal the last vestiges of the lingering day. Hayvon wrestled Losna aside and stared out, squinting against the barely perceptible light.

Losna sniffed at him, nuzzling at his pockets, her tail wagging. *Vesta?* she thought again, snorting and stomping about him in search of his shadow. Hayvon pushed her away and stared past Ahraia.

"It is *not* dusk. It's still full light out. Are you crazy?"

Ahraia looked behind her.

Daispar was murky black with the barest hint of where the Dae-Mon might linger in the west—as light as it ever got beneath the tightly woven darkening trees. No sprites would be up and about yet. Like Hayvon, they would still be underdaeing beneath their shade trees.

"Does the ward not turn his face to the light to provide dark for the sprite?" she said with half a smile.

Hayvon scoffed. "I'm no ward, and you're certainly not a sprite."

"Well, do you want to see Kren's test or not?" Ahraia asked, growing impatient.

"Not if I have to burn my skin off trying."

"Fine." *Come on, Losna.*

With a last snuffle towards Hayvon's cloak, Losna emerged. Ahraia let the branches fall back and turned toward their nit, irritated with Hayvon.

She noticed movement and stiffened. The branches of Altah's shade tree peeled back, followed by a dark flutter of wings. A moment later, her older brother emerged with a small carry-sack over his shoulder. He stopped when he saw Ahraia. His shadow, Mehra, a dark, silver-tipped raven circled and settled on his shoulder. She croaked quietly.

"What are you doing up?" Ahraia asked warily.

Altah fished a light-veil from his travel sack, his ears turning down and tucking in.

"I'd ask the same, but I imagine I already know." *You're trying to see Kren's test.*

He wrapped the veil carefully over his nose and mouth, so that only his moon-white eyes shown out below his silver-white hair. He brought his hood around both, then lifted his eyebrows.

"Am I right?"

Ahraia ignored his conveyance. She eyed his light-veil. "I thought we aren't supposed to leave the darkening."

"*We* aren't," Altah said flatly. "Kaval and I are heading to the Stone Tree to await an emissary from Angolor." *Father's orders.*

"From Angolor?" Ahraia said in surprise. "A match for Kren?"

Angolor was the central darkening of the whole Silh, and a world apart from the Gelesh. It was ruled by the Masai, the Astra of all the other Astrael, and was a long and perilous journey from Daispar, around the plains and past the human realm to the south. Ahraia couldn't remember an emissary ever coming—and certainly not for a simple match.

"You don't think they mean to uproot her?" Ahraia asked, unsettled at the notion. "I've heard the Masai takes every daughter she can." She scowled. Daughters folded and kept the darkness of the darkening; they weren't meant to be traded away like dae-wards.

"Maybe." Altah shrugged. "Maybe they've come regarding the trouble in the West Vales with the lightwalkers. It might have nothing to do with Kren. Father didn't say."

Ahraia had heard rumors about the West Vales. Daispar buzzed with stories of the humans seizing the deep valleys towards the west. She furrowed her brow.

Kaval glanced about warily. His next words were conveyed conspiratorially. *There are whispers that the Masai thinks it started here, in Daispar . . . on the Astra's watch.* He gave Ahraia a meaningful look.

How could you know that? Ahraia conveyed, eyes narrowing. "That's absurd." As much as she disliked the Astra, along with the rest of her siblings, she couldn't come to imagine that the Masai would trouble herself with happenings in Daispar or the Gelesh.

Altah's ears tucked back. *It's true. I heard it from one of the dae-wards . . .*

"The dae-wards couldn't tell the stars from a forest full of fireflies," Ahraia said. "I can't imagine an emissary coming all this way, just for that."

Altah shrugged, clearly put off that she wasn't convinced. His voice turned peevish.

"And *I* can't imagine what would drive you into the light this early . . ." *Without a veil, even.*

"You and Kaval are going out—"

"Kaval and I are both going to be dae-wards," he said, cutting her off. "We don't have a choice but to walk the fringes of the night and the deep shadows of the day. But you . . ." *Light-scarred and star-brushed.* "It's unbecoming . . ."

Just then Kaval's shade tree rustled and Ahraia's oldest brother emerged with his light-veil hanging under his chin. His shadow, a fox named Reyn, trotted after him but veered straight for Losna. Reyn dipped his head and nuzzled beneath her chin in greeting while Losna licked at his ears.

Altah was still glaring at Ahraia reproachfully.

"Well, don't get caught. It's bad enough that you look like daeward already." He stalked off, leaving Kaval and Ahraia standing awkwardly in silence.

Another shade tree swished open, and Kyah peeked out.

"What's happening?" she asked, bleary-eyed. Her own fox, hardly more than a pup, peeked from under her elbow.

"Go back to sleep," Ahraia and Kaval responded together. The younger shade rolled her eyes, but disappeared inside her shade tree.

Ahraia sighed. She had hoped to be out of the nit before anyone noticed. All she needed now was the two spritelings to wake up and she would have encountered her whole nit: spritelings, shades, and all of their shadows.

Kaval studied her with knowing eyes as their shadows wrestled playfully. Reyn nipped at Losna's ears as she pinned him easily to the ground with a paw. The silence resettled.

Is this about the third task?

She hesitated, then nodded.

Kaval walked to the center of the nit, where the arching trunks of their mother's tree grew, spreading overhead in a perfect dome, with branches draping all the way to the ground beyond the shade trees. With a coaxing hand, he brought the nit's orb from a slit in the trunks, drained of the last vestiges of its moonlight. He closed the shell and slipped the empty light-pod carefully into the folds of his cloak.

"There isn't any mystery about it," he said, turning back to Ahraia. "Kren either sends Flit back, or they're dead."

Both Reyn and Losna stopped wrestling, and their ears perked attentively.

"Trust me," Kaval said. "Dwelling on it won't slow the turnings of the moons. You should just be reveling in the fact your test won't be anytime soon. You're still fourth in line. And the fog will fail the heart of the forest before Hayvon's summoned into his test."

Ahraia opened her mouth to protest, but Kaval's eyes turned to a smile.

Just let me know if there's any trick to it.

Ahraia's drew her brow in sharply. "Don't think for an instant you'll get it that easy," she said crossly.

Kaval undoubtedly smiled now. She turned back to the center of their nit and felt a grin tugging against her mood.

Wants to know, but doesn't want to risk finding out himself, she conveyed loosely to Losna, letting the echo out to Kaval.

A snort of laughter carried after her.

Ahraia led Losna past the trunks of the nit. Her mother's tree had once been regal, woven with vibrant yellow night lilies, purple spade stems and silver horned flowers—but now, it looked decrepit, a skeletal reminder of what had been. Its leaves hung withered, its branches wain and colorless, like a creature tired and starved, with the folds of the darkening faintly visible above.

The nit was ragged, but it wasn't for lack of trying. After their mother's death, it had passed to Kren to tend it, and her foldings had kept it as dark as could be hoped. Now, the responsibility had passed to Ahraia. For three turnings of the Bright Moon—ever since Kren had entered her test—she had been working on maintaining the dark. She spent whole days awake ministering to the tree's branches and leaves, weaving tighter bonds and sending roots in search of good earth and deep water. Kaval fed it moonlight from the orb he carried, but he wasn't as good at gathering it as Kren had been. The effort was exhausting for both of them, with little progress to show.

And with the work came the dreams: dreams of the Shadow Woods, dreams of the Shad-Mon, and dreams of the fog and mist and the quiet creeping of the forest.

Losna growled next to her and Ahraia realized her thoughts had been reflecting onto her shadow.

"Sorry," she muttered, shaping the nit's hanging branches into a closure leading to the central hollow. The nits of the other families grew about the vale, smaller, impenetrable domes sheltered beneath the draping sheets of the sprawling darkening tree.

Where is everybody? Losna thought. It was murky black, as light as

Ahraia had ever seen the central hollow, entirely empty, and without a single sprite or shade within.

They're all still underdaeing, she conveyed. She glanced to the darkening tree above. Although her brothers had delayed them, she could tell the Dae-Mon was still in the sky. Outside would be lethally bright.

Are you sure we should be doing this? Losna thought.

"Of course I am," Ahraia whispered.

What happens if they catch us?

Probably better we don't find out, Ahraia conveyed, wishing she had thought to get her hands on a light-veil. Only wards—or potential wards—grew them, but she wished she had one nonetheless.

They won't send us to the Shadow Woods, right? Losna worried, padding at her heels with her ears perked up.

Ahraia folded aside a bushel of leech ferns with an enchantment, sensing a shiver of anxiety reflected within her shadows thoughts.

I don't think so, she conveyed. She led Losna along the edge of the hollow, beneath one of the core trunks of the darkening, towards the span of woods known as the Makers. Shades were forbidden from entering the Makers, especially on a night like tonight, when Kren would be finishing the last stage of her shadow test: the test that would make her a sprite.

Losna trotted alongside Ahraia, her eyes gleaming and ears twitching. *Movement,* she warned.

Ahraia ducked behind a nascent web of winter-weave as a veil-wrapped sprite emerged from the fire-pits, filled up a bucket from the springs and returned to the hidden fires.

Ahraia waited. They were halfway across the darkening and she was getting nervous. Being outside with the Dae-Mon in the sky was absurdly dangerous but she had a plan. They just needed to make it out on the shady side of Daispar. From there, a short walk through the darker ravines would lead to the edge of the Makers, where she had folded an underdae to protect her until true night came. After that, it was just a matter of waiting to see if Kren would be able to send Flit back to the forest.

But first, they had to get to the Makers unseen. It wouldn't be hard if they just—

Hey!

Ahraia flinched as loose conveyance echoed across the hollow. She whipped about to find Hayvon hurrying after them, like a great lumbering bear, not bothering with any caution or sense. He had his hood drawn up, as though the barely perceptible light would scorch him. A tiny set of brown ears and whiskers poked out from the pocket of his cloak. His shadow, Vesta, furtive and sly, was anything but bear-like. Inside the darkening, she rarely left his pocket.

Hayvon—you scared me! Ahraia conveyed.

He had hardly reached them when he held up a hand. "Wait for us," he said, and hurried back towards their nit.

Where is he going? Losna thought.

Ahraia shrugged, her ears twitching with impatience. Hayvon returned holding a light-veil and fumbling with it around his hood.

"I hate this damned thing. Don't know why I grew it so thick," he whispered once he reached her. "What's your plan here?"

"Decided to come?" she asked in irritation.

He nodded, oblivious. "Only to keep you out of trouble."

She took a deep breath, trying to force down an angry tirade. Losna leaned forward on her foreclaws, eager to be gone. Ahraia pursed her lips.

"The Makers won't be sealed yet, and I'm guessing the dae-wards are still awood. I've been folding a bit of darkness at the edge—"

"A shelter?" Hayvon cut in. "A new underdae? You can't do that—not without permission. How many times have you been caught? Have you already forgotten—"

"Stop," Ahraia said, putting a firm binding over him to force his lips closed. "It's not like we're allowed any of this. You're either with us or you aren't."

Hayvon frowned but shrugged. *Fine. But—*

"Good," Ahraia said, tightening the binding further to cut off his thoughts. "We'll use the shelter until first dark falls, then we can—"

Losna growled barely a moment before a loud, unchecked voice cut through the darkening.

"Shade Ahraia, Hayvon."

Hayvon bowed his head, tucking back his ears deferentially. Ahraia closed her eyes and let out a heavy sigh. She wanted to curse Hayvon for slowing them down. Recognizing the voice, she turned to find their father, Beran, match of the Astra and head of the nit-wards, walking through the dusk light towards them.

"What are you two doing about at this hour?" he asked.

Ahraia subtly bound Hayvon. *Let me talk to him—*

Nothing! Nit-Ward, Hayvon conveyed roughly before Ahraia had finished her thought.

She glared at him and his markings paled under her stare, though his eyes never left the ground.

"Is that so?" their father said.

Ahraia bit her tongue. A deep frustration mingled with her annoyance at Hayvon's lack of subtlety. Strong as he was with bondings and bindings, his conveyance was forced and rough; he lacked the necessary control to lie convincingly. Vesta ducked deeper into his pocket, sensing Ahraia's mood.

Losna glowered at her father. Her demeanor wasn't remotely appropriate, but like Hayvon couldn't control the subtleties of his inner-voice, Ahraia couldn't constrain the better nature of her shadow. At least one of them could show how they felt.

Come here, her father conveyed to her.

Ahraia glanced up.

Her father wore his hood like Hayvon, his white hair framing the light-scarred skin about his eyes and ears from a forgotten time when he had once been a dae-ward. His eyes glowed a too-brilliant shade of yellow and he frowned at Ahraia as she approached.

"Don't you think your time would be better spent training for your test, rather than trying to see what will happen?" he asked.

Ahraia swallowed down a hundred different excuses and lies with a single knowing glance. If she guessed right, he had already interrogated Hayvon in the uncomfortable silence.

Yes, Nit-Ward.

His ears were rigid, and he pursed his lips, weighing his words. "Nitesse Gavea tells me she caught your shadow hunting for you again. Is that true?"

Ahraia's ears curled at the mention of Gavea. Named after the blood moon, she was every bit as malevolent. Ahraia hesitated, wondering if she could lie convincingly. His gaze penetrated her, cold and pale. She decided better of it and nodded instead.

Her father's mouth twisted downward in a frown. *The nitesse had reason to suspect you didn't have the prey bound.*

Ahraia flushed with embarrassment and her ears twitched against her will. Hayvon glanced at her sideways.

Of course I had it bound. Gavea just has it out for me, Ahraia conveyed quickly, hoping her brother hadn't heard the charge. Her father let out a long sigh, obviously aware of the lie at the edges of her thoughts.

"Ahraia . . . you understand what's at stake here, don't you?" He let the question hang between them, like a serapin vine in the forest, ready to strike at the barest misstep. She sensed the Dae-Mon finally dropping beneath the horizon and a deepening gray settled about the darkening.

"This isn't just about you—or your shadow—or even your test," her father continued. "There is something greater happening in these woods. This is about the future of the whole darkening: every shade and shadow, every sprite and spriteling. The dark of the Gelesh has been constricting for years. Lightwalkers encroach on every side, alps and humans both. It's not beyond my memory that a dozen other darkenings once existed within the Gelesh. Now we are but a few—Daispar being one of the last."

What does this have to do with me? Ahraia conveyed.

The pale-yellow of her father's eyes grew speckled with a ring of darker gold. His voice stretched with impatience.

"If we are to have any chance reclaiming these woods, then this darkening needs its strongest shades to become sprites. Do you understand? If not . . ." He didn't finish the thought in words. Instead, he bonded Ahraia more firmly and showed her a stark vision of what he saw: moonlight streaming through broken branches, a solitary, light-scarred sprite eking life out of the barest recesses of the forest, a nit laying bare and withered beneath a broken darkening under a canvas of stars. The last image wasn't Daispar, but it held too much detail to be his imagination. It was a memory, of Holcrek or Dimdale or one of the other darkenings that had failed in recent years. Ahraia shuddered, breaking free of his enchantment to see his cold eyes burning with earnestness. "Do you see? Is that what you want to become of us?"

No, she conveyed, lowering her eyes. *But why is it my—*

"Your binding of Losna shifted the power of the whole Collective." His voice rose, and Hayvon grimaced against the grating sound of it. "Astrael from darkenings across the Silh send all manner of tokens trying to curry favor with Daispar—all on the assumption that they might one day have to answer to you. Word is you've even caught the eye of the Masai. It's imperative that you become a sprite."

Dusk had fully settled now. The first sprites began to emerge from their nits. Some headed towards the Makers to witness Kren's test, while others headed towards the cook fires. The smell of roasted beets and venison drifted from the confines of the deep recesses, from which light never escaped, not even as flickers. No other shades or spritelings were about, nor would they be. A few sprites looked towards Hayvon and Ahraia but most pointedly ignored them.

"Until the day comes that you are summoned into spritehood, you have two tasks: prepare yourself for your test and keep from the light. Neither of which you seem capable of. This darkening needs you. The Astra is counting on you."

Ahraia flushed in anger at his mention of the Astra. *I don't care what she thinks she needs*, she conveyed, letting her thoughts tumble out unchecked.

Hayvon flinched but kept his eyes to the ground. Her father's ears angled sharply downward, as though she might have just declared herself a lightwalker.

A nit rustled open and several sprites emerged, saving Ahraia from facing his wrath. She looked up and realized Kren walked among them, headed off to her test. Her sister looked pale, worn down to her bones, her skin seeming as white as her hair.

Where's Flit? Losna thought. Ahraia glanced about and noticed that Kren's enormous eagle owl was missing. It was the first time she had seen her sister without her shadow since she had first bound her.

Already in the Makers, I suppose.

Kren froze on seeing Ahraia and Hayvon.

"Move along," their father said, stepping between Kren and Ahraia.

Kren's eyes didn't leave Ahraia. She swallowed painfully, looking as though a lump of stone rested above her heart.

Ahraia leaned past her father. "Good luck," she said, ignoring his admonishment. Kren gave her a wide-eyed nod, then allowed the sprites to escort her towards the Makers. Ahraia found her father still glaring at her.

"You're out of line Ahraia. You—" he stopped himself short, the muscles in his jaw clenching in frustration. He shook his head. "You may not think it, but I have your best interests in mind."

My interests? Ahraia thought in disbelief. *Is that why you deserted our nit? And left us for her—*

"Enough!" he said, his voice rising loudly. A half-dozen sprites turned at the sudden burst of noise like a brace of grouse startling into flight. Ahraia could feel the anger boiling across the space between them. "What happened with your mother is done. The strongest lives to rule, and when the Astra challenged your mother, she won. Behra understood that. You should as well."

"It didn't mean you had to leave." Ahraia swallowed hard as she struggled to get her emotions under check, fuming at his nerve.

"I'm a nit-ward, not some nitesse," he said, his scars flushing with red. "Now, Kren is gone—whether she passes her test or not—it's one less sibling standing between you and your shadow test. Unlikely as it seems, that could come any day. You must be ready."

Ahraia struggled to keep her ears from tucking back.

"And being ready means that you can't waste your time on silly adventures such as this one. Watching her shadow test?" He scoffed. "Even if you did, it wouldn't help you. It doesn't matter in the least if you can't perform the basic functions of a sprite. That means your shadow can't hunt for you anymore, understand? You must make your own kills. You need to be able to bind and hunt as a sprite." He glared at her malevolently.

When he finally broke his gaze, he stepped back and nodded to Hayvon, who stood up, with eyes and ears still downcast.

"You're supposed to have more prudence than this, Hayvon . . . your only responsibility is to keep *her* out of trouble."

Hayvon stared at his boots and nodded.

"It's obviously too great a task for you . . ." their father said. He sighed in irritation and waited for quiet to settle. "Tomorrow night, I want you two to take my oldest shades hunting. Shim and Tev have only just bound their shadows and they need direction. Maybe it will help you both. Take them to the northern woods, and don't come back until you've brought in enough game for the month. Understood?"

Yes, Nit-Ward, Hayvon answered quietly.

Ahraia refused to acknowledge him.

"I can't promise lenience if this happens again. Now get back inside your nit. Otherwise, it's a week's patrol of the Winnowlin for both of you."

Ahraia turned away defiantly, her ears straight, and stalked back across the hollow. Her father's thoughts carried after her.

No more hunting with your shadow, Ahraia. She won't always be there for you. Understand?

2

THE ASTRA

Tonight is a dark night. A good night for shades and shadows. A perfect night for hunting, Hayvon thought. His blackened pupils were ringed with pale yellow.

Speak for yourself, Ahraia answered darkly, leading him through a towering grove of firs as the path faded step-by-step into ferns and roots. A thin fog crept through the forest, bleeding through the creases and spreading across the hollows and dells.

Ahraia glanced at Tev's and Shim's bows longingly, feeling the paltry hunting blade at her hip. Her father had insisted on replacing her own bow with the small drain in the first turnings of winter. Spring and summer had passed, but she had yet to use it, though soon enough, she would have to.

What's wrong with tonight? Hayvon asked.

The understory was pitch black, without the moons or stars to light their way. But they moved easily through the deep forest, without a single sound of turning leaves or breaking branches.

Dark nights are a joyless thing, Ahraia conveyed. *And Tev and Shim aren't my idea of company. I'd rather drink from the Winnowlin.*

The bitter taste of the night before lingered, and taking her father and the Astra's oldest shades hunting was as close to condemnation as she could think. She had half a mind to lead them past the Shadow Woods, just to watch their ears curl.

All last night you complain of being restless. Now it's the company you keep? Hayvon shook his head playfully.

This is your fault, Ahraia said, wanting him to know her mood. *If you had just come when I told you, we never would have been caught.* She cut in front of him and stepped into the lead, catching the look of surprise on his face. Tev, the smaller of the two shades, hurried after her with her shadow clutched close to her chest.

We would have been caught either way, Losna thought. She brushed past Ahraia in irritation and loped off ahead. *I don't know why you're so obsessed with this test, anyway.*

I'm not obsessed, Ahraia projected forward. She clenched her teeth, irritated with her shadow as her tail disappeared through the brush.

She followed Losna down a narrow ravine covered in ferns and sparse maples. They passed a human head, staked and unrecognizable, placed by the dae-wards as a warning. Wicker blooms burst vibrantly over a stream bank, their fetid odor reflecting Ahraia's mood. Hayvon brought up the rear in absolute silence, leaving her alone to brood over the night before.

With Kaval and Altah gone to the Stone Tree and Kren gone for good, the nit had seemed deserted. Only five of them remained, and for the first time, more than half of their shade trees lay empty.

Ahraia had spent the better half of the wasted night trying to teach Alua and Thelon how to properly bind the nit tree, so they could come and go without shaking every leaf from the branches. Being the only remaining spritelings, and without the guidance of her mother or father, they struggled with the simplest bondings and were incapable of true bindings. As such, they didn't have much luck forming closures.

But Thelon managed to move a branch with his mind and Alua's conveyance was improving, so it hadn't been without benefit. At the very least, it had taken Ahraia's mind off Kren's test and kept her from wishing the worst for Hayvon, though, at the present she had returned to it with a renewed will.

Kren, thankfully though, had passed. It had taken the whole night. When she had returned from the Makers, her cheeks had been tear-stained and her eyes puffy and angry—but she was a sprite. The nitesses had ushered her into the small shelter of a nascent nit tree—her nit tree—less than a year old and waiting to be cultivated to her will. She would spend the next several turnings molding it and the rest of her life living under its protection, until one day she became a nitesse with her own spritelings and shades. The mood of the darkening had been jubilant, but Ahraia had simply felt restless. She had wanted out of her nit and out of the darkening. Now she just wanted to know how Kren had managed it.

Shim's voice suddenly shattered the silence, breaking the quiet like a branch snapping violently underfoot.

"Where do shadows go when their shades become sprites?" He was the Astra's oldest, nearly as old as Alua and Thelon and only just having bound a shadow. As such, his conveyance wasn't very strong and so he spoke aloud instead.

"Part of the shadow is said to join the shade," Hayvon said from behind them, "but the shadow itself goes back to the forest."

Ahead, Losna stopped, holding perfectly still with her ears turned back attentively. She didn't like hearing about the shadow test—and most of all she didn't like to hear about shadows returning to the forest.

Is that true? she thought, waiting for Ahraia to catch up.

More or less, Ahraia answered, slightly unsure herself. The first two tasks were a mystery, but she knew it spanned three turnings of the Bright Moon and had something to do with hunting by bindings, but beyond that, shades weren't allowed to know anything until they were called to become a sprite. Every time a shade entered a task, the rest of the darkening's shades were relegated to their nits, hidden away until it was over.

"So her owl might be out here?" Shim asked, looking up to the forest as though Kren's owl might be perched, watching them. His shadow, which was smaller and slinkier than Vesta, looked up nervously.

"Flit's certainly out here somewhere," Ahraia said, saddened to think of her being all alone after so long. Flit was motherly, and just as Kren had looked out for the shades, Flit had watched after the shadows. It didn't seem right, or fair, to expel her back to the woods. The thought left a hollow beneath Ahraia's throat, an aching in her heart that no amount of reason or reckoning could fill.

Losna let out a quiet whine. The hollow inside Ahraia deepened. She didn't want to think about sending Losna back to the plains. She pointed upward at the first chance to change the conversation.

"Look, a suckle pine," she said, hoping to distract the younger shades.

Hayvon glanced up. "It's well out of reach," he said. The lowest branches hung a dozen feet above them. "And there's a serapin at the trunk." He gave a half-hearted attempt at reaching one of the lower branches but stayed well away from the coiled stems of the serapin tree—the poison stingers on the bigger ones were enough to kill.

"Why?" Shim asked. "I mean, why do the shadows go back to the forest." His own brown ermine crawled about the nape of his neck, its head bobbing and whiskers quivering. A collar of white had already begun to show, even though winter's chill wouldn't arrive until the dark moon finally reemerged in the sky.

"Because," Hayvon said, brushing his hands clean, "they're meant for the forest. They aren't meant to be shadows forever."

Losna let out a huff of irritation. She held her tail stiffly behind her, her eyes piercing Ahraia.

"It's not too high," Ahraia said, pointedly ignoring her. *I can climb that.* She scanned the woods and found a large maple that suited her purpose.

Losna huffed again.

Ahraia focused on forming her bonding. First, she linked her mind to the tree, taking a moment to acquaint herself before she turned it to a true binding. She sensed deep roots and limber branches.

Come here, she thought, forming the movement of the branches in her mind. They responded by stretching towards her.

"What's happening?" Tev asked fearfully. "Why is the tree moving?"

"Shade Ahraia is binding it," Hayvon reassured her.

The tree's resistance revealed itself through the faintest creak of its trunk, forcing Ahraia to move the branches more willfully. They strained, the leaves shuddering right to their tips.

Tev looked even more frightened at this. "Like a shadow?"

"Subtler than that—more like the darkening wall." Hayvon's eyebrows drew in skeptically as he looked between Ahraia and the maple. "Will those hold you?"

Ahraia grabbed the outstretched branches, persuading the wood to twist about her wrist and grip her firmly.

"Of course they will," she said, trying to inflict confidence into the tree.

Just like last time? Losna thought.

Ahraia grimaced. The scabs still traced across her shin and elbow from when the last spring tree had broken halfway up its lift, dropping Ahraia square in the middle of the nettle she had been trying to avoid. *That was my fault*, she conveyed. *This is a young maple, supple and strong*. She let the thought carry, making sure the tree heard the compliment.

The leaves preened themselves, whispering without the wind to blow them.

"Besides," Ahraia said, grinning, "I'm as light as a feather."

Shim looked to Hayvon again, confusion on his brow. "I thought the wall only responds because it's awake, like our shade trees."

"In a manner," Hayvon explained. "The wall and the shade trees *are* awake, and they're used to us—they expect to move because they've been conditioned to it. But everything is awake if you're strong enough with your binding and willful enough. Every living tree and creature is awake—you couldn't bind a log any more than you could bind water or fog. But most shades and sprites don't take to such bondings easily. Shade Ahraia just happens to think herself a bit of an expert," he said. "And one of these days it's going to get her into trouble."

"One of these days . . ." Ahraia said. She flexed her arms and bent her elbows slightly. She took a deep breath and then released the enchantment holding the doubled over branches.

Whoosh.

The boughs ripped her from the ground in a rush of leaves and hair and fog. Her arms strained and she focused firmly on her intended endpoint. The branches twisted accordingly, slowing, losing power. Her feet came to rest twenty feet above the ground. She released her hold along with the enchantment and the branches swung back freely over the forest in a tempest of leaves. She stood on the first large branch of the suckle pine with the serapin branches slithering hungrily below.

She picked a maple leaf from her hair, letting it fall to where the shades stood, staring up, with mouths agape.

Show off, Hayvon conveyed, but even he looked impressed.

A smile tugged at the corner of Ahraia's mouth. She made her way nimbly to the trunk.

"How did she do that?" Shim said in awe. "I've never seen anyone do that."

"That's because no one is stupid enough to try," Hayvon said disapprovingly.

"Why not?" Tev asked. Her bushy-tailed shadow watched Ahraia with beady eyes.

"Look around us," Hayvon said, gesturing to the canopy. "How many branches could you reach if they bent the proper way? Not many. And of those, how many could support you?"

Tev shrugged. Shim searched the woods with his mouth hanging open and his eyes wide. Hayvon went on.

"Most of the branches near enough to the ground wouldn't support you and the rest are half-dead. What happens if the one you bind breaks? Are you going to be ten feet off the ground? Twenty? Higher? And which trees should you bind? Some are stiffer than others. Some are more stubborn. Firs have strong branches but they're too high. Maples are okay—but not if they're wet. Oaks—if you're foolish enough to bind—are mean and gnarled and would be glad to break beneath you."

"They would?" Tev said.

Hayvon nodded. "And that doesn't figure in each tree's manner. Some are old and slow, some are young and wild, some are brittle and others are just plain mean. Which ones should you trust?"

Ahraia listened vaguely as Hayvon listed all the reasons the shades shouldn't do as she had. To her, it seemed easy: some trees could, and some couldn't, some trees would and some wouldn't. That came naturally. And to worry about it was why there were three shades on the ground and only one in the tree. Still grinning, she began to climb.

Be careful, Losna thought distantly. Their bond twanged with worry.

Ahraia climbed higher until the warnings buzzed distantly, keeping her from doing anything extraordinarily foolish. The trunk narrowed and the branches and cones grew thinner. She grabbed one of the slender cones. *Still soft.*

She climbed higher still, above the fog of the forest, delighting in the exhilaration of being so high, so free. The fog lay below and the clouds above, but between, the trees swayed like the grasses of the endless plain, dancing and whispering and playing together. She could almost forget the conversations below; she could almost forget that shadows were returned to their place in the woods.

Almost.

She checked another cone.

Firmer. Good.

She bound the tree, a tall and proud sentinel. A binding here wouldn't do; if she took without asking, the tree might get angry. It might throw her to the ground or break a branch beneath her.

May I have some of your cones? she asked, rousing it to wakefulness. The words didn't matter, they just helped form her intention. And the tree didn't answer, of course, but the connection from the stem to the cone softened. She pulled the first prize loose. She smiled.

Thank you.

She quickly rearranged the eaves-web of her cloak, re-weaving it with her mind and hands to form pockets. Then she went about gathering more cones, leaving the softer ones to harden, taking only the ones the tree parted with easily.

Once her pockets brimmed with the long, slender cones, she climbed back down to the lowest branches. She linked the maple, bringing the boughs towards her once more. They twisted around her wrists. She grabbed hold, stepped into the air and swung back to the ground with the fog curling after her. She landed with a flourish.

Tev gasped and Shim's mouth hung open. Hayvon hid half a smile while Vesta peaked out from his pocket.

Losna sniffed at Ahraia's pockets and then turned about. *Waste of time,* she thought, her tail bouncing after her as she jogged off to scout the woods. *Show off . . .*

Ahraia grinned. She offered each of the younger shades a cone after snapping the tip off to reveal the sweet sap beneath. She split her own and tipped it up to her lips.

Hayvon held out his hand. Ahraia raised the cone above her mouth, letting every drop of the sweet juice drain before she tossed it to the ground, smacking her lips like Losna sometimes did.

Hayvon waited expectantly.

Ahraia frowned. "This is for Vesta," she said, holding out a cone halfway. A pair of slender paws emerged from his pocket and greedily snatched it away from her. The cone, which dwarfed Vesta, somehow disappeared easily back into Hayvon's pocket. He was still looking at Ahraia. She grabbed another cone but held it out of reach.

You don't deserve this after last night.

I'm sorry, he conveyed, only to her. She considered him for a moment. He was hopelessly wardish sometimes, and terrible at conveyance. But with Kren gone, Hayvon was her closest sibling, and he looked out for the others as well as any. *I am sorry,* he conveyed again, skillfully keeping the thoughts to a whisper.

That's better, she conveyed, her ears flickering impishly. She handed him the cone but nearly dropped it when Tev let out a terrified squeak.

"Shade Ahraia! Something's coming!" She pointed through the fog.

Ahraia spun about to find Losna bounding back through the woods, their bond reverberating with fear.

Alp! Losna thought, terrified. *Alp!*

An alp? Here? Ahraia thought doubtfully. She touched Losna's memory with her mind, and her shadow showed her what she had seen. A lightwalker, sharp-eared with a wicked face, ran through the woods. She saw a silver-tipped spear disappearing, and then the memory faded, ending with Losna standing before her. The hair on Ahraia's neck stood on end, mimicking Losna's bristling fur.

It passed there. That way. Losna pointed her body to the north, towards where she had just come.

What is it? Hayvon asked, sensing their shared vigilance.

The younger shades flinched skittishly as a branch broke somewhere in the woods. Ahraia dropped the cone she held.

An alp, she conveyed only to Hayvon, not wanting to scare the shades.

Alps! His surprise got the better of him and his thoughts burst forth, so loose and unbounded that Shim and Tev jumped, hearing echoes.

"What do you mean alps?" Shim said. "Lightwalkers?"

The scratching snap of footsteps over leaves disrupted the quiet of the forest.

"Shhh. Give me your bow," Ahraia whispered, quickly grabbing Tev's bow and taking an arrow from the quiver at her hip. Alps were a wicked type of lightwalker that had realms in the north, beyond the Shadow Woods. They were said to be dangerous and clever, and they didn't belong so close to Daispar.

The footsteps faded. Several tense moments passed. Ahraia let out a breath, lowering the bow.

"Do you think—" Hayvon stopped, falling silent at the sound of more branches being disrupted.

Ahraia's ears twisted towards the sound. She turned and saw movement, and she raised the arrow to Tev's bow. Several figures hurtled through the dark forest, from the same direction where Losna had seen the alp.

Quick. Hide! Hayvon conveyed. The shades ducked for cover but Ahraia stood her ground. There was no time to hide. She took aim, her fingers poised to release the bowstring, when she realized the runners weren't alps—they were sprites. A dae-ward led the way, with his hood back and a veil loose across his neck. A nit-ward followed him. Pale skin and scarred skin flashed between tree trunks, along with white-eyes and yellow-eyes both, all with moon-white hair.

Ahraia froze. Half a dozen enchantments crashed down upon her, like a heavy web that stilled both her body and mind, holding her fingers tight to the bowstring and dimming her thoughts.

Hayvon, along with Shim, already had his eyes lowered and ears down. The group was led by the Astra. One of the wards stepped in front of Ahraia's arrow. Ahraia recognized him as Golan, one of the newer wards, without the heavy scars or the yellow-eyes of the others. Her gaze, however, was drawn to someone standing beside him. *Something* standing beside him.

An alp.

Ahraia stared, dumbfounded. It was a golden-haired alp. She had never seen one so close. And she had *never*—not in all her life—heard of one allowed in the Gelesh, much less accompanied by sprites.

The alp stared back at her with gleamless eyes. Her cloak was woven of a strange material, uniform throughout, unlike the spritish eaves-web. Dark fur lined the outer edges of her hood, holding back her light-touched hair and hiding her telltale ears. Her icy-gray eyes were small, dim in contrast to the yellow-eyed wards and the white-eyed sprites. Her skin was stained by the Dae-Mon, not dark, but certainly not pale or ashen.

The enchantment holding Ahraia weakened and she lowered the bow to her side. Her skin crawled from the brief paralysis, but even more so from the presence of the alp. Losna raised her hackles and bared her teeth.

"What are you doing here?" the Astra said, flushed.

"Mother!" Tev said, leaping towards her. The Astra shoved her away dismissively, sneering at her.

"Beyond your shade tree, I'm your Astra," she said sharply, her words cracking the silence. "That means you address me as such—and your voice isn't to be heard."

Tev flinched, stepping back as though she had been cut. Her shadow leapt from her arms and darted into the undergrowth.

"Pick up your pathetic shadow," the Astra said. Her unblemished skin shone out in sharp contrast to the alp. The alp watched curiously. The surrounding sprites looked on with scorn, frowning at Tev as though she was some vile mud mare of the deep swamps. The Astra looked back to Ahraia, "What are you doing here?" she asked again.

Ahraia realized she was staring at the alp with ears pinned back. She closed her mouth and composed herself.

Nit-ward Beran sent us hunting, she conveyed, turning her ears down deferentially. *To help your shades properly bind their shadows*. She suddenly remembered that she was holding Tev's bow. *Well, not right now. And this isn't mine—it's Tev's.* She dropped it as though the bow might be poisonous.

The Astra glared at her. The circle of dae-wards tightened around them. Their veils hung loosely at their necks, revealing their wicked light-scars from all the time spent abroad in full light. They unnerved Ahraia, but not nearly as much as the sharp-eared alp.

Gavea, the nitesse that had caught Losna hunting for Ahraia, stepped forward. "You aren't allowed a bow, Ahraia."

Ahraia's scars flushed hotly. *Losna thought she saw an alp. It was just precautionary*, she explained quickly.

"An alp? Which way?" the Astra said, cutting Gavea's castigation short. The alp at her side tensed, her eyes narrowing.

Ahraia pointed. The air quivered with conveyance that Ahraia couldn't catch.

"Golan, take Anasazi and go," the Astra said. The dae-ward nodded, then gestured for the alp to follow. They hurried off through the woods, heading in the direction Ahraia had pointed. Ahraia watched, the confusion spreading in her mind like the thickening fog in the woods.

What are alps doing here? And what are dae-wards doing about at night?

"The alp is none of your concern," the Astra said dismissively. "Her dealings are with me." Her ears stood sharp and tall and batted once: an order for obedience. Disturbing as the lightwalker's presence was, Ahraia swallowed down a dozen other questions. The Astra's glare shifted to the younger shades with disdain.

"If your only concern is taking these wretched shades and trying to shape something of them, then you're wasting your time. They haven't the will or the wit to become sprites."

Shim's ears curled, but his face remained even. Tev had retrieved her shadow, but her mouth began to quiver. She pressed her lips together, pursing them to be stoic, but a tear dripped across her cheek.

Stop that, the Astra conveyed sharply. She stepped forward and flicked Tev hard across the face with the back of her hand.

Tev let out a sob.

"Stop that," the Astra said aloud, hitting her harder. Tev dissolved into tears.

Losna growled.

"Dae-Mon above," the Astra cursed, stepping away in disgust. "It's a wonder she became a shade at all. She won't even make it to her shadow test." She leaned down and picked up the bow that Ahraia had dropped. She turned back to Tev. "Stop your whimpering right now." She struck Tev across the shins with the bow.

Tev let out a yelp of pain.

"Stop that!" The Astra stuck again.

Before Ahraia knew what she was doing, she stepped forward to grab the bow. She would have stayed the Astra's hand, but a collective enchantment spread across her, keeping her from reaching out. The third time, the Astra's lash slashed Tev's face and the shade spun to the ground with a scream, clutching her jaw.

Ahraia clenched her teeth, seeing blood come away on Tev's

hand. She struggled against the enchantment. She stepped back and the spell dissipated. The Astra hadn't seemed to notice; she tossed the bow on top of Tev, who sobbed helplessly into the dirt.

"I don't know why Beran insists on keeping her. This one either . . ." She shoved Shim roughly aside. He stumbled but kept his footing, never looking up at his mother. "No wonder the Masai thinks the Gelesh is failing . . . How in the night are we going to ever press back the light with whelps such as these? They would be better off given to the Shad-Mon. At least the rest of the spritelings would think twice about returning with such woeful shadows."

Losna shook with fury and Ahraia with her.

"Still," the Astra said, glancing between Hayvon and Ahraia. "Maybe my next will bear better shadows. Both of you are Beran's offspring, and look—one binds a rat and the next binds a wolf," she scoffed.

Vesta's not a rat—she's a martin, Hayvon said, glaring at the Astra. Vesta peeked out with dark beady eyes.

Hayvon! Ahraia conveyed, for once being the voice of caution. Light seared her blood as well, but standing up to the Astra wasn't like standing up to their father—the Astra was vindictive and violent, and could condemn Hayvon with a single thought. Ahraia held her breath. Gavea scowled at them both but the Astra, luckily, didn't seem to care. She was still sneering at Tev, who lay on the ground sobbing.

"It's no difference. The point remains," she said, snorting in disgust. She shook her head once more. "Get these two out of my sight. I don't care if they ever become sprites."

3

BINDINGS

"What in day's light is the Astra doing with an alp?" Ahraia asked. It was midnight, and the Astra had sent them away with a warning to stay away from the alps and not to speak of their passing.

Hayvon's ears stood on end.

And how could she treat them like that? Ahraia went on. *How could she hit Tev without any conscience?* Her insides still writhed in anger at the Astra's attack on her shade.

Hayvon still didn't answer. Ahraia wasn't sure if it was because the Astra had called Vesta a rat, or if he took her command for silence seriously. She fell in beside him, fuming alone in her thoughts.

They were headed north, away from the alp and the Astra. Losna roamed ahead, scouting for game near the edges of the forest where the last valleys spilled out onto the Endless Plains. It was a safe night for skirting the great expanse, and there was little chance of any light spoiling the dark.

She finally sensed the touch of Hayvon's mind.

It's really not that surprising. Look at the shadows they bound, Hayvon conveyed.

Tev's squirrel scampered through the treetops after Vesta, while Shim's ermine bobbed beneath them on the ground.

Hayvon was careful to keep his conveyance from the shades. *She's the leader of the darkening and they're her first shades. Of course she wants them bound to stronger shadows. It's a poor reflection on her. Especially when father already has shades from another nit with owls and foxes and wolves.*

It doesn't mean she has to cast them to the Shad-Mon, Ahraia conveyed, wondering what the Astra would have done if she had actually grabbed the bow.

Hayvon wrestled his way past a stubborn alder tree.

It was the same when I bound Vesta. Mother was furious—said she was going to give me to the Shad-Mon that very night. Father still threatens that . . . His eyes turned dark and he kept the remainder of his thoughts to himself.

Ahraia considered comforting him, but stopped when she saw a defiant smile spread across his face. His gaze rose to Vesta, who had a small cone held between her paws, nibbling at the tip.

Of course, if I had just brought home the bear I bound rather than my little martin, sprites might speak to me as something more than daemon-bait—

A pinecone suddenly struck his head from above, followed by a sharp series of chirps from Vesta. Hayvon laughed, dodging to the side as a second cone shot down from above. Ahraia gave a weak smile. She knew he was trying to make light of it, but it grated against her nonetheless.

They don't stand a chance if she isn't willing to help them, she conveyed.

Hayvon shrugged. *It is what it is. Those of us with weaker shadows are a mark against our nits. Dwelling on it won't change anything.*

Ahraia fell silent. She knew Hayvon was right but it made no difference. She sighed and walked on, wondering how she had been lucky enough to bind Losna. She had never told Hayvon how close she had come to returning to the darkening without a shadow at all.

Shim's voice broke the quiet of the forest. "Is it hard to kill?" he asked, looking pale but resolute. Neither him nor Tev had spoken since they left the Astra. He swallowed nervously. "I mean, is it hard to hunt?" He had their father's cold eyes, but they were still white, untouched by light.

Ahraia considered it, looking longingly at their quivers full of arrows. *With a bow it's not*, she thought to herself. "It's not hard," she said aloud, hoping to sound reassuring. She enchanted a small maple and raised it above the shades.

"Do we have to?" Tev asked, following her along the crest of a log making a convenient path through the undergrowth.

Ahraia felt a twinge of regret for the young shade. The question wasn't entirely appropriate, but she had no one in her nit to guide her.

"Yes, you have to. But Hayvon and I will be there to help," Ahraia said. Tev, if anything, looked even more frightened. Her shadow scampered along the log after her, its bushy tail bouncing wildly in tow.

Were we ever that small? Ahraia conveyed to Hayvon.

Smaller, I think, Hayvon answered.

They seem awfully frightened. She leapt down from the log.

Neither of them have a wolf for a shadow, do they? Hayvon conveyed, grunting as he hit the ground behind her.

Ahraia smiled. *I suppose not.* She stopped and stooped down in front of Tev. The little shade had an angry welt forming across her cheek.

"Look at it this way, Tev: with Losna on our side, there's no way we return to Daispar empty handed—" Ahraia stopped, sensing a familiar warmth away in the woods—her shadow. She signaled the others to stop.

Shim gathered his shadow to him. Tev imitated him but her little squirrel wouldn't come out of the darkness. Instead, it scampered halfway up a tree and scratched around the far side of the trunk, hiding.

Losna jogged back through the pines, her gaze darting towards

Tev's squirrel, while licking her lips. She had a bounce in her step that told Ahraia she had found something.

What is it? Ahraia conveyed.

Two deer. Laying down at the edge of the meadow up ahead, Losna thought, still eyeing the tree. A bushy tail was just visible, twitching nervously.

Ahraia relayed to the others what Losna had found. Hayvon and Shim's ears perked up while Tev's breaths rasped out nervously. The wind whispered far above, but on the ground, not even the fog stirred. The forest was quiet and still.

"Here's what we're going to do," Ahraia said, wondering if Tev could make a kill by herself or not. "Losna and I will lead. The deer are just down the hillside from here. We'll make our way down—slow." *And silent.* "Once we've spotted them, I'll guide us close enough to make the shots. I want you two to make the kills." *We'll convey from here on out. Okay?*

Shim nodded, but Tev gave no indication she had heard.

"What if I can't?" Her gaze dropped to the ground. "I'm not a very good shot."

"She's terrible. She's worse than Malar and he's still a spriteling," Shim added.

"That's all right," Hayvon said, frowning at Shim. "We're going to help you, Tev. Ahraia and I will have the deer bound. It will be an easy shot."

Tev seemed to brighten at this, but a knot twisted in Ahraia's chest. Hayvon glanced at her, and again she wondered if he had heard their father's accusations the night before. She nodded, not wanting to project the sudden nervousness that gripped her.

Just like what Kren did for us on our first hunt, Hayvon reminded her.

Ahraia nodded again.

Losna watched nervously. *Bound? Like enchanted?* she asked, her bright yellow eyes boring into Ahraia.

Ahraia didn't answer.

I knew it would come to this, Losna thought, discontent rumbling from her chest.

Ahraia kept her ears up with an effort. Her father's warnings echoed in her mind. One night, she was going to have to hunt with her bindings and tonight was as good as any to start.

Couldn't you just let me do it? Losna thought. *I'll be careful.*

No, Ahraia conveyed.

Losna's low grumble turned to a disapproving growl. She knew the ruin that hunting with enchantments held for Ahraia. The problem wasn't the hunt, of course—it was the binding. The act of enchanting and then killing left Ahraia empty and maimed.

It's not worth it. Last time, you ended up sick for a whole turning. There's no decency in tricking something into death.

Ahraia steeled her courage, embarrassed that Hayvon might have heard her father's words the night before. *It's how all the other shades hunt. At some point, I'm going to have to get over myself.*

Losna huffed loudly, growing more agitated.

"You lead," Hayvon said to Ahraia, unaware of the conveyance passing back and forth between her and her shadow.

Ahraia headed towards the meadow, wondering if she could knowingly keep the deer bound. Losna trailed at her heel, supplying a steady stream of admonishment for even considering a binding. Ahraia ignored her, intent on getting the shades furtively down the hillside. Tev and Shim were quiet, but Ahraia helped them, moving every leaf, branch and tree root that she could. Hayvon and Vesta pointed out loose sticks or logs underfoot and together they managed to get down the hill in true spritish silence. The meadow spread out before them with fog clinging to the tall grasses. Ahraia took a moment to spot the deer.

Okay, there they are. Her heart thumped loudly in her chest. She pointed across the field to the two subtle shapes at the meadow's edge. Two flickering sets of ears and a single set of antlers rose above the grass. Losna licked her lips, forgetting her reservations for a moment. Ahraia moved the group into a better position, until the shot would be reasonable for the shades. Silence gripped the night.

Get yourselves ready, Hayvon conveyed. Shim took his bow from his shoulder and nocked an arrow to the string. Tev mimicked her older brother.

I'm going to have to bind it, Ahraia conveyed to Losna. *Maybe since I won't make the kill it won't be as bad.*

Losna resigned herself, staring at the deer, disconcerted. Ahraia tried to calm herself but her body was alight with fear, every nerve tingling in anticipation. She took a settling breath while Hayvon and the others awaited her order.

I'll bind the stag and keep him still, she conveyed. *Shim, I want you to take that one. Tev, you see the doe . . . the one closer to us with its head down? Hayvon's going to have it bound in place. All you need to do is place the arrow under its shoulder, right in the heart. Understand?*

Tev nodded along with her brother. The tiny shade trembled but raised her bow. Losna was tense, her shoulders squared and ears forward, ready if anything went wrong.

Everybody ready? Hayvon asked. They nodded again.

Ahraia reached out carefully; the initial brush of enchantment elicited a shiver, as though she had suddenly slipped into an icy forest pool.

Wariness ruled the stag; its body was tense and ready to spring. It listened to the soft sounds of the meadow, to the rustle of the grasses and the distant trickle of a slow creek. It turned an ear towards the forest.

It's safe, Ahraia thought, feeling the first twinge of regret.

She deepened the enchantment, turning the bonding to a full binding. Her own surroundings faded. The breeze, with the first hint of autumn, turned across the grasses of the meadow. A squirrel scratched up a tree in the distance. The stag lay perfectly still. Ahraia's stomach clenched knowing what was about to happen; a fragment of the worry transferred to the deer. An ear turned towards her.

On my mark, she conveyed to the shades.

Tev and Shim drew back their arrows. The bowstrings whined quietly. Dry, sticky saliva flooded Ahraia's mouth; she couldn't swallow. The stag raised its head and peered towards them, both ears turned now.

Ahraia? Hayvon conveyed, staying perfectly still.

It's fine, Ahraia lied. A jolt of fear passed through her, followed closely by cold sweat crawling from her skin. The stag stood up, snorting.

What's happening? They're spooked, Hayvon asked.

I've got it under control, Ahraia conveyed, closing her eyes. But she didn't. The enchantment was slipping. She didn't want to be bound to it; her own fear was compromising the link.

It's now or never, Hayvon conveyed.

The stag took a step, nearly wild with alarm. The doe raised her head as well.

On my mark, Hayvon conveyed to the shades, taking over.

Ahraia's lips were numb with dread. She couldn't keep the binding. She didn't want to.

Now! Hayvon thought forcefully. Ahraia flinched and the stag flinched with her. It leapt in the air as the bowstrings twanged and the bond suddenly snapped. Tev's arrow hit her mark. The doe took one bound and then crumpled. But Shim's arrow disappeared into the grass. The stag was free. It bolted across the meadow.

Light take me! Ahraia thought as Losna sprang after the stag. She leapt after them both, frantically attempting to reform her binding.

In a matter of bounds, the stag reached the far side of the meadow, out of reach. A moment later, it disappeared into the woods, with Losna chasing close at its heel.

What happened? Bind it! Hayvon conveyed.

The grasses whipped at the underside of Ahraia's arms. She leapt into the woods, spinning ferns and maples out of her path just in time to see Losna's tail slip out of sight. Ahraia cursed herself for letting the enchantment break.

She leapt onto a log and rushed down a steep slope, seeking the stag with her mind but feeling only the empty night. The binding was broken. The chance was lost. She searched for Losna but had no sense of her shadow now, either. The hunt was over. She had failed to make a kill—again.

4

SINGING

Losna dragged the stag by the neck down the hillside. She wrestled it over a log and proudly dropped it at Ahraia's feet. It slumped down the slope and its antlers gouged the soft earth. Its black eyes turned upward.

Any better? Losna asked. She sat back on her haunches, panting lightly, with her ears turning backwards and forwards, her brow raised hopefully.

Ahraia looked down at the lifeless deer. Blood spilled from its ravaged neck.

"Dae-Mon above," she cursed, worried what Hayvon would think. The bite marks were both obvious and unmanageable. A sinking shame settled over her for losing the binding; it mingled with abhorrent relief that she hadn't been bound when Losna had made the kill.

Losna cocked her head sideways. *No good?*

Ahraia pulled the drain from her hip. "Maybe if I cut its throat here . . . or maybe here . . ." she said, drawing it out. "Maybe then it might look like I killed it?"

Losna stared back at her, her big golden eyes full of doubt.

"No? No. I didn't think so." Ahraia sighed. She looked down at the bloodied mess. They both knew that it would never pass as her kill.

Food?

Ahraia raised an eyebrow at her shadow. "Is that all you think about?"

Losna yawned wide and licked her lips.

"Yes. Food," Ahraia agreed. There was no sense bringing it back to the darkening. Her father would only count it as another mark against her. Losna's tail thumped against the ground as Hayvon jogged through the woods towards them.

"Did you bind it?" he called excitedly, seeing Ahraia holding her drain. *Did you make the kill?* He took one look at the deer and frowned. "No?" *Damn.*

Where are the shades? Ahraia conveyed, unable to meet his eye.

"Back with Tev's kill," he said hesitantly. He opened his mouth to speak but stopped. He stepped cautiously closer, peering at the deer with a frown. *What happened?* he conveyed finally.

"I lost the binding," she said, the words tasting bitter.

"You lost it?" he asked, his eyebrows coming together. "Or you broke it?"

"I didn't break it," Ahraia said quickly, flushing in embarrassment. *I just lost it.* She turned away, discomfited that he was so close to the truth.

"This isn't the first time," he said.

Losna lifted her bloody snout, her ears perked attentively.

Ahraia carefully cleared her mind, but she couldn't ignore what had happened with the stag. The binding had crumbled, and she wasn't sure if it had unraveled from her inability or her own volition. She walked away from Losna and the kill, running her hand over the coarse, barbed bark of a fallen dorn tree.

Losna whimpered, perturbed that Ahraia had left her unguarded while she ate. But Ahraia couldn't face her brother.

"It's all right," Hayvon said. *It's all right.* Alarm, shrouded poorly like the Bright Moon behind a thin wisp of clouds, seeped through his thoughts. Ahraia could feel it ringing in the space between them. She could hear it in the measured calm of his breaths. She clenched her teeth, flushing in embarrassment.

"No, it's not all right," she said. She glanced back to find both Losna and Hayvon staring at her. The silence stretched between them, with Hayvon's question growing. The weight of the truth crushed inward on her. "I don't know if I broke it . . ."

The muscles in Hayvon's jaw flexed but he didn't speak. He watched her carefully, as though he couldn't decide if she was being honest or if she was sick.

I can't do it. I just can't, she conveyed, suddenly desperate for him to understand.

"Tonight?"

I never could. She bound a fir and used the lower branches to spring atop of a half-fallen cedar. She landed nimbly, her toes curling inside her boots. The toppled tree jutted out from the hillside, high above the ground where she imagined for a moment that Hayvon's judgement couldn't touch her. She walked to the very end of the trunk. The forest spread before her, hundreds of dark pillars glowering back above the colorless underbrush.

Hayvon stared up blankly. "What do you mean you never could?" His ears batted in disbelief. "You never have? Father was right? You've never bound your prey? But how did you . . . how could you make so many kills?"

"I'm a good shot," Ahraia said quietly.

Hayvon had a pained look on his face. "Never?" He ran a scarless hand through his hair. "Not even once?"

"I've tried . . . It's always been a disaster."

"I remember," he said slowly, walking up the hillside from beneath the log. "That strange deer . . . the one from the plains . . ."

Ahraia nodded, remembering the terror that had taken her after she made her first kill. She bound a higher branch and propelled herself into the crook of a large maple, putting more distance between herself and Hayvon. She stood, bracing herself between two of the trunks, distressed that she couldn't do as the rest of the shades did.

"Maybe you could start smaller, simpler," Hayvon suggested. "I could help you."

"It's not like it's big," Ahraia said. *The stag was a yearling—a small one at that.* "Besides, it doesn't matter. The second I make the bond I can't go through with it. It's like I get . . ." she trailed off, leaning between the trunks, too embarrassed to finish the thought.

"Scared?" Hayvon suggested hesitantly.

Sick, Ahraia thought only to herself. "No, I just . . ." *I can't kill what I attach myself to,* she conveyed, finishing the thought unsaid, aware of how awful it would sound aloud. How *un-spritish* it would seem. She pulled apart a maple seed, tossing it into the air.

Hayvon frowned. "You've never had trouble hunting before."

Ahraia didn't answer. Enchanting a creature, no matter what her intent, tied her to it. And to get close—close enough to keep it fearless and trusting—and then make a kill was revolting.

"It's a lot different," she said finally.

"It's not supposed to be. It's the way we . . ." Hayvon stopped short. "It's how we . . ." he trailed off, his face twisting, the words escaping him.

Ahraia didn't have to hear anymore to know his thoughts. To be a sprite was to bind, enchant, and kill; it was the only way their people managed in this light-strewn world. She couldn't meet Hayvon's eyes. She grabbed another handful of seeds, flicking them one by one into the air as she spoke.

"You know what a binding is like, it's a connection—" she stopped, searching for the words, "No, it's more than that. It's an attachment that stitches me to whatever I bind and when I sever that, a part of me is torn with it. It's a betrayal—an ache that settles like a mara in my chest. But it doesn't go away when I awake. It becomes a part of me: a terrible blackness in my heart."

She looked up. Hayvon stared at her, stricken.

"That's what it is to be a sprite!"

The condemnation in his voice was too much. She tossed the remaining seeds away and bound a limb, twisting it towards herself before swinging to the forest floor, away from Losna and Hayvon, not wanting either to know the helpless fear that gripped her heart. She flitted down the hillside, using springs and shifts to take her farther away. Hot tears of embarrassment ran down her cheeks and her vision blurred but still she ran.

When she finally stopped, her failure pierced her like a shaft of unhindered light. She sat down and dug her nails into her palms. She had always known her faults—always kept them close and secret—but now they were spilling out, unchecked.

She wiped her eyes, running her fingers over the dry earth and leaves, soaking in the silence and relishing the separation from Hayvon's questions and judgment, wondering why things had to change, wondering why she would have to become a sprite one day.

Blissful quiet draped the night. No leaves turned on the wind. Not a branch stirred. The clouds and the canopy hid the stars and held the dark motionless.

For a moment, Ahraia hoped it would last forever. But of course, it didn't. Her ears twitched, hearing a sound.

A soft sound.

Ahraia held her hand above the ground, perfectly still. Her ears curled towards it.

The sound drifted through the woods, subtle and subdued. It rose and fell like the wind, so faint that she wondered if she was imagining it.

Did you hear that? Losna thought from afar.

Ahraia stood up, listening. She leaned forward against the trunk of an ancient fir tree, turning her ear towards the east. Was it coming from the plains? She strained to hear a hint of it. *A voice? The shades?* No, it couldn't be. The shades were still in the meadow, in the deeper folds of the forest. The noise caressed her ears again, strange and beautiful, unlike anything she had ever heard—and now louder than before.

What was that? Hayvon and Losna thought together.

Quietly, Ahraia stalked towards the noise, trying to get a better sense of it. Her ears twitched as the sound grew. The louder it got, the stranger and more haunting it became. Ahraia had never been so enchanted and enthralled with a noise in her life.

What are you doing? We're almost on the plains, Hayvon conveyed, catching up.

It's a voice, she conveyed, unsure if Losna or Hayvon had truly heard it yet.

Losna hurried from behind her, sniffing at the night. Her thoughts suddenly constricted to a single point, her instincts rising. *That smell.*

Ahraia stopped and sniffed. She smelled it too. The sweet scent of woodsmoke and something else . . . something pungent and unnatural . . .

Humans, Losna thought, bristling.

The voice rose, accompanied by a strange strumming that stirred Ahraia's heart and straightened her ears.

Hayvon had caught up. *There's something out there. I see light.*

Ahraia ignored him. They were approaching the edge of the forest, the trees growing sparser and the plains suddenly spreading out before them as a dim and undifferentiated mass. The wind smelled familiar, dry and unhindered by the tangled turnings of the forest, but it was tinged with something foreign, something that didn't belong. Then she saw what Hayvon had mentioned—a light that caught her eye. At first it, it glowed, faint and flickering. With every step closer it swelled like the noise, until it reverberated as a bright, unsheltered radiance reflecting upon the eaves of the forest. The air stung with smoke.

Ahraia peered carefully from behind a thicket of saplings. She squinted. A fire blazed upward, surrounded by humans, all sitting or standing in a circle unabashed, all looking inward. The voice carried clear and true now and she realized that one of the humans was singing.

Singing, she thought in disbelief.

Its voice mixed and twined with a sound it spun from its hands. Ahraia held her breath, staring at the humans and listening to the song. Humans were said to be a rough and destructive type of people, scraping and turning the earth to their hands, but this was different . . . this was wonderful.

Ahraia! Get back here, Hayvon conveyed. *If they catch you they're going to torture you to death!* He made a stronger bonding and forced a thousand thoughts of lightwalkers' destruction into Ahraia's head: burning and hacking, bright fires and cold stone, strong hands, sharp steel, and pits beneath the ground. She closed her mind to his enchantment.

It's singing, she thought in disbelief.

Even worse. Get back here. Hayvon's ears were bent almost flat.

Ahraia . . . be careful, Losna thought in distress. Her fear ran even deeper than Hayvon's.

The human who sang was a he, Ahraia decided. Hair grew about his face like wired nettle, of a color she had only ever imagined in the embers of a nearly dead fire. His voice rang out, rough and full. The others humans sat in absolute stillness, as though they too were enchanted, enraptured by his hands spinning violently across the strange object, which sang out a second sound that filled the air, intertwining and mixing with the rise and fall of his voice like a tempest. His hair shook with his movement, then he slowed and brought his voice down, looking intently at his hands.

Ahraia ducked closer, until only a few trees stood between herself and the plains, between herself and the fire. She sensed a binding around her—Hayvon was furious.

What are you doing! Your skin is going to burn. He stood twenty yards behind her, still in the deep folds of the woods. *What if we're seen?*

She ignored him, moving branches and leaves to dampen her steps.

They'll hunt us. They'll come looking for the darkening, Hayvon continued to fret. *I—*

Shhh, she said, blocking out his conveyance. She hadn't yet dared to bond the human, but her curiosity overcame her caution. She cast a mirroring enchantment, revealing the words through the bond. Her ears turned towards the singer, now entirely spellbound.

The words ground against her ears, made of a substance Ahraia had never heard before, a coarse and tumbled language that ran against itself in its haste. And yet, a cadence and a rhythm coursed through it.

He's telling a story, Ahraia realized, just getting a sense of the language.

You aren't actually listening, are you? Hayvon conveyed, aghast that she had bonded the human.

Ahraia stepped forward, but paused.

The human's voice was quieting. His hands were slowing. She kept her foot just above the ground, holding her breath while she waited for him to continue.

But the song ended and the last note of his voice went quiet, like a sudden still within a storm. The night seemed to hang silently from the tip of his fingers and the curve of his mouth.

The singer looked up, and his spell suddenly broke. The other humans shifted, as though roused from sleep, and some clapped their hands together. Ahraia's ears tucked back in fear and she instinctively stepped behind a thicket of fern and elderberry, peering out, unsure what the clapping sound meant.

Losna tensed, ready to leap to Ahraia's aid. *It's a threat. They've seen us!*

But the humans weren't looking towards the forest; their small, gleamless eyes were focused towards the singer.

Ahraia let Hayvon loose from her binding, too distracted by the scene before her to hold him still and silent. Immediately, he started where he had left off.

They've spotted you! Get away from there, he conveyed desperately.

Go back to the shades. I'll meet you there. She peered from behind the bushes, gawking at the humans.

And let father condemn me when you return light-seared and reeking of humans?

Ahraia ignored him. She had never seen humans so close before —not any that were alive, anyway. Once in a Dark Moon, a human would roam too close to the darkening and end up on the end of a dae-wards stake, but that was different.

These humans looked peculiar and brutish, taller and broader than sprites with skin and hair both burnt by the Dae-Mon. They wore coarse clothes and stunk of earth and sweat and woodsmoke. The men had hair growing from their face, like the beards on the bison and keress of the plains. All of them had small, round eyes with too much white, and no gleam, and all of them had small, motionless ears, without any point in the least. She wondered how they could see or hear anything at all.

There were probably twenty of them, she guessed, all gathered closely about the blazing fire and settled between the strange moving shade trees that followed them wherever they went. A small boy played with a figurine, which was suspended by strings. He danced it across the ground as the others faced the fire. Their beasts of burden, like misshapen elk with no horns, brayed and snorted softly beyond the firelight. *Horses*, Kren had called them. *And wagons. With wheels.*

Losna and Ahraia had seen their skeletal, white tops and round legs before, but only from afar, when they had been gathered on the plains in a place where normally only rocks and grasses stood. That night, she and Losna had kept a safe distance, and by the next, the humans had gone, leaving behind only flattened grasses, deep tracks in the mud, and rocks charred black by fire.

One of the larger, bearded humans walked from behind the wagons and clapped the singer over the back. Something bright and metallic glinted at his hip, like an enormous drain. When he spoke, Ahraia marveled at the deep, stone-cut sound of his voice.

"I'll be honest lad, you play like that each night, I'll give ya your three rounds back when we get to Rhun and a place to sleep under a wagon as long as you want. Lord and Lady know we need a bit of cheer on this forsaken stretch of road." He turned to the rest of the humans, pulling at his beard. "That being said, it's getting late, and tomorrow's gonna make for a long day—a day I'm not looking forward to. We'll be making our way clear through this stretch of wood. I want every wagon loaded and ready to go by sunrise. If you're late, you're left. And you don't want to be left behind in cursed woods."

The man spoke quickly and Ahraia struggled to keep up.

Listening to a language she had never heard before was mesmerizing, and while she understood the basic intention of words, the little pieces slipped by her like leaves on a swift river, leaving nothing more than dim impressions of their passing. When the man said "lad", he had been talking to the singer, but it wasn't his name. *It was* . . . she struggled to understand it. Spritish language flowed, purer and more fluid. It never wasted time with such vague thoughts. Ahraia turned her ear again as the singer spoke.

"Cursed woods?" he asked.

A second man stood up, shaking his head. "There you go scarin' 'em with your stories. Nothing good ever came from talking about those things after dark—"

"Just as well, Layton," the bigger man said. "I won't go scaring anyone unnecessarily like. I just want everyone to be mindful . . . these are the north woods of Astenith," he said, gesturing to the forest. Ahraia stiffened as the eyes of the humans turned towards her and the woods. "You'd be a fool not to keep your head about you—and as it is, we'll be doing double watch for the next three nights. You know your lots."

Ahraia crouched further beneath the cover of the trees as the humans stood and started to move about.

Let's go, Losna urged her. Ahraia reluctantly stepped back into the woods, but heard a voice and froze.

"What's out there?" the singer asked.

Ahraia held perfectly still, worried she had been seen when the singer's eyes flashed towards the woods. Her heart pounded so loudly that she was glad for their small ears. The bigger man turned, staring right towards her.

"Nothing good," he said, pulling at his beard. "I've never had trouble myself, but enough sturdy men have stumbled from these woods cursing their eyes and mad as hell, talking of demons and spirits and what not. And those are the ones who've come back—a fair number never do."

"I don't believe in demons or spirits," the singer said. His eyes seemed to rest directly on Ahraia.

The bigger man shrugged. “I don’t either, lad. But that being said, there are all manner of mares roam these woods. Wood wraiths . . . fidmares, tomptes, night elves, trolls—even lady lasts, though I don’t believe that one for a second.”

Ahraia had half formed thoughts of what the different words meant. Trolls were jontuns. Mares sounded like maras, but prowling and physical rather than the wispy-clawed spirits that drifted through the darkest hollows. Wood-wraiths and fidmares were nothing at all to her, hooded shadows and impish figures hidden between half-thoughts. But when the man said night elves, Ahraia had a bare impression of sprites: white skin, long ears, bright night-gleaming eyes. She wondered if he had seen a sprite before.

“Tomptes and fidmares! Trolls and night elves! What a bunch of horseshit,” an old grizzled man scoffed.

“Lady Lasts? I’d pay a fair bit to see a forest maiden,” another man added. His voice rose playfully and he nudged the singer, who gave half a smile.

“Believe me, Tommen. That ain’t what you want to see,” the bearded man said. “You’d do well to think before you open your mouth. Now, a group as big as us won’t have any trouble, but we’ll push hard nonetheless. There’s some old ruins half-way through the woods that will give us a bit of shelter, not much, but it’s a damn sight nicer to make camp near something familiar, even if its empty. We’ll get in a few hours before nightfall if the road looks kindly on us. So, everybody to bed.”

The humans began to move about purposefully. Ahraia tried to catch more of what they said, but they were talking too hushed and scattered for her to hear properly. Some of them disappeared into the wagons while others unrolled blankets on the ground. The child danced his figurine near the fire, until a woman swooped him up and carried him off, out of sight, while he made a racket the whole way.

Ahraia felt a tug at her elbows. Hayvon had one sleeve and Losna the other, both were pulling her back.

Hayvon’s conveyance came through sharply. *I’m not going to get in trouble for not looking out for you.*

I'll vouch for him, Losna thought.

Ahraia let herself be pulled away, a nagging feeling tingling in her mind. Something about the man's words lingered with her . . . something about "old ruins" sounded familiar.

Old ruins . . . in the middle of the forest . . . She had no idea what he meant by "ruins", but she had the impression of shelter. Deep unease gnawed at her stomach, as she struggled to recall the impression the man's words had given her. *Old ruins . . . a shelter, a stone shelter . . . broken*, she thought more precisely.

Her naggings dawned on her all at once, so sharp and clear she almost spoke aloud.

You don't think they mean to make for the Stone Tree, do you? she conveyed, her worry swelling. It made sense. The road from where they stood headed south, directly past the Stone Tree.

What? Hayvon asked, still dragging her forcibly away. *What are you talking about?*

The human said they were going to "old ruins" to the middle of the woods, Ahraia conveyed quickly.

What's a "ruins"? Hayvon asked.

It felt like the Stone Tree to me.

You bound them! Hayvon conveyed, apparently registering what she had said. *You were listening?*

Yes, Hayvon, I was listening! she thought sharply. *You weren't?*

That's not safe. You're not supposed to bond humans—they're dangerous.

Not with their voices, you fool, Ahraia conveyed sharply. *The human said they were making towards a place called "old ruins". He said they would be there by tomorrow night. It felt to me like he meant the Stone Tree.*

So?

So? So! Altah and Kaval are at the Stone Tree, waiting for the emissary from Angolor. Ahraia's panic was rising. *If the humans reach the Stone Tree before nightfall tomorrow . . .*

Hayvon's face fell as realization dawned on him. *Altah and Kaval will be trapped.*

Ahraia imagined the horror of being discovered by the humans while trapped in an underdae. *Still light with no where to go . . .*

"They have to be warned," Hayvon whispered.

The night wasn't old yet, but the Stone Tree was miles and miles away. Ahraia hurried through the woods, back towards where they had left the shades, folding back the forest with enchantments as she went. Losna and Hayvon chased at her heels.

What's your plan? Hayvon said, struggling to keep up. *Even if you get there in time, there isn't another underdae for miles. You'll be caught by the lightrise.*

Ahraia cursed. She knew he was right. The Stone Tree stood in the fringes of the forest. It was the only underdae for a half a night's journey big enough for all of them.

You take the shades back to Daispar. I'll warn Kaval and Altah.

"I'm not going back to Daispar without you," he hissed aloud. *Father would be glad to give me to the Shad-Mon.*

Ahraia doubted their father really would, but she didn't want the trouble of finding out. Her mind raced.

Here's what we're going to do . . . I'll go with Losna to the Stone Tree—

Ahraia—

"Listen!" she said aloud. "We can't all go. By dawn we'll need darkness, and the shades are only going to slow us down. We need to reach another underdae by the time the Dae-Mon rises."

"I'm not going back to Daispar," Hayvon said again, breathing hard as they scrambled up a hillside back towards the meadow.

"I'm not suggesting you do."

"But there isn't another underdae within a night's march."

"Yes, there is," she said.

Hayvon seemed to have guessed her thoughts and was already shaking his head. "No, no, no," he said, "I'm not going there . . . not onto the plains. That's more trouble than it's worth."

Fine. Then good luck in Daispar, Ahraia conveyed as they burst into the meadow and saw the young shades working over Tev's kill.

The Astra forbid you from going back.

Well, then she'd better not find out, Ahraia conveyed. "Come on, you two," she said aloud, letting a tone of command carry through her voice. In an instant, the shades were up and jogging next to Hayvon and her.

"What's happening?" Shim asked.

Ahraia ignored him as Hayvon continued to plead his case.

There's not enough night left, Ahraia. And even if we all manage to reach Plain Dark in time, you don't even know if it's still dark. If it isn't, we're all dead.

If the underdae isn't dark, I'll make it, Ahraia conveyed forcefully.

5

THE STONE TREE

The deepest corners of the night enveloped them by the time Ahraia led the shades across a black-rock ravine that signaled one of the southern markers. The moons had set. She swallowed nervously. Hayvon sensed it too.

We're behind the turn, he conveyed, looking up. *There's no going back to Daispar tonight.*

Impenetrable clouds still veiled stars but Ahraia knew he was right. Losna roamed out ahead again, scouting off towards the Stone Tree. The shades were lagging and for what seemed like the tenth time, Tev's squirrel darted from her arms.

"Get your shadow already," Shim said sharply. Ahraia cringed at how much he sounded like the Astra.

"He's not listening to me," Tev whined, scrambling after her shadow into the underbrush.

We don't have time for this, Hayvon conveyed, worried.

"Tev, you have to make him feel safe," Ahraia said. "You have to look after him—and listen to him. Hear him when he tells you what he wants, or what he's scared of. Reassure him with your thoughts." She tapped her head, trying to remember that not every shade's link came naturally. Her bond with Losna had existed before she had even recognized it.

"Well, Bashir wants to go back. He doesn't like it at night," Tev said, crawling out from under the ferns having finally coaxed the little squirrel back to her.

Shim's eyes narrowed maliciously. *Not very shadow-like.* Ahraia glared at him.

Somewhere off in the night, a moon-raven cawed, calling out for the coming morning. Ahraia turned back to the younger shade.

"Tev, remember, you are the shade that casts the shadow," she said.

"He doesn't listen."

"He will—" Ahraia stopped, sensing movement in the woods before she saw it.

Losna, she thought.

Neither the stars nor the moon lit her shadow's fur and no sound emitted from her paws, but Ahraia knew she returned—revealed first by thought—then by the barest hint of movement, followed by another dash through dark trunks, until at last, she streamed towards Ahraia and the others—effortless and silent—a silver arrow reduced to a streaking shadow in the dark of night. Tev and Shim flinched at first sight of her. Losna slowed and trotted the last fifteen yards, taking in their surroundings in a single, tense glance. Her fur bristled.

Ahraia could sense Losna's emotions storming in distress. Ahraia's ears straightened.

"What did you see?"

Unnatural . . . danger. Losna was beyond agitated. She let out a low woof that trailed off in a growl. Ahraia trembled, cold sweat prickling her skin from the sudden and intense fear that flowed through their link. She reached out to touch her shadow's memories, but there wasn't any one thing, just vague instincts: *deep unease* and *malice*.

"What's wrong?" Hayvon asked. He pushed his hood back, his ears turning about just as Losna's did. Vesta, who had climbed out of Hayvon's pocket to comfort Tev's shadow, hopped back to him, her head bobbing up and down like a bird, her small nose sniffing at the night. Shim and Tev hunkered down quietly, their shadows small and hidden in their hands.

A long moment passed without a single breath stirring in the woods.

"Keep your eyes and ears about you," Ahraia said, taking in the woods, unnerved. A thin line of fog seeped through a seam in the forest. *Losna, what did you—*

Losna turned and cut her off, emitting a low, dangerous growl from the deepest bellows of her chest. Vesta scurried into Hayvon's pocket and Shim nearly tripped as he stepped back in alarm.

Ahraia reached out and steadied the shade. *What is it?* she thought, her free hand reaching instinctively for her drain.

Danger. Losna's thoughts were simplified to a single point.

Which way?

Losna didn't move. She kept her body pointed south, towards the Stone Tree.

Ahraia sniffed. The forest smelled as it always did: pine and maple, fern and foxglove. And mist.

"Hayvon," Ahraia whispered with forced calm, her skin still crawling with Losna's agitation. "Take the shades to Plain Dark."

"But—"

"Listen to me. Just do it." *It's not safe for them.* She bound him so he could feel the fear radiating from Losna, letting the link transfer the emotion; he shuddered. His breaths grew shorter and his eyes darted about the woods.

"What is it?" he said, resigned.

"Get to the underdae," she whispered. "We'll meet you in a bit."

"I don't want to leave," Tev said, looking towards Ahraia.

"Shhh," Ahraia whispered before forcibly quieting her with a binding. "Go with Hayvon." The little shade followed Hayvon with a nudge from Ahraia's mind, her eyes glazed over and her shadow clutched tightly in her hands.

Ahraia watched them slink furtively eastward towards the plains, keeping her eyes shifting about the forest for any signs of danger.

Come on. We're losing the night, Ahraia thought. Losna didn't argue but let out another low growl.

The Stone Tree wasn't far now—another two valleys and they would reach the underdae. They moved quickly through the empty woods. When they reached the valley, Ahraia could feel at once why her shadow was so unnerved. Her hair stood on end, her every fiber telling her to run. She had never felt a place shuddering so strongly under such menace as this.

Losna let out a quiet, deep growl. *Kaval and Altah would be fools to still be here*, she thought, having regained some of her sense.

We have to find them, Ahraia conveyed. They moved in silence across the valley floor and paused at the edge of a wide, treeless expanse.

The meadow stretched out beneath a thick, seeping layer of fog. A black veil of clouds blotted out the stars and the moon, and Ahraia had the intense and immediate feeling that something wasn't as it should be. She could see the dark silhouette of the Stone Tree on the far side of the meadow, slipping in and out of the fog.

The Stone Tree wasn't a tree at all. In fact, it didn't even look like a tree—not in the least. But the humans used it like a shade tree, a shelter built of stone that they used during the night instead of the day. The human road passed beneath the colossal structure like a tenuous serpent through the dry grasses. The Stone Tree rose on the far side: high walls laced with dark closures. One whole side had caved in; the rubble-pile slanted downward, overgrown with bramble and grasses. The remaining structure loomed as tall as a tall maple tree, held by some human magic from collapsing in its entirety.

Do you think they're in there? Ahraia asked. She wanted to call out to them. She wanted to hear their voices without moving any closer.

Don't, Losna thought warningly.

Instead, Ahraia scoured the meadow with her mind. The Stone Tree was a long way off, too far for conveyance or binding, and she felt only an ominous lacking—an emptiness. She wished she wouldn't have reached out at all.

Losna sniffed. She turned her ears forward and back. Ahraia did the same.

No scent. No noises. No movement.

Just fog.

Something's wrong, Losna thought. Ahraia silently agreed. Had her brothers sensed the same menace and fled? Could there be humans about? Or alps? She didn't smell smoke, didn't see bright fires. She didn't see carts, or wagons, or horses.

We have to find my brothers, she said, putting her hand on Losna's back for reassurance.

Losna tensed but didn't argue. Ahraia stood up, readied herself, and then slipped from the forest onto the field.

It took only a matter of moments to cross the meadow. The gentle folds of the grass gave way to the hard dirt of the human path and then back again to meadow. They passed a low ring of crumbled stone. Losna prowled next to Ahraia, a ghostly silhouette in the deepening fog, seeking for any signs of what might be amiss.

Ahraia searched with her mind as they neared the Stone Tree. For the briefest moment, she thought she sensed movement. She paused, crouching low, but the feeling passed. The fog shifted disconcertingly. Ahraia cleared her mind and searched out again but felt nothing but the barren night.

But something wasn't right. The barrenness didn't surprise her. It was something else . . .

Her ears turned. *Silence.*

She sniffed. *Nothing.*

She searched out with her mind again. *Deserted.*

Ahraia shivered.

The Stone Tree wasn't just empty—it was trying to convince her of its emptiness. She vaguely felt her mind wandering and her worry lessening. With a jolt of fear, Ahraia realized her thoughts were being warded off intentionally.

Something's inside, she conveyed as a hiss, so unsettled that the words nearly escaped aloud. Her breaths thinned and her eyes darted about. She focused to stave off any enchantments and bondings that might emerge from whatever was inside. It didn't feel like her brothers, and if it could keep itself secret, it might be able to manage a bonding or a binding just as well.

Are they in there?

I don't know. She held her breath, hesitating in the silence of the moonless meadow. The solitude of the night seemed to swell. The moment stretched on and Ahraia began to wonder if she had imagined the feeling of being warded off. She strained her mind, trying to sense anything within or without. The Stone Tree felt desolate, but maybe it felt desolate because it truly was empty. She turned her ears towards the closure. *Maybe the movement was just the fog*, she thought.

Losna turned her nose, searching for anything on the air. *Shades? Sprites?*

Maybe they've already left. Ahraia wasn't convinced. *Circle around and see if you can't see anything. But keep your distance.*

Losna made off at once, stalking towards the back of the Stone Tree, circling wide around the brambles with eyes and ears up and tail down.

Altah? Ahraia probed tentatively into the darkness. No response emerged.

Kaval? she conveyed.

She crept closer, so silent that she couldn't hear her own footsteps. She stood, dwarfed in the shadow of the tallest wall. The underdae was pitch-black inside. Ahraia struggled to peer past the closure into the inner chambers.

Anyone in there? she probed. Her thoughts seemed to echo off themselves. She let out a slow breath.

Empty.

Truly empty, without ward or thought or binding. A bubble of tension in her chest dissolved.

Still, she stared at the void, waiting for Losna. Her nose twitched. *The remnants of humans? Their stinking metals?* She couldn't tell. Her eyes fell to the ground, where something lay just at the edge of the closure. She strained to see what it was. She knelt, expecting a broken stone or a fallen branch. Instead, she realized it was a bird's wing, contorted oddly.

She leaned forward. The bird was dead—its head was missing. The tips of its wings were silver.

It was Altah's raven, Mehra.

Losna! Get over here! Ahraia conveyed, recoiling. Deeper in the dark, Ahraia glimpsed another shape; a paw—Kaval's fox, Reyn. The night swallowed Ahraia's courage.

"Kaval? Altah? Are you in there?" she said aloud in panic. Her voice cracked the silence of the night like a thunderclap, echoing off the insides and rushing back at her. She stood up and stepped back, distancing herself from the closure as her skin erupted in chills. She realized then what the smell had been: blood. The air was thick with it.

Something lurked just inside the threshold of darkness, near enough that it could have touched her where she had crouched a moment before. If pitch-black could possibly be wreathed in shadow, it was, and an overwhelming sense of danger swept through Ahraia.

She opened her mouth to shout, but even as she did, she felt an enchantment strike out, grabbing her by the neck and pinning her where she stood. A deep void formed inside her, commanding her: *Be still.*

Ahraia stopped, paralyzed far beyond any binding she had ever suffered. The shadowy figure shifted behind the mantle of darkness. She caught a glimpse of jet-black skin or fur, and lightless, lifeless eyes. Ahraia had no sense of what it was: a daemon, like an inky-black wolf standing on its hind legs, the jaws of its binding pinning her still. Every muscle and fiber in her body strained, wanting to scream.

Losna! she conveyed desperately, unsure if her shadow could sense her or not. All she knew was the binding. It gripped her, utterly and unbreakably. Her self-control unraveled under its coercion; her foot moved closer to the closure, possessed by the enchantment. Her teeth were clenched so tight that she knew they would break. She screamed inside herself as she was dragged another step closer.

Losna! she tried to convey, but her thoughts didn't escape her any longer. *Another step.* Her panic threatened to suffocate her. She needed to break away. She couldn't let herself be pulled into the darkness. She knew in a matter of steps she would be dead.

Ahraia gathered herself, closing her eyes and trying to clear the fog from her mind.

Stop, she commanded, both to herself and the figure in the darkness.

Her feet halted and the link crackled with a sort of primal, wicked laughter. The emotion swelled, bringing Ahraia out of the enchantment just enough to have a sense of the figure—of the shape of its thoughts; it was unlike anything she had ever bound. Its mind felt broken and twisted: a vile and violent creature, totally fearless and repulsive.

A renewed sense of certainty enveloped Ahraia. If she reached the darkness, she would be dead. The binding redoubled malevolently, and once again, her foot jolted forward. Her attempts to resist crumbled; she stood just upon the threshold.

Dread consumed her. She couldn't fight the binding.

Her next step would be her last.

She stood perfectly still, waiting.

But the footstep never came.

Hesitation reflected through the binding, and then something else, faint and peripheral. Instinctive protection rustled against every nerve in her body. A willingness to die fighting surged through her, but it wasn't her own.

A snarl erupted right behind her, followed by the most bone-chilling growl Ahraia had ever heard.

Losna!

The binding reverberated with gut-wrenching torment and suddenly dissolved. Ahraia stumbled back in surprise before she realized she was free, tripping over her feet and falling to the ground.

Losna stood over her with her teeth bared and hackles raised. She growled again, her whole being threatening whatever stood inside the darkness.

Ahraia heard rustling within the underdae, a stone falling and then silence. She scrambled up with her knife drawn, cold sweat covering her entire body. She cast out with her mind and felt the menace fleeing.

"Kaval? Altah?" Ahraia said aloud, scrambling forward into the darkness that only a moment before she had desperately sought to escape.

Ahraia! Losna thought in surprise, leaping after her. But the threat was gone. Ahraia could sense that it had fled.

She stumbled to her knees beside two dark figures on the ground. Momentarily, the clouds seemed to break, and moonlight burned her skin. Her hands ran against something slick and warm on the floor of the underdae: blood, pooled next to her brothers' bodies.

They were dead.

Her breaths didn't seem to draw any air. A helpless sob escaped. She put her hand on Kaval's chest as tears streamed down her face. Something cold and smooth stuck out from between his ribs. *A knife.* Without thinking, she pulled it from her brother, slipping the dark blade out with ease.

Ahraia! We're leaving. Losna grabbed Ahraia's cloak and pulled her bodily from the underdae, growling as she did. Ahraia's skin was burning, her mind numb.

Losna thoughts were reduced to instincts. *Leaving!*

Ahraia tried to resist, but Losna dragged her away. She was suddenly aware she was still holding the blade she had pulled from Kaval's chest. She flung the knife into the grasses, disgusted. Then her feet churned on their own accord—first stumbling and then running, fleeing across the meadow—away from the dark of the underdae, away from her brothers and the terror of the enchantment.

We have to find the others, Ahraia thought, wiping the cold sweat from her brow. Guilt swept over her for sending Hayvon out alone with the shades. *What was that?* she thought, unnerved.

Evil, Losna thought. *Pure evil.*

We shouldn't leave them. Ahraia hesitated. She couldn't believe that her oldest brothers were dead.

Losna growled and then jostled Ahraia, keeping her from turning back. She let out a low woof. *I know what that was.*

Ahraia's feet raced, but her mind couldn't make sense of it. The dark. The menace. The death. Whatever it was, it had been vile to touch and overpowering. The brush of its mind had left her feeling sick and weak.

"What was it?"

That was the Shad-Mon, Losna thought grimly. *I'm sure of it.*

6

THE UNDERDAE

W*hat else could bind you like that?* Losna thought, repeating an argument Ahraia had already deflected a dozen times.

Ahraia swung down a shift, her hands transferring seamlessly between the first branch and the next, her feet never touching the ground.

"It *couldn't* have been the Shad-Mon," she said again, unwilling to cede the point but too uncertain to earnestly convey the thought. *It doesn't leave the heart of the forest. Ever.*

Her shadow ran the length of a fallen log, bounding to the forest floor just ahead of her. *Just like sprites can't leave the forest?* she thought, leading Ahraia across a creek that spilled in steep, chattering steps down towards the plains below.

"You don't understand. It's bound there—beholden to the Seed of the Forest. It can't leave the Shadow Woods."

Then why do we patrol the Winnowlin and the Daemon's Creek in the first place?

Ahraia didn't answer. Arguing with her shadow was no better than arguing with herself.

"No one's ever seen it and lived."

I saw it—white teeth all wreathed in black. And I could smell it—dead fur and death, Losna thought, adamant and discomfited.

Ahraia had heard every exaggerated story and seen every half-formed memory from those claiming to have seen the Shad-Mon, but none of them matched the menace they had faced in the Stone Tree. Some told of a gray-skinned monster, the size of a jontun, other's claimed it was an imp with the head and wings of a great eyeless owl, and still others claimed it was a spirit that moved as fog and mist and materialized as death. Each and every story was just as absurd as the next, but none of them had ever called the Shad-Mon black as the night, with black fur and lifeless eyes.

What other faceless daemon roams the woods? What about the fog? Losna pressed, leaping easily from one stone to the next, onto a moss-slickened log and over a narrow channel of foaming water.

"It's always foggy in autumn. Maybe it was a wraith of sorts . . . some spirit or fiend from the Reaches."

Losna scowled at her. *It killed Kaval and Altah, Ahraia—and their shadows. What else has ever killed a pair of shades?*

Ahraia didn't know. The mention of her brothers was like tumbling into a nettle, sharp and barbed, but the piercing needles resided on her insides: thick and blunt and excruciating. Guilt pressed into every corner of her chest, suffocating her.

"I never should have left them."

Losna paused, dropping her insistence for a moment. Her great golden eyes shone back from the water's edge. *There's nothing we could have done.*

Ahraia lapsed into silence, dwelling on her brothers, wondering if she might have stopped the wraith if they had been sooner. Now, they lay upon the barren floor of the Stone Tree with the lightrise coming.

"They aren't meant to suffer light, even in death," she said quietly.

Neither are you, Losna thought, looking to the east. A hint of gray was creeping over the horizon. Soon enough, it would be burning bright, even before the Dae-Mon decided to rise. Losna stopped at the stream side and lapped at the water. Ahraia felt woefully tired, drained from the emotions twisting within her.

"We're going to have to go back," she said.

Losna looked up, startled, her snout dripping-wet.

"Tomorrow night," Ahraia said. She brushed her hair behind her ear, resolute in her decision.

Losna, who would be willing to argue until the fur fell off her tail, stared at her in disbelief, her thoughts reduced to pure instinct. *No.*

The sky was growing lighter by the minute.

We need to get to the underdae, Ahraia conveyed. She started back down the hill, using fistfuls of ferns and alder trunks to slow her descent. Losna eventually gathered her thoughts. She hurtled after Ahraia, slipping in haste and letting her know how foolish she was for even thinking of returning.

The hillside eased. The stream dropped in shorter and shorter falls, quietly churning over rocks and tumbled logs, until at last it slid smooth and glimmering onto the plain before them.

We'd better hurry, Ahraia conveyed, cutting off Losna's warnings. She lengthened her stride.

The plains were frighteningly unprotected, an endless expanse that would soon enough be swathed in deadly daylight. Even with all their nights spent running wild, it still made Ahraia nervous being in the open so late.

They climbed a series of long, low hills, until Ahraia spotted the underdae in the distance, first as a silhouette, then as a small stand of trees, and finally growing as a massive grove that towered overhead. She could see a tiny figure standing beneath the eaves of the outer trees.

She recognized Shim but he disappeared back into the woods. A moment later, he returned with Hayvon behind him, just as Ahraia and Losna reached the grove.

"Where have you been!" Hayvon called out, looking disheveled and weary. "Where are the others? Where are Kaval and Altah?"

Ahraia could tell something was wrong. Hayvon's face was pale. Ahraia slowed to a walk, moving under the broken cover of the woods, exhausted.

"What's wrong?" she asked.

The stand of trees looked ragged and unkempt—dark—but not nearly dark enough.

"The underdae, it's been—" Hayvon stopped suddenly as though he had seen the Dae-Mon. "Are you okay?" *What happened to you?*

Shim was staring at her as well. Ahraia looked down. Dried blood covered her hands.

"It's blood," she said dumbly. *I mean, it's not mine.* Her stomach clenched, realizing it was her brothers' blood.

"Where are Kaval and Altah?" Hayvon asked, his ears flattening.

"They're . . ." The words failed to form on Ahraia's lips. She swallowed down a lump in her throat. *They're dead.*

"They're what?" Hayvon's skin faded to a paler shade of gray. The tips of his ears curled down.

Dead, Ahraia repeated, unable to meet his eye. "Where's Tev? It's getting light."

"Dead? How?"

"Why is it so light in here?" Ahraia said, moving past him into the first layer of trees. The once tightly sewn limbs dangled loose and unwoven. She walked farther into the grove and felt her heart sinking. "What happened here?" she asked in disbelief, looking at the state of the underdae.

It had been ravaged. Two anchor trees lay cracked upon the ground, uprooted. Branches hung withered and sickly. The source vines that the inner trees leeched off of had been hacked away. All her tedious coaxing and tending had been spoiled. A golden line of light in the east could just be seen through the far side of the grove.

Losna sniffed about, worried. *The Astra must have destroyed it . . .*

"What do you mean they're dead?" Hayvon asked again, his gaze chasing her for an explanation.

"I mean they're dead!" Ahraia snapped, her composure crumbling under the fear that came with finding the underdae in tatters. "Dead. Like we're going to be if we don't get this folding back in order."

Hayvon stared at her, his mouth agape. The shades were staring too. Ahraia turned away, immediately wishing she hadn't lashed out. Her fear had gotten the best of her. And the guilt that had been steadily weighing on her heart now hung like the Dae-Mon, just beneath the horizon, on the verge of killing her.

"What are we going to do?" Shim said.

Ahraia assessed the shelter, rubbing her hands together to flake away the blood, feeling both disgusted and defeated. Folding an underdae took time and energy, neither of which she had.

She drew in a deep breath, blowing stray hairs from her face. Folding darkness normally required calm, but she was going to have to make do without. She focused on the grove about her, taking in every twig and branch, every half-grown leaf and twisted trunk. She nodded, beginning to see the shape of things as they were, and the shape of what they would need to be.

"I'll need your help, Hayvon. We don't have much time."

"It's too much. We'll never be able to form darkness that quickly," he said. He paused, his eyes showing pale in the last vestiges of true night. "We aren't going to survive the day, are we?" he asked, a quiet certainty in his voice.

Shim and Tev looked up from where they huddled with their shadows under a low bramble of fox fern and maple.

"Of course we are," Ahraia said firmly, setting her mind to the task. "You start tightening the inner bit. I'll take care of the rest." She turned away from him and sat down.

"But what happened to—"

Hayvon . . . Ahraia conveyed, clinging to her thread-bare calm. *You're wasting time.*

She reached out and made her first binding. Hayvon stood just behind her, his questions about the Stone Tree lingering at the tip of his mind. The moment stretched on and finally he turned away. Ahraia was glad, turning her attention to weaving the branches of a small fir to the trunk of a nearby cedar. Her emotions prickled like a nerve laid bare, and if Hayvon had pressed her, she didn't know if she could keep the weight of everything from overwhelming her. She fought back tears and made another binding, trying to lower herself deeper into the task.

The trees remembered her. They swayed at her first touch, quivering right to the tip of their needles and leaves. But Ahraia's heart was a storm and her mind was the wind. The branches moved to the tempest of her will, as though terrified of what she might do if they refused.

The underdae worked the same as a darkening: outer husk, inner shell, and a tree within that provided true dark. In the darkening, each layer consisted of a single tree: the shell, the nit, and the shade tree, and each were expanded over whole lifetimes. But in the case of Ahraia's underdae, each layer was a fusion of trees and bushes coerced into coexistence. It had taken months to fully weave. And it was far more dangerous than using single trees—but seeing as only the Masai controlled the seeds for new darkenings, and the Astra kept the seeds for new nit and shade trees—Ahraia hadn't had much of a choice.

She turned her attention to the outer layer first, moving larger branches to re-form weavings that had been lost without her tending. These were simple, broad threads that wouldn't be dark in their own right, but would support the next layer, which was more broken than the rest. Once she had a loose web, she began to truly work. She wove cedar and fir and fern and hemlock. She tied off branches to limbs and trunks, splaying leaves and turning needles. The light was growing outside. In a way, it made the work easier, showing where the underdae lacked integrity. Losna stood next to her, still on edge from the night and worried about all the light. She huffed and whined but left Ahraia to her work.

The branches twisted and turned. Leaves spun and needles shook, and slowly the bowels of the underdae grew darker. Outside, she sensed that true light had finally come. Her skin felt a gentle burn but the underdae was holding for the moment.

"Ahraia . . .," Hayvon said, bringing her out of her reverie. "There's too much damage here. With this tree down . . . I don't think I'll be able to form the wall properly."

She looked back and saw that Hayvon had admirably gathered darkness to the inner layer, in his own haphazard way. A cedar that had anchored the western wall, however, was toppled over with its roots high in the air.

"That's not going to do," she said, retreating deeper into the shadows with the shades watching her. She lightly bound the surrounding trees, testing which ones might be willing to help her. A pliable maple, with great broad leaves, shifted eagerly at her touch. She moved it into the gap, but there was nothing to anchor the fold. She tried feebly to bring a fir branch across to help but it couldn't reach. She tried the same with a sapling but it simply bent and shivered and then sprang free.

"I've already tried everything," Hayvon said, his voice tense.

Ahraia ignored him and bound an enormous fir tree well outside of the underdae. It was massive, the largest tree in the grove, its trunk as wide as a darkening core. Ahraia sat perfectly still, coaxing the giant to her will. Morning sounds drifted in as she produced a true binding, with birds chirping beyond the folds of the underdae and small creatures rustling through the bushes. The shades watched, probably unaware of what she was even trying.

"You don't think you can actually bend that, do you?" Hayvon asked, peeking out and seeing branches wriggling far above the outer shell. "That's never going to work. You might as well try bending a bridging tree on your own. Those branches won't even come close."

Ahraia set her mind on her intention and waited, straining slightly as the fir resisted. "Who says I want the branches?"

"I told—" Hayvon stopped short as the earth suddenly shifted and a large root emerged just beneath the gap in the trees. Ahraia grimaced. It was as close to a smile as she could manage. She brought the maple down and hooked it to the root. Hayvon's ears quivered straight and she went back to weaving the rest of the wall complete.

Losna, go and get any fallen branches you can, we'll just have to patch what we can't fill.

Her shadow went off through the grove in search of fallen limbs. Morning slipped on and the Dae-Mon's brilliant light turned the outer world un-walkable, but the inside of the underdae remained dim and safe. Losna came and went by a low tunnel of leaves, thrashing and shaking the folding each time she passed. Hayvon used the branches that Losna brought, stacking them in the barest spots while Ahraia put the finishing touches on the shelter, weaving fir to cedar, maple to fox leaf. She worked without thinking—bonding and binding and bending and braiding.

Eventually, Hayvon's voice came through the fog of enchantment. "I think that will do."

The branch she was tucking away slipped and swung back idly. She re-bound the tree and tucked it in again, persuading it to curl around the pine branch in order to lock in place. It wasn't perfect, but it would be sufficient. The day would be kept out.

Ahraia heard something large moving outside of the underdae. She probed out for Losna with her mind, but only got a dim sense of struggle from her shadow.

Losna, are you out there? she conveyed, forming a tiny closure, just big enough for her eye. She peered out, worried. Losna was wrestling with a fallen tree, far too big to be of any use. She fought with the tree stubbornly, as though dragging the body of some overlarge, prized kill.

Get in here, Ahraia thought.

Losna looked up guiltily. She grabbed the tree and jerked it closer.

Come here, Ahraia conveyed firmly.

Losna reluctantly let go of the log and slipped back into the underdae through her tunnel of leaves. Pine needles and burrs coated her fur.

Ahraia turned back to the underdae, exhausted. Tev was asleep and her shadow was curled inside her cloak. Ahraia wasn't sure if it was a sign that the squirrel was growing attached or if it was simply terrified of Losna. Shim was watching Ahraia with tired eyes, looking frightened and on edge. He had a small knife out on his lap, apparently in case anything from the plains came for them.

Vesta was wrapped around Hayvon's neck, her eyes closed but her tail flopping about idly. Hayvon, however, was staring at Ahraia with bloodshot eyes. She knew what was coming, and thought about binding him to stop it, but she was too exhausted.

What happened at the Stone Tree? Hayvon asked, careful to keep the younger shades from receiving his conveyance.

I don't want to talk about it, Ahraia conveyed, picking needles from Losna's fur as her shadow settled against her.

I need to know. Hayvon paused. *You're . . . you're sure they're dead?*

She could feel the doubt in his words, a hidden hope that she was wrong. It brought the night crashing back over her, and the emotions that had dimmed came bursting back like the Dae-Mon suddenly burning through.

Positive, she conveyed. *I saw them—and their shadows.*

All of them? He asked in shock. *How?*

I don't know. There was something there with them. Something . . . terrible. She shuddered, remembering the binding and the figure in the dark.

Something there? You mean something that killed them?

She nodded. Hayvon looked as though she had pushed him into a beam of light.

You saw it? What was it?

I don't know, Ahraia conveyed, unwilling to admit what Losna suspected it had been. Losna lifted her head and glared at Ahraia.

Tell him! she growled. Vesta's eyes opened and her tail stopped on Hayvon's shoulder.

Ahraia drew a deep, shuddering breath. She stared blankly at her bloodstained hands. *We think it might have been the Shad-Mon.*

Hayvon's mouth hung open and Vesta's head snapped up from his shoulder, obviously having heard a reflection through her shade. Hayvon seemed unable to form words. Ahraia kept her eyes down, digging at the blood beneath her fingernails. After a moment, Hayvon seemed to find his thoughts.

The Shad-Mon? That's impossible.

Tell her that. Ahraia nodded to Losna. She would have been just as certain as her brother if she hadn't felt the terrible crushing weight of the binding and seen the barest shape of the creature.

The daemon doesn't—

I know. Hayvon, believe me, I know. But I don't know what else it could have been. You weren't there . . .

Hayvon swallowed hard, staring at her with a determined intensity. *Will you show me?* Vesta crawled off his shoulder onto his lap, facing him uncertainly.

Show you? Ahraia thought, suddenly terrified, feeling sick at even the thought of reliving the scene for him. *No.* She shook her head. "No," she said aloud, trying to push away all thought of it. A bird outside startled into flight and Shim and Tev raised their heads. Ahraia kept shaking her head. *No*, she repeated more subtly. *I won't. They were murdered. I can't relive that.*

Hayvon was staring at her with wide eyes, idly pushing Vesta out of his face.

Ahraia looked down at the blood on her hands, feeling guilty. *They were already dead when I got there. Whatever it was . . . it was in the Stone Tree with them . . . inside the darkness. Made of darkness. Black fur and black eyes, standing blacker than a black shadow.* Ahraia shuddered remembering how it seemed darker than the deepest corner of the underdae. *It would have killed me too, but I think Losna surprised it. It had me bound, Hayvon, like a sprite would, like prey—bound firmer than any binding I've ever felt. I felt myself still . . . I knew I was in danger—but I didn't have any control. It dragged me forward, without any effort.*

You have to show me. It couldn't have been the Shad-Mon.

Ahraia bit her lip, her heart constricting with the pain of the memory.

Losna nudged her with her snout. *Show him*, she thought. *Let him see for himself.*

But Ahraia couldn't. Her fear, guilt, and pain all tumbled together, overwhelming her. She couldn't relive the memory again. She shook her head, unwilling. She closed her eyes and blocked out Hayvon's conveyance. She blocked out Losna as well, dizzy from the sudden feeling of loneliness and quiet in her mind.

Ahraia's jaw ached from clenching. It was the only thing to keep her from sobbing. A single tear formed and slipped down her cheek.

She wiped it away, not daring to open her eyes. She lay down, facing away from the others. Losna nuzzled her and licking idly at her hand. Eventually she laid her head on Ahraia's arm.

Ahraia didn't move for a long time, listening to the strange sounds of the day. The wind sounded more dangerous than at night, as though it wanted to peel back the bindings of the underdae to bring light scorching down on them. Birds that she had never heard before chirped and sang outside. She lay in a daze as the Dae-Mon rose dangerously overhead, trying to sleep, hoping for the sweet relief of nothingness, but instead, every time she came close, she found herself rigid with fear, feeling the deep, falling sensation of being paralyzed by the enchantment. Every time the daemon was waiting, just beyond the veil of darkness. The memories kept tumbling about her against her will. She was reliving the night whether she wanted to or not.

She rolled over and found Hayvon watching her. She guessed it was getting near mid-morning.

"They're my brothers too. I need to see," he whispered. Losna raised her head but the shades kept sleeping.

Ahraia nodded. "I know," she said, having already thought through the memory a dozen times.

When she spoke, she spoke aloud to make sure he understood what he was asking. "I'll show you, but . . . it's not going to be comfortable. It's not going to be easy."

He nodded, looking fearful but determined.

Ahraia took a deep, steadying breath. She scooted towards him, until their knees almost touched. Losna watched on nervously. Ahraia looked into Hayvon's bright white eyes—so different from the horrible lifeless eyes of the creature in Stone Tree.

Are you ready?

Hayvon nodded. Ahraia took another deep breath. She formed the bonding, melding their minds so that he would see what she envisioned. She closed her eyes, searching for a thought that would prompt the memory. *Fog over the meadow.* The memory grew more palpable. She let it envelop her. The binding to Hayvon and the underdae faded.

Ahraia could feel the dark of night surrounding her. Things she hadn't noticed before seemed more pronounced. The fog wasn't just drifting—it was flowing like water over the lip of a falls, with no wind or current to push it. But the grass didn't move with it. The unnatural silhouette of the Stone Tree loomed like a ghostly monster, formidable and menacing. The dark closures of the underdae stared unblinking back at her. She reached out and touched Losna for reassurance. A dim part of her knew that it was a memory, but that part was fading.

Losna's fur was coarse and warm beneath her hand. Ahraia moved silently towards the underdae. The grass brushed against her knees and the crunch of hard dirt sounded beneath her feet.

The moments slipped by in a blur of sharp details and raw emotions: a pulse of fear, *hesitation, doubt.* Losna jogged around the far side of the Stone Tree, searching for a sense of things. But Ahraia had her own sense of things: stone and dark and shadows. She knelt and saw the broken wing of a raven and the limp paw of a fox.

Losna! She stepped back, horrified. *Something was inside.*

And then the darkness descended upon her. She sensed the creature in the inky-black interior of the Stone Tree. *Terror.* She couldn't move. The Shad-Mon was there with her.

The binding wrapped around her mind anew, so complete and unbreakable that Ahraia nearly screamed. She would have if she could, but every fiber in her body gave way to the enchantment, entirely against her will. *I'm going to die*, she thought. Her feet dragged her towards the closure. Helplessness coursed through her. The Shad-Mon was just inside the darkness. A black wolf on its hind legs. She could *see* the shadow in the deep dark. Black as black. White teeth beneath lidless eyes. Vile. *Evil.* She felt the brush of its mind and nearly vomited from the sensation. She was as good as dead.

The growl came unexpectedly: violent and protective, sure as death. Losna was just behind her. Ahraia's heart soared and she tumbled backwards. The Shad-Mon retreated with a sense of surprise and panic. And then Ahraia was on her knees at her brother's side. She burned with moonlight suddenly, sharp and bright, and her eyes blurred with tears. Blood coated the floor: *warm and wretched*. She grabbed the knife: *Icy-cold and charcoal dark*. Losna was dragging her away. Ahraia tossed the knife aside and then she was running. Running and rising. She came out of the memory breathless and sick.

The night faded and the dark gray of the underdae swelled around her with the sounds of day. Ahraia leaned over and vomited, her fear overcoming her.

"I left them. We can't leave them like that!" she said hysterically.

It's okay, Losna thought, whining in worry.

What in day's light was that? Hayvon conveyed, clutching his chest, wide-eyed and terrified. Tev and Shim cowered in the deepest shadows, watching them. Vesta had scurried into Hayvon's pocket and was now curled up and hidden, quivering at his chest.

Losna was next to Ahraia, trying to comfort her and keep the fear from reflecting through their bond. *It's okay*, she thought again, nuzzling against Ahraia.

But the simple reassurance of her shadow did little to quell the terror and guilt that swelled within her.

That was the Shad-Mon, wasn't it? Hayvon conveyed, barely managing to keep his thoughts from the shades this time. *Black eyes and black heart.*

Ahraia was shaking. Her hand felt cold where she had held the creature's knife. She scratched at her skin as though she could still feel the brief, unnatural moonlight.

Where did that light come from? Hayvon conveyed as though he guessed her thoughts. She hadn't properly broken their connection.

The moonlight? Maybe the clouds broke, she conveyed, still scratching.

Ahraia . . . there wasn't any moon last night.

Ahraia stopped scratching. Her heart suddenly clenched tightly as she realized he was right. There had been no moon or stars, but her skin had definitely felt light, dim but undeniable.

The orb, Hayvon said flatly.

Our nit's orb! Ahraia's heart stuttered. Kaval had been carrying their orb, the one that fed moonlight to their nit tree. She had been too shocked to notice it, but the faint light she had felt had undoubtedly come from the orb, somewhere on the ground in the underdae.

We have to go back for it, she conveyed feeling an overwhelming sense of despair.

What about the Shad-Mon? Losna asked.

A shiver of fear raised the hairs at the back of her arms. *We don't have a choice. If we don't get that orb back, mother's tree won't last a turning.*

Hayvon looked frightened, but didn't argue. Their nit tree couldn't survive without the orb's light, and without the nit tree to leech off of, their shade trees would wither as well.

Already wracked by guilt for fleeing her brothers, Ahraia felt doubly foolish. She should have noticed the light, no matter how faint it was.

Hayvon's eyes grew darker. *The orb's going to be lethal after a whole day under the Dae-Mon.*

He was right. It was dangerously light outside—and the orb would be engorged, close to shattering, Ahraia guessed.

We'll just have to find a way to cover it. One of the shadows can carry it . . .

Hayvon's ears turned down. His eyes grew even darker. *What about the humans?* he worried.

The humans! Ahraia felt faint. She had entirely forgotten about the lightwalkers. Her chest felt as though her heart had given up, collapsed inward on itself. "If the humans find them, we're dead. If the light doesn't kill us, the Astra will."

7

BRIGHT FIRE

A low crescent of the Blood Moon sat just above the horizon when Ahraia and the shades finally emerged from the shelter. Ahraia hadn't slept but now the light had finally surrendered to night. She led them to the edge of the grove, where stars spilled in between the clouds streaming in from the west. She caught the scent of rain on the wind.

"What are we going to do if the humans are already there?" Hayvon whispered as they hurried across the plains.

What are we going to do if the Shad-Mon is there? Losna thought darkly.

"I'll figure something out," Ahraia said, answering them both. She looked back. The shades were already lagging behind. Both of their shadows were hidden in the folds of their cloaks and their hoods were drawn up against the dim light.

"Hurry up, you two. A little starlight isn't going to kill you." Ahraia had told them just enough to keep them moving without whining, scared but not terrified. They knew something bad had happened to Kaval and Altah, but she hadn't mentioned the Shad-Mon.

The journey back to the Stone Tree was longer than Ahraia remembered, and her disquiet grew with every step. If the humans were camped in the meadow, they undoubtedly would have discovered her brothers and the orb. The nit tree would be leafless in a single turning without the moonlight to feed off of. *And Kaval and Altah* . . . she let the thought go, not wanting to think of their bodies being discovered.

"What do humans do with the dead?" Tev asked, as though an echo of Ahraia's fears had escaped.

"You don't want to know . . ." Hayvon said grimacing, leading them up a long gully of a dried up stream bed. "It's not a peaceful rest under the unbroken dark, that's for sure . . ."

They clambered up a dry falls with Shim in the lead.

"Father told me they burn them," he said, peering back from above with a horrified gleam in his eyes.

Tev shuddered, "That's not true. Is it?"

"Of course it is. They burn the body in the brightest, hottest flame they can make—"

"Shim. That's enough," Ahraia said, disgusted by the thought. She hoped it wasn't a fate her Kaval and Altah would suffer.

"I'm just telling her—"

Quiet, Hayvon conveyed, cutting Shim off and pulling Tev to the top of the rise. *It's not far now. This way*. He gestured, leading them away from the stream bed towards a broad slope carpeted in ferns.

Ahraia's ears kept twitching forward, listening for any signs of a song or the singer, but none came. The slope eased and the understory grew thick with maples and musty smelling charberries. The wind gusted in the trees, sweeping in and then leaving, each time stronger than before.

Losna lifted her nose. *Smoke,* she thought to Ahraia. Her tail stiffened.

Ahraia held up a hand in caution. She mimicked her shadow, sniffing the cool air. The smell was faint, but unmistakable. *Fire.*

"Bright light and bitter day," she cursed. "The humans have already reached the valley. Keep your shadows close."

Tev trembled and Shim's ears tucked inward, but neither argued. Ahraia took the lead and guided them downwind, where the scent of smoke grew heavier. Losna was just ahead, furtively picking her way through the woods, sniffing high and low. The trees creaked and shifted, stirring the night with swaying branches and the crackle of falling leaves. To Ahraia's relief, thick clouds had hidden the stars.

I don't like this, Hayvon thought, as the scent of smoke mixed with the strange smells of the humans. *If the humans are already here, then there's nothing to be done.*

Tev pinched her nose. The odors were repulsive. *They smell awful.*

Like burning flesh, Shim conveyed with fiendish eyes.

Ahraia glared at him, her ears batting three times for silence. Her nose stung from the smoke.

Is that light? Hayvon conveyed before they had even crested the hill. A faint glow spread through the woods. *That's too big to be a fire.*

The meadow was still out of sight, and yet, radiant light spewed through the treetops. Ahraia and the other shades paused, watching ahead. The light was garish and glaring—penetrating too deeply into the woods.

Hayvon caught Ahraia's eye, his conveyance dropped low, hidden from the shades. *You don't think they're burning them, do you?*

Ahraia's ears curled against her will, unable to answer out of fear. She imagined Kaval and Altah in a great pyre, burning before the humans, light and heat devouring them. She would die of guilt if that was their fate.

We should leave, Losna thought, nervously.

Ahraia shook her head stubbornly. *I'm not leaving without the orb.* She snuck forward to the hill's crest, trying to get a glimpse of what could be sending out so much light.

That's far enough, Hayvon conveyed from the deeper safety of the woods. *It's too late. The humans are already here.*

Ahraia ignored him and edged towards a break in the woods. Upon reaching it, she peeked out from the cover of the trees and saw great, billowing flames rising from the meadow. They soared upwards, towering into the air as roiling clouds of light, far worse than any fire she had ever seen.

Dae-Mon above, she cursed. She ducked back behind the trees.

Sweat beaded in her hair and she pulled her hood close before slipping forward. She stole carefully between safer shadows, contorting herself between the flickering beams. She looked back.

Hayvon's ears tucked tightly against his head. *Have you gone mad? You aren't getting anywhere near that meadow*, he conveyed. Against his normal prudence, he lumbered forward to Ahraia, shielding his face with an arm. *If you come back to Daispar light-scarred, it's my head.*

Ahraia shook her head. *What do light-scars matter if we don't have a nit tree?*

Hayvon's bonding rang with disbelief. *We can come back tomorrow night! Once the humans move on. Once this light is gone. Let's—*

A distant crash cut Hayvon's conveyance short; it sounded like a tree cracking in a storm. New flames surged upward and then settled. Hayvon and Ahraia froze, waiting for anything else, but nothing came. No voices. No sound. No call or cry from the humans.

Another day under the Dae-Mon and it won't matter if we get the orb back. It'll be shattered, she pressed. *And if the humans already have the orb, then it won't do us any good to come back tomorrow night.*

Hayvon glared at her.

Then I'll go. That way father won't condemn me. I'll just burn up along the way. He took out his light-veil and unfurled it.

"Give it to me," Ahraia said. She snatched it from him and held him back with an arm. *We wouldn't be in this if I'd used my head. I'm not going to let you suffer for it.*

Hayvon opened his mouth to protest and lunged for the veil. Ahraia formed a binding and held him still. She half-wrapped the web about her neck with her free hand and stepped towards the light.

I'll go without if you force me, she threatened stubbornly.

Hayvon's conveyance was desperate. *This is a bad idea. What if the humans see you? What if the orb isn't there? You're not going to find it and you're going to mar yourself in the process. If you'd just—*

Ahraia stepped closer to the light.

Hayvon looked tormented, letting out a growl before relenting. He stared at her skin. The faint lines of light-spotting were emerging at her wrists, drawn out by the barest glimpses of the fire. He frowned.

"What about the light?" he pleaded aloud.

It's not like it's the Dae-Mon. "I'll survive," she whispered. *Get them to the deeper dark. Losna and I will be fine. Come on, Losna . . .*

Hayvon reluctantly retreated with the shades to the safer dark, while Losna and Ahraia crept closer to the meadow. Losna moved one paw at a time. If she was quiet, it was nothing compared to what Ahraia was capable of. Silence was woven through every step. She bound branches, ferns and leaves to keep even the faintest rustle from disturbing the night.

They reached the edge of the meadow and Ahraia paused, not yet daring to look at the bright fires. The oppressive menace that had permeated the night before was absent, chased away by the light.

Do you see anything? Ahraia conveyed. Scarlet firelight flecked Losna's skin and danced in her eyes. Their bond reverberated with fear.

The work of the Shad-Mon, Losna thought, peering out.

Ahraia looped Hayvon's veil about her face and risked a glance. She squinted. The light of the fires burned hot—so bright that she was forced to covered the veil with her arm. It rose in great, angry flames, illuminating the whole meadow, all the way from the eaves of the forest to the imposing figure of the Stone Tree.

Ahraia gasped at the ruin before her.

Flames engulfed the human encampment, but nothing else moved. Humans and horses both scattered the ground, like the last leaves after an autumn storm. Two of the wagons lay tipped on their sides, their white coverings smoking heavily, the dark fumes curling amongst the wicked flames. The smell stung her nostrils: damp cloth and flesh. A surreal stillness reigned, even amongst the ever-dancing blaze. The wagons looked as though a great beast had ravaged them and cast fire over the whole meadow, like the sky-daemons of the north. But Ahraia knew it couldn't have been.

Losna stepped back into the shadows. *Are you convinced now?*

There was no movement, and no sign of whoever or whatever did this. Nothing about the meadow seemed like the night before. Light replaced dark. The low crackle of flames replaced silence. The Stone Tree loomed over the meadow, flickering in the firelight but untouched by flames, staring down with empty, black eyes.

Is there anything alive out there? Losna asked.

Ahraia swept out with her mind. The meadow was too broad to tell, but a lingering sense of dread and devastation hung in the air, but it was far different from the intentional emptiness of the night before.

What do we do? Losna thought.

"We can't do anything yet; these flames need to settle first. We're just going to have to wait," Ahraia said. She tucked herself into a dark hollow of the forest and listened, probing with her mind for any life or threat. Losna searched as well, her eyes fixed on the encampment and her ears turning one way and then the next, but nothing stirred except the slowly dying flames. After a time, the light settled to the point that Ahraia's face didn't burn when she peeked out.

Go check on Hayvon and the shades, she conveyed. *Then circle the woods and see if there's any sign of what happened. When you get back, we'll go look for them.*

What about you?

I'll be fine. I want to keep a watch over things for a bit.

Losna huffed in discontent, not liking Ahraia's plan one bit. She let out a whine but nuzzled against her cheek in acknowledgement.

And be careful, Ahraia conveyed after her.

Losna trotted off into the woods, leaving Ahraia listening to the whispers of the fires. She waited and watched. The flames slowly turned to embers, and she sensed the skies overhead growing darker. It smelled of rain, and she hoped for a downpour.

Not one of the humans had moved. Their deaths would mean trouble in the Gelcsh. More humans would come—with bright armor and sharp spears. And more fire. The borders of the forest would be dangerous. But horrible as that thought was, her mind kept returning to their deaths.

What kind of daemon could kill a whole troop of lightwalkers? she wondered. *What kind of daemon could kill two shades and their shadows?*

The thought festered in her mind, until she sensed Losna creeping back from the woods. The firelight barely glowed on the eaves of the forest now.

Anything out there? Ahraia asked.

Deserted. Hayvon's still safe in the deeper dark. Losna looked about, her ears twitching in all directions. She let out an agitated huff. *I want to be done with this place. We've already lingered too long.*

"Then let's get this over with," Ahraia whispered. *I can probably stand this light.* She pulled up her hood and carefully re-wrapped Hayvon's light-veil about her face, so only her eyes shone out.

Are you sure?

Ahraia looked back to the fires. Only a few low, lingering flames and bright hot embers remained, licking at the wagons and ruins.

We'll find out. She nodded to Losna and then moved decidedly from their hiding place.

The heat and light pressed against her eyes, but her skin didn't burn. Losna jogged right beside her, worrying and watching and sniffing as they went. Ahraia hurried towards the Stone Tree, staying low in the grass and awaiting Losna's warning if anything seemed amiss. She sought out ahead of her with her mind, fearing the sudden paralysis of the night before. But no enchantment came. They crossed the meadow quickly, staying well away from the ruins of the human encampment. Ahraia's heart thudded in her chest and the skin around her eyes felt hot. Her mouth was dry and sticky, knowing she was about to see her brothers again.

Careful, Losna thought as they approached.

Ahraia drew her small drain and peered into the dark. The closure itself was black, but the glowing cinders of the human fires cast the ground in relief. Ahraia leaned in and saw at once that neither her brothers nor their shadows lay where she had left them.

She moved cautiously inside the underdae. Losna pressed up against her side.

The entry was empty; her brothers were gone.

Where are they? Losna asked as she sniffed about, moving carefully into the darker recesses of the Stone Tree.

Ahraia's mind was racing. Had the humans found their bodies? Moved them? Burned them? And where was the orb? Had the humans taken it? She walked nervously into the bowels of the Stone Tree, moving down a narrow, rubble-strewn passage. She turned a corner and the closure was hidden entirely. She let her eyes adjust.

Small chambers led off either side, but they too were empty. The stairs leading both up and down were crumbled inward. She circled back, searching each corner for Kaval and Altah. She checked beneath an overgrown bramble that spilled in through a second closure, and beneath a small pile of stone where part of the structure had collapsed.

They aren't here. Ahraia stood up, disheartened and worried. *Neither is the orb.*

Blood stained the ground where Kaval had lain, but no other signs remained of her brothers or the orb. She swept her hands over the rough dirt floor wondering if perhaps the orb had shattered from all the light of the day and the fires. But there were no fragments of it. And if it hadn't shattered, then she expected it to be gleaming with brilliant light.

She stood up and looked back to the human fires, wondering if the lightwalkers had perhaps burned her brothers before whatever trouble had beset them. Her heart constricted with guilt.

Do you think the humans took them? Losna thought, following her gaze.

I hope not. She hesitated in the cool dark just inside the closure, wondering what to do next. Losna sniffed once more and then headed out of the underdae into the grasses of the meadow. Ahraia walked about the structure again, knowing she wasn't going to find them. An agitated woof came from outside.

Here they are! Losna called to her.

Ahraia hurried from the underdae, not caring about the burning light. Losna sniffed through the waist-high grasses of the meadow, her fur glowing in the dying flames.

Just their shadows, she thought as Ahraia approached. *Here's Reyn.* She stood over Kaval's fox, nuzzling him gently, as though he might awaken with her touch.

Ahraia stooped down and turned him. The soft white fur at his throat was punctured cleanly, too perfect to be caused by anything but a blade.

The knife. Ahraia remembered the charcoal black of the blade. She couldn't imagine the daemon using a knife. It didn't seem right.

Losna sniffed through the grass. She woofed again, quietly, upset. *Here's what's left of Mehra.* Altah's raven lay several yards away, one wing twisted awkwardly out.

Losna moved away, checking progressively outward from the shadows and the underdae. A faint mist began to fall.

"Do you see the knife?" Ahraia asked. She searched across the meadow's rough tussocks, trying to retrace their path. Losna hurried after her, sniffing about below the dry grasses.

It's here, she snorted and shook her head, disgusted by whatever she smelled.

Ahraia hurried to her shadow, kneeling next to her to block the light of the glowing embers. She peered at the knife, examining it closely before picking it up. It was long and charcoal black, as slim as a drain but of some strange material Ahraia had never seen. It wasn't bone of any type she knew, and it wasn't metal, wood, or stone.

She picked it up. It was cool to the touch, far lighter than she expected. And yet, she could tell it was strong. Unbreakable perhaps. She tested the tip, pricking the end of her finger with hardly any pressure. A point of blood formed on her skin.

She considered it for a moment, then carefully wiped the blade on the ground and slipped it into her cloak. She looked back to the human encampment, wondering about her brothers. The embers and flames sizzled against the mist.

They must be among the humans, she conveyed. Ahraia moved

towards the burning remnants of the wagons. Most of the flames were extinguished, but the night was still brighter than any she had ever seen. She held her hood close and put a hand over her nose and veil. She ducked behind the only wagon that remained upright and hadn't yet succumbed to the fire at its feet. The mist prickled at her skin and hissed at the edges of the fire.

The repugnant stench of humans filled her nose. Two twisted figures lay on the ground nearby, and a third slumped awkwardly over a broken barrel of wood, all dead.

Losna's fur bristled nervously. *Let's get out of here. They aren't here. And neither is the orb.*

Ahraia peeked inside the wagon. A smaller human's body lay across the floor with blood pooled about it. It was only a child, like a spriteling and it clutched something close to his chest, almost like Tev clutched her shadow. It was the small, wooden figurine she had seen him playing with the night before, carved in the perfect likeness of a human. It dangled from four strings tied to a cross of wood. Ahraia felt a pang of hurt, wondering what horrors he had seen in his last moments.

Losna let out a low, agitated growl. Ahraia looked up to find her shadow's eyes on the woods. Her tail was stiff and her ears pointed to the darkness.

Something's out there.

Ahraia's eyes snapped towards the forest where firelight danced and flickered against the outer eaves. She couldn't see anything, but she could feel it. It came as a chill running through her body. They *were* being watched.

Ahraia ducked behind the wagon, her first thought wondering if it was the Shad-Mon returned. She didn't feel the paralyzing enchantment of the night before or the overbearing menace. She thought about Hayvon and the shades, but she knew they wouldn't venture so close to the fires.

What do you think it is? she conveyed to Losna, peering towards the woods. The mist was turning to a light rain.

Losna sniffed at the air. *I don't know.*

It could know what happened here, Ahraia thought.

Losna growled. *Or it could* **be** *what happened here . . .*

Ahraia put her hand to the knife at her hip, wishing she still carried a bow. She probed out with her mind and felt a fleeting sense of fear and worry.

It's human, Ahraia realized, brushing against its mind. It startled, as though it had felt her mind probing it, and Ahraia heard branches breaking and movement away in the woods.

It must know what happened, come on. Ahraia was already running for the woods.

Ahraia! Stop, Losna thought, distraught. *Have you gone mad? It could be dangerous!*

So are we, Ahraia thought.

8

LIGHTWALKER

Ahraia entered the woods with her skin still ablaze from all the light. She pulled down the veil and pushed back her hood, eager to be rid of them. She paused, letting her eyes re-adjust to the comforting dark.

Where is it? she conveyed, scanning the woods for the human. The canopy above shielded them from the mist, and the understory was still mostly dry.

You're sure it was human? Losna sniffed, worried that something more sinister might be roaming the woods. A shiver of uncertainty ran through Ahraia.

It felt human, she conveyed, wondering if she was being tricked. Her brief brush against their quarry's mind hadn't felt anything like the night before: there was no menace, no waiting evil—no lingering death. She had only felt fear and the desire to be hidden.

But now, she sensed nothing at all.

Can humans ward off bondings or bindings? Losna asked.

Ahraia shrugged, proceeding warily into the tangled forest, searching with her mind and eyes and ears. Losna's gaze darted to and fro, and her body was tensed and ready to spring. She raised her nose, hunting after any signs of danger.

It couldn't be far, Ahraia conveyed, pausing to listen. The rain was soaking through the forest, falling in sporadic drops. Muted pops and snarls came from the fires in the meadow.

I've got the scent! Losna thought, sniffing through the underbrush. *It's human. And it reeks.* She huffed in disgust and shook her head. *This way . . .*

Ahraia followed, relieved it was only a human. She parted each leaf and branch, keeping her eyes up. Wherever the human was, it was silent. No footsteps. No breaking branches.

It has to be close. It must be hiding, Ahraia conveyed, listening to quiet sniffs coming from Losna. *Maybe it's—*

Crack!

A flash of searing light suddenly burst through the woods. The air split as though lightening had sprung unbidden from a single point, spinning Ahraia to the ground. She yelped in terror.

What was that? Losna whimpered, crawling closer to Ahraia.

The light faded to blinding dark. Ahraia squeezed her eyes shut and covered her face, but heard familiar shouts rising through the woods.

The shades! she thought fearfully. *Hayvon!* She risked a glance up and saw total dark had returned. Eyes still bursting with light, she lunged from the ground and took off sprinting through the woods, heedless of the noise she stirred up. Losna leapt after her, sending a flurry of warnings through the night. Ahraia ignored them. She spun branches out of her way and burst through a thicket, tumbled over a small rise and nearly fell on top of the shades, who huddled in terror beneath the undergrowth.

"Where have you been!" Tev shouted, with light-speckling seared across her cheeks. Shim stood next to her, wheezing. He rifled through his clutch for an arrow with his free hand, his bow already poised in the other.

"Where's Hayvon?" Ahraia asked sharply. She searched the woods but saw no sign of her brother or the light's source.

"We've been seen!" Tev said hysterically.

"Quiet," Ahraia ordered, her mind racing. *Seen by the human?*

"Mother's going to give us to the Shad-Mon—"

"You aren't going to be condemned," Ahraia snapped. "*Get a hold of yourself.*" She inflected a binding inside her words, forcing calm over the shade. Tev's body seized, and she squeezed her shadow so tight that Ahraia expected the squirrel was crushed.

"What happened?" Ahraia demanded, turning to Shim. "What was that light?"

"We were seen!" he said. The markings on his face were flared but fading. "By a human. It just came creeping through the woods. It almost ran straight into us. We thought it was you—'

Tev's thoughts burst out, muddled and panicked. *The human saw us . . . she saw us . . . Mother's going to kill us . . .*

Ahraia blocked her out.

Shim carried on aloud, just as hysterical, "But then we saw it wasn't you, it was a human. And it shouted something and there was a terrible flash of light and then it was gone." He fell quiet, looking terrified and guilty.

"We have to catch it," Ahraia said, more to Losna than to the shades.

"Mother's going to condemn us, isn't she?" Shim added, fully aware of what it meant if it was discovered that they had been seen.

There's no reason she ever needs to know, Ahraia conveyed firmly to the shades. She doubted that either of them could hide it from the Astra or her father. Even their barest guilt would bleed through the simplest of bondings. It would be plain as day for the sprites to see. She drew a deep breath, forcing calm over herself. "Which way did Hayvon go?"

"That way . . ." Shim said, looking guilty. He pointed off through the woods with an arrow.

"I don't want to die . . .," Tev whimpered.

Ahraia squared herself towards Shim. "You're going to have to stay here with Tev." *Wait for us.* "No matter what happens, you weren't seen. Get Tev to understand that." *You. Were. Not. Seen.* "You won't be condemned if you can convince yourself of that, understood?"

He nodded, his ears tucked tight to his white hair, frightened and guilty.

"Make *her* understand," Ahraia said. Tev had dissolved into a mess of tears. "Come on Losna." *Find Hayvon for me.*

Losna leapt from the hollow like a silver-flecked arrow shot through the fading night. Ahraia raced after her, trying to unravel what they should do when they caught the human. Spritish rule dictated they kill it, but she had no intention of killing this one—especially if this one could answer what had happened at the Stone Tree. Maybe it knew about the orb, or her brothers. She needed to catch it before Hayvon did.

Don't kill it, she thought to Losna.

Ahraia sprinted after her shadow, leaping over fallen logs and through narrow seems in the forest. She sprang over a silent brook, binding a fir branch to propel her over the dark water. Losna splashed across below her, sniffing at the far bank until she found the scent and loped into the underbrush.

They climbed a short hill and ran the length of a ridge.

Something's up ahead, Losna thought, no longer bothering with the scent as she bound forward. Ahraia looked up and saw Hayvon; he was limping heavily. There was something else ahead of him, crashing through the forest blindly.

The human!

Ahraia wondered if a binding would subdue it. She would have to stay Hayvon; he would insist on killing it. Losna caught up with him. He flinched at her sudden appearance and then glanced back at Ahraia.

We were seen! There's a human up ahead! he conveyed in distress. His right leg dragged with every step as though he had been stabbed.

What happened to you? she conveyed, alarmed to see blood staining his cloak.

Shim—that little bastard—got startled and damn near killed me with an arrow!

The human disappeared out of sight. The rain began to fall in earnest, dripping in fat, spattering drops from the forest above.

"We can't let it get away!" he said aloud.

I'll get it, Ahraia conveyed to him, not bothering to explain she had no intention of killing it. Losna disappeared ahead of her, gaining on the human, but it was still beyond the reach of a binding. It led them down a long hill, through a narrow ravine and out into the open woods, where it stood no chance of outrunning Losna.

Careful! Ahraia conveyed.

Losna was gaining on their quarry. She hardly noticed Ahraia's warning, her mind reduced to a single instinct: *Catch*.

Ahraia sprinted after them both, her legs and lungs burning. Branches scraped across her face and leaves scattered beneath her feet.

Losna closed in on the human. In a single, enormous leap, she brought it tumbling to the ground and came up snarling, with ears pinned back and tail low. Her teeth shone long and white and terrifying.

The human rolled to her feet and froze, facing off with Losna. Her hesitation gave Ahraia the opening she needed—she closed the distance to the human, reached out with her mind and bound it with a forceful enchantment.

Be still, she commanded, leaping over a log and drawing her drain. She over-projected the thought, causing her own feet to falter below her. She stumbled forward, but the binding anchored the lightwalker firmly to the ground.

The human was a she—a fiery-haired girl—taller than Ahraia, with speckled markings beneath her eyes, almost like the spatter of light-scars beneath Ahraia's. Fear reflected through the binding, but it was hardly the only emotion the girl harbored. Her thoughts were instinctive, like Losna's, and she struggled against the enchantment. *Fight. Escape. Break free.*

Stop! Ahraia commanded, bringing the girl's intentions to a halt. The human stilled. Her breaths shivered through half-bared teeth, and her eyes darted between Losna and Ahraia.

I'm not going to hurt you, Ahraia projected.

The thought had the opposite effect—the girl struggled harder to get away.

"Don't move," Ahraia said.

The girl reached for something at her hip.

I said stop. Ahraia mustered the full strength of her binding, assuming a blade or some other weapon lay at the girl's side. Losna prowled forward and growled, a cavernous and hostile threat. Her snout bared back, showing every one of her long, white teeth.

The girl's resistance faltered, and then failed. Fear stilled her hand and she stopped struggling to break free. Ahraia waited a moment, delaying to make sure it wasn't some human ruse, luring her into complacency.

"What happened in the meadow?" she mirrored for the girl to understand, softening the binding to let her speak.

The girl gasped, her surprise giving way to anger. "What happened? You happened!"

Confused, Ahraia ignored her, distracted by something glowing at her side. It shone through the thick, sheep-reeking cloth of the girl's cloak as a brilliant point of light.

"What's that?" Ahraia said, pointing. *Is that the orb?* she conveyed to Losna.

The girl looked down, stunned. "Is this it? Is this what you were after? All of that for a little ball of light? I knew I should never have touched it. Those people were innocent. They were good people," she said, letting out an angry sob, more a growl than a cry. Hate and anger radiated through the enchantment.

"I already told you, we had nothing to do with it," Ahraia said.

"Didn't have anything to do with it!" the human scoffed. "Of course you did. Now let me go, elf."

Ahraia's eyes returned to the point of light at the girl's hip. "Where did you get that?"

"I found it. In the ruins of the holdfast."

The Stone Tree? "What about the bodies? What did you do with my brothers?" *Did you burn them?* Ahraia thought unnerved.

"What bodies?"

My brothers. "They were lying there, in the Stone Tree, in the . . . holdfast," Ahraia said, using the girl's own word.

The girl glowered at Ahraia, confused. "I don't know what you're talking about. The holdfast was empty. I just found the stone and took it."

"It's not a stone—" Ahraia stopped, sensing movement throughout the woods. She glanced sideways and saw Hayvon, but her ears twitched and her heart froze; he wasn't alone. The woods surged with the conveyance of a dozen sprites following behind him, unseen yet, but spreading and closing in.

Keep her bound! Hayvon conveyed, closer than the rest.

The human's desperation reflected in a horrifyingly familiar way; Ahraia knew all too well the terror of being held paralyzed before a certain death. That fear reverberated deep within her. *You have to run,* she conveyed without thinking. In that moment of pause, the enchantment slipped, and suddenly the girl renewed her struggle. Ahraia couldn't keep her bound, unwilling to be the wraith holding her. The girl reached into her pocket and the next moment, the forest burst with brilliant, blatant light. Ahraia screamed and spun to the ground, hiding her face.

Cover that! she commanded. The orb pulsed, swollen with too much light. Her order brought the human's hand in front of it, but the girl's voice rang out powerfully through the night.

"Light!" she shouted.

Crack!

For the second time, the forest split asunder. Dazzling, white-hot light shot out from the orb. Ahraia heard something snap, and heard sprites calling out in dismay. Losna whined in despair, leaping over Ahraia to try and shield her from the searing light. Ahraia tried to look up, covering her face with her arm. Her skin felt hot and charred, and her enchantment suddenly stretched thin, strained by distance; the human was running.

The orb! Ahraia thought. *Drop it!*

The orb slipped to the tip of the girl's fingers but she resisted as the last vestiges of the binding disintegrated. She kept hold, and kept running, crashing through the woods away from Ahraia, still clutching the orb as it spilled dying light into the forest.

"What was that?" A sprite called out. *Was that a human?*

"It's getting away!" Hayvon said desperately.

She has our orb! Ahraia thought in dismay.

Losna was ready to leap after the girl. *Should I go after it?*

No! Ahraia conveyed, her skin still tingling from the blistering light. *It's too dangerous.*

"Shade Ahraia. Shade Hayvon! Get over here!" Ahraia recognized her father's voice before she lifted her head. Her eyes slowly came back into focus, though her skin felt singed.

"That was a human—these shades have been seen," one of the sprites said loudly.

"None of us were seen," Ahraia said, terrified that they had just lost the orb. "We were stalking it . . ." The rain made everything a blur and the sprites had been far enough away that she thought the lie might hold.

Gavea, the same nitesse who had accompanied the Astra the night before, flicked her ears once disapprovingly. Ever since she was a shade, she had resented Ahraia for bringing home a stronger shadow, and at the moment, she bore an impish glint in her eyes. "Shades aren't supposed to speak aloud, and they are definitely not supposed to stalk lightwalkers."

"Where are my shades? And what was that light—" her father started.

"Not seen?" Gavea held up a hand, her eyes boring into Hayvon. He wouldn't meet her gaze, and instead clutched at his leg where the arrow had struck him. But after a moment Gavea spoke quietly, and confidently. "That *was* a human. And these shades *were* seen. Levath, Tallin, with me. The rest of you with Lecke, make sure it doesn't get away. Bring it to me, alive."

A half dozen sprites and wards hurried off after the human. Ahraia's throat tightened.

Hayvon looked stricken. *That's not true. Ahraia wasn't seen*, he conveyed, his thoughts fumbling over themselves to get out.

He looked ashamed and frightened, and in that moment, Ahraia knew that Gavea had already pressed the truth from him. His eyes turned towards Ahraia, giving her a guilt-ridden look. *She knows*, he conveyed as a whisper. His jaw clenched and Ahraia watched in horror as his hesitation gave way to his voice.

"She wasn't seen," he said determinedly, "I was."

The remaining sprites' ears stood sharply in surprise.

Hayvon! What are you doing? Ahraia conveyed to him. *Have you gone mad?*

"Are you admitting you were seen?" their father asked.

Just stay quiet, Ahraia conveyed frantically. Admitting to being seen was condemnable; shades and sprites had been given to the Shad-Mon for less. A muscle twitched in Ahraia's father's jaw.

"Then Hayvon, your shadow is forfeit," he said, stepping forward and drawing his drain. The small, silver blade glimmered violently even in the dark. Ahraia flushed with fear and saw Vesta duck deeper into Hayvon's pocket. She stepped between them, holding up her hands.

"We weren't seen, I don't know what Hayvon is saying. He must be light-sick," she said quickly. "None of us were seen. Your shades are back in the forest, safe," she added, hoping to distract the conversation back to her father's question.

Stay out of this, her father conveyed.

"But he wasn't seen!" Ahraia said more firmly.

Gavea's ears flickered in warning. She stepped towards Ahraia, her hood pulled back just enough to show her ears.

"I could swear as I came over that hill you were face to face with it," she said with dangerous calm.

The forest dripped and shook with rain, but every remaining sprite stood perfectly motionless.

Careful, Losna warned. Her ears lay flat and her lips pulled back just enough to show her long teeth. Her father shot her a warning glance but she ignored it.

Our nit's orb was stolen, Ahraia conveyed cautiously, neither a lie nor entirely an answer.

"But it saw you?" Gavea pressed.

No— Ahraia started, the lie sitting right at the forefront of her thought.

Silence! Her father ordered her, even as he spoke aloud to cover his own conveyance. "Hayvon's already admitted to it," he said dismissively. Gavea glared at Ahraia but didn't force the point.

"That was the light talking," Ahraia said. "You can't condemn him on words alone."

"Can I not?" he answered aggressively.

Losna growled, a low, ominous sound that spoke for Ahraia. Her father's ears flickered at her like Gavea's, calling for silence.

"Don't presume you're a sprite yet," he said.

Ahraia bit back her words, knowing full well the precarious nature of their situation. Her father's warning and Gavea's accusation both hung in the air, threatening condemnation with the slightest misstep.

The skin of each sprite was splashed with light, but her father's scars ran the deepest. His eyes shifted to Hayvon, who stared into the dark, shaking slightly.

Ahraia could sense conveyance passing between the two and she was sure her father was interrogating him. Hayvon's eyes and ears were down, and he was as pale as the Bright Moon. She wondered if his leg was injured worse than she had thought, but she guessed it had more to do with whatever was being conveyed. She strained to hear their conversation. Unexpectedly, she caught a sliver of her father's conveyance, a faint and diminishing echo.

. . . It's your choice. But she's your responsibility, and to the light . . .

A shiver of fear ran through Ahraia, unsure of what she overheard and unsettled by the tone of it.

What is he saying? Losna thought, sensing Ahraia's unease.

To the light turns the ward? I don't know, I couldn't hear it all. Ahraia formed a link to her brother. *Hayvon, what's happening?* she conveyed, feeling the fear radiating off him. But before he had the chance to answer, Gavea spoke, her words startling Ahraia and causing Losna's ears to turn.

"Beran, you saw what I saw. She stood just as close to that human as I stand to you. Look at her scars. It looks as though she's been walking in the day. You can't just let her get away with it," she said.

"Nitesse Gavea," her father said with exaggerated deference, "surely the shade who admits to being seen must be punished."

Gavea didn't look mollified. "Perhaps. We'll know once the human is caught."

Ahraia felt her scars flushing and her ears straighten. Her father's face was placid as Gavea said this, but his eyes had turned a dangerous, golden yellow.

"This is a matter for the Astra. The humans are blind as trees without their light—unreliable at best and plagues at the worst. Once we're back in Daispar, judgment will be passed at her discretion."

Gavea pursed her lips.

We should have killed the human when we had a chance, Losna thought. Ahraia swallowed nervously, realizing now the folly it had been to let the girl escape. Their only hope rested on her ending up dead before the wards caught her.

"We had better get back to Daispar," her father said dismissively, too obviously trying to move the conversation away from such dangerous territories. "The night is growing old and the company will have already arrived."

Gavea didn't move, and Ahraia sensed that she wasn't going to give up so easily. Her gaze traced between Hayvon and Ahraia.

"I thought you two were supposed to be hunting in the north woods . . ." Her mouth turned down in a frown. Ahraia's father froze.

Vesta shuffled inside Hayvon's pocket. Hayvon started to answer. *We—*

Their father cut his conveyance short. "Not you—you lack wit, half-shade. Shade Ahraia . . ." He gestured for her to speak, flickering his ears to spare her from conveyance. *Whatever you say, you had better not condemn yourself.*

Ahraia hesitated, for a moment having forgotten what had brought them back to the Stone Tree and unsure how much she should divulge. Every act was enough to condemn herself: failing the hunt, bonding the human singer, folding an underdae, letting herself be seen . . .

"Last night—" Ahraia stopped, as Gavea signaled for conveyance, overriding her father's permission. Ahràia took a steadying breath.

Last night, we discovered a group of humans while we were hunting, she conveyed carefully, deciding the closer to the truth, the easier her lies would be. *They were on the human road—on their dirt river that passes the Stone Tree—headed towards the underdae.*

"How could you know that?" Gavea interjected, obviously sensing Ahraia's underlying fear for having bound the human singer.

We have eyes, Ahraia thought loosely before she could stop herself. She hoped the mild insolence hid her guilt. *They were headed south on the road . . .*

Gavea's eyes narrowed and Ahraia's father frowned but neither reprimanded her. She quickly went on.

I knew Kaval and Altah were here, waiting at the Stone Tree for some emissary. I had no choice but to warn them the humans were coming. We hurried south, but when we got there, they . . . she trailed off, having no trouble inflecting her emotions to the conveyance, remembering her brothers' lifeless figures. *They're . . .*

"They're dead," her father said. "We know."

Ahraia looked at him in surprise. *How could you know that?*

"That's why we're here." His face turned dark. "A scout of Angolor passed through here two nights ago, ahead of their company, and found the shades with their shadows killed."

A scout? From Angolor? Ahraia's mind was racing. *What do you mean "a scout"? Where is this scout?* Her mind grappled around the memory of the shadowy figure in the innards of the Stone Tree, wondering if it could have been a sprite. The black fur and lifeless eyes didn't fit, but the binding did.

"It must have been them!" she blurted out. "The scout must have killed them—"

Gavea's ears flickered a warning and her father spoke over her.

"Ahraia, that's absurd."

"—or the emissary. It could have been either. Where are they? I want to see them!" Ahraia shook with anger, surprised she hadn't put together the thought before. She remembered the touch of the shadowy figure's mind, hidden just behind the screen of darkness. She wanted to see them. She wanted to bind them—to recognize the foul touch of their mind—then she would return their knife by way of a swift and silent death.

"Ahraia, the scout didn't kill them. It was just a shadow."

Ahraia cut her father off. "I know it was a shadow! I saw it! It was a wraith. And I felt its enchantment. It killed Kaval and Altah."

"Stop!" Her father commanded, his enchantment clapping down so forcefully that Ahraia bit her tongue. She tasted blood. "The scout *was* a shadow to a shade, like Losna to you," he said pausing, pointing to Losna and letting the words sink in. "It was just a moon raven, a shadow kept by their wards as a scout."

Ahraia was having trouble thinking straight, she was so upset. She heard her father's words, though she couldn't make sense of them. "The scout was a moon raven?" she asked, breathing hard. The other sprites seemed perturbed by her outburst, and she tried to calm herself. Gavea shook her head in disgust.

Her father nodded. "The wards from Angolor use shadows as scouts. When the raven found the underdae, it found our shades dead. The company sent word to the Astra and came by way of the Deep Brook instead."

Ahraia was shaking in anger. *They must have killed them. They killed Kaval. They killed Altah.*

Gavea stared at her. "They didn't."

Losna, surprisingly enough, agreed with her father and the nitesse. *Ahraia, that was no mere shadow. That was something worse...*

Ahraia's emotions were unraveling though. "Then who did this? —"

"Ahraia—"

"—then who killed them?"

Shades of charcoal filtered across her father's eyes, his ears tucked back and he stepped towards her. "It must have been the humans. In fact, I'm sure it was."

No. Ahraia shook her head adamantly. "That was no human. It was something worse. I know." *It bound me.* "And besides . . . the humans weren't even here yet. They couldn't have killed them. Hayvon can tell you, they were still miles and miles away. It doesn't matter though. They're dead too," Ahraia said. "Their whole company is dead. Whoever killed Kaval and Altah must have killed them too."

Hayvon eyes paled. *The humans are dead?*

Gavea sneered. *Except the one your sister just let get away*, she conveyed loosely.

Ahraia's ears batted in irritation.

"Ahraia, you're wrong," her father said dismissively, ignoring Gavea. Beneath his words, however, he berated Ahraia with a seething tirade of conveyance. *How could you let yourself be seen? How foolish could you be? Do you have any idea the danger you're in? You should have killed the human and been done with it.*

Ahraia ignored his undertones. Something scraped at her side, and she remembered the knife she had found in the meadow. The wraith's blade.

"No, I'm not. Look," she said pulling out the drain. "Does this look like something a human would carry?"

That looks like a drain, Hayvon conveyed.

Daemon's bone, Levath, one of the remaining sprites thought loosely. Both Gavea and Ahraia's father both glared at them, then stared at the blackened blade.

Ahraia's father hesitated. "I have no idea what kind of blade a human carries but that's not a drain. Ahraia, why are you insisting on this? You're not making any sense. You think—"

"Not making any sense? Of course I'm making sense! You can't think it's coincidence that Kaval and Altah are killed and then, the very next night a company of humans is massacred in the same meadow. How—"

A weak binding sprang over her, cast by her father, trying to silence her.

"—could you possibly be so light headed—" she pushed through the enchantment, too angry to be bound in silence. "It was *not* the humans! I was *here*. I saw *it*." The tighter the enchantment fell, the angrier she got. "So, what? You think the humans killed Kaval and Altah, and then . . . and then what? And then they killed themselves? Is that what you think? That is so—"

"*Ahraia, Stop!*" Her father mixed a full binding with his words, forcing quiet over her. She flushed, feeling her whole body bound as she had the night before. But it wasn't half as potent as what she had felt in the Stone Tree. She wriggled against the enchantment.

Her father was glaring at her with a murderous stare.

"The humans didn't kill themselves," he said. "We did."

Ahraia stopped struggling. *What do you mean you "did"?* she conveyed, unable to speak aloud. *You killed them?*

"Of course we killed them," he said dismissively. "They killed the shades—something had to be done. Daispar isn't going to stand aside and let lightwalkers murder our shades. Every day they creep closer to our darkening. The forest grows smaller with every passing night."

Why would you kill them? The humans had nothing to do with Kaval and Altah. They were innocent! Ahraia was overwhelmed with the injustice of it. She thought of the vile shadow in the Stone Tree: the pure, overpowering evil with the repulsive intent to kill.

Ahraia, calm down, Hayvon conveyed. *You're going to get yourself in even more trouble.*

Ahraia ignored him, feeling the filaments of her father's binding holding her in place. The enchantment was lessening; he either assumed she couldn't—or wouldn't—resist. She hardened her will against him and felt the brittle nature of the fading enchantment. She focused her mind and broke the remaining link.

"How could you be so stupid! They didn't do it," Ahraia said, protectively walling off her mind to prevent her father from binding her again. "If that was a human that killed them, then I *was* seen!" Ahraia spat. "Because I was there in the Stone Tree with it."

Gavea and the other sprites looked taken aback by her words, but her father stepped forward angrily.

"Enough!" He scowled at Ahraia. His next conveyance was

directed only to her. *Don't say one more word—not about the humans, not about anything!* He turned and walked back through the forest. "The Astra will sort this out when we get back to Daispar."

"What about Kaval and Altah? What about whatever killed them?" Ahraia said stubbornly, not caring about his warning.

He didn't bother to turn about. "We already gave them darkness."

"Not that they deserved any," Gavea added.

Ahraia stared after him dumbfounded. Losna's ears tucked back in anger.

"Now, where are my shades?" he asked.

Ahraia pointed, too angry to form words or thoughts.

Why isn't he listening to me? she conveyed to Losna. She turned to Hayvon. *What did father convey to you? What did you say to him?*

Hayvon was staring after their father, his eyes distant, and his jaw clenched firmly down. *Just keep your head down. You can't let yourself be condemned.*

Ahraia hesitated, not wanting to leave Hayvon or leave the mystery of her brothers unsolved.

Her father's voice drifted back through the sweeping rain. "Hurry up. We'll want to be back if the company has already arrived."

"What does it matter," she said stubbornly. "Why is the company from Angolor even here?" she called out after him.

Her father turned back to her, his eyes gleaming through the woods.

"Didn't you hear? The Masai has come to Daispar."

9

WORRIES IN THE NIGHT

"The Masai?" Ahraia said, certain she had misheard her father. "The Masai of the whole spritedom is coming here?"

To Daispar? Losna thought.

Hayvon stared after their father, but his eyes were distant and unseeing. Ahraia turned back and found that Gavea stood right before her, pressed close by the dripping forest. The nitesse spoke quietly, her voice hidden from Ahraia's father as he headed away through the woods.

The loathing plain upon her face, she began, "You think you're the moons' gift to the night. You think you're entitled to wander these woods unafraid—that somehow you're impervious to the rules. Well, you're not. You're just a shade, and a pitiful one at that. Never hunting, never making kills—just a spoiled spriteling with a shadow far more menacing than she is fierce. In all my years, I've never seen a shade and shadow so smitten with each other—so prideful and foolish."

"You haven't?" Ahraia said coldly. She spoke aloud, well aware it irritated Gavea to no end.

The nitesse smirked. "So naïve . . . you think your father is going to get you out of this," she said quietly. "Just like every other time you've overstepped your bounds—running the plains, folding underdaes, being seen by a human." Gavea ears twitched. "You should have had your meeting with the Shad-Mon a dozen times over."

Ahraia clenched her teeth, but didn't respond. Levath and Tallin, Gavea's sisters, watched on idly. Gavea leaned forward, disgust pressed into every crease and line of her face as her whispered words fell amongst the scattered raindrops.

"Your reckoning is coming."

"Is that right?" Ahraia said. Her heartbeat pounded all the way to the tips of her ears. A storm raged inside her chest, echoing out as a growl from Losna. A contemptuous smile spread across Gavea's face.

"I can't wait for you to find out how dark the night truly is." She pushed past Ahraia, leading her sisters back towards Daispar. Losna bared her teeth and Ahraia barely held back the urge to lunge after the nitesse. She bit back a tirade of thought.

I could end her, Losna thought eagerly, on the verge of leaping after Gavea.

"Don't," Ahraia said, barely managing to suppress her shadow's instincts. She took a settling breath, stilling the urge to fight, and turned to Hayvon, whose face was still awash with a vacant look. His cloak's folds shifted. Vesta turned about within his pocket, and though Ahraia only saw her ears and whiskers, she could hear her chittering loudly.

"What did father convey to you?" Ahraia asked. "I heard him say, "to the light turns the ward."'

Hayvon didn't answer. Vesta scrambled out of his pocket and onto the ground, bobbing up and down, in obvious distress. Losna, who normally teased Vesta every time she touched the ground, watched nervously.

"The human got away," Hayvon said emotionlessly.

A horrible, sinking guilt cut through Ahraia's thoughts. *I know . . . I should have killed her. I just . . .* she trailed off, unable to finish the thought aloud or within, aware it was far worse than being unable to bind the stag.

"She has the orb," Hayvon said absently. "The nit tree isn't going to last." Ahraia grimaced. She hadn't thought her guilt could worsen, but it did. Hayvon was the oldest now, the orb was his responsibility, and she had let it slip away. The shame overwhelmed her, like a binding too difficult to keep, threatening to tear her apart. She clenched her jaw tightly.

"Hayvon? What did father say? If we're going to be condemned, I need to know."

"We aren't going to be condemned," he said without inflection. But Vesta chittered even louder.

Something's wrong, Losna thought.

We aren't going to be condemned, Hayvon conveyed evenly, as though he sensed Ahraia's doubt. The thought came too easily to be a lie.

"What did father say?"

"Nothing of any importance," Hayvon said, shifting his weight cautiously and grimacing as he grabbed his leg.

"Hurry up," Gavea called out impatiently. Their father echoed the nitesse.

Ahraia ignored them both, frowning at Hayvon. "What are you doing?"

"I'll be there in a moment," he insisted, meeting her eye. He looked ghostly but resolute, his silence scaring Ahraia far more than Gavea or her father.

Ahraia paused, considering a bonding but decided against it. "You're not thinking of running, are you?"

Hayvon knelt down in front of Vesta, grimacing and clutching at where the arrow had struck him. His hand came away smeared with blood. Vesta balanced on her hind legs facing him, finally quiet, though her whiskers bristled nervously.

"Do you really think I could run? Besides, I'm as curious as you are to see the Masai. I want to know why she would bother coming to Daispar." *Maybe the Astra has it coming*, he conveyed, the corner of his mouth turning up. "Now go on, I'll catch up."

Ahraia reluctantly turned back to follow her father, glancing one more time towards Hayvon as he held out his hand to Vesta, who tentatively bobbed towards him.

Ahraia pulled her cloak close and wiped rainwater off the tip of her nose. The forest dripped with the thick chorus of rain, every branch and leaf soaked through. Hayvon's last conveyance brought the mystery of the Masai back to the forefront of her mind. Never in all her life had Ahraia heard of the Masai traveling to other darkenings, or at least, not as far as any in the Gelesh. The Gelesh were separated from the rest of the Silh by a narrow strip of darkness south of the plains. It passed frighteningly close to the human realm. Altah had presumed the visit was spurred by the Gelesh's failing darkness and the ever-encroaching lightwalkers, and though Ahraia hadn't considered it likely, she wondered now if the Masai was indeed blaming the Astra. A dim hope lit in her heart but it mixed with worry. She hurried to catch up with her father and the other sprites.

"What is the Masai doing in Daispar?" Ahraia called to her father once she was in earshot.

He turned around and glared at her with a reproachful flicker of his ears. He pulled his hood up and kept walking

I mean, why would she come all the way here? she asked.

Her father pushed back branches as he walked; like most wards, he didn't bother with bindings of the forest. Ahraia hurried after him with Losna close at her heel, folding the forest out of their path, sending water shaking from the leaves and branches.

She projected her conveyance to him as she caught up. *Altah claimed it was because of the trouble in the West Vales. He said the Masai's blaming the Astra for it.*

Her father didn't bother to stop, but she could tell that the thought irritated him.

"That's between the Astra and the Masai," he said, navigating down into a deeper ravine. "But I wouldn't listen too closely to rumors from a fool who got himself killed by a human. Gavea's right, he didn't deserve true dark."

"How could you be so callous?" Ahraia said aloud, stopping short in disbelief. Her throat tightened and her heart suddenly felt as though it would sear right through her chest. Losna's hackles raised, influenced by their bond. "How could you care so little that they're dead? I don't care what nit you call your own—they were still your shades. Are you truly that pitiless?"

He turned around. His scars were flushed.

"Altah and Kaval would have only ever been dae-wards—and if they couldn't keep themselves alive as shades, they wouldn't have managed as sprites," he snapped. "You're already in enough trouble as it is. It's bad enough that the Masai is coming to the darkening—which should be our only concern—but now besides the trouble with the lightwalkers, I have to bring our fabled wolf-binder before the Masai, light-scarred and reeking of smoke and humans. You seem to have forgotten how to convey anything and seem to think your voice is as beautiful as the night. It is not. And I don't want to hear it again. Understood?"

I understand perfectly well, Ahraia conveyed, disgusted that he didn't care about Kaval or Altah.

When he spoke, his voice shook uncharacteristically. "Listen to me, and hear me clearly. You're so busy worrying about what is behind you that you fail to see what lies just ahead. The Masai of the whole Silh is in Daispar. That in and of itself should frighten you straight. You have more at risk than any shade or sprite in the darkening."

Ahraia paused, his words taking her by surprise. *What does the Masai have to do with me?*

His ears straightened to their full length beneath his hood.

"You're not foolish enough to think this is passing happenstance—an idle visit, do you? Then let me put it plainly, since you seem so determined in your naïvety." He stepped closer, not seeming to notice as Losna let out a warning growl. "You need to start worrying about the simplest of things." He held out his hand, all five fingers spread. With each point, a finger curled away. "You're a shade. Burned by light. Having spoken aloud more times than I can count, having been caught hunting humans." He wriggled the last remaining finger, then formed a fist, his words turning to conveyance. *Having been seen by a human.*

He continued silently, his words all the more dangerous.

Tonight, you've managed to put yourself and your shadow before the tip of a drain. The wrong turn of a leaf and you could easily end up in the Shadow Woods. All that is standing between you and that is me.

His voice rose to a whisper. "Maybe it's time you stop fretting over your brothers and start worrying about yourself."

With that he turned, leaving Ahraia standing against Losna in the dripping forest.

He's going to get us out of this, right? Losna thought.

I don't know, Ahraia conveyed. She grabbed her shadow's fur for reassurance, wondering for the first time if it was safe to return to the darkening. Her thoughts turned to running but the night was growing old. There were only so many underdaes, and any number of them could be occupied by other sprites or shades.

Gavea lingered and looked back through the woods.

"Where's your brother?" she said.

"I'm not his ward. Find him yourself," Ahraia said, quietly enough so that her father couldn't hear.

Gavea's eyes went wide. "You're going to see the Shad-Mon in the end. Just wait."

Ahraia ignored her. Losna snarled at Gavea and trotted after Ahraia, leaving the nitesse staring back through the woods for Hayvon.

Finding the shades wasn't difficult, but it was farther than Ahraia expected. Tev and Shim were huddled in the same hollow, fearful and quiet. Tev had thankfully calmed, and sat running her hand over the back of her shadow, which clung to her forearm, leaving sharp, angry marks on her wrist. Both of the shades' skin had mercifully returned to normal, the blistering marks from the initial burst of light having faded. Shim seemed to understand the gravity of the situation, and was taut as a bowstring as the sprites gathered about him and his sister. Ahraia conveyed subtly not to say anything about the human, but her father hardly paused to interrogate them.

"Where's Nitesse Gavea?" he asked once he had finished.

Here she comes, Levath conveyed, looking back through the woods. Ahraia looked back too and saw movement. Hayvon followed Gavea, limping heavily and making enough noise to be a lightwalker. His feet snagged on branches and ferns.

Ahraia hung back, not having realized how badly injured he was. *Are you all right?*

He didn't answer. Ahraia had never seen her brother look so distant. He was pale beyond his normal ashen color. Shim shuddered nervously at the sight of him.

Hayvon? What's wrong? Ahraia said, growing more worried.

Just hurting. That's all, he conveyed, cradling his cloak were Vesta huddled. Apparently, they had settled their argument, as she was silent and hidden from the rain. Ahraia followed behind them, folding the dripping wet forest away from their path, attempting to keep them dry while worrying about Hayvon's leg and about whatever their father had conveyed to him.

Gavea brought up the rear and Ahraia let the branches swing back, perhaps more than idly, spraying water over the nitesse's path.

THE JOURNEY back to Daispar passed miserably. The rain turned to a downpour, dripping in maddening drops from the canopy above. The first autumn leaves plummeted to the ground as well, and water beaded on the eaves-web of Ahraia's cloak, streaming down her shoulders like rills over rocks.

Hayvon seemed oblivious to everything: the rain, the forest, and most of all, bondings and thoughts. His hair dripped, lank and sopping, giving him an empty and skeletal look.

What's wrong with him? Losna asked.

He must be really injured, Ahraia conveyed, having given up on talking to him. She bound several ferns and moved them out of Hayvon's path. She guessed that he and Vesta were deep in conversation as he kept his thoughts to himself. But his limp was getting worse, and he made no effort to keep his leg from dragging through the dripping wet-brush. They entered the low valley of Daispar by way of the southern paths. They had hardly rounded the first corner when Losna let out a woof, signaling to Ahraia that something was behind them in the forest.

Nit-Ward! Ahraia conveyed. She spun about to see a single sprite running headlong through the woods. It was Lecke, one of the sprites Gavea had sent after the human. He slowed, dripping wet and breathing hard. Ahraia swallowed nervously, worried they had caught the girl.

Nitesse Gavea, Nit-Ward Beran, Lecke conveyed, his ears dipping deferentially.

Ahraia's father turned about. "Did you capture the human?" His worry revealed itself in the rise of his voice. He gestured for Lecke to speak aloud.

The ward hesitated, and Ahraia could sense his fear. "Yes and no."

Ahraia's heart stopped.

"What do you mean?" Gavea said crossly.

Lecke licked his lips nervously. "Prin and Havis have it pinned in the meadow of the Stone Tree—but it's setting fire to everything about it, and they haven't managed to get close enough to bind it. But that's not—"

"They haven't bound it?" Gavea said, cutting him off abruptly. "They're sprites, are they not? Get the dae-wards there before the daylight comes."

"We have a runner out already," Lecke said. "But that's not why I'm here." He hesitated, and spoke quietly under the dangerous glare of the nitesse. "We came across a group of alps. Their leader claimed to have met the Astra last night, and claimed to have been given free passage through the woods."

The alp! Ahraia conveyed before she could help it. She had completely forgotten about seeing the Astra and the alp the night before. An echo of her surprise must have escaped, because her father turned towards her, his ears flickering for silence.

Lecke went on, each word worsening Gavea's ire. "Prin sent the rest of the wards to track them."

"What about the human?" Gavea said, her ears turning dangerously downward. "Is it just Prin and Havis after it now?" Lecke nodded. Gavea spun towards Ahraia's father. "I thought this was already dealt with, Beran."

Ahraia barely registered Gavea's words as she turned over the thought of the alp. She turned her conveyance inward, just to Losna. *That was only last night,* she conveyed in disbelief, remembering the golden hair and icy eyes; it felt as though years had passed since then.

Ahraia's father ignored Gavea. He turned back to Lecke, looking unimpressed.

"Was it Anasazi?"

Confusion spread plainly across Lecke's face. He nodded. "Yes, Anasazi . . . of the Cirice. Are alps being left to roam the Gelesh?"

Gavea's ears batted in irritation. "This is your fault, Beran. You can't even handle your wards. They should have been warned about the alps last night. Now the human is going to get away."

"You worry about your nit—I'll worry about my wards and the human," Ahraia's father said, causing Levath and Tallin to draw sharp breaths. He ignored them and turned to Lecke. "Tell Prin to call them off; the alps have the leave of the Astra."

Lecke looked startled by the order. Gavea's eyes gleamed dangerously, and her thoughts echoed out, unchecked.

It would suit you all too well to let the human get away—for the sake of your shades. She turned back to Lecke. "Forget about calling them off, this night is getting too old. I'm not going to leave this to chance. Lecke. Come with me." Gavea turned and headed back through the dripping woods, away from the darkening, with the ward in tow.

"Where are you going?" Ahraia's father called, his eyes narrowing.

"To catch that human," Gavea called back.

Ahraia's father watched her go, his jaw set tightly. He turned back to Ahraia, meeting her eye.

You'd better hope that human ends up dead before Nitesse Gavea binds her.

10

THE MASAI

Why are alps being given leave to roam the Gelesh? Ahraia conveyed to Losna, holding back branches for Hayvon and Vesta.

Her shadow jogged ahead of her towards the looming darkening, just as perturbed.

The wall funneled rivulets of water to either side of the closure, protecting the passage out of the dripping forest. They passed inside, and Losna shook herself, a mist of water spraying from her fur.

Ahraia hesitated, letting her eyes adjust. The true dark felt blissfully soothing, dry and warm. The waterspouts streamed with rainwater, directing what the shell couldn't turn back into urns and pools that had been dry since spring. Beneath the spouts, however, an unnatural, forced silence quivered inside the protective dark. The air reverberated with the tangled conveyance of dozens upon dozens of sprites. Ahraia slipped between the outer nit trees past a bank of drying eaves-web, following her father and Hayvon by a narrow path with Losna close behind.

Those are bad omens, Losna conveyed, looking up.

A pair of white moon ravens hid in the upper eves of the darkening. They weren't shadows—not of Daispar, at least.

They've arrived, Tallin conveyed ahead of them. The hairs on Ahraia's neck prickled.

The Masai's already here, she conveyed to Losna.

The group emerged into the central hollow to find the entire darkening gathered, packed together in the rain-pattered silence. Every sprite, spriteling, shade and shadow crowded about the deep-set depression from which the central springs flowed out to the west. Even most of the dae-wards congregated inside, something Ahraia hadn't seen since the Astra had supplanted her mother. They stood about the edges, their light-scarred skin and yellow-bright eyes showing out from the small creases of their light-veils.

The Astra stood in the middle, nearest to the springs, surrounded by her closest wards, and facing a group of sprites and wards Ahraia had never seen before. Among them, one stood a step forward from the rest.

Is that the Masai? Losna thought, catching a glimpse through the crowd.

Ahraia's throat tightened as she swallowed. *It must be.*

By the looks of it, the company from Angolor had only just arrived. Most were still wearing traveling cloaks, their eaves-web still dripping and their hair falling lank and unkempt about their shoulders. Ahraia stood on her tiptoes to get a better look, catching glimpses of the Masai through the silver-bright hair and hoods of the sprites and wards standing before her. It was strangely surreal to see the leader of the whole Silh. Somehow, she seemed impervious to the damp. Her traveling cloak looked to be sewn of inkan silk: a deep nightshade of silver, dark and rich and sinuously shifting as she moved. Beneath it, she wore a dress of shadowy-velvet web. Her hair was long and held high by an intricate tarry vine, with dazzling purple flowers.

She was speaking, and her voice rolled quietly through the hollow. "First it was Holcrek . . . then Dimdale and Enshad. Now the West Vales. It's not hard to see that the Gelesh is being torn apart by lightwalkers."

Not Daispar, the Astra conveyed, her thoughts carrying from below. She looked surprisingly simple, dressed in a demure black eaves-web that clung to her unblemished skin. Her drain was threaded tight at her hip.

The Masai sounded unconvinced. "If Daispar is the heartwood of the Gelesh's strength, then it is also must be the root of its weakness."

The Astra blushed visibly, the markings at her neck and ears graying.

The Gelesh stretches too far for any single darkening to oversee. We need more darkness, more daughters and more wards. We can't begin to range all the ways from the Endless Plains to the ever-swelling oceans of the west.

"Which is why I'm here," the Masai said, turning. Ahraia got her first clear look at her and was surprised to see she didn't look nearly as regal her clothes did. She was beautiful, though not in a very spritish way. She had dark, lingering scars, darker than Ahraia's, wrapping behind her ear and up her neck. Her eyes were sallow yellow and faded, as though they had once been bright and wardish, or even wolfish maybe. And while her voice was calm, even quiet, Ahraia couldn't help but feel a tightness growing in her chest as she listened.

"The Gelesh is vital to me—I'm not willing to cede it to the Dae-Mon and the lightwalkers."

The Astra didn't answer, at least, not aloud or in any conveyance that Ahraia heard. The Masai paused, and eventually continued.

"I understand you have a freshly cast sprite, unrooted as of yet . . . I want to make arrangements for her uprooting. In return, I'll give you what you need to protect your lands."

All eyes and ears turned towards Kren. She didn't look as though she had registered what the Masai had said; she still had the same, empty stare that had haunted her since her shadow test.

Kren can't be uprooted, Ahraia conveyed towards Hayvon out of habit. *Daughters aren't supposed to be given. She belongs here.*

Havon didn't seem to notice. Ahraia didn't see the Masai's ears flicker, though they must have because the Astra's conveyance gave way to words.

"We need every daughter we have. Folding darkness is the only way we'll ever keep—"

The Masai held up a hand, cutting the Astra off as though she had bound her.

"Two of your shades are dead within a night's march from here, undoubtedly the devilry of lightwalkers. Alps and humans both have been reported in the area by my scouts. More lightwalkers are spreading to the West Vales and two darkenings of the Gelesh have failed since you've become Astra of Daispar." She stopped and let her words sink in. The unbearable silence settled, but this time, it was devoid of any conveyance. Only the drip of rain could be heard, falling steadily on the outer husk of the darkening and streaming down the funnels. "Folding darkness isn't your problem—Daispar is plenty dark." She gestured about them. "Protecting the Gelesh is your problem."

The Astra's jaw moved as though her mouth was full of mud that she couldn't spit out. Ahraia held her breath, hoping that the Astra would refuse.

We don't even know what killed the shades, the Astra replied, not fully objecting. *Lightwalkers might not have had anything to do with it.*

The corner of the Masai's lip twitched. "I'm willing to give you two dozen dae-wards, and the seeds for as many nit trees. That's more than any unrooted sprite is worth."

An audible gasp circled through the surrounding sprites. The air once again resonated with conveyance, and sprites and shades shifted uncomfortably. The change in the air was so palpable that Losna growled in irritation.

The Masai's ears twitched, turning towards them. She looked over her shoulder, peering up through the crowd. A shiver ran down Ahraia's spine, and she instinctively ducked aside and lowered her ears.

"Is that your wolf-binder?" the Masai said.

Ahraia stepped self-consciously behind several sprites, bringing Losna closer with a fistful of fur. Faces and ears followed the Masai's gaze towards them, and sprites stepped aside, giving her no place to hide. Ahraia bowed her head even more, staring at her boots. They were stained black with mud and gray with ash.

The Astra looked up as well. *And my nit-ward, returned from looking into the trouble with the shades*, she conveyed. "Beran, come down here."

"Bring the wolf-binder," the Masai said with a curious smile.

Ahraia ears ached from trying to keep them straight.

What does she want from us? Losna thought nervously.

"Come on," her father said, indicating for her to follow. The sprites in front of him had parted, showing the path down to the bottom of the hollow. The stones seemed to shift beneath her feet as Ahraia followed her father. She heard a nervous swell of conveyance pass through the dell:

What happened to her skin?

It looks as though she's passed under the Dae-Mon . . .

Not the Dae-Mon. Those scars are from fire-light. Look at how red they are . . .

Ahraia kept her eyes down, but glanced up to see the Astra glaring at her with a sharply furrowed brow.

Stay quiet, her father conveyed subtly before bowing. *Masai*, he conveyed with eyes and ears down submissively. *This is Ahraia, daughter of Behra.*

Ahraia bowed, her ears tucking backwards self-consciously.

"Your shadow is beautiful," the Masai said, her sallow eyes faintly gleaming as she looked at Losna. Her light scars were even darker than Ahraia had first thought, charcoal gray. She had a scar across her cheek that looked like a claw mark, and her left ear was just shorter than the other.

Ahraia's thoughts tumbled against her nerves and came out as rough as a spritelings conveyance. *Thank you.*

A nervous silence settled over the hollow. The Masai's gaze was fixed on Losna and Ahraia.

"Did you find the shades?" the Astra asked Ahraia's father to break the silence.

He nodded. *It was just as the Masai indicated; the shades were already dead. The work of lightwalkers undoubtedly—we found two dozen of them camped in same meadow.*

Ahraia looked up, her fear giving way to anger that her father was still insisting it was the humans.

That's not true, she conveyed.

Keep your thoughts to yourself, the Astra conveyed, her mouth turning down at the corners before turning back to Ahraia's father. "Humans?" she asked. He nodded. "What did you do with them?"

We disposed of them, all but one . . .

"One got away?" the Astra said, perturbed. Her ears twitched for an explanation.

Nitesse Gavea and my wards are seeing after it, her father conveyed.

"Why is a Nitesse hunting after a human?" the Masai asked. "That's the task of a ward."

Let me explain, her father conveyed, holding up his hands placatingly. A murmur of thoughts and whispers passed through the crowded dell. The Astra shifted uncomfortably. Her father's conveyance tightened so that his thoughts were known only to the few in the center of the hollow.

Our shades came across a human while they were hunting and it got away—unfortunately, one of them was seen.

Ahraia barely managed to hold back her objection, knowing any lie would reveal itself and she would end up condemning them all.

"Seen?" the Masai asked, her listless eyes turning to Ahraia.

"Who was seen?" the Astra asked sharply, worry plain on the edge of her voice. A flurry of conveyance passed across the darkening as the sprites and wards who hadn't been privy to the conveyance sensed the implication. Ahraia's ears twitched unintentionally. She glanced back and found Hayvon standing near the bottom of the dell. His ears were pointed sharply upward. He met her eye and made the lightest bonding.

Be ready to run, if this turns to the light, he conveyed.

What's happening? What did father say to you? Ahraia hoped she wasn't as pale as Hayvon.

Her father frowned and held up a hand. *I was hoping to discuss this in some privacy*, he conveyed with a glance to the Astra. Her eyes widened and Ahraia was sure some conveyance passed between them.

"Then tell," the Astra said, ears flickering for privacy.

Ahraia's father nodded. Every sprite in the darkening watched on, but not a sound of his conveyance slipped forth. Water still streamed down from the shell even as the rain's patter lulled, but a silence formed in the hollow, oppressive and still. Ahraia strained to catch what was being conveyed, but her father's thoughts were too subdued.

What did you tell him? Ahraia conveyed to Hayvon, growing more nervous by the moment. Hayvon didn't respond. He was staring sharply at their father. Losna shifted anxiously on her paws, pressing closer to Ahraia.

The Astra began to nod, her ears dropping slightly and her eyes darkening to a deep flaxen shade. When at last she spoke, her voice shattered the silence that had formed.

"Bring me Hayvon and my oldest shades."

What's happening? Ahraia conveyed. Her father shot her a warning glance and signaled for her to keep quiet.

Stay out of this, unless you want to lose your shadow.

Ahraia bit her lip and grabbed hold of Losna. She looked at Hayvon.

Stay quiet, he conveyed with his jaw set firmly. He stepped forward, shoulders squared and ears up, seemingly unafraid. Tev and Shim were shuffled down the hillside: both looked startled and frightened. Shim's ermine scuttled from his hands and into his cloak, and Tev's squirrel bounced closely after her. Both the Astra's and Ahraia's father's eyes glowed maliciously. Losna growled without knowing it.

"Your father told me what happened," the Astra said. Her words carried an unasked question, and the barest accusation.

This has nothing to do with your shades, Hayvon answered firmly.

Ahraia, strangely enough, was keenly aware of his thoughts, as though a bonding had formed between them, though it hadn't. The dimmest hint of a confession lay at the tip of his conveyance, mixed with an emptiness, raked out of his heart, haunting and hollow.

The veins of the Astra's eyes turned golden. "Is it true?"

Hayvon's emotions tumbled across Ahraia's mind just before the thoughts were conveyed.

It is.

Ahraia opened her mouth to protest, but couldn't. An enchantment seized within her, preventing her from objecting. Her body and mind stilled, overwhelmed by a heavy binding, like a protective shelter that cocooned her and forced her into silence. She struggled against it, but froze when Hayvon's conveyances echoed in her mind. *This is the only way out of this.*

What are you doing? Ahraia conveyed in panic, but the thought didn't escape. She tried to free herself, but a second and third binding suddenly enveloped her, smothering her. Her father's eyes lay fixed upon her and she sensed another gaze flicker towards her, though she couldn't tell whose it was. A heavy fog clouded her mind: her thoughts faded, her eyes blurred and her ears didn't seem to hear. Her fingers, resting in her Losna's fur, seemed distant and foreign. Even their bond felt subdued. She watched in a haze of terror as the Astra pressed forward.

"But you're admitting it? Openly?"

Hayvon's answer echoed in Ahraia's mind, close and yet dim. *Just me. Not the shades. Not Ahraia.*

Ahraia would have screamed if she could have.

"You understand what this means?" the Astra said.

Hayvon nodded.

He wasn't seen, Ahraia tried to convey, trying to force her thoughts through the stifling enchantment. Her father's eyes flickered to her and her mind blurred.

Stay out of this if you want to keep your shadow, he conveyed again. Yet Ahraia didn't have a choice. She watched in helpless terror, her chest drawn in tightly as the taste of what was to come turned chalky on her tongue.

The Astra stood in front of her shades, contemplating them

evenly. Shim kept his eyes down and Tev stood clutching her shadow tightly. The Astra's stern posture softened and she knelt in front of the younger shade, who, like her brother, was staring at her feet. When the Astra spoke, her voice snaked out, quiet and tender, nothing like the tone she struck with Hayvon.

"Tev, my love," she said, lifted her daughter's chin to meet her eye. "What happened with the human?"

Tev's eyes brimmed with tears. Her shadow crawled into her arms.

"You *were* seen, weren't you? You can tell me. Nothing bad will come of it," the Astra said. The whole darkening was silent, eerily so. The Astra nodded reassuringly. "It's all right." She caressed Tev's hand.

Don't believe that, Ahraia thought in desperation, her voice swallowed by the binding. She wanted to scream at Tev to stay quiet. *Please, Hayvon*, she thought, begging to be released from at least part of the binding.

Tev began to cry.

"*Tell me*," the Astra commanded more forcefully.

Tev took a shuddering breath, lowered her eyes and nodded once. She sobbed, a pitiful and quiet noise.

No, she wasn't. She wasn't seen, Ahraia conveyed desperately. The bindings twisted down upon her, holding her like the unforgiving webs of a vice spider.

The Astra still held Tev's hand, though her gentle reassurances sounded blunted.

"And Shim? Was he seen? If you tell me the truth, I promise I won't hurt you—or your brother."

Tev nodded once more. A murmur of surprise and excitement passed through the watching sprites. Shim still hadn't looked up, but Ahraia thought she heard a sob.

"What of Ahraia?" the Masai asked, a dim glimmer in her eye like the Dark Moon at its peak. The furor hushed, and a shiver of fear swelled through the enchantments holding Ahraia.

Tev shook her head. "Shade Ahraia wasn't there," she whispered.

The Astra let out a sigh. Ahraia's father shifted uncomfortably and the link swelled with both relief and anxiety.

Hayvon's ears batted for pardon. *The shades weren't seen. I told you,* he conveyed. *None of them were seen. I—*

"Enough," the Astra said, dismissing his pleas. Ahraia could feel Hayvon's panic rising.

"But they weren't seen!" he said aloud. "Father. I already told you, they weren't seen!"

Whispers of disapproval hissed out through the crowd of sprites.

"*Quiet,*" the Astra commanded, her face clouding in disgust. "Don't you dare speak aloud in front of the Masai."

A searing wave of silent admonishment turned the air, but Ahraia could sense through the binding that Hayvon hardly noticed. His mind was surprisingly empty, and the only fear he held was for the shades, and for Ahraia.

"You've already admitted to being seen by a human—you've put this whole darkening at risk. But you're not going to endanger us any longer. Give me your shadow."

Losna let out a whine, terrified for Vesta. The rest of the sprites stared on eagerly. The Masai was the only one without any emotion in her eye, watching with the quiet stillness of a lidless owl.

Ahraia expected Hayvon to panic, but to her disbelief, he let out a grim smile. No thought or conveyance came forth, but Ahraia could feel bitter satisfaction flowing through their bond, a sense of relief followed closely by a haunting, aching emptiness in his mind that he had been avoiding.

The Astra held out her hand. "Where is it? Where is that pathetic little tree rat."

The air bristled, but Hayvon didn't move, except for a bitter smile playing at his lips. Ahraia shuddered feeling his emotions boiling to the surface. She felt a void of loss yawning open inside him.

The Astra's spell rang out with her voice. "*Give me your shadow.*"

"She's gone," Hayvon said.

Gone? Ahraia thought faintly. Then she understood the void she sensed. He had cut Vesta loose—given her back to the forest. Ahraia's breaths seemed empty, like she couldn't draw enough air. Her chest ached, the weight too heavy to bear, the void too haunting to touch. She couldn't fathom what he had done, but she understood; he had known Vesta would be shown the light, and he had set her free before the Astra could kill her.

The Astra's ears lowered angrily. "Impossible." She stared at Hayvon, her eyes fierce and disbelieving. "Find me his shadow. It can't be far," she called out. Several sprites and wards swept away through the darkening.

The Astra turned back towards her shades.

"*Come here*," she ordered. The shades didn't move, but their shadows wriggled into motion: Tev's squirrel leapt from her hands, scampering the short distance to the Astra, and Shim's ermine crawled from his pocket, snaking free from Shim's attempt to keep hold of him.

Ahraia sensed Hayvon telling the shadows to flee, and watched in impotent horror as the Astra reached down and grabbed Tev's shadow. The squirrel didn't struggle. It waited calmly, watching as the Astra drew her drain. The knife was narrow and sharp. There was no hesitation. With a single, clean stroke, the Astra sliced the head from Tev's shadow.

Tev gasped and fell to her knees. She shuddered, her breaths escaping as a horrible strangled noise. The Astra tossed the dead squirrel at her feet.

Shim's shadow tried to scramble away. A dae-ward stooped to grab it, but it slithered free. It scampered towards the darkening wall, wriggling through the legs of sprites.

Shim did the same but a sprite caught him by the arm, yanking him to the ground. He cried out in pain and his shadow froze. In that instant, Ahraia's father slammed his hand down, pinning the ermine by the neck. The shadow bit him, sinking its sharp teeth into his knuckles. Blood streamed across his fingers but he carried the shadow unflinching to the Astra.

The binding around Ahraia lessened. Hayvon was directing more of himself into urging the ermine to flee. Shim's shadow twisted and squirmed, but the Astra took it, and in a single, swift motion, beheaded it. Blood spurted across her wrists.

Hayvon gasped, and Ahraia sensed his brief connection to the shadow sliced open. Even twice removed, it felt as though she had been stabbed. She flinched, and realized she could move. The enchantment holding her had thinned; Hayvon and her father were distracted. Concentrating on the threads of the binding, she willed her mind free, snapping one hold after another. Losna was suddenly close and comforting next to her, but terrified by what had just happened.

Shim collapsed, hanging limp in his captor's arms.

"You daemon!" Hayvon said through clenched teeth. Wards lunged forward to grab him. The air quivered once again with enchantment and he went quiet, though his eyes were wild and terrible.

"Daemon?" the Astra said, her pale eyes now glowing yellow. "You'll know a daemon soon enough. Get him out of my sight."

Ahraia panted, still reeling from the shadows' deaths as wards wrestled Hayvon away. Her ears were flat, and tears of anger streamed down her face.

"Shade Ahraia," the Astra said, blood covering her hands and wrists like Ahraia's markings covered hers. "Get a hold of yourself..."

The shadows' blood dripped to the forest floor. Ahraia barely restrained the urge to scream at the Astra, to attack her father with her bare hands for condemning Hayvon, and for letting his own shades be cut from their shadows. Ahraia's emotions were a storm that roiled within her. She hadn't realized it, but her teeth were bared and Losna was poised for a fight.

Ahraia, comport yourself with a bit of decency, her father conveyed heatedly. *You're in charge of your nit now; you're too old to show your emotion.*

The Masai's ears perked straight up. "She is the head of her nit?" she asked. Her calm broke for the first time, showing with surprise. "Is she the eldest?"

The Astra's face turned from anger to fear in an instant, as though she suddenly realized some terrible, unstoppable truth. Ahraia's father paled, and his lips drew tight. Neither answered, and Ahraia was too distraught to even understand the Masai's implication. Shim lay limp upon the ground, and Tev sobbed incoherently.

"Is she the eldest?" the Masai asked again.

The Astra nodded, a pained look on her face.

The Masai's ears were quivering. "Then I want her as part of my darkening."

Ahraia's breath caught. The words didn't make sense.

She's not even a sprite yet, her father conveyed. *She's not old enough.*

"She doesn't have to be," the Masai said. "I'm calling her to become one."

What's happening? Losna thought, as realization settled upon Ahraia's heart. The Masai's words constricted around Ahraia beyond any binding she had ever felt. The world closed around her and her eyes blurred. Unbound fear spread through her, so intense that she couldn't help it reflecting on her shadow. Losna let out a terrified whimper.

She's not ready, the Astra conveyed desperately. Ahraia's lungs wouldn't fill.

"You mean you're not ready. Don't pretend you never had any intention of letting her be uprooted," the Masai said.

She's just a shade still, the Astra conveyed.

The Masai smiled, a cold and shimmering smile like starlight on a frigid winter night. When she spoke, her voice projected to the furthest corners of the darkening, to the very blackness of the night.

"I'm calling for Shade Ahraia to enter her shadow test."

11

TRADED FOR DARKNESS

The silence that gripped the darkening was absolute.

Ahraia felt faint. She steadied herself on Losna, whose whole body trembled with fear.

The Masai stared at them like trophies.

"Her shadow test?" her father said aloud, his voice snapping the silence violently. He looked stunned. "She's not old enough." *Not by half.*

Horrified gasps chased the echoes from the hollow. A rustle of unsettled wings fluttered above and a sprite coughed. Ahraia's shock stabbed so deeply, she hardly registered that he had spoken aloud to the Masai, unbidden. But the rest of the darkening had. A dae-ward from Angolor stepped dangerously forward, his eyes shining brilliant golden beneath his veil.

The Masai held up a hand, staying the ward. The scars on her face were graying, revealing the storm just beneath the surface.

"You dare speak to me?"

Even the dripping of the forest seemed to stop. Ahraia's father quailed beneath her gaze, bowing submissively with the top of his head showing. Giving no indication she was appeased, she turned back to the Astra. When she spoke, her tone was flat and dangerous.

"This is a troubling darkening, where shades and wards presume their voices are to be heard and where the will of the Masai is not absolute. Perhaps the Gelesh has fallen farther than I imagined."

The silence welled from every corner, sharpened by the low hissing streams and Tev's choking sobs. Ahraia's father kept his eyes down and the Astra pressed her lips together, staying submissively silent.

Ahraia still couldn't believe what was happening. Losna let out a whine and the Masai's eyes flickered towards them.

"Now, unless, I've misunderstood," she said, "Ahraia is the eldest in her nit. Which means *any* Astra could ask her to become a sprite at *any* time. And I'm not willing to let her become a sprite to any darkening but my own."

The Astra's mouth hung agape. *It's only by chance, ill fate really, that she's eldest at all—two brothers dead and the other seen . . . she's not ready to become a sprite. No Astra would ask her to enter her test so soon.*

The Masai's lips curled down at the corners. "Unfortunately for me, I have no choice. You've condemned her brother to death, and rightly so. But in doing so, you expose her as eldest and make her entirely uprootable to any who would choose to call out the challenge. Offers will undoubtedly come—offers already *have come*," she said knowingly.

The Astra's eyes widened in affront, but in a forced manner that Ahraia could tell it was an act. The Masai went on, unimpeded.

"I know of at least three agreements you've already heard from other Astrael—in West Vale, Herth, even Menton—though I can't imagine what of any value they could possibly offer. I won't let another darkening think they can challenge Angolor with a wolf-binder."

That's preposterous, the Astra conveyed, but Ahraia could feel the truth bleeding through her thoughts.

An easy smile spread across the Masai's face and sent a shiver through Ahraia. "I know you mean to rid yourself of her. A wolf-binder is too dangerous for you . . . and she's worth too much."

"You've already taken one daughter. Two would be too much, least of all her."

Ahraia couldn't process what was unraveling. For once she agreed with the Astra; she wasn't ready. But the Masai's accusation caught her off guard. She bound her father.

You were going to let her trade me?

By the way his brow furrowed and his lip curled, Ahraia wasn't sure he even knew about the Astra's intentions. He didn't answer.

The Astra hesitated. Tev was still sobbing. A ward pinned Shim to the ground, though he looked like he was as limp as his shadow.

The Astra nodded towards her shades. "Get them out of my sight."

Several sprites stepped forward and dragged the shades away. Tev's sobs became faint, leaving only the sparse raindrops rattling on the shell above. Ahraia couldn't think straight.

Are you willing to let me speak plainly? the Astra conveyed. The Masai's ears flicked in assent. Every sprite and shade in the darkening held their collective breath.

"What are you willing to give me for her?" the Astra asked.

Ahraia swayed on her feet, clutching Losna as the only thing steady in her world. The Astra pressed on before the Masai had a chance to answer.

"You're asking for a second daughter—a wolf-binder, no less."

The Masai's smile hollowed out Ahraia's insides. "I don't need the first daughter. You can keep her . . . and the dae-wards."

Kren looked up, seemingly aware for the first time. She looked at Ahraia, her mouth falling open, motherly despair plain upon her face. Her ears curled in apparent dismay that Ahraia would be uprooted in her stead.

The Masai went on. "I've can give you more. More wards or seeds, or orbs . . ."

The Astra scoffed. "There aren't enough wards in all of Angolor to trade a wolf-binder." Ahraia noticed a perceptible shift in her manner: her ears angled back and a hard edge had crept into her voice. The change was startling, as though she realized the Masai had her cornered.

"You're right, you know," she went on. "I *have* received offers. From your allies and enemies alike. Some promising allegiance—even fealty—some promising darkness and wards. But who is to say I don't keep her? It's my right to do so." She stared fixedly at the Masai, her words threateningly close to treason. The sprites about the dell shifted uncomfortably. "And if I choose to, there's no reason Daispar wouldn't become the roots of a whole new spritedom. What will you do when a new Masai rises here, in the Gelesh?"

The gleam of the Masai's eyes disappeared entirely. "It would mean war," she said.

The Astra held a hand up and bowed in full formality, showing the top of her head as Ahraia's father just had.

"A war which I have no intention of causing." When she raised her head, there was a greedy turn to her ears. "But neither do you expect me to accept wards for a wolf-binder. If you insist she enter her shadow test, then it's my only recourse to protect my darkening. If I didn't, I wouldn't deserve to hold what I do."

The Masai remained silent. Her ears twitched, signaling the Astra to go on.

The Astra's voice dropped. "You came here to address the failing darkness, but you're going to take away that which will bring us the most darkness."

The Masai gave the Astra a wolfish grin. "So this is about darkness."

"I have no interest in seeing a new spritedom rise—or a new Masai, for that matter. But you're right, the woods of the Gelesh aren't what they once were; lightwalkers trespass on every side, and our cover shrinks with each passing night. I need darkness, and the ability to weave it, protect it, and spread it. I need the ability to reclaim these woods. I need your help in pulling over the veil of night. Is that not what a Masai is meant to do?"

Every sprite in the darkening listened eagerly.

"What would you ask?" the Masai said.

The Astra rolled forward onto her toes.

"I need new darkenings. I need the *seeds* of darkenings."

The Masai's face twitched. "*Darkenings*?"

A maddened gleam shone in the Astra's eyes as she nodded once. Ahraia hoped that it was too much to ask, that the Astra was being too greedy. Darkening seeds were invaluable, and only the Masai held them. Ahraia hoped that the Masai would walk away, wanting nothing to do with the Astra's preposterous request. But when she spoke, her voice was measured and practical.

"And who would be their Astrael?"

Ahraia's throat felt like it was pinched closed.

The Astra's ears batted, unable to contain her fervor. "Whoever you choose. Your own daughters, if you wish." *I mean these woods to be allied to Angolor, an extension of your great realm in the east. Together, we can spread darkness as it once was.* Her inner-voice dripped with sincerity.

The Masai seemed to consider this for a moment. Ahraia was terrified, still holding on to the barest hope that the Astra asked too much. She lowered her gaze again as the Masai eyed her.

"If she becomes a sprite, I will give you a single seed of a darkening."

"Two . . ."

"Two seeds."

The Astra considered it for a moment. "She's not the eldest yet. Not until her brother is dealt with, and he won't be condemned until the turning, which is still three nights away."

"It's only proper if the first task falls at the full moon."

The Astra nodded. "Then it's agreed. Two darkening seeds and you have my wolf-binder." The Astra bowed, ears pointed in acceptance. Ahraia's breath rushed from her chest. She couldn't process what had happened. She didn't understand. She didn't *want* to understand. But Losna's thoughts unraveled more clearly, deadly aware of the loneliness of being cut away, of being exiled. She threw back her head and filled the darkening with a haunting, lonely howl.

~

"I SHOULD HAVE KILLED the human. I should have just killed her and been done with it." Ahraia bit her lip in frustration, running her fingers over the trunk of her mother's tree.

The narrow slit where the orb fit stared back at her like a black, lifeless eye.

We should leave, Losna thought, her whole body quivering, from nose tip to tail tip.

"And just run from it?" Ahraia said wistfully, running her fingers along the inside of the empty cache. She had watched Kren and Kaval slip the moon-bright orb into the tree countless times, covering the opening lest any light escaped. Now, the hollow was painfully dark. Ahraia wished she had forcibly enchanted the orb from the human: peeled back the girl's fingers and ripped it from her mind. She sighed and picked idly at a rough spot on the bark.

"Where would we go?"

To the forests? To the plains? We could run. What about Plain Dark? Or farther still. What about a new darkness, something you could fold?

"They would hunt us."

Even on the plains?

Ahraia clenched her jaw bitterly. "There's no darkness there. Not for me." Her skin itched from all the light she had already suffered. Her scars were darker now, the angry-red giving way to silver-gray permanence over ashen skin, almost like the Masai's.

Losna let out a low whine, and rested her head on her paws with her tail tucked beside her.

What happens if Gavea finds the human?

Ahraia didn't want to think of it. She didn't have an answer. It was full day outside the darkening, and her remaining siblings were asleep in their shade trees. There were only three left: her sister Kyah, and the two spritelings, Thelon and Alua. It seemed impossible that in less than a turning, all three of their older brothers were dead—or close enough to dead. Three nights remained until Hayvon would be condemned to the Shadow Woods.

"If we had only gotten to Kaval and Altah quicker," Ahraia said, "then none of this would have happened." She resisted the urge to scream, to howl with all her fury at the injustice of it. She turned back to her shade tree.

The innards were blissfully black. She settled in against the trunk, leaning against Losna and combing her fingers through her shadow's fur. Losna didn't even seem to notice. The shadow test had poisoned their bond.

"If Hayvon just would have listened . . . why did he tell them he was seen?" Ahraia ran through a thousand ways things could have gone differently.

To protect you. To protect us. Losna thought, laying her head against Ahraia. *If he hadn't, it might be us. It should have been us . . . we were seen as well.*

Ahraia swallowed guiltily. She shook her head. She couldn't begin to imagine cutting Losna loose, no matter what the circumstance. The void within Hayvon had been haunting, an absence like missing his limb, or his heart, or his mind. She had no doubt that it had clouded his thought.

Ahraia ran her fingers over Losna's back. The test was like a spider's web from which she couldn't escape. And though she couldn't bear the thought of sending her back to the forest, the alternative was far worse. She shuddered to think what failure would mean. Losna would be shown the light—pinned down by a dozen bindings, snarling and afraid, and then suffering the Astra or the Masai's drain . . .

"I can't suffer what Shim did," she said.

Losna huffed in irritation. *Then why must we go through with it?*

"Because . . . it's the only way we both live," she said, defeated. "I can't run. If the wards didn't eventually catch us, the light would. It's not like I can underdae forever, and there's more than just darkness that this place provides." *Food, shelter, protection from lightwalkers and the light of the world . . .*

Losna's chest rumbled and she pointedly looked away. Ahraia knew she didn't understand the shadow test; she never had. In truth, Ahraia didn't understand it either. Sending Losna back to the woods wouldn't make her a sprite—it would simply destroy her. When she was younger, she had thought she could change it, and take her shadow with her. But as time went on, she realized the truth—no shade ever became a sprite with their shadow, and the only way for a shadow to live was to pass the test and release it back to the world.

She sighed, shaking loose her tarry vine. She hung it to the shade tree, where its filamentous roots hooked on greedily.

"It could be worse. Look at Hayvon." *Shadowless and condemned.*

A low rumble of discontent came from Losna, but stopped abruptly. She raised her head, her ears twitched and she let out a quiet growl.

Instinctively, Ahraia reached out with her mind. She flinched, sensing an unfamiliar presence lurking inside the nit, just beyond the wall of her shade tree.

The branches of her shade tree suddenly twisted back, pulled against their will, and before Ahraia could react, she saw the Astra standing outside. The Astra peered inward, looking gaunt in the midmorning murkiness, her perfectly white eyes gleaming from the sunken hollows of her face.

Losna heaved off the ground and bared her teeth, holding her tail stiff and low behind her. *Shadow killer*, she thought.

What are you doing here? Ahraia conveyed without thinking or bowing. The Astra's ears lowered, and she hesitated at the closure, either wanting Ahraia to come out or waiting to be invited in.

Ahraia didn't move.

The Astra pursed her lips and stepped through the unobliging closure, her displeasure spread plain across her face. But it was nothing compared to the storm erupting in Ahraia's mind. Since the day of her mother's condemnation, Ahraia had resented the Astra, even hated her, but a deep part of her had always understood: postulants were the way of the darkening, the way of sprites. Her mother had chosen to fight. But Shim and Tev, Hayvon and Losna were different—they were never given the choice. Ahraia's ears flattened and her heart pounded right beneath her throat. She swallowed down the urge to set Losna on the Astra.

A low rumble emanated from the depths of Losna's chest—she was more than willing.

The Astra glared at them, ears just as flat and her hand resting not too casually above her drain, until Losna's growl faded into nothingness. Once it did, the Astra's gaze moved from Losna to Ahraia to the shade tree, studying it in one prolonged, sweeping look. The silence deepened.

"This is an unusual shade tree," she said at last.

Ahraia couldn't tell if she disapproved.

"Night-bells and winter jasmine . . . these need light, and warmth." She eyed the medley of flowers and vines braided amongst the shade tree. Ahraia held her breath as her gaze came to rest on the brightest flower, a ball of white petals dangling from the central branch of the shade tree.

"A moon flower?" The Astra's anger seemed momentarily forgotten. She raised her hand, cupping her fingers a hair's breadth below the petals.

I doubt my weaving brought you here, Ahraia conveyed, snapping the Astra from her reverie. She drew her hand back and a frown played at her lips.

"I won't lie. I have no love being inside your mother's nit tree. It doesn't sit well in my heart to feel her presence." *Not in the least.*

It wouldn't sit well with her, either. Ahraia's conveyance slipped out before she could stop it. Losna swished her tail in agreement.

If the Astra was offended, it didn't show; her face had stilled, her ears were uncurled, and her eyes had faded to white.

"I don't blame you for being angry," she said uncharacteristically. "I would have been too."

Ahraia remained silent, not out of respect so much as a lack of anything to say.

"But she wasn't a good Astra. Under her watch the dark faltered . . ." As the Astra spoke, Ahraia's heart fluttered in her chest. Losna's lip curled up in a snarl.

"Dimdale and Enshad's dark eroded, and Daispar's and the Gelesh's strength are weakened because of it. Now my hand is forced. It was my only choice to act then, much as I do now." The Astra looked down at her hands. The shadow's blood stained her wrists, as though it was still the blood of Ahraia's mother. "In the end, I did it for the good of Daispar—for the Gelesh. Our woods have been failing for years. We needed change—we needed an Astra who would lead us back into the darkness."

And you thought it would be you, Ahraia conveyed, wondering what the Astra was getting at.

"I know it will be," she said. Her eyes narrowed again, her placid rigidity returning. "The price you've garnished alone will set much of what has failed back in order."

That's all this is about? Returning darkness? Ahraia conveyed bitterly.

"That's what it's always been about," the Astra said. Veins of gold crept into her eyes. "I know it's hard for you to conceive of a night beyond the next, but I'm looking out for your future. That's partly why I'm here—to remind you of your *purpose* in all of this." Her contempt showed plain in the downturn of her ears and lips, chastising Ahraia as a silly shade.

"You're poised to be the next Masai—and the Gelesh will be just one sliver of your province. These darkening seeds are as much for you as they are for me. And while the shadows of my labor won't be realized for years to come, when they are, the woods of the Gelesh will be ruled by a new darkness, where no lightwalker would dare roam. That's what's at stake."

Ahraia barely kept her thoughts from turning to spoken words. *My shadow is at stake.*

The Astra's ears flickered in annoyance. "You naïve little shade," she said, the calm of her face breaking with lines of anger. "You're so busy worrying about your shadow, you've failed to take notice that our world moves in true dark." She stared pointedly at Ahraia's scars.

"Did you only come here to lecture me?" Ahraia felt Losna's tail flick against her leg.

The Astra's eyes yellowed with the sound of her voice, glowing against her ashen silhouette. Ahraia's heart thumped heavily in her chest, knowing she had crossed the line. Losna didn't care. Her thoughts were reduced to the simplest aggressions. Every one of her teeth glimmered white.

The quiet pressed about them. The Astra kept her eye on Losna.

"No," she said at last, seeming to give up on Losna settling. "I came here to discuss your brothers." The gold drained from her eyes and the cant of her ears lessened.

"Beran told me you went looking for them—that you saw something. I want to know what happened." The Astra's ears flickered for Ahraia to speak. It was a good thing because Ahraia's doubted she could convey another word without letting the sheer contempt and anger howl from her thoughts.

"Didn't he already tell you?"

"He said the humans killed them."

Ahraia shook her head and pressed her lips together angrily. She hated her father just as much as she hated the Astra. He was just as guilty in Hayvon's and the shades' condemnation.

The fur behind Losna's neck still bristled. *Careful,* she thought, *I don't trust her.*

The Astra watched Ahraia piercingly. "You don't think the humans did it?"

"I *know* they didn't," Ahraia said. The Astra raised her eyebrows. "We saw what killed them—and it wasn't human."

The Astra's ears twitched. "You saw the killer? What did it look like?"

Ahraia hesitated, still angry but now careful to measure her words. The Astra's face was a mask, but her eyes glinted with something . . . was it eagerness? Fear? Knowing?

"It was a shadow of sorts—but not in the sense of a shadow like Losna; it was a wraith . . ." Ahraia said.

"A wraith? An imp—maybe a mara? Some fiendish trick that slowed your thoughts? Something eating off the corpses?"

"No. It formed a full binding, stronger than any I've ever felt, a vice, from which there was no escape."

The Astra's eyes widened. Bindings of a sort were possible by a number of woodland creatures. Even some of the trees and flowers could leave you in a cloud of despair or fog of confusion—but not many wildlings had the ability, or the will, to bind a shade or sprite intentionally.

"Did you tell your father this?" she said, seeming perturbed.

"I told him, but he insisted it was the humans."

"A spritish binding?" The Astra frowned, her eyebrows furrowing darkly.

Ahraia shrugged. "It wasn't like any sprite I've ever bound. It was twisted . . . vile." *Evil.*

"And you didn't see anything more? What it looked like? The form it took . . .?"

Ahraia searched for the words to describe the inky-figure within the dark but then remembered the drain she had picked up. She hesitated, unsure if she should show the Astra the blade.

"I know what it killed them with. It left this . . . when Losna startled it." She slid the dagger from her cloak, holding the blackened blade for the Astra to see. In the shade tree, it showed veins and channels that had been imperceptible in the forest.

The Astra reached out, as though she was thinking of taking it but stayed her hand. "Did you show anybody this?"

"Only my Father and Gavea." *And Gavea's sisters—Levath, and Tallin.*

All trustworthy, Ahraia heard, unsure if she was supposed to. The Astra's ears straightened. "Don't show it to anyone else." A pause formed on her lips. Ahraia's mind tingled with the lightest bonding. *Did you see any sprites that night?* The Astra conveyed as a whisper. Through the bond, Ahraia could feel the Astra's emotion; she was worried.

Losna shifted next to Ahraia, glaring at the Astra. *Only her and the alp . . .*

Ahraia ignored her shadow's suspicions and shook her head,

knowing what the Astra meant. "You think that blade belongs to a sprite?" she asked. "Levath thought it might have been some sort of daemon bone."

"It does look like daemon bone... but I don't know what to make of it." The Astra's jaw clenched, and Ahraia could tell she wasn't letting on whatever she thought or knew.

"Could it have been an alp? Or maybe one of the Masai's company?"

"Not likely," the Astra said calmly, but her eyes went wide and her ears batted for silence. *Have you lost all reason? You can't say that aloud! She could have spies anywhere.* She looked about nervously. Ahraia sensed her probing out with her mind, seeking anyone who might be listening.

She glared at Ahraia. *That kind of accusation will get you condemned.* Her voice covered her thoughts with a forced calm. "Besides, their company was in Deep Brook." Her ears flickered and flicked again, scolding Ahraia not to speak aloud. "Now enough about this, your test begins when the Bright Moon is full. I want you to be ready for it." She took a deep, steadying breath. Still looking perturbed, she turned, making to leave the shade tree.

Ahraia let a thought out before she had time to consider the implication, desperate to know what the Astra suspected.

I can show you, she conveyed, hoping to glean some hint of her suspicions.

The Astra froze, her ears twitching curiously.

Losna growled, sending a flurry of admonishments towards Ahraia.

The Astra peeled back a branch and looked out of the shade tree, then turned back.

A memory? She let the branches fall. *Show me.*

Ahraia took a deep breath. Reliving the scene once more wouldn't be easy, and sharing the memory would put their minds far closer than she ever wanted to be. But it would be worth it, if she could learn whatever the Astra suspected. Losna let out a growl. She stepped protectively closer to Ahraia.

Ahraia cleared her mind of all the emotions she could: of her brothers, of Hayvon, of the shades and her shadow test, of the Astra and all the anger and fear she was feeling. She took a deep breath, setting her mind to the memory of the meadow and the menace. The Astra was waiting.

Ahraia tentatively bound her, swallowing down a lump of fear. The initial connection was too hesitant to have any clarity. Ahraia had no sense of what the Astra was thinking either; she had no other choice but to let down her guard and let their link strengthen.

The fog came first. It wrapped around her spine, sucking her back into the meadow.

She was standing next to Losna, looking towards the Stone Tree. But the thin layer of fog didn't seem to flow; it hung, untouched by the faint breeze that ruffled the grasses. The hulking Stone Tree loomed ahead.

They were moving. Dirt crunched beneath her feet. She was falling back into the memory, her distaste for the Astra fading entirely, as she recalled the quiet uncertainty of the night: the gathering clouds above, the darkness collecting within the underdae, and the pervasive menace. Her worry for her brothers returned.

Ahraia stood poised, alone at the edge of the impenetrable dark.

Kaval? Altah? She stepped forward. *A broken wing.* She knelt down. *Mehra.* She stood up quickly, her scars flushing with fear. *Something* stood just inside the dark.

Losna! she conveyed. The binding slapped down on her. Ahraia had a clear sense of the figure, *death*, standing on its hind legs, *a wraith*, wreathed in shadows blacker than the night. It waited, just inside the darkness, step by step drawing her inward. She saw it. Fur bristling around white teeth. One more step. *This is it.*

Losna's growl erupted behind her and the binding disappeared. She was suddenly free. But the wraith didn't flee. It was still there, just inside the darkness, waiting for her. The change in the memory scared Ahraia, startling her out of the vision back to the shade tree.

She emerged disoriented and panicked, her heart racing. She was in the true dark and Losna's fear reverberated just behind her. For a moment, she thought she was still in the Stone Tree, and the wraith was in front of her. She scrambled backward, still breathing hard, unclasping herself entirely from the memory.

Losna bared her teeth at the Astra, who looked equally startled.

They both stood breathing hard before the Astra spoke. "Did you show your father that?" Her voice was surprisingly shaky.

It took a moment for Ahraia to reorient herself. Losna's defensiveness had her on edge.

"No. He wouldn't listen. He was intent on getting back here." Ahraia stomach tightened in a sour knot.

You didn't get a better look at it? You had no sense of it? Ahraia could feel the doubt in the Astra's thoughts—and again the worry. *Guard that memory close*, she conveyed, turning to leave the shade tree.

Where are you going? Ahraia conveyed, reeling still from sharing the memory and the aftermath. *What do you think that was?*

"That's none of your concern. Keep your head about you, things may be worse than I imagined. For now, forget about it. I need you focused on your test. The Gelesh is counting on you."

She turned and pulled aside the branches of Ahraia's shade tree. When Ahraia looked back at Losna, her shadow was standing stock still, her whole body rigid with burning fear.

Ahraia, Losna thought, *it was her.*

12

FADING LIGHT

H*er? The Astra?* Ahraia conveyed.

How could we not have seen it? Losna thought. *She must have killed Altah and Kaval. She was getting them out of the way. Didn't you hear her? "It's always been about darkness'.* Losna let out a woof, obviously aggravated. *That was her knife. That's why she told you not to show anyone.*

A chill passed through Ahraia, as though she had brushed beneath the ghostly fingers of a mara. She spoke hesitantly, her thoughts tainted by the terror of the memory. "I've seen her drain, and that wasn't it."

Losna couldn't sit still. She paced back and forth, tail held back as though she was hunting. *There's no way this is coincidence. She planned this. And if it wasn't her in the Stone Tree, then it was some daemon of hers . . . maybe the alp. Maybe she can control the Shad Mon.*

No one controls the Shad Mon, Ahraia conveyed.

Losna pressed on. *She knew the Masai was coming. She knew that if you were the oldest, she could trade you for darkening seeds.*

Ahraia shook her head. "So she killed Kaval and Altah . . . and then what? Hayvon was supposed to just disappear?"

Losna stopped. The fur on her brow wrinkled in discontent. *Hayvon is disappearing, isn't he?*

Ahraia scratched idly at her scars, wondering if the Astra truly could have planned this.

"What about the fur and eyes? You smelled it. And besides, even with Kaval and Altah dead, she couldn't have done it without Hayvon out of the way too," she said, thinking aloud. "It was sheer stupidity on my part to let the human go. And even worse luck that Hayvon admitted to being seen. There's no way she could have planned for that."

She condemned him easily enough. Losna huffed in aggravation, shaking her fur.

"Maybe she could have . . ." Ahraia admitted. The Astra was certainly vile enough to kill for her own good; she had discarded her oldest shades easily enough, and she had condemned her own sister. But as horrible as she was, Ahraia struggled to imagine the Astra hiding behind the veil of darkness. Then again, the enchantment had been powerful, and if it did emanate from a sprite, then the Astra was the strongest . . .

Her, or the Masai, Losna conveyed, continuing Ahraia's thought.

"And the Masai was in Deep Brook, and her contingent with her . . ." Ahraia trailed off. The silence between them stretched, and Ahraia reached out to make sure the Astra had truly left. The nit was empty.

Losna paced the edges of the shade tree. *No one else could bind you like that. Think about it . . . who else has more to gain? Not the Masai. She gets to keep an eye on you, but you're another daughter in a long line waiting to supplant her. She's acting in defense to keep you rising against her from here in Daispar. But that security is trivial compared to what the Astra gets. She gains whole darkenings. And she gets rid of us.*

Ahraia flushed, her stomach roiling in anger. She couldn't fathom going to such lengths just for darkness; she couldn't imagine killing shades and shadows. But the truth flashed before her like the light-burst from their nit's broken orb. She couldn't do these things, but the Astra certainly could.

She hesitated, remembering how she had been dragged towards the underdae, step by inevitable step. "Why would she draw me in? Do you think she meant to kill me too?"

She probably didn't realize it was you until I showed up. That's why she fled.

Ahraia could swear she had seen black eyes—black, lifeless eyes —and fur, but regardless, the truth was crashing down like the binding from the Stone Tree.

"And we thought it was the Shad-Mon." She scoffed, shaking her head. She suddenly had a terrible thought. "You don't think my father knew, do you?" Her heart felt like it was in her throat.

Maybe that's why he blamed the humans so quickly. Losna growled, a low, deep rumble that came from the hollows of her chest.

"He was in on it," Ahraia said, flooded with disbelief. It spread as though she had been stung by a serapin, starting at her fingers and flushing all the way to her cheeks, tingling right to her lips. The emotions overwhelmed her. She sat down, her legs feeling weak. Losna came closer and nuzzled her.

What are we going to do?

Ahraia let out a heavy sigh, running her fingers through Losna's damp fur. She wanted to confront her father: to scream at him until her voice was hoarse, to bind him and *feel* if it was true.

"We're going to find him and find out if he did it."

And if he did?

"Then I'll kill them." Ahraia squeezed her fist around the blackened drain until her fingers hurt.

It comforted her that Losna didn't challenge her. She carefully placed the blackened drain in a fold of the shade tree, turning back to find Losna watching her. Her shadow was worrying, but no longer about the Astra or her brothers.

What are we going to do about the Shadow Test?

Ahraia swallowed. What *could* they do? She closed her eyes, her teeth clenched so tight that her jaw ached. She could feel Losna watching her, but she couldn't begin to know how to answer that.

"I don't know," she said at last.

~

Losna's breathing eventually became too deep and uniform to be awake, the steady rasp of her breaths rattling against her nose, but sleep wouldn't come for Ahraia. The day stretched on. She lay awake, agonizing over everything that had come to pass: her brothers' murders, Hayvon's and the shades' condemnation, and her and Losna's eminent shadow test.

She lay in a haze, her hand stuck in Losna's fur, debilitated by her fears while she wondered if the Astra could have murdered her brothers. Her memory from the Stone Tree had changed—the wraith took a more familiar silhouette. The fur was gone; the eyes weren't lifeless—they were lightless—pale and drawn. Ahraia could see the Astra now, standing over Kaval and Altah, a foreign drain in her hand to hide her identity. Ahraia could feel her mind: the ragged rush of evil and the absolutism of needing dark.

It made sense. And it made sense that the Astra had come to her shade tree, no doubt seeking what she had seen. She felt stupid for showing the Astra the blade, and even more foolish for showing her the memory.

She eventually dozed, and when night came, she awoke to an overwhelming sense of despair and the sound of rain falling on the darkening beyond. A part of her never wanted to move again, but she forced herself up and Losna followed. They emerged from the shade tree to find a ghostly nit. Only Kyah, Alua, and Thelon remained. The two spritelings were sitting together, whispering in hushed voices. They looked towards her, heads down and ears back, their faces cast with worry.

Ahraia greeted them and walked towards Kyah's shade tree. The tree was small, but perfectly kept. Her sister was like Kren, mature and motherly beyond her years. Soon enough, she wouldn't have a choice. Ahraia bound the shelter and lifted back the branches.

Kyah sat awake with her shadow cradled on her lap, its gray-black tail tucked tightly about it. They were both young; it hadn't been more than three winters since Kyah had become a shade. Her gray fox had its head down and ears up. Their despair seeped through the dark like fog from the Shadow Woods. Ahraia had no need to guess that they too were mourning Kaval and Altah and their shadows. Her sister looked sunken and drawn.

"Have you eaten?" Ahraia asked.

Kyah shook her head.

"You need to. And you need to make sure the spritelings get something too . . ." Ahraia hesitated. The words and thoughts felt sharp as knives in her throat. She swallowed painfully. "Kyah . . . I won't be here much longer."

"I know . . . I heard." Kyah kept her head down.

It wasn't a fair burden to place on the young shade, or the spritelings for that matter. They stood so little chance of surviving without older shades and sprites to guide them—especially now that the nit tree was failing as well.

"When I'm gone, you'll have to look after Alua and Thelon." *They need you.*

"I know." Kyah bit her lip and sniffed away a tear. "I know." She set her shadow on the ground and stood up. *I'll look after them.*

She walked to Ahraia and embraced her. Ahraia held her younger sister, her hands wanting to protect her forever, her body nearly shaking in the anguish of all the loss their nit had suffered. She wanted to scream for the helplessness she felt. She blamed her father, and the Astra, and the Masai—and every sprite who had ever come before her. She didn't understand the shadow test. She didn't understand why she was worth killing for, or why she was worth trading for. She kept these thoughts within, clutching her sister, determined not to show how deeply cut she was.

When Kyah let go, her eyes were dry and her face was forced into a stern grimace.

I'll see after them, Kyah conveyed. A light enchantment brushed Ahraia—a steady conviction spreading unintentionally—Kyah's determination ran resolute right down to her core. Like a young tree with strong roots. Ahraia couldn't smile, but pride radiated through her for the honor her sister carried, even with their world being turned to light.

~

EVERY CURSE and accusation Ahraia could think of ran through her mind as she led Losna across the darkening in search of her father. Her thoughts blurred with the anxiety of confrontation, but her anger drove her forward with ears flat and hair pulled back in a loose tarry that made no effort to hide her scars.

She paused to scan the central hollow first. A few sprites filled waterskins at the springs, and others edged along the fringes of the nits, but it seemed most where already afoot in the woods. Rain rapped on the shell above, but no water dripped through to the hollow below. Ahraia wondered idly where the Masai and her company were being sheltered, though only so she could avoid them.

She checked the cook fires and the dim groves first, winding circuitously towards the Astra's nit. Ahraia had no intention of actually entering—the thought reviled her—but soon enough they rounded a stony path and the dense wall of the Astra's nit loomed ahead, hanging heavily with tallow vines and velum creepers.

Ahraia stood awkwardly for a moment, wondering if she should just bind the tree and check inside. Sticky saliva suddenly choked her mouth. Repulsed, she formed a loose bond but was spared going any further when Tallin, Gavea's sister, emerged through a narrow passageway nearby.

"There you are," she said in greeting. "I've been looking for you since dusk." Like her sister, Tallin still resented Ahraia from when she was a shade.

Couldn't have been looking that hard, Ahraia thought, just loose enough for an echo to pass outward. Tallin frowned. Losna's tail swished contentedly.

"Your father wanted me to tell you—you're not to leave the darkening."

"Why?"

Tallin's ears quivered upright, then batted for Ahraia's conveyance. "It's not my concern to know your father's mind."

A sprite who was passing nearby stopped to look. Ahraia bowed her head, just enough to ward off any repercussions. Once the sprite had moved on, she looked up, not bothering to apologize.

Do you know where he is? she conveyed.

"He's away. With the Astra."

Do you know where? Ahraia asked.

Tallin furrowed her brow. "No."

Ahraia didn't press the point. She turned away with a mock bow and made to return to the nit, feeling Tallin's gaze on her back the whole way.

As though I'd follow her orders, Ahraia conveyed to Losna.

They entered the nit through a thin closure and headed straight for the other side, then exited and headed for the darkening wall. In a matter of steps, they were outside. The forest rattled with falling leaves and dripping rain. Spurts of cold wind sent great showers shaking down from above. Ahraia pulled her hood up and sealed the darkening behind her.

All right. We need to find my father . . .

Losna put her nose to the ground and began hunting for his scent, leading towards the east, where Ahraia guessed he would have left the darkening. She didn't have much of a plan yet, other than to put the question to him by conveyance and see if she could feel the lie.

I've got his scent. Losna indicated a trail emerging from a narrow fold of Daispar, heading off towards the Endless Plains. Losna led them into the fitful rain, nose down, with Ahraia following at a run.

The path wasn't hard to follow. It led through the rifts and gullies of the hills, gradually downward, past the Deep Pool and Warm Springs. Ahraia looked wistfully at the steam rising amongst the pattering rain. The water, dripping from above, was beginning to seep through to her shoulders, sending a miserable, chattering cold through her jaw and neck.

We shouldn't let them get what they want. We should leave, Losna thought, sniffing after a scent she didn't recognize.

Ahraia didn't answer. Try as she might, Losna wouldn't be convinced how dangerous leaving the darkening would be. True enough, she could fold darkness—but eventually it would fail. The wrong storm or the wrong creatures abroad—whether it be sprites, alps, or humans—jontuns, bears, or goblins— and then what? She would be dead. Something, someday would disrupt any dark she folded. She couldn't cook, and she couldn't live off roots and berries forever. It was too dangerous to run.

Losna snorted and shook her coat, then turned back to the trail, jogging after the scent before it washed away. Ahraia could tell she was angry.

Losna, I can't just run for it. It's not that simple. If I—she stopped as something snapped away in the woods. Losna had heard it as well. She turned her neck, looking towards the noise—a falling branch likely. Ahraia turned back to Losna.

It's not that I want to go through with it—

Losna growled her off.

Ahraia frowned. It wasn't like Losna to be short with her.

"What do you want me to do?" she said, her emotions laid bare.

Losna growled and shot her an angry glance. *That wasn't a branch. There's something out there.*

Ahraia listened, feeling foolish and upset. But Losna was right, something *was* moving distantly through the forest. It was coming closer, lumbering through the underbrush, loud and unafraid. Only a few things could move so disastrously and worry-free through the woods, and all of them were dangerous in their own right, a jontun or a bear, or one of the keress, wandering into the forest from the plains.

Losna sniffed, trying to catch a scent in the rain. Ahraia stood perfectly still, pressed against the trunk of a large fir tree. Her ears turned for a better sense of it, but what she heard was not what she expected.

A voice rose through the night and was followed closely by conveyance, loud and unchecked.

"Keep it bound! I don't care how difficult it is. If you even let it think, we'll both be burnt again—"

I'm trying. It's a damned fiend. We should just kill it and be done with it, Nitesse.

Ahraia heard something struggling through the underbrush, shaking leaves and branches as no sprite ever would.

We can tell the Astra it was already dead.

"I want it alive, you fool."

Sprites, Losna thought, hearing only a reflection of what Ahraia did but catching a scent through the dark. Ahraia recognized the conveyance, only having a moment to duck into hiding before the brush was pushed aside and two sprites emerged, Nitesse Gavea and a dae-ward, dragging a figure between them. At first glance, Ahraia thought it was another sprite, bound and hooded, but then she saw light-burnt hands and a strange cloak. The figure struggled and kicked as they went.

It's human, Losna thought, catching a scent, just as Ahraia got a glimpse of long red hair tumbling from beneath the veil.

"That's *the* human," Ahraia whispered, unable to contain her dismay. *The one with our orb!* Her heart clinched with fear, knowing what it meant once Gavea brought the human back to Daispar.

The dae-ward's light-veil was off, showing a face crossed and scarred with light. His veil was wrapped around the head of the human, binding its mouth and eyes. Gavea was equally seared with light streaks, as though freshly exposed to the orb's light. Ahraia felt momentary hope for her nit. She couldn't help but look for any glimmer of the orb shining through the human's rain-swept cloak, but no light came forth.

What good is it alive? the dae-ward asked, struggling with the human as it stumbled to the ground. "It's clearly deranged."

The human thumped her head inconsequentially against the ward, oblivious to what he had said.

"Beran—" Gavea said, yanking the girl up by the hair, eliciting a stream of muffled shouts, "will get that damned shade out of trouble if the human isn't alive. The Astra too. But if it comes from the human, they can't deny it—" The nitesse continued deliberately through the forest, dragging the human away, casting her conveyance sharp and unchecked through the night.

It's time that wolf binder's shown for the fraud she is. She never deserved her standing—I'm sick of the Astra overlooking true sprites because of her and that light-laced shadow of hers.

Losna bristled next to Ahraia, but held back her growl. *If she's got the human, what choice do we have but to run?*

Ahraia held her breath, listening. She waited, but Gavea and the dae-ward trundled off through the woods, back towards the path Ahraia and Losna had been following.

We have to stop them, Ahraia conveyed. Before she had any sort of plan, her feet carried her out from behind the cover of the underbrush.

What are you doing! Losna thought, nipping at her to hold her back. But Ahraia ducked away, following the sprite and the ward, staying quiet and out of sight.

Unless the human drops dead or manages to escape, we're as good as condemned, Losna thought. Her worry filled their bond, but her thoughts struck reason into Ahraia.

That's it, Ahraia conveyed, breaking into a run. *Come on!* She folded back the branches just ahead of her, rushing past before most even began to bend.

You mean to kill the human? Losna thought, surprised but not all together against it.

Maybe, Ahraia conveyed, slipping down a hillside and muddying her hands. *It doesn't matter if she's still with Gavea—we have to get her away from the nitesse.*

And you think that won't lead to trouble? Losna thought sharply. Her chest rumbled as she ran.

Ahraia ignored her, hurrying silently ahead of the trio in the blissfully loud night. *It won't—as long as we aren't seen.*

She was already laying the foundations of the bindings in her mind; they would have to be perfect. She had already bound the human once, and she knew how impish she was. Hopefully she wouldn't put up a fight—and hopefully the dae-ward was light-sick and weak.

Ahraia ducked behind the cover of a log just as she saw branches shaking from the path. A limb broke and Gavea led the impossibly-loud human forward with the dae-ward following close behind.

Ahraia crouched in hiding, peaking out just enough to see the ward and the nitesse. Losna pressed close beside her.

You're not binding Gavea, are you? she worried.

No. Ahraia wasn't sure she could manage Gavea in binding. A ward, maybe . . . but a nitesse? It was too much risk.

She reached out to the human, casting a subtle enchantment. At once, the girl's fear echoed through the link, but Ahraia quelled it, focusing instead on the part of the girl that wanted to scream and fight—like before, she felt fierce.

Can you make light? Ahraia conveyed. She didn't see any hint of the orb glowing out. She hoped the human hadn't lost it.

The girl, who had been struggling, went perfectly still. Confusion and simultaneous hope bubbled across the link; the girl shivered, sensing the bonding, but she didn't startle.

The dae-ward pushed her hard from behind.

"Keep moving," he said, not bothering to mirror his words.

Ahraia reassured the girl, stilling her anger. *I'm going to free you. Can you make light?* she conveyed again.

"Light?" the girl tried to say, her voice muffled by the veil. Ahraia sensed hope and helplessness twining in the girl's heart.

I'll get you free, she conveyed, hoping the orb still had light.

Ahraia slackened the enchantment and turned her mind towards the dae-ward instead. She bound him, turning it quickly to a full binding without time to fully familiarize herself to him. She was surprised by the difference. His emotions felt blunted, dim as the night compared to the human: tired, wet, and ill at ease being behind the lightwalker. Ahraia lowered herself into the enchantment, her mind entangling with his as she took total control.

Her hiding place faded. She watched, but only with dim eyes. Her sense of night came instead through the ward's eyes, but it was blurred by a degree of separation. Ahraia began to move his hands—their hands—forward, imagining her intentions while the dae-ward compliantly provided the action, unaware of the binding. She could vaguely see the knot holding the human and coaxed his hands into untying it. They fumbled at it awkwardly, as though in a dream where their fingers had no muscle. The knot was stuck.

Untie that, Ahraia thought.

The ward jerked the human to a stop and yanked at the veil.

Gavea looked back, her face contorting in bewilderment.

The dae-ward froze, suddenly sensing something awry, a twining sense of the enchantment and Ahraia. She could sense his uncertainty through the link, and watched as Gavea's face twisted from confusion to blinding fury in the span of a breath. Ahraia forced the dae-wards fingers to move, working faster, ripping at the knot. The veil loosened, slipping slightly. His fingers twisted, and he pulled hard. The knot gave way.

Free! Ahraia thought.

Gavea stepped quickly towards the pair, poised like an adder about to strike. Ahraia untangled her mind from the dae-ward just as Gavea's fist struck his temple. Ahraia felt the briefest, most brilliant pain before withdrawing from the binding completely. The dae-ward crumpled to the ground beneath the curses of the nitesse.

Fully returned to herself, Ahraia turned her eyes to the scene in front of her. The girl had freed her arms and was scrambling away, pulling the veil from her mouth.

We need light! Ahraia conveyed.

The thought was already forming at the tip of the girl's mind.

"Fire!" she said, though it didn't sound like the human tongue in the least. Ahraia watched in shock as fire sprang into the air, springing from the human's very words. Ahraia ducked behind the log, realizing the human wasn't just a lightwalker—she was a lightcaster—some form of enchantress herself, who held the name of fire in her voice.

Ahraia cowered from the light, wondering what she had

unleashed. She stayed low, keeping her eyes and ears down. Losna crouched next to her defensively, ready to leap at the girl.

Ahraia risked a glance and saw the human holding the fire to a broken branch, soaked with rain. Flames leapt onto it, sizzling hot, and smoke curled heavily into the night. The dae-ward was crawling away, and Gavea lay crumpled in the firelight, writhing in pain. The human was backing away, and Ahraia's link strained with every step, the distance stretching it.

This way, she thought, using the bond to re-direct the girl eastwards, towards the plains. The light and fire danced dangerously closer. Ahraia ducked aside and Losna scrambled with her. The human didn't need any more encouragement, and ran past them without notice. Ahraia sprang after her, leaving Gavea and the dae-ward floundering on the ground.

The human crashed through branches, over roots and fallen logs. Ahraia stayed hidden and tried to guide her, but even folding back what she could, the human managed to sound like a bear twice her size.

Losna dashed at Ahraia's heel, looking back towards Gavea and the ward. *What are you doing? We should just kill it and be done with it.*

Ahraia felt a flutter of fear. *She's too dangerous*, she conveyed back. But in truth, something else stayed her hand.

Then I'll kill her, Losna thought.

I've already bound her, Ahraia explained.

Losna's demeanor changed at once, realizing what Ahraia meant. She looked back through the woods, worried Gavea or the ward would come running after them at any moment.

How are we going to get out of this? she thought.

We've got to get her to the plains.

Losna was nervous but didn't argue. *This fire is a beacon to any sprites. What if your father is out here?*

Ahraia's ears tucked back anxiously. If they were found with a human that had just been freed from a nitesse, it would be the end of them, especially once the dae-ward was interrogated.

Get out ahead—make sure there aren't any more sprites out there, she conveyed.

Losna hesitated.

Ahraia reassured her. *I can handle the human. Just make sure we don't run into any more trouble.*

Losna gave her a wary look and then darted forward, easily outpacing them, disappearing first from sight and then from mind. Ahraia followed, guiding the unassuming human after her faint and dimming link to her shadow.

The trail led downward, winding through rain slickened woods. The flame bobbed in front of the girl, but it was growing dimmer, cooling, until it was too feeble to provide true light for her to see by. She scraped and cut herself blindly, exhausted. The fire seemed to be bleeding her energy and the girl tripped and then fell.

Get up, Ahraia urged. The enchantment was growing more difficult to uphold. A cold, seeping weariness that had nothing to do with the rain and the wind dragged at Ahraia's feet. The fatigue was waxing through their link.

Losna! Ahraia thought, trying to call her shadow back. But she was already too far ahead, too distant to sense.

The fire was fading, showing less now than even moonlight would. It dimmed, until it was nothing more than a firefly, and then it flickered, and extinguished all together.

The girl stopped.

The night became woefully dark.

The girl's fear reflected back through the bond: desperation twining with inevitability. Her breaths were labored and slow, her chin chattering from cold. The fire had drained her of all warmth and there was nothing left inside to burn.

You have to keep going, Ahraia urged. She looked about the woods for her shadow. *Losna!* she called once more.

"I can't," the girl said, less than a whisper.

Just a little farther, Ahraia conveyed.

The human didn't budge.

Ahraia thought she heard something away through the woods—

Losna coming back. *We're over here*, she conveyed once more. They didn't have time to rest; soon enough, Gavea and the dae-ward would recover from the light and would undoubtedly set out after them. Ahraia took a deep breath, knowing what she had to do.

She stepped forward out of the woods, plain for the girl to see her.

The girl looked up, and through the bare link, Ahraia had the most ghostly impression of herself. *Pale sprite. Demon. Fiend. Death.*

Ahraia pushed the fears down and mirrored her words. "Come on. Get up," she said, holding her hand out. "I'm going to get you away from here."

The fear in the link mixed with confusion. It spread first in the girl's thoughts and then across her dark eyebrows, which flatly turned inward. Hesitantly, the girl lifted her hand.

Just then, Ahraia sensed movement. *Losna, there you are*, she thought. But she immediately knew it wasn't her shadow. She turned just as a binding enveloped her, clamping down on her. Gavea stepped from the woods, her face scalded by light, her hand gripping her drain.

"I should have known," she said with a wicked sneer.

13

ALP AND ASTRA

The enchantment coiled around Ahraia's mind, constricting like the vines of a serapin tree.

"And your father thought you would be the next Masai." Gavea smiled wickedly. The light lingered across her previously bleak and flawless skin.

Let me go, Ahraia conveyed, unable to even speak. *Losna!*

"Where's your shadow now?" Gavea said scornfully.

The nitesse's hold was absolute; there was no use trying to break it. Instead, Ahraia formed her own binding, hoping to keep Gavea away. Through it, she sensed the emotions at the tip of the nitesse's mind: *triumph, contempt, disgust*. Gavea readied her drain, stepping closer.

Stop, Ahraia ordered ineffectively. She was at a disadvantage; the roots of Gavea's enchantment snaked deeper than her own. Ahraia felt the cold leeching through her, sapped by her bonding of the human, dulling her wit.

Gavea forced a foot forward. Ahraia resisted, woefully aware of how weak she felt. She clenched her teeth, hanging onto her tenuous hold of Gavea.

"I've been waiting for this for a long time," Gavea said, inching closer. "You were never—"

A vicious growl erupted a moment before Losna lunged from the woods, taking Gavea completely by surprise. The attack was startling, ferocious and short lived. Losna's teeth sank deep into Gavea's neck, throttling her to the ground. Before Ahraia could worry about the binding, her enchantment vanished—replaced by Losna's violent and deep-rooted need to protect and kill. She jerked back and forth, unyielding with her jaw. She shook again and then stilled, her teeth still wrapped around Gavea's neck, poised in case she was still alive.

"She's dead," Ahraia said, breathing hard. She waited, expecting the pain of the severance, but it didn't come. Relief flowed through her, even an inkling of justice.

She deserved it, Losna thought.

Ahraia didn't have time to wonder about it as the human suddenly scrambled away, tripping back weakly, hardly making it a dozen feet before she came to a stop, still drained from her flickering fire.

Losna raised her head, her snout bloodied. Ahraia took a moment to force calm back through her shadow's mind, blinded by defensive passion. Losna's growls subsided and Ahraia turned to the girl who braced herself against a fallen tree. She was a pitiful thing, all spun of fire and yet all out of light.

Ahraia offered her hand.

The girl looked up at her with dark, gleamless eyes, too exhausted to resist. In a daze of not understanding, she timidly took it.

Ahraia pulled her to her feet. "Follow me," she mirrored.

The girl fell in step at her side.

What are we doing? Losna thought, following after them as her thoughts returned to some normalcy.

Getting her away from here, Ahraia conveyed, half dragging, half coaxing the human through the cover of the forest. *And taking back the orb.*

What about Gavea?

What about her? Looks like she got on the wrong side of a couple of imps, Ahraia conveyed, not about to worry over the body of the nitesse. She felt relief knowing she could be bound to something during a kill. For the first time in her life, she felt like a sprite.

IT WAS NEARING midnight when they reached the slope falling to the plains below. Ahraia still held the girl's hand, having broken all but the barest binding. The rain swept through the woods in great billowing spurts. Trees shook in the tempest, sending leaves spiraling to the ground. Each surge was followed by a still, the woods whispering, waiting for the next swell. The girl struggled with the dark, and Ahraia could feel the tremor of fatigue in her hand. She helped her as best she could, guiding her feet and folding back the forest.

"Where are you taking me?" the girl asked at last, her voice tremulous.

"To the plains," Ahraia mirrored. "You'll be safer there." *At least from sprites.* Ahraia doubted even the dae-wards would bother venturing onto the plains. She could feel the unasked question forming at the tip of the human's mind: *Why?*

She ignored it and focused on the task at hand. Together, they struggled down the hillside, slipping over rain-slickened logs and between dripping fern leaves until they reached the plains.

When they finally stumbled into a grove of aspens at the edge of the plain, Ahraia worried the human would be too exhausted to keep going. The wind and rain were colder now, and the girl was shivering violently.

"Can you make it a little farther?"

The human nodded, too tired to answer, mouth hanging agape and eyebrows lifting in an attempt to overcome her sagging eyelids.

With Losna's help, Ahraia guided the girl out to Plain Dark. She made a closure and led the human inside of it, where it was dark but dry.

"Why are you doing this?" the human asked finally, as Ahraia helped lower her to the ground, settling her into the same nook where Tev and Shim had rested.

Ahraia mirrored her words. "The orb you had—the light—do you still have it?"

The human's face fell. "It's broken." She pulled the orb from her sopping cloak.

Ahraia flinched, expecting light to spill unchecked from the girl's hand. But she saw at once what the human meant. The orb wasn't just devoid of light; its pods had burst—it was ruined.

Ahraia felt as though her heart had burst along with it. The girl held the orb out, as though her offering it could undo its breaking. Ahraia took it, feeling the sinuous, leathery shell against her light-scarred fingertips. The seeds inside were shriveled and spent, no longer warm.

The human looked at her with worried eyes. "I didn't mean to break it."

Ahraia nodded, placing the orb in her cloak. Morning wasn't far off, and they still needed to find out if her father had a hand in her brothers' deaths.

"Tomorrow, once the Dae-Mon's risen, make for your lightwalker's realm. Stay to the light and no sprite will bother you."

The human pressed her lips together in thanks.

Ahraia took the broken orb, and headed back out of the underdae, with Losna close at her heel.

What happens to the nit now? Losna wondered, leading Ahraia up a steep embankment, back into the deep and dripping woods.

Ahraia didn't answer at first. She bound the hanging roots of a hemlock, using them to pull herself up the steep hill they were climbing. She had been thinking about Gavea—about the trouble that would come when the nitesse's death was discovered. For some reason, the kill itself had no effect on her. She felt nothing at all. No guilt and definitely no pain, though she had been bound firmly. If anything, she was glad. It frightened her, weighing on her mind.

But the orb weighed on her mind as well, just as it weighed in her pocket—a dead and lifeless reminder of her nit's trouble—a portent of things to come.

Losna was waiting for her at the top of the rise, her eyes piercing and worried.

"Without the orb," Ahraia said, trying to wipe mud from her hands, "the nit's dead."

What about the spritelings? What about Kyah?

Ahraia clenched her teeth at the thought. *Nothing good.*

She was soaked through to the bone. The cold and wet numbed her, both body and mind. Her troubles stacked one on top of one another: the orb, her brothers, the wraith, the trouble with the Masai, the Astra and her father, and most of all, her shadow test. They all melded together in a living nightmare. If her eyes weren't open, she would swear a mara was sitting right in the middle of her chest, sinking its wispy claws into her heart and demonizing her thoughts.

Will they die? Losna let out a low whine, brushing against Ahraia's raw emotions.

Ahraia nodded. Without the nurturing of the nit tree, the shade trees would eventually wither too, and Kyah and the spritelings would be put out of the darkening. The spritelings likely wouldn't last a day, and Kyah wouldn't manage much longer.

Ahraia pulled her hood closer, trying not to think of all that had happened—or all that was soon enough to come. Hayvon would be condemned in two nights, and then her shadow test would begin . . .

Eventually, they found the path they had been following before. Ahraia waited under the deepest shadows, hiding from the rain while Losna sniffed about for signs of her father, but his scent had washed away, and soon enough they turned back towards Daispar.

The rain gradually lessened, but the forest dripped and shuddered incessantly. They were just reaching the creek leading towards Daispar when Losna stopped, sensing something.

What is that? she thought.

Ahraia followed her gaze. For a moment, she thought her eyes were playing tricks on her. A dim glow shone through the woods, dimmer than even the night lit only by the Dark Moon. But none of the moons or the stars broke through the thick clouds. Ahraia stepped from the path, moving towards the faint light, and froze as she heard a soft noise. She turned an ear, listening.

Voices, Losna thought.

Maybe it's my father? Ahraia conveyed. The light immediately dispelled the notion, but she moved towards it nonetheless, too curious to be hindered by Losna's string of warnings.

The light was too pale to be a fire and too diffuse to be an orb—too faint to even burn, like starlight.

The voices were growing louder. Ahraia crept closer and stopped abruptly, seeing a group of half-hidden figures gathered in a glade ahead, vaguely illuminated. Losna raised her nose to the air, sniffing silently.

Alps! she thought suddenly, her ears perking up. *And more than one.*

Ahraia's ears tucked back tightly and she pulled off her hood to listen. She peeked around the tree.

In the middle of the glade, a whole gathering of alps stood together, illuminated vaguely by the light. She saw bows and bright weapons, and immediately wondered what such a large group of alps was doing so near to Daispar. With the Astra's leave or not, it was unusual. The light's source wasn't clear, but it emanated from behind a shielded veil, as though it was both intentional and yet intentionally diminished as well.

There is no way the Astra allowed for—Ahraia stopped her conveyance short, realizing there were sprites gathered with the alps. She leaned out farther and saw a dozen different wards gathered close.

"Dae-mon above, what is happening here?" she whispered under her breath. *That's the Astra*, she conveyed, seeing only the back of her hood but recognizing the weave of her eaves-web.

And your father, Losna thought. Ahraia crouched down, binding and peeling back a fern leaf to get a better view. Her father was indeed standing among the sprites, with a group of wards behind him. Ahraia froze in inaction, having never seen anything so strange.

She stared at the alps. A few had their hoods back. Their ears were sharp, without the absurd roundness of a human's, but not half as long as a sprite's. And their skin was scarred by the Dae-Mon, but not truly dark.

There's the one with the golden hair, Losna thought. Ahraia leaned forward and saw the same alp they had seen with the Astra before.

The alp stood just ahead of the others. Her hood was up, fur lining the edges while her hair streamed out, the color of moonlit grasses upon a midwinter night—but colder still. She had a narrow face, with dark lips and small, icy eyes, like a human's eyes, without any gleam. Even as she spoke, those eyes shifted. She paused, almost as though listening, and then her head turned right towards where Ahraia and Losna were hidden.

"Something is over there—watching us," the alp said, in a sprite-like tongue that Ahraia had no difficulty understanding.

Ahraia let the fern branch drop, flush with fear as she ducked further behind cover. *We've got to get out of here*, she conveyed to Losna.

She took two steps through the woods when an enchantment settled over her like a heavy net, rooting her where she stood with Losna next to her. A flourish of movement filled the woods, and a moment later, her father suddenly emerged around the tree with his drain drawn, followed by an alp with an arrow nocked to its bow. Ahraia's father held out a hand in restraint.

"It's all right," he called out, "It's one of ours."

The alp eyed Ahraia distrustfully, but lowered its bow. The air quivered with conveyance as her father took her roughly by her arm, dragging her away from the group.

"You weren't supposed to leave Daispar," he said. "What are you doing?"

What is happening here? Ahraia had a fleeting glance of the golden-haired alp, leaning forward with a long neck to see what was going on. The binding holding her felt horribly familiar, menacing and absolute. The Astra was watching too, looking cross, and Ahraia was surprised to see the Masai stood next to her. She felt the brief and paralyzing enchantment disintegrate.

Her father shook her again, his ears perking inside his hood. *I asked what you're doing here.*

Ahraia looked back at him, still surprised by the gathering of alps and sprites, but even more rattled by the brief paralysis.

We were just passing through the woods, she conveyed, too quickly. Her guilt for leaving the darkening mingled with thoughts of Gavea and the human, tainting her conveyance. She didn't care. She couldn't shake the sensation of the enchantment—the sudden and absolute way that it had enveloped her, taking full control of her movement and mind.

Did you feel that? she conveyed to Losna, shaken. *That was just like the Stone Tree.* Her skin erupted in chills.

It was the Astra, Losna thought, glancing back through the woods.

But Ahraia wasn't sure—had it come from the Astra or the alp? Maybe even the Masai or her father?

Her father's fingers crushed into her arm. "You know damned well you weren't just passing," he whispered.

I needed to talk to you, Ahraia conveyed, remembering why they had initially been looking for him and dropping her pretense of innocence.

And it couldn't wait?

No. It couldn't wait, Ahraia conveyed, ears flattening as she met his eye. *You knew what was going to happen, didn't you? You knew Kaval and Altah were going to be killed. This was the Astra's plan all along, wasn't it? To trade me for darkness. You sent them to the Stone Tree, for her to kill them.*

Her father hesitated, a blank look in his eyes before anger swelled across his face, but in that moment, Ahraia was sure of his guilt.

"What is your obsession with them?" he whispered. *No. This wasn't the Astra's plan. She's making darkness out of loss, and you're going to be the next Masai. How could you be so oblivious?* His conveyance felt sincere, but Ahraia wrenched her arm free from his grip.

She killed them. And I know you helped her.

The Astra was in the darkening—dozens of wards and sprites could tell you that.

Ahraia pressed on, unhindered, her thoughts giving way to her voice. "Well, then it was the Masai. Or you. Or that alp she's meeting with," she said. A flicker of fear belied his anger.

Are you trying to get yourself condemned? "That's absurd," he said aloud. *Now you're accusing the Masai? And myself? Or an alp? As though an alp is capable of some enchantment.*

His guilt simmered on his mind just beneath his thoughts. Ahraia was reeling, her suspicions all but confirmed. The Astra had been in the darkening, and the Masai and her company had been away in Deep Brook along with Ahraia's father and a dozen other sprites but the alp wasn't—and they had seen her with the Astra that very night.

"So it wasn't the Astra," Ahraia said, "It was the alp," Suddenly remembered the alps hood, wreathed in fur. "But the Astra set it up, and you knew—you sent them to the Stone Tree."

His ears snapped three times for silence. *You're not making any sense,* he conveyed. But his thoughts and eyes betrayed the truth. Ahraia's heart quickened.

"I know what this is about—it's about *her* darkness—the two of you figured if the Masai was coming here, you could tempt her with me. You knew that Kaval and Altah were in the way—just as Hayvon was. Well, their blood is on your hands."

Ahraia! Stop!

An enchantment spread like heavy snow over her, blanketing and muffling her. Ahraia shook it away, trembling with anger.

"I should have known!" *You betrayed mother, why wouldn't you kill your sons?*

Losna growled as Ahraia's emotions swelled across their bond. Her father shook his head but Ahraia was beside herself with anger.

"Well, guess what?" she said. "You did this for darkness? I'm not going to play along. You think you can *use* me for some twisted plan of yours? I'll leave the darkening before I help you."

"Is that so?" a voice behind her said. Losna whirled about, her hackles raised. The Astra swooped towards Ahraia, a hardened gleam in her eyes.

"I warned you to stay out of this, Ahraia," the Astra said.

Ahraia met the Astra's eye, ears sharp and head up, refusing to show deference. "I should have known it was you, killing shades for darkness," she said, not bothering with conveyance.

The Astra actually laughed, a mirthful laugh full of spite and ridicule.

"Me? You think I killed your brothers?" Her eyes were hard and cold, and the smile turned to a sneer. *You're more naïve than I thought.* She stared Ahraia right in her eyes, a firm bonding letting Ahraia feel the sincerity in her thoughts. *I didn't kill your brothers—or have them killed—I gain nothing by having you enter your test so young. You're not ready, you lack the will to pass your test, and you're no good to me dead.*

The Astra stepped closer. "That being said, I'm not willing to lose you to some childish stubbornness between yourself and your father. You're not going anywhere. Beran, see her back to Daispar and make sure she stays there until I return. I'm not finished with her."

Ahraia shook with rage. She wanted to hit the Astra in the mouth, to drag her beneath the moonlight and burn her perfect skin from her face. Ahraia turned and stalked away without another word, incensed by the pair of them, furious their designs had left two of her brothers dead and another condemned. The Astra glared after her.

"*Wait, Ahraia,*" Ahraia's father commanded, an enchantment intertwined with words. Ahraia brushed it aside, too angry to let him hold her back.

Where are we going? Losna thought, trotting after her.

"We're going to make sure the spritelings have a nit tree once we're gone."

Without the orb? How are you going to do that?

~

THE FOLDS of the darkening drooped low above Ahraia, like a spider web sagging between each point of support. She straddled the highest curve of her mother's nit tree, her legs dangling dangerously on either side of the arching trunk, like resting on the spine of some enormous beast whose branches extended as ribs to form the dome of the nit.

"You're supposed to protect us . . . to provide shelter," Ahraia murmured to the nit tree. "I'm trying to help you."

A deep sense of stubbornness quivered beneath her legs—unease belying an unwillingness to change.

That's not going to get you anywhere, Ahraia reprimanded. *Do you want to keep protecting us or not?*

The tree didn't move in the least. Ahraia sighed.

Losna stood warily below. It was day outside of Daispar and Ahraia's anger had slowly smoldered, hardening into a firm will to make sure the spritelings would have a nit once she was gone.

Her shadow's neck craned upward. It was strange to be in the tree, and stranger still to ask it to unfold itself—but with the orb gone, it had only one option for light.

Losna's thoughts drifted up from below, sounding worried and motherly. *Are you almost done up there?*

Ahraia snorted. Binding a single spring branch was one thing, but binding whole trees required enchantment of another magnitude. She was still getting used to the vast spread required of her mind, the ability to not only move a part, but to understand the whole: from leaves to twigs to branches to trunks to roots and back again.

I'm just getting started, she conveyed, knowing if she called out aloud half the darkening would hear her. *Go find yourself some food or something, I'm going to be a while.*

Food?

Ahraia sensed a twinge of excitement from below. A moment later she heard Losna's thoughts receding.

Food, food, food . . .

Ahraia smiled. She turned back to her task and lowered herself into the binding, hiding her deep bitterness and growing despair. *You need moonlight—and I'm trying to give it to you. Now let me show you.*

She leaned back, knowing that forcing it would do nothing but strengthen the tree's resolve to resist her. For a time, she just sat. She breathed in and out, keeping her mind as blank as she could. Then she began thinking of moonlight. She felt the leaves whisper. She started to work again, wriggling the tendrils of enchantment down each branch and trunk, holding more and more of the tree's power in her grasp.

Straighten up, she thought.

The tree shuddered, unhappy with the change. Ahraia's stomach turned nervously, but she knew the tree wouldn't let her fall, no matter how much it disliked her suggestion.

If you won't do it, I'll have to grow another.

The tree creaked. And then it started to unfold, imperceptibly at first. Ahraia smiled. And she waited.

You won't regret it, she thought.

It was tedious, and tenuous—the undoing of untold winters frozen and summers growing. But Ahraia could sense it: the slow unravelling of time and the aching strain against the growing grain. The trunk unfurled, like an enormous crane raising its neck, its wings still spread wide, encompassing and protecting its brood beneath.

Ahraia moved lithely up the trunk once it had extended enough, climbing to what would become the highest branches. She situated herself, and waited until it reached just beneath the draping ceiling of the darkening. From here, she could tell the shell wasn't a single layer, but many layers laying one branch over another, like lily pads crowding each other over a dark-bellied pond.

Even though she couldn't see it, she could feel the warmth of the Dae-Mon just outside. It terrified her to know that if she chose, she could send light cascading down into the center of the darkening. The hollows and paths spread out below, but no sprites were about. It was the middle of the day. She wondered idly what would happen if she broke a hole open above the Astra's nit. The darkening's cover tightened.

Don't worry, I won't, she conveyed to the tree, binding the nearby branches. At once, she could feel that they were old, and resiliently proud, resistant to her touch. *You look like you could use a little rest . . . and a little company up here.*

Delicately, she teased the nit tree underneath its branches. The nit tree felt the warmth and the light and settled itself into the weave, its branches fixing themselves within the shell, beneath the outer layers where the light was dim but not direct.

Just like moonlight, Ahraia thought. She waited, feeling the trunk stiffen contentedly. Once she was convinced it would stick, she retreated back down and went to work on the break left by the unfurled trunk. She wove the branches back together, sewing them across the void. Then she climbed down to the base, and was surprised to find Losna curled on the ground, waiting.

"How long have you been here?" Ahraia asked, realizing how preoccupied she must have been to not notice her shadow.

Losna looked up, put off. Her stomach growled. *The wall wouldn't let me out.*

"It wouldn't open?" Ahraia said, surprised. The darkening recognized Losna just as easily as any shade or sprite, and had no trouble forming a closure for her.

I'm hungry.

Ahraia had a sinking suspicion and guessed why the shell had resisted her above.

Come on, she thought, leading Losna back out of the nit by the quickest path to the darkening wall.

Open, she commanded once she stood before the thick cover. The wall, however, tightened, sending a quiver outward that passed like ripples on a pond. "What's the meaning of this?" she said to the wall, her suspicions confirmed.

I told you, Losna thought.

Ahraia tried again. She sat down, growing more irritated with every passing moment. Binding the wall was simple, instinctive like folding closures in a shade tree, but the wall was being obstinate, and intentionally so. Ahraia's attempts became progressively more aggressive and less couth.

Open. Move. Open! She grabbed the branches and shook them violently without consequence, pushing them with all her strength.

Losna let out a low, warning growl. Ahraia turned to find the Astra walking towards her.

"Trying to leave during the day? I knew I couldn't trust you, but this is a new low."

Ahraia realized how suspect she looked.

"I wasn't trying to leave. Losna was just trying to hunt . . . the wall wouldn't let her out."

The Astra's ears flickered at Ahraia's voice. "Do you think, after the stunt your brother pulled, I'm going to let your shadow just walk out of the darkening? She can eat at the cook fires with the rest of the shadows. Neither of you are going anywhere."

Until when? Ahraia conveyed, her ears batting in irritation.

"Until whenever I say. Trying to leave by day?" The Astra shook her head. "I underestimated how dastardly you are."

Ahraia glared at her. A muscle twitched in her cheek.

"I'm not willing to lose you for nothing. You think you can just leave this darkening? You think you can run?"

You think you can stop me? Ahraia challenged with ears burning. She knew at once it was foolish and irrational, but she hated the Astra. She couldn't think straight, and it wasn't as though the Astra could condemn her for her insolence. *You think you can kill my brothers and expect me to imp along. I won't. I'd rather die by the light.*

The Astra stepped forward aggressively. The darkening wall suddenly wrapped itself around Losna, who let out terrified yelp.

"Don't test me, Ahraia."

Ahraia fought down every urge to leap at the Astra, with Losna's panic flooding her mind. Her breaths came ragged. "She's no good to you dead." She had meant it as a threat, but it came out as a whimper.

"No . . . she's not." The wall released Losna, who scurried towards Ahraia with her tail tucked low. The Astra was glaring at the pair of them. "But that doesn't mean others aren't."

A bond formed, threats forcing themselves into Ahraia's mind: she saw the faces of Kyah, Thelon and Alua, cold and lifeless, lying dead with fog dripping all about them.

Ahraia broke the binding, pushing the Astra from her mind. Her heart was hammering in her chest.

The Astra leaned in, meeting her eye with her ears rigid and sharp.

"I didn't kill your brothers, Ahraia," she said forcefully. "But I won't hesitate to kill the rest of your nit. If you don't pass your test, I swear to you, I will cut their shadows' throats, just like I did those of my shades. I will wash my hands with their blood, then I'll give those wretched spritelings to the Shad-Mon. Do you understand me? I never wanted it to come to this, but you leave me no choice. Don't even think about running, or it's their lives too."

14

CHASMS

The Bright Moon will be turned tonight, Losna thought, letting out a long, trailing sigh from her muzzle.

Ahraia lay flat on her back, staring up at the moon flower hanging above her. Hayvon had given it to her, the day after their mother had been condemned. It was a rare and precious thing, something she had never found in the forest, though she had wasted enough nights looking for one. How he had even come by the seed, he had never said. It had taken her months to coax it out, but now, it seemed like nothing more than a hanging reminder that he—her closest family besides Losna—was about to be given to the Shad-Mon. Another sibling dead.

We should have run when we could have, Losna thought.

"And what? Just leave Kyah and the spritelings to die?"

Losna let out a whine but didn't argue. Ahraia stared upwards, in a haze of anxiety and fear.

"Why did he do it?" she said aloud, her thoughts slipping past her lips. "Why did he admit to it?"

Losna picked idly at her paw with her teeth, her eyes glowing faintly in the true dark. *At least Vesta didn't have to suffer like the others.*

Ahraia sensed her thoughts tarrying on Tev's squirrel and Shim's ermine.

"It's not like she didn't suffer. She's still alone out there."

Losna fell silent, still digging at her paw.

Ahraia stared upward, helpless. Since their run in with the Astra, they hadn't left the nit. Ahraia had gone to the top of her mother's tree again, and the trunk seemed to be holding steady, the light suffice to keep it living—but now, even if it managed to stay alive, it might not matter. The Astra's threats hung over her, like Hayvon's death. And Ahraia couldn't fathom passing her shadow test. She couldn't imagine sending Losna away. The pain of such a thing would be excruciating. She would be driven mad if she even tried. And yet, somehow Hayvon had done it.

She sat up, a thought suddenly coming to her.

"I can't lie here any longer."

Losna turned quickly onto all fours, eager to be moving. *But we can't leave the darkening*, she thought.

"I don't mean to. I'm going to see Hayvon."

Losna's tail stopped swishing. *You're going to the chasms? You won't be allowed, will you? They'll be guarded.*

Ahraia paused, wondering if the wards would stop her. "I'm not going to give them a choice." She made a closure and stepped out of the shade tree. Losna hesitated.

Should I come with you?

Ahraia shook her head. "There's no sense. You'll just have to wait for me anyways. I'd feel better if I knew you were here."

Losna stood poised at the edge of the deep dark, but didn't make to follow. Ahraia didn't like leaving her, but in a way, she was glad that Losna couldn't come. The questions she meant to ask Hayvon wouldn't be comfortable—least of all for Losna.

Once out of the nit, Ahraia flitted through the faint dark of the outer halls. It was mid-afternoon outside, and no sprites were about. Nonetheless, she tread the lesser-seen paths, through archways of leech ferns and beneath tunnels lined with hanging mushrooms. She wound past webs of wicker, winter, and velum weaves, all in varying states of growth, and around a dozen nit trees, including Gavea's, before she circled back towards the central hollow. The nitesse's body still hadn't been found and the dae-ward hadn't been seen either. All sorts of rumors had been passing through the darkening, rumors that the nitesse had run afoul with alps or humans or even the dae-ward. Ahraia guessed the ward had fled rather than face condemnation for being seen. She hoped Gavea was never found.

The chasms were just downstream of the central springs, where the quiet gurgle of water broke the haunting quiet. Ahraia wasn't sure if the deserted sense of stillness came from a lack of sprites or her missing Losna.

At the heart of the darkening, the grove of darkening cores towered upwards as the source of the outer shell. The trunks were black barked and dozens of feet across, without a single branch forming until they unfurled above, curling back in great draping sheets to the edges of the darkening, with vine trunks growing down throughout to support them like the joints of a spider web. A gaping series of rocky chasms extended below their monstrous roots.

As expected, two dae-wards were guarding the entrance. Their light-veils hung loosely around their faces as they idled before the outer roots of the cores. They stood up as Ahraia approached.

"Where do you think you're going?" the first said, his scars deeper than the other's, marking him as older.

Ahraia braced herself for an enchantment, knowing she would have to be firm with the wards.

"I'm here to see my brother," she said, walking with shoulders back and ears pointed towards the sky. She began to form a binding and was encouraged by the doubt radiating back at her. She hoped her eyes looked golden-bright, unbecoming for a shade.

The scarred ward stepped forward. "You're not allowed here. Not while the lower recesses are occupied."

Ahraia remembered the tone and strength of the Masai, and mimicked her as she spoke. "Who are you to tell me what I can and can't do?"

Already being linked, Ahraia heard the conveyance passing

between the wards. *She's going to be the Masai someday*, the second ward conveyed. His ears tucked back nervously.

The older ward furrowed his brow. *You don't know that. She's not even a sprite,* he conveyed. *I heard she can't even make bindings.*

Ahraia didn't have to feign being angry. "Of course I'm going to be the Masai," she said without thinking. Their eyes widened in surprise. They faltered, shoulders shrinking and ears batting back. Ahraia strengthened her hold, forcing stillness over the wards. *And of course I can make bindings.* She let her conveyance echo out threateningly, and she forced them to bow, bending their necks and tucking back their ears. They moved easier than most trees as their surprise gave way to fear. Ahraia continued her act, sensing they would fold with the right pressure. "Get out of my way." *Or you'll never be nit-wards in my spritedom.*

Just as she hoped, the wards shuffled aside, their resolve overrun. They bowed on their own accord.

And don't bother me while I'm down here, she conveyed, moving right past them into the entrance of the first ravine.

She proceeded down a narrow passage with moss-fringed stone rising on either side. The bindings faded with each step, and almost at once, the silence swelled. She let out a breath, relieved it had worked. Yet almost at once her chest tightened again.

The chasms were a series of caverns beneath the darkening cores. The roots of the darkening ripped at the earth like enormous hands, sinking their fingers deeper and deeper into the stones, forming great rents in the world.

Ahraia walked right to the edge of the first precipice, staring down into the blacked chasms. Roots snaked out of sight, and she reached out for a binding to lower herself into the depths, but sensed resistance far stronger than that of the wards. The cores wouldn't answer to her any more than the outer wall had.

"Fine," she said aloud, her voice piffling amongst giants. She grabbed hold of a smaller root which trailed over the edge and began to rappel into the chasm without a binding.

At once, the air cooled. The cold mud on the knotted root was rough and slippery, but she climbed easily, having spent enough nights making springs and climbing trees. This was no different, and she found footholds and handholds on slick, pressed mud. The root she was holding grew too sinuous, so she switched to another. She brushed aside crawling seep trees and the interlaced night thistle, half-expecting to look up and see the wards' heads appear above, but neither did. She scraped and clawed her way down, and, sooner than she expected, her feet found firm ground at the base of the first chasm.

She was engulfed in the bowels of the roots and the ground wasn't truly ground; it was a twisting line of chest-thick runners covered in matted dirt and hardened mud. The musty earth filled her nose, and the damp pressed all about her. She stood in perfect stillness, letting her eyes adjust. A faint crescent was all that showed of the darkening above.

Hayvon? She conveyed, edging along the narrow crevice. Her hairs stood on end in the hollow dark.

Another fathomless well disappeared beside her, with water gurgling deep below. She moved farther along, passing the first recess, which was an alcove covered by a tangled, impassible wall of roots.

Hayvon? Are you in there?

Something—someone—was inside, ragged and almost lifeless. The barest whisper scraped out from deep within.

"I want my shadow. I want my shadow back."

Hayvon? Ahraia formed an enchantment, but immediately flinched away, pierced by aching loneliness. It was Tev. Her mind was fractured and Ahraia couldn't bear to form any lasting connection. She dropped the binding and gripped the vines diving into the earth, clenching her teeth. The emotion was wretched.

She listened to Tev's mourning, taking a heavy, steadying breath as she considered trying to comfort the shade, but nothing she could say would ease Tev's pain. She stayed silent, and eventually, without other choice, left her crying to the pitiless dark.

A pit formed in the center of her stomach.

She moved farther down the chasm and lowered herself into a deeper ravine. The air was colder here, and the crescent of the darkening disappeared entirely.

"Hayvon?" Ahraia whispered, her voice swallowed by void. Her heart thumped loudly against her chest, accompanied by the eerie silence and occasional drip of water.

Are you down here?

The dark and the silence melded, but she heard a muted scraping noise of something moving. She stepped back.

"I'm here," a hollow voice said from nearby.

She stumbled over the uneven ground trying to find the opening to Hayvon's hold. Her eyes adjusted and she could see him pressed against a narrow slit, trapped by the massive roots. He stared out, a single yellow-white eye visible against the inky black interior.

"Tonight's the night, isn't it? That's why you're here." His voice was quiet, rough from disuse.

Ahraia opened her mouth to speak, but stopped as the words felt foul on the back of her tongue. She nodded, drawing in a shuddering breath.

Hayvon didn't say anything.

"Can you get out of there?" Ahraia asked, finding her voice. She attempted another bonding to the roots but instead of moving to her will, they groaned and tightened, and the slit between her and Hayvon narrowed. She stopped at once, frightened that the fissure would close entirely. Rootlets twisted down above her, poised to strike, a warning from the core to leave them be.

"It's not worth it, I've already tried," Hayvon said. "Do you have water?" She could hear the desperation in his voice.

Ahraia fumbled at her hip and found her water-skin. It wasn't full, but she handed it through the narrow slit, half expecting the roots to close around her wrist. She felt the weight of the bag snatched away from her and heard Hayvon fumbling to open it, and then the loud and exalted sounds of him drinking.

He finished, and she heard him shaking and tipping the bag over his mouth. After a moment, she heard him laugh, a bitter sort of laugh that took the heart from her. Then his voice slipped out with a touch of madness as he chanted a rhyme that every spriteling grew up reciting.

"Don't drink the water, noiselessly part. Don't break the branch, stay from the heart. Don't try to run, or try to swim, waiting and watching, the Shad-Mon grim."

"Stop," Ahraia said, the horror of his fate suffocating her. Hayvon fell silent. Ahraia hadn't heard the rhyme in years . . . since before her mother was condemned. She heard Hayvon squeezing the waterskin, trying to get every last drop.

When he spoke again, the singsong of his voice was gone. "Do you think the water in there's really cursed?"

She didn't answer. They both had watched the Shad-Mon summoned enough times to know the truth. Ahraia slumped down, as close as she could to the slit in the roots.

"Why did you do it? Why did you have to admit it?" she said, her thoughts from the last several days tumbling out. She saw a sliver of a smile, a half-dead smirk showing through the gap.

"To the light turns the ward . . ."

Ahraia didn't hear any bitterness, but she thought she saw it playing at the corner of his lips. Guilt tormented her, pressing down like the dark of the chasms; she leaned her forehead to the roots and closed her eyes, clenching her teeth tightly. When she spoke, all she could manage was a whisper.

"I'm sorry. I shouldn't have let the human go. I just . . . I didn't think it would lead to all this."

Hayvon didn't answer at first. The silence engulfed her, and she didn't dare bond him to find out what he was thinking.

"You didn't know it would come to this," he said finally, his voice without any accusation. It almost made it worse.

"But why did you take the blame? You didn't have to. I was seen too."

"It was a bad situation. And if I didn't, it would have been all of us . . . it still practically was." His voice was quiet, muted by the earth, but now she could hear the creep of bitterness at its edges. He let out a heavy sigh and went on.

"Gavea was hell bent on condemning you and Father knew it. You're too important to this darkening, too important to the Gelesh. He thinks you're going to be the Masai one day. And I know it doesn't matter, but mother thought the same . . ." He trailed off, lapsing into silence for a moment. "She wanted me to watch out for you. It's almost like she knew what was coming . . . "protect her," that was the last thing she ever said to me."

Ahraia remembered all too clearly the night their mother had been condemned, how she had stopped before each of them with her final words.

Hayvon let out a deep breath. "I just never imagined that it would mean following in her footsteps."

I'm sorry. Ahraia's heart felt like a stone too heavy to move. There was no air to fill her lungs.

Hayvon spoke quietly but his voice was strong. "I would do it again in a heartbeat."

Ahraia's lip quivered in shame. The silence between them swelled. She was mortified at how cowardly she was. Even if it was unintentional, she had let him take the fall, and here he was, facing the Shadow Woods without so much as a whimper. Brave through it all, just as he had been when he had sent Vesta away.

"How did you do it?" she said at last. "How did you set Vesta free?"

"I don't know."

Ahraia hesitated. "Is she gone for good? I mean, if you weren't . . ."

"If I wasn't being condemned to the Shad-Mon? Would she really be gone? I don't know."

Ahraia fell silent, peering into the slit of the recess. Hayvon was drawn back, covered in shadow. She could sense the void inside of him and she pressed her next words unwillingly from her mouth.

"I'm entering my shadow test, once the Bright Moon's turned. I need to know how you did it."

"No!" Hayvon's face was suddenly pressed against the slit. "You can't be. You're not ready!"

"I know," Ahraia said miserably. "But with you being condemned, I'm the oldest. The Masai's uprooting me."

For the first time, Hayvon looked truly at a loss. "No!"

Ahraia nodded, the words tumbling forth. "Father planned this all along, him and the Astra. They set it up. He sent Kaval and Altah to the Stone Tree to be killed. And if you hadn't taken the fall, he would have done away with you too. He needed all three of you out of the way—it was all part of the Astra's plan for darkness."

"They wouldn't do that . . ." Hayvon said in disbelief.

Ahraia explained everything that had come to pass since he had been condemned. She would have shown him the memories too, but she hesitated to bond him deeply, terrified of feeling Vesta's void again. She finished, and he stood back, not saying anything for a long time.

"He couldn't have planned for this," he said finally. "Being seen by a human? He couldn't have just done away with me . . . It's just bad luck."

Ahraia was about to answer when a ragged voice startled her.

"He *was* going to get rid of you," it said.

Ahraia turned, unsettled, her skin crawling from surprise. She stepped away from Hayvon's holding and saw a face pressed against another recess. It was Shim. His face was tear-stained.

"That arrow was no accident," he said quietly.

Ahraia opened her mouth to protest but Hayvon spoke first.

"I *knew* it wasn't. You little day-walking bastard."

"I didn't want to," Shim whined. "It was an order from my Nit-Ward—what was I supposed to do?"

Hayvon lapsed into silence. Ahraia shook her head. It was the confirmation of everything she had suspected, the last piece to confirm her fears.

"That's why he sent us hunting," she said. The Astra was a convincing liar, but now Ahraia had proof. She bitterly wanted to turn back the nights. She wished she could have let Losna loose on her father and the Astra like she had on Gavea. Hayvon's voice broke the silence.

"It was a piss poor shot . . . but I don't blame you."

Shim muttered an apology but Ahraia turned back aghast. *You don't blame him?* "He shot you! You could have caught the human, if not for that."

Hayvon's voice was maddeningly calm. "Even as shades, we are wards. It's our duty to do as our nit-wards command."

"That's absurd. Look at you," she said, furious that Hayvon could be so forgiving. "What did listening get you? You're without a shadow, due to be condemned at nightfall, and—"

"And *you* are alive," he said. "That was my duty. Always. And I should have done a better job at it." She felt his eyes lingering on her light-scars, tracing them from her jaw down to her neck. "Your duty is to become Masai, to lead the Gelesh and the Silh to a more wholesome darkness."

Mine is to my shadow, Ahraia thought to herself, but it must have echoed out to Hayvon as he stopped short.

"It is to Losna as well," he said. "But only in this sense: she lives . . . or she dies . . . it's your choice. The test doesn't bend and it won't budge. It's not some branch or tree you can manipulate to your will, Ahraia. Losna is going to leave you. It's only a question of how."

"So how did you do it?" she asked miserably.

"How do you bend the forest to your will? Strength of mind? Unbounded sense? I don't know. But I knew what would have happened if I didn't set her free. That was enough."

They lapsed into silence. Ahraia sat in the chasm for a long time, unsure of when or how the night would come. Eventually, she stood up, knowing that Losna would be worrying and the night would be coming soon. She remembered Hayvon's light-veil in her pocket.

"This is yours . . .," she said, reaching through the small hole to hand it back to him. She dropped it, and took Hayvon's hand. She held it for a long time, squeezing tightly to say the things she couldn't.

She felt something brush against her wrist, and when she withdrew her hand, the light-veil was tied loosely about her arm. Hayvon's teeth showed in what she supposed was a smile.

"I would tell you to stay to the dark . . . but I know you won't," he said.

Ahraia's lips quivered against her will as tears threatened to spill forth. She bit down firmly, searching for words that simply wouldn't come. *Look after yourself*, she conveyed at last. *Don't go looking for the heart of the forest.*

"I won't," Hayvon said, withdrawing to the dark, out of sight.

Ahraia pressed her forehead to the trunk and then turned away in despair. She headed up through the chasms, climbing until she emerged back into the darkening. She took a deep breath, composing herself before she wound her way back through the tendrils and boulders. The air was dim. Evening was coming. The dae-wards stood tensely off to the side, looking defeated and surly. Ahraia moved past them without a word, but pulled up short when she noticed a sprite standing nearby.

"Kren?" she said in surprise, relieved it was just her sister. "What are you doing here? I thought you're supposed to be bending your nit —" she stopped abruptly as Kren's ears flickered for quiet.

Ahraia looked about. The entrance to the chasms was empty. They were alone, with just the dae-wards. She turned back to her sister, trying to regain her thought. She hadn't seen Kren since the night the Masai had arrived, and she hadn't spoken to her in earnest since the beginning of her shadow test.

"What are you doing here?" Kren asked, an edge in her voice.

"I was just visiting Hayvon—" Ahraia stopped short again as her sister's ears flickered again. *What?* Ahraia conveyed, looking about once more, sure she was missing something.

"You're a shade," Kren said simply. Her ears were canted back in irritation, an obvious sign that she wanted Ahraia to convey.

Ahraia stared back at her, caught completely off guard, struggling to tell if her sister was serious or not.

I'm sorry, she conveyed. Kren glared at her. The wards watched on, their expressions hidden beneath their veils. Flustered, Ahraia tried to think of something to say, anything to break the tension. *I'm entering my shadow test*, she thought dumbly.

"That doesn't mean you're a sprite," Kren said. Her eyes narrowed suspiciously. "And don't expect me to help you with it."

"I never—" Ahraia started in shock, before realizing her mistake. *I didn't mean for you to*—She stopped again, dumfounded. *I just came to see Hayvon.*

The braver dae-ward seemed to find his voice again. "Well, you're not allowed here. Not while the lower recesses are occupied."

Ahraia ignored the ward, still staring at Kren in disbelief. Her sister seemed a hollow reflection of herself—the touch of her mind *felt* like a hollow reflection as well. Even her face looked different. Her eyes were pitiless, cold and dim; her face emotionless and still. Only her ears held any emotion, and it was anger.

"What did you want to see Hayvon for?" Kren asked flatly.

You know he's about to be condemned, right? Ahraia said.

Kren's face was devoid of any understanding. "That doesn't explain why you were down there. Does the Astra know?"

Ahraia flushed. She looked at the wards. "Can I have a moment . . . with my *sister*?" She emphasized the word, but Kren didn't seem to notice. Or she didn't care.

Emboldened by Kren's presence, neither ward moved.

Do you really want to be forced again? Ahraia conveyed, her anger rising. *By a shade?*

They shifted uncomfortably. Ahraia glared at them until one after the other, they shuffled away.

Once they were out of earshot, Ahraia turned to face Kren, who watched her with a mix of indifference and displeasure.

"What's come over you? Hayvon's being condemned and you don't even care. Kaval and Altah were murdered, and all of it in the name of darkness. And yet you stand here as though my voice is the greatest offense . . ."

Kren's jaw was quivering, but her eyes glinted like their father's. Ahraia formed a bonding to her sister, knowing it wasn't safe to say her thoughts aloud.

Father set this up. Kaval and Altah are dead. And Hayvon too—

"Hayvon's not dead yet," Kren said matter-of-factly.

Well he's going to be! Ahraia snapped. *And Kyah and the spritelings as well. They're alone. And our nit's orb was lost. They're without guidance. And the Astra's threatened to kill them if I don't pass my test.* She was breathing hard, her teeth clenched.

Kren broke away from the binding, as though the emotions were too much for her. She glowered at Ahraia.

"It should be me going to Angolor."

Ahraia stood in shock, completely at a loss for words. She stared at Kren, wondering how she could possibly be so detached. But as she looked at her, she realized, it wasn't her sister standing before her —not even a hollow shell. A sprite stood before her, a memory only in likeness.

"You're shadow broken," Ahraia whispered, fighting back anger. A void like Hayvon's was opening inside her chest, but this one was for her sister. "You were supposed to look after us . . . you still are," she whispered.

A ghost stared back at her.

"I was supposed to go to Angolor, to live in the ever-spreading dark."

Ahraia shook her head, too upset to speak; she made to move past Kren, but her sister grabbed her by the wrist, wrenching her to a stop.

"You don't deserve it."

Ahraia twisted her arm free. The wards perked up nearby and two weak enchantments tried to stay Ahraia's hand. They hurried forward to intervene. Furious, Ahraia cast her own bindings, directing the wards to lunge against one another. Carried by momentum and forced by her mind, they crashed together with a satisfying thunk. Through the link, she sensed two unsuspecting skulls colliding. The wards crumpled to the ground and she disentangled herself from the binding. She felt Kren briefly try to bind her, but her sister flinched away, her mind seeming to recoil from the touch.

A growl rose in Ahraia's chest. She sensed her shadow hurrying through the woods.

Losna emerged, leaping effortlessly onto a long beam of root that led to the hollow. The air swelled with her snarl.

There you are! she thought. Her worry ebbed across their bond.

Ahraia kept her eyes towards the wards, who were standing up and looking towards her again, rearranging their veils and their cloaks.

The Masai came looking for you, Losna thought.

Ahraia glanced at her and saw her fur was standing on end. Her tail was low and her ears sharp and turning.

She did? What did she want?

She didn't say. Another low growl emitted from Losna's chest.

Kren sneered at Ahraia, seeming to think Losna was growling at her. "You wouldn't be anything without the protection of your shadow."

Ahraia bit back her retort, struggling to fathom how her sister could have changed so much in the span of half a turning. "I never said I am."

Kren's voice quieted, her every word clear and sharp.

"If she weren't here, I'd put you in your place. Everyone is so sure that you're going to be the next Masai. But I *know* you, Ahraia. You're not hardened by the night. Everything that's come to you—everything you've ever done—has come on the shoulders of your shadow. You won't pass your test."

Ahraia's heart felt like it had risen into her throat. Each heartbeat surged hotter than the last. Losna's distress twined with her own and the result was hard to restrain. Kren nodded to the wards.

"Take her away from here. She shouldn't be here. Bind her if you must."

A flood of emotions rose in Ahraia: despondence mixed with anger, loathing and sickness all at once.

The wards stepped towards her but she bound them firmly where they stood, rooting them to the ground. She grabbed Kren by her wrist. Binding a sprite was condemnable, but Ahraia formed an enchantment before she could help it, wrestling control over her sister.

Kren flinched visibly at her touch and writhed against the connection. "*Let me go,*" she commanded, unable to break free.

Ahraia grappled to keep the wards in check. The injustice of Kren's words made her latch onto the bindings, finding strength she only ever used in folding darkness.

"What's become of you?" she asked, shaking. Kren refused to meet her eye, but Ahraia forced her to lift her chin. Her face was twisted bitterly and her eyes were hollow, without the faintest familiarity.

"This isn't you . . ." Ahraia whispered, hurt. "You were my sister—do you forget yourself so completely? You, who raised us and brought us through the light. You, who tempered our fears and guided us as shades and spritelings. If this is what the test makes of us, then you're right, I won't become a sprite." Kren was shaking too now, desperately trying to break Ahraia's hold.

Let me go.

"Our brothers are dead," Ahraia said. "Our nit is on the brink. You should be ashamed of yourself."

"It should be me going to Angolor."

Ahraia didn't have to say anything, her disgust flowed through the enchantment unchecked. Kren was as pale as the moon. Her ears were quivering. The enchantment snapped, too upsetting to Ahraia. A voice suddenly rose from beyond the central cores.

"A little sisterly love. How very spritish . . ."

The Masai was watching with a bemused look, half hidden by the darkening cores. Kren was already bowing, her ears batting ruefully.

Ahraia stared with a mix of embarrassment and fear. *Do you think she heard me?* she conveyed to Losna. Her shadow, however, had her hackles raised and wasn't listening.

The Masai moved easily through the tumble of the forest, wearing the whitest dress Ahraia had ever seen. It was the color of clouds on a moon-burned night. It glowed obscenely, inappropriate to be sure, reflecting on the dark scars of her face. Ahraia bowed belatedly, lowering her eyes to the ground.

"Did you have those buffoons bound as well?" the Masai asked, gesturing toward the dae-wards, neither of whom had moved. Ahraia dropped their binding, and hesitated, unsure if it was acceptable to admit the truth or not. Their sudden flurry of prostration revealed the truth to the Masai. Ahraia nodded. A cold smile played at the corners of the Masai's lips. "Controlling three at once, and a sprite among them . . . I'm impressed."

Kren blushed all the brighter, her pale markings flushing almost as bright as Ahraia's.

The Masai looked to her and the two wards. "Leave us."

The dae-wards hurried away, looking chastised. Kren turned, hiding her face as she went.

I wasn't enchanting them . . . Ahraia started, suddenly worried that the Masai meant to punish her.

"It's our nature to move that which we can—that's what makes us sprites." Her tone was easy, but she watched intently as Losna leapt down one root to another, until she was right next to Ahraia.

Losna leaned close, her agitation reflecting through their bond, though her fur and tail thankfully didn't show it. Ahraia was nervous too. She had never imagined standing before the most powerful sprite in all of the Silh.

The Masai's voice was gentle as she spoke. "Your sister wanted to go to Angolor? I don't blame her. It's a wonder—and not just of my making. True dark spreads as far as you can walk in a night, a long winter night." Her pale eyes gleamed with the most life Ahraia had seen yet. "Darkenings overgrown and bustling, veiled webs stretching over midda trees for miles and miles. And it spreads. Almost on its own. Eventually, dark willing, it will cover all the woods—like an ever-sprouting veil to protect us all, a true empire. Like we sprites once had."

The hairs on Ahraia's neck stood on end; she wasn't sure if it was from the thought of such expansive dark or from simply being alone with the Masai.

The Masai's ears flickered, inviting Ahraia to speak openly. "Sounds good, doesn't it?"

Ahraia nodded. Custom dictated she keep her head bowed, but

she couldn't take her eyes from the Masai. Her dress was a spin of web that Ahraia had never seen. It glowed so bright that her skin seemed dark as the last shadows of dusk, making her scars show like the stripes on a swamp-cat. Her white hair twisted in a silver cascade over the dress, and her pallid yellow eyes accentuated the brightness. They were tinged with soft golden rays around the edges, almost like the way the Dae-Mon sent flares of light into the sky right before it rose deadly over the horizon.

"I'll talk to your Astra about your sister. My offer still stands and she can afford to uproot another daughter . . . and it would be nice for you to have a familiar face once you settle in Angolor." She smiled reassuringly.

That would be nice, Ahraia conveyed, angry with Kren but glad for the Masai's consideration.

The Masai nodded, looking towards Losna.

"Your shadow is beautiful. I asked for her name, but she wouldn't say." A smile played once more at her lips, her ears flickering again for Ahraia to speak aloud.

"She wouldn't?" Ahraia asked, looking at Losna.

Losna looked like a Jontun had cornered her. *I don't have to tell her my name.*

Losna! She's the Masai! Ahraia conveyed, startled by her hostility.

"Losna," the Masai said easily, obviously having heard an echo of Ahraia's thoughts. "A fitting name." She bent to scratch Losna behind her ears, eliciting a low growl.

Ahraia flushed in embarrassment. *What are you doing? You can't do that!*

"It's all right," the Masai said with a mild look of distress. She stepped away from Losna who stopped growling, but continued to show her teeth.

Stop that, Ahraia chided.

The flares in the Masai's eyes seemed to diminish. "She reminds me of my shadow. His name was Ansbach."

I don't like her, Losna thought. Ahraia flushed, worried that the Masai might somehow be able to discern her shadow's thoughts.

"Ansbach? Was he of the plains?" Ahraia asked, so flustered that she spoke aloud, searching for anything that might distract the Masai from Losna's behavior. *Losna!* she thought in terror. *You can't disrespect her like that, we'll be shown the light.*

"From the plains?" the Masai asked. "No. He was from the forests of Cairn. She has beautiful color, doesn't she? Such a beautiful coat."

Thank you, Ahraia conveyed, regaining her composure. *Greet her,* she urged to Losna as muted as she could.

Losna came reluctantly forward, sniffing at the out-held hand of the Masai. The Masai held perfectly still, but her fingers trembled ever so slightly.

"What happened to Ansbach?" Ahraia asked, distracted and flustered.

The Masai's face gave no hint of emotion. "He returned to the forest. As all shadows do." *And he is still with me.*

Ahraia waited for the Masai to speak again, unsure if she had been meant to know her last thought. But the Masai turned, and left them standing at the entrance of the chasms in rigid silence.

15

FINGERS AND FOG

Ahraia shivered beneath the cloudless night. The stars shone with untarnished brilliance, and the Great Swell cut the night and the river, slashing through the sky above and reflecting in ever-turning glints off the water below.

Hayvon and the shades stood on the far bank of the Winnowlin, in the Shadow Woods. The bridging tree groaned, its branches strangled beneath the churning river.

"Let it go!" the Astra called.

The sprites on the bank braced themselves for the spray of water, but the bridge lingered a moment longer than it should have. The binders had relinquished their hold, but the tree remained. They looked to each other. A scowl formed at the Astra's lips, but then the tree shook and whipped back, spattering the woods with dark water.

Ahraia took a shuddering breath, overwhelmed by her attempt to keep the bridging tree down. She clutched at Losna, swallowing down a dry lump in her throat, staring across the fog-covered waters.

Hayvon and the others had collapsed at the water's edge, in exhaustion or despair.

Ahraia, her father conveyed, interrupting her thoughts. *The summoning . . .*

She looked away from Hayvon to find that all the sprites were kneeling next to the river, drinking in unison. Even the Masai was down on all fours, leaning forward to the water, her tarry vine keeping her hair from falling in.

The Astra and her father glowered at Ahraia. *Drink*, they conveyed.

Numbly, Ahraia walked to the water's edge and knelt, she lowered her lips just above the water. She waited, pretending to drink but refusing to take part in the ritual, feeling the cold stream just beneath her lips.

A roar shook from the Shadow Woods. Ahraia trembled, then stood and wiped her still dry lips. She found the Masai watching her too, now. She hastily turned her eyes back to the opposite bank.

Hayvon was up, and Shim was as well. The younger shade lurched towards the water.

Don't touch the water, she thought, yet knowing it was already too late. It was too far to convey anyway and Shim stumbled into the shallows. He lowered himself and drank deeply, coughing and sputtering on his hands and knees. Tev was still lying on the banks, sprawled out as though she was already dead.

Go, Hayvon, Ahraia thought. *You have to go.*

Hayvon limped to where Tev lay, shaking her and trying to rouse her. A roar shattered the air, echoing much closer. The sprites on the near bank eagerly watched on, ears sharp and eyes glowing. They jeered at Shim as he scrambled out of the water. Hayvon dragged Tev to her feet, but she refused to move, crying, in great wracking sobs that shook her whole body.

Losna growled next to Ahraia. *They're wasting his time.*

You have to leave her, Hayvon. You have to go, Ahraia thought.

He looked back across the water, as though he had heard her. He met her eye, and raised his hand in farewell. Ahraia knew it was disgraceful, but she didn't care; she raised her hand as well, ignoring the sharp censures of her father and the bristling contempt of the other sprites. Hayvon lingered half a moment longer, still staring across the water, and she heard a distant thought.

Farewell, Ahraia.

Farewell, Hayvon. Be safe, she answered, with a clenched jaw and hot tears slipping down her face, hoping beyond thought and reason that he might somehow escape the Shadow Woods. But she knew the truth of the matter—a death too horrible to imagine was coming for him from the heart of the forest.

Get a hold of yourself, her father conveyed. *It's unbecoming.*

Ahraia ignored him.

With a last word to Tev, Hayvon turned and guided Shim into the woods, leaving the smaller shade where she stood next to the roaring call of the river. The heavy currents of fog boiled over her. She sobbed until her body heaved and stillness settled over her.

The sprites' eyes gleamed, and Ahraia could feel their eagerness as the steady hum of conveyance and twitching ears. She tasted bile in the back of her throat. She wanted to scream at Tev to run.

Losna whimpered, stamping and shifting nervously next to Ahraia. *She needs to go. Now.*

The Astra stood near the Masai, frowning.

Ahraia had the distinct impression that her every movement was being watched by others beyond her father. If not for that, she would have called out to Tev to do anything—to swim, to run, to hide, to jump in the river and drown rather than be caught in stillness. Anything but wait.

It's coming! One of the sprites conveyed. The Masai actually smiled. A cruel and terrifying smile.

Losna's eyes were intent on the woods. She let out a low, angry woof. *It's here.*

Ahraia searched, wondering what her shadow saw. Tev stood before the ever-shifting silhouettes of the trees, a tiny figure in front of the gaping maw of the forest. Every hair on Ahraia's body stood on end. She could feel the menace. Her ears turned, listening. A limb moved, against the grain of the rest of the woods.

And then she saw it.

A flush of fear coursed through her. She wanted to scream for Tev to run. But she couldn't, her voice was gone. Even her thoughts were subdued. She stood, totally petrified. Whatever they had seen in the Stone Tree, be it alp or sprite, wraith or shadow, it certainly had not been the Shad-Mon.

A long, slender hand, with fingers as long as Ahraia was tall, gripped a tree impossibly high above the ground. Impossibly quiet. Sinuously, it reached forward to the next tree, seeming to move when the fog moved, drawing forward like a spider on its web.

Tev had seen it too, but too late. A scream erupted from the shade a bare moment before the clawed hand swept down and lifted her bodily back into the mist. Her voice, high-pitched and horrified, stopped with a sudden, terrible crunch. A harrowing silence swelled in its wake, but it didn't last long. Ahraia could hear bones cracking. She could sense the Daemon looming just beyond sight—a hulking silhouette of some corporeal beast. The noise of its chewing ground across the river. Then the silhouette turned back to the forest, holding just a pair of dangling legs, and disappeared back into its fog.

The Shad-Mon had come. And it was worse than any nightmare Ahraia had ever imagined.

Losna sat with her ears perked up and her back to Ahraia, guarding inward on the darkening, listening and watching for any movement. It was still night but dawn was coming swiftly, and outside, the Bright Moon would just be dipping behind the horizon. It was getting ominously close to full.

Two nights to go, Losna thought restlessly, standing and yawning.

Keep your eyes out, Ahraia conveyed, pulling her hood closer. Almost half the turning had passed since Hayvon had been condemned, but still they were confined to the darkening and their shadow test was looming.

And the Shad-Mon was looming, for that matter, creeping through Ahraia's thoughts, sweeping through her dreams like the clawed hand had swept through the mist.

In the nights following the condemnation, Losna had dwelled on the shades' fates. *Do you think Hayvon could have escaped? Do you think he got away while that evil was hunting after Tev?*

"To what end?" Ahraia had answered, terrified by the memory of the silhouette. "To be hunted by darkness and hiding from light?" The thought of escape was almost worse than a swift death—alone and shadowless, trapped in the Shadow Woods with his days and nights spent cowering until the light overwhelmed him or the Shad-Mon found him. No sprite had ever returned from the heart of the woods, and Ahraia had little hope for Hayvon.

It was a fate she refused to suffer. If she was going to fail the shadow test, they were going to run for it—and the spritelings and Kyah with them. They needed an escape route, one that would answer to her in a pinch. That was why she was leaned casually against the darkening wall in a tucked away corner of Daispar, where neither shades nor sprites would bother them.

It's almost day . . . no one's going to be about, Losna thought, yawning wide again, and lowering herself to the ground. *Besides, it's not like you're making a closure.*

She was right, of course, but it didn't mean Ahraia wanted to be discovered softening the wall.

"Just keep your wits about you," Ahraia said, reaching out to bind another tendril, slowly starting to stretch and bend the branch, gently turning it to her will. Her thoughts drifted as she worked, trailing from Hayvon and the Shad-Mon, to Vesta and the Stone Tree, and eventually to her shadow test. It was the Astra's fault. Every little bit of it. And Ahraia wanted nothing more than to send her quivering across a bridging tree into the Shadow Woods. Then Ahraia would drink until she was sick, summoning the daemon down on the Astra and watching in delight while the Shad-Mon chewed her down to her shins.

The tendril tensed, sensing Ahraia's mood, tightening purposefully and spreading the thought to the other branches. Ahraia let go of the binding. She cleared her mind and stretched her neck. It had been a long night—a long turning, for that matter.

Shouldn't we tell Kyah the plan? So the spritelings are at least ready? Losna asked, noticing a break in Ahraia's concentration.

"There's nothing to tell," Ahraia answered. *It's too risky for them to know anything yet.* She rebound the tendril and started to rework it. The plan wasn't so much a plan as it was a last resort, an escape route if their shadow test fell apart.

What if something happens to us?

Ahraia shook her head and the branch she had bound shook with her. *Then they're dead anyways.*

The light outside was growing, and inside the darkening, it was getting too bright, even for Ahraia. She unbound the wall, leaving it ready for a quick exit and headed back for their nit. They wound through the darkening, but when she turned down the last path, Ahraia pulled up short, seeing Tallin waiting for her.

She immediately thought of Gavea and wondered if Tallin suspected their role in her sister's death. Gavea's body had finally been found, light-torn and ravaged. Tallin had been stomping around the darkening in a foul mood ever since.

"Where have you been? I've been looking everywhere for you," Tallin said with her usual impish sneer.

Ahraia picked a twig from the darkening wall from her sleeve and flicked it casually to the ground.

What for?

Tallin's eyes narrowed. "The Astra is waiting for you. You were supposed to be at the dae grove before the light rise."

Ahraia's heart beat faster. "The dae grove? Now?" she said, noting Tallin's ears flickering for deference. *What for?* The dae grove was hardly ever used, but Ahraia suspected what it meant.

A malevolent smile spread across Tallin's face. "Your shadow test begins tonight."

But we still have two nights until Bright Moon is full! Ahraia conveyed, suddenly panicked. Losna tensed, her tail stiff and straight and her fur standing on end.

Tallin gestured for her to follow. "Hurry up. They're waiting."

Ahraia hesitated, a sinking sensation spreading through her

chest. She made to follow, with Losna close behind, but Tallin raised a hand and spoke again.

"Just you. Leave your shadow here."

Ahraia stopped, suddenly terrified to be separated from Losna. "I get her for my test."

Tallin nodded but gestured for her to follow, nonetheless. Losna let out a whimper.

Why doesn't she get to come? Ahraia conveyed.

"Because, you're becoming a sprite, and sprites don't have shadows." Tallin turned towards the central hollow, and Ahraia had no choice but to follow, alone, without Losna.

"THIS LIGHTRISE MARKS the beginning of your Shadow Test, Shade Ahraia. You've been summoned here with all the sprites of Daispar as witnesses." Her father radiated pride, but his hidden thoughts were a stark contrast to his voice. *Are you listening to me?* he conveyed.

Ahraia was listening only in the sense that she heard the words, but they were hollow. She felt naked without Losna, and her mind seemed strangely quiet. Every sprite in the darkening was gathered under the dae grove, and the silence in her mind set her worrying worse than ever about being separated.

"Your Shadow Test will make you a sprite," her father went on evenly. "The final step to joining a darkening." *And you will become a sprite*, he conveyed angrily. *Or I'll see the Astra's promise done.*

Ahraia felt a hot surge of blood through her cheeks.

The Astra stood nearby, her ears quivering greedily. Next to her were the Masai and the sprites from Angolor. The Masai was watching the processions with the same bemused smile she had when she had found Ahraia enchanting Kren at the chasms.

They were gathered in a dark hollow known as the dae grove, a dell covered by a dark swell of trees, circular and broad, with a certain staleness and formality to it. Although no true light entered the grove, a hundred eyes gleamed pale white all about Ahraia.

"Our Masai has come for you," her father said, bowing his head respectfully to the leader of the Silh. "But ultimately, our Masah will be the judge of you." He used the true name of the Bright Moon and his pale eyes turned towards the west where it had just set. "You will be judged by her throughout, and so the test will span three turnings, recommencing each time she is full and in all of her forbidden splendor. At times, her sister's will be watching as well. Let them whisper in your favor, dimming her anger and softening her edge, giving you blood and darkness both."

Ahraia noticed a pause and realized that the sprites were waiting for her response, listening eagerly.

What must I do? she asked, feeling disconnected. Without her shadow, she was less than whole. Her father's ears batted and he frowned at her dejection before carrying on.

"There are three tasks—meant to ensure that you are ready for spritehood. Today, you will learn of the first . . . and tonight, you will begin." *Understood?*

Ahraia nodded.

"If you fail any of your tasks, your shadow will be shown the light and you will be given to the Shad-Mon." *Understood?*

Ahraia nodded again, her eyes flickering towards the Astra who was watching the proceedings with an intense gaze.

"The first task is the simplest. You must make a sacrifice of an innocent to the people of Daispar."

Ahraia hesitated, waiting for him to say more. With no explanation forthcoming, she asked, *What do you mean, a sacrifice of an innocent?*

"You must make a kill for the darkness. A simple kill."

Of an innocent? As in game?

Her father nodded. *You must do this by binding*, he conveyed, only letting her know his thoughts.

She let out a sigh. She had always known that it would come to this.

Do I get a drain?

He nodded, holding out a small knife, hardly big enough to gut a rabbit. It was a typical spritish drain, not much more that a hand-span long and woefully inadequate to make a kill. *And your shadow can't make the kill for you.*

She ignored his barb and took the drain, staring down at the useless blade. He kept his hand out, and she realized he meant to exchange the one she currently carried, which was twice as long. She handed it over reluctantly, though she had never even used it.

When do I begin?

"When the day is gone, the Bright Moon will be three nights from full. By the end of the third night, your kill must be made. As it was the Masai who chose you to enter your test, she will name the sacrifice to be made."

He stepped back and bowed. The Masai moved out of the circle of sprites, her tarry vine holding her hair elaborately above her head. Her posture was straight with ears to match. The other sprites drew back, the whole hollow seeming to flinch at her presence.

She wore a black dress, deeper than the night, and the Astra seemed diminished next to her. She didn't carry herself with any of the strange wariness that she had at the chasms, and instead, her face was still as a midnight pond. The darkness seemed to pool about her.

"Shade Ahraia, do you fear your shadow test?"

Ahraia gathered herself, preparing the lie.

No, she conveyed. Fear wasn't an acceptable trait to show, least of all to the leader of the Silh.

The Masai face didn't move. "You should."

A murmur of thought passed through the gathering. It was a strange thing to say. The Astra watched the Masai keenly. The Masai didn't seem to notice.

"It will turn you from a shade to a sprite. As a wolf-binder, your will alone is all that will see you through. Not drain, or shadow, or any other possession." The Masai fixed Ahraia with a hard stare. "Do you fear the Shad-Mon?"

All things but fools and the dead fear the Shad-Mon, Ahraia conveyed, reciting words she had heard a hundred times.

The Masai frowned. "You shouldn't. It is a weakness that will draw you to it, like the moons are drawn into the night after their long sleeps. The stronger you fear it, the more likely it will consume you."

Ahraia lowered her eyes and nodded, not knowing what to say. She wished she had Losna with her. The Masai went on.

"As a wolf-binder, you are marked by the moons to lead. Your light-scars are deep." The Masai walked closer, and Ahraia was reminded of how Losna sometimes stalked prey, moving slowly but purposefully, her body tense and ready for the chase. The Masai reached out and took Ahraia by the hand, looking at her wrists, turning her hands gently to reveal the pattern tracing up past her elbows.

"I see the marks of the Blood Moon—red and lethal. I see the marks of her sister, the Dark Moon—shadowy and lurking. But more than anything—I see the marks of the Bright Moon—she who is strongest, swiftest of all— more dangerous than any. These are deep scars. The kind one gets from tarrying too foolishly beneath her light." She reached up and pushed back Ahraia's hair, looking at her neck and jawline where the markings tapered out. As threatening as the Masai was, there was tenderness to her touch. Her voice was quiet as she went on.

"They will fade with time, as mine have. But the memory of your shadow will always be sharp," she said, stepping back from Ahraia. "Like a knife that cuts at the slightest mishandling. And the memories will rise, just as the moons." Her eyes had a strange glimmer to them—wolflike almost, golden and yet gleamless. Her voice grew stronger.

"If your will is strong, the cut will heal and scab enough times that it is only a scar by which to remember not what you are, but what you once were. This is a test I do not envy. But your shadow marks you as a leader, Ahraia, and that is why I have asked you to join me."

Ahraia's mouth went dry again. She wasn't a leader. She had no desire to even become a sprite. She wanted her shadow back and she wanted to run from Daispar, to flee from every darkening, from the whole Silh. The Astra was watching her sharply, as though she guessed Ahraia's thoughts. The Masai went on.

"The moons have marked you. And I have marked you. Should you pass your test, a day will come when you will lead the Silh. As such, you must be stronger, sharper, more willful, and wiser than all of us. Thus, your test will be a reflection of that." *You must be ruthless.*

If her words were meant to make Ahraia feel more frightened, they most certainly did. She felt faint. Cold climbed down her spine. She wished she had never grown old enough to be chosen for this task. She wished her brothers were still sheltered under their nit tree; it was a guilty thought, one she wanted as much for herself and Losna as for them. Shame spread like clouds over her heart. The Masai went on, staring at her.

"So when I choose your first task, understand, I choose it for you, not for anyone else. If you are not tested, then you are not fit to lead. If you are not the strongest of us all, then you will go to the Shad-Mon. You must be better than the rest. You must be like a Masai."

The air stilled, enough that the beat of wings or fidgeting of a shadow would have sounded like a thunderclap.

"Because of this, I choose a keress as your sacrifice."

An audible murmur went through the sprites, and the air vibrated with conveyance.

A keress? Ahraia thought blankly. The other sprites fell silent with a signal from the Masai.

The Astra stood with her mouth open, shaking her head in disbelief. She started to laugh, a hollow and empty sound. "I should have known," she said quietly, a sickened, joyless smile spreading across her face.

A keress? Ahraia thought again in disbelief. The keress were the great elk of the plains, impossible to hunt.

That's like setting her after a Jontun or a mountain bear, her father conveyed, looking equally aghast. *They are creatures of the plain. She might as well try hunting the Shad-Mon.*

Ahraia looked down at the drain in her hand. It was pitifully small. The Masai looked nonplussed by her father's objections.

"That is her task," she said easily.

Ahraia tried to imagine if she could kill a keress with a dozen sprites and a handful of arrows. The elk of the plains were three times as tall as even the tallest sprite, likely a dozen feet at the shoulder with antlers just as wide. They were mean, unpredictable—territorial and defensive. No one hunted them. Not alone. Not in a group. Not with all the luck in the world.

16

RUNNING SHADOWS

Losna got up, circled twice and lay back down, letting out a huff as she did. She glared at Ahraia. The day was gone, and evening was quickly descending outside the darkening, but neither of them had managed to sleep.

Ahraia's nerves were frayed. She turned the drain slowly in her hand. The blade was slight, sharp but not even a hand-span long—and her hands were small. It was likely stolen from the body of some lightwalker, and it stunk of iron. To a keress, it would be nothing, just a splinter.

"How are we going to do this?" Ahraia muttered.

We aren't. Losna huffed again, putting her head on her paws.

"We have to. I'll make a binding and be done with it."

Losna looked up in agitation. *Have you forgotten? You can't make a kill by a binding.*

"You're not helping," Ahraia said sharply, stung by the echo of her own fears.

Losna growled. *Even if you could—even if you do—it's poisoned. The last time you tried was a disaster and the time before that was even worse. It was just a hare and you were curled up for days. How are you suddenly planning on bringing down a keress?*

"I was bound to Gavea, wasn't I? That didn't ruin me."

Losna ignored her. *My pack—my whole pack—wouldn't hunt them. Not unless they were already half-dead or dying. They're too aggressive. It's madness to think you can suddenly manage that! And with nothing more than that tooth.* She pulled her lips back at the drain.

Ahraia's skin was flushed, feeling the sharp and bitter sting of Losna's barbs. "We don't have a choice. And the only reason I *can't* is because I've refused to—which ends tonight."

You've refused to because it destroys you. We're not going to survive if you mean to bind it. And I don't want you to, Losna thought stubbornly.

"Well, then we are dead either way."

Losna growled at her. *That's my point. We should run.*

Ahraia didn't answer.

We have three whole nights, Losna thought. *We could be halfway across the plains by then.*

"I'm not leaving Kyah and the Spritelings." *Drop it.*

Losna pinned back her ears, showing her teeth. *Then take them with us! Why else did you spend all that time softening the wall?*

Ahraia didn't answer. She couldn't. Losna was right, and the worst part was that now they couldn't run. Kyah and the spritelings had been ushered out of the nit, moved under the watchful eye of the Astra. The barest interaction was condemnable—and if Ahraia went looking for them, she might well as walk into the Shadow Woods voluntarily, with Kyah and the others with her.

She stared down at the blade. The markings on her hands had faded, leaving nothing more than faint spotting at her wrists and forearms.

"We're going to have to find a way," she said at last. "If we can get past this first test, that will give us a whole turning to plan if we need to run." *That will give me enough time to make sure we can find darkness . . .*

Losna growled, not needing to make her thoughts known.

"Ahraia?" A voice called from outside. Losna let out a woof and got to her feet.

Ahraia bonded the shade tree and pulled back its branches.

Her father was outside, standing just beyond the nit tree, looking gaunt and pale.

"It's time."

~

BROKEN CLOUDS DRIFTED over the plains, speared by moonlight that blazed across the grasses below.

"It's getting late," Ahraia murmured, standing right at the edge of the forest. Two nights had already passed and her scars had emerged in full again, ashen-gray instead of fire-red. She was becoming accustomed to it. *Too accustomed.*

The eyes of the keress shone like a line of twinkling stars, glinting when they stepped and then stopped, disappearing as they lowered their heads to eat and then shining back to life. Losna sniffed at the wind, watching the sprawling herd as they stomped and called, spreading and constricting like the clouds above.

Which one are you thinking? Not that bull in the back . . .

No. The one just ahead of him. The smaller one, Ahraia conveyed. The night was woefully quiet, and unbearably bright. She sniffed at the barren breeze as it ruffled through the grasses.

Losna's tail hung low and still. *This isn't possible. They're too big.*

Ahraia moved several paces through the forest, stalking along with the movement of the massive herd. The river formed a black line through the moonlit fields, funneling the herd past the forest. The males called in trumpeting voices and the calves squealed softly.

We'll be fine, Ahraia thought, more to herself than to Losna. At this point, they didn't have a choice. They had spent the first night finding and tracking the herd, and the second just watching them on the open plains, trying to find a weakness in their movements. Twice Ahraia had tried to bond a cow, and once a calf, but each time the males that patrolled the edges turned back her quarry.

Tonight was the last chance to make the kill.

Let's go over it again, Losna thought. *You bind the smaller one, the one ahead of the big bull. Right?*

Ahraia nodded. The males roved the borders, closer to the eaves of the forest, protecting the females and calves.

Then you draw it into the woods.

Ahraia nodded. If she could kill it outright with a binding, she would. If not, she was going to use the closeness of the forest to overwhelm it.

Losna glared at Ahraia. *And then you kill it with your spare tooth, ripping yourself apart in the process.* Her hackles were raised, but her tail swished back and forth with feigned acceptance.

Ahraia swallowed. "The drain isn't that small."

And if that doesn't work—Losna went on, her eyes glowing yellow—*then I'll just run into the middle of the herd, incite fear into the wolf-trampling, sprite-skewering beasts and hope that they accidentally trample one of their own, or one drowns in the river that they cross like a crick . . .*

Ahraia frowned at her shadow. "If it comes to that, I'll make the kill on the plains," she said, unable to convey the thought with any sincerity. She turned back to the keress.

The males roving towards the forest were enormous. The largest bull roamed in the rear, shepherding the herd, constantly calling and posturing, directing the other males. Its antlers stretched more than a dozen feet across and its great beard hung half that distance above the ground, waggling each time it bellowed.

"It's now or never," Ahraia said. "Are you ready?"

No, Losna thought. But she was poised, with ears turned forward and tail back. Ahraia ran her fingers through Losna's coarse fur one last time, wondering if they would survive the night.

"Go."

With a nip at her arm, Losna loped off through the woods, downwind of the herd. With a last bounce, her tail disappeared beyond a pine thicket. Their link stretched thin, until it was so faint it almost wasn't there. Ahraia waited, gathering herself until she was sure Losna was in position.

The Bright Moon, which had been hiding behind a cloud, emerged as though it knew her task was at hand. She was alone in the sky.

Look after me, Ahraia thought, looking up. The smaller keress raised his head too. It was still well over twice her height, with broad, sharp antlers, fanning out above and behind its ever-turning ears.

Ahraia cleared her mind as best she could and made her binding. The enchantment was subtle, a muted bond so that the keress didn't feel her presence. It *couldn't* know she was there. As soon as it did, it would spook, and the whole herd would rally to it.

Ahraia let her eyes go blank, letting the great elk grow accustomed to her, acquainting herself to its emotions. It was wary, right down to its bones: overseeing by nature and nervous to be patrolling near the darkened forest.

Protect the herd, it thought.

Good instincts, Ahraia answered, letting the beast's nature govern her thoughts. She saw through the blurred eyes of her binding. It lowered its head to eat and then looked up again. She let it call as it always did. Carefully, she interjected simple thoughts into the bond.

Protect the herd, she thought. *Watch the forest. Listen to the wind.*

It raised its head and sniffed. She began to exert her will on the creature.

This way. The grass looks good here.

The keress took a step forward towards the thicker grass. It lowered its head and ate, then looked up again.

Good. Protect the herd . . . one step over here.

Ahraia was patient. The herd moved slowly. She tracked along, drawing it step by step towards the woods. The Bright Moon passed in and out from behind the clouds. She flitted in and out from behind the trees. The keress ambled closer, until it was only some forty paces from the forest.

So close. For a moment, Ahraia saw it through her own eyes, and realized how truly enormous it was. The drain was too small. It wouldn't even pierce the hide. The keress's antlers were too broad. She would never get within reach without being skewered, and even if she did, she couldn't reach its throat. She hesitated.

The keress looked up, staring at the forest.

It was as far from the herd as any keress had been in all three nights. It sniffed and snorted.

It's okay. The forest is safe, Ahraia reassured it. She dimly sensed the bull keress turning towards her. The herd was following the line of the river, and had turned away from where Ahraia stood. The bull called out, summoning her keress to follow.

The forest is empty. And you're too big to worry, Ahraia countered, holding it steady.

The bull called again, jogging several strides towards them, shaking its massive antlers back and forth, and jutting its jaw forward.

Ahraia's keress turned. Her spine tingled with reflected fear; he realized he was too far from the herd.

You're safe, she thought again.

The bull snorted and great gusts of fog stirred from each nostril. Her keress took a step away from the forest.

Ahraia's ears turned down. She was going to have to turn the bull about, and quickly. She formed a second binding, intending to force him away. But he sensed her, and bellowed into the night. All the keress on the plain turned to look. A flush of fear reflected from her first binding; Ahraia ignored it, oppressing its panic with forced calm.

Go, she commanded to the bull. *Back to the herd.*

The bull trumpeted angrily, sensing danger. The two enchantments entangled, the bull's warnings reflecting through Ahraia to her first charge. The smaller keress startled, its fear reverberating to the bull in turn, causing it to stomp and bellow even more. The herd turned, swelling with calls and shaking antlers.

They're spooked, Losna thought distantly.

Ahraia dropped her enchantment of the bull, realizing too late that it had only made things worse. She focused instead on her first binding.

It's all right. Come to the forest. She rushed the thought; the keress wasn't yet at ease. It threw back its head and bellowed into the night. It turned and jogged back towards the bull.

"*No!*" Ahraia voiced aloud, stepping onto the plains into full sight of the keress. Moonlight blazed upon her skin.

Stop! she commanded, her binding no longer subtle or hidden. The smaller keress froze. *You are coming to the forest*, she thought forcibly with a tingling awareness of the self-destruction that she was proffering. But what choice did she have? The night was almost over; the kill had to be made.

Hurry up, she thought, forcing the elk to canter towards her, each step wrapping herself deeper into its mind.

For a moment, she thought it was going to work. The keress was nearly to the forest. Its hooves beat against the grasses. Its beard waggled back and forth with every ragged breath.

Ahraia stood poised, the drain raised in her hand.

But the bull trumpeted again and her keress stopped dead in its tracks, still a dozen paces from her. The fog from its breath filled the space between them. Its black eyes stared at her. It was torn between instinct and enchantment.

Ahraia wrestled with its will, but the pull of the herd ran too deep in its blood.

Losna. I need you! Scare the herd. I need that bull gone, Ahraia thought, her whole being intent on keeping her charge rooted where it stood.

A moment later, Losna's howl rose through the night.

"Ahooo!"

Her keress stomped its feet, twisting back towards the sound. Sweat erupted on Ahraia's skin. She nearly collapsed, overwhelmed by the perfusion of fear. The binding snapped.

"Ahooo!" Losna darted onto the plains, a dark shadow against the moonlit grasses. The herd circled, all braying and clattering in distress. The males trumpeted and shook their antlers, tightening around the cows and the calves which mewed and squealed. Ahraia's keress and the bull cantered back towards the herd, shaking the ground.

"*Stop!*" Ahraia commanded, sprinting out farther onto the plain, chasing them and reforming her enchantment as a feverish sweat broke out over her body. *You're not going back!* she thought forcefully. *You're coming with me.* She pushed down her fears, clenching her teeth.

Her keress stopped.

Come here, she commanded, her drain poised for the kill, running to meet it on the plain.

The bull had stopped too. It bellowed and stomped its hooves.

This is my kill, Ahraia thought, unfazed by the bulls posturing. It snorted and lowered its antlers, pawing the ground. It bellowed once more.

Then it charged.

"Light take me . . .," Ahraia said, forgetting her task. She tried to bind the bull to slow it, but it was already seething with rage. It thundered towards her, covering the ground at an alarming rate.

No, no, no, she thought, trying more desperately to halt it.

"Ahooo. Ahoo!" Losna called distantly. *Ahraia, run!*

It was like being in a dream where her legs wouldn't answer. She couldn't form the binding.

Ahraia, run! Losna thought again, her howls turning to terror.

Ahraia turned, sprinting for the cover of the woods. Her hair whipped across her face. The ground shook beneath her. She could hear the bull closing in with great lumbering strides and ragged, bellowing breaths.

Get down, Losna urged her.

Ahraia flung herself to the ground, expecting to feel the piercing stab of antlers or the crushing weight of hooves, but instead felt a burst of air overhead. She looked up. The keress turned and swung its antlers violently about.

There was nowhere to run. It lowered its antlers. Even the smallest of its tines were twice as long as her drain. It pawed the ground, sending hard earth flying as dust. It stomped towards her.

A snarl rose through the night and Losna was suddenly circling behind the keress, yapping and lunging at it. The bull bellowed deafeningly.

Keep it busy. Ahraia scrambled to her feet and sprinted for the forest. *Let it after me once I'm in the woods.*

Losna danced about the bull, lunging in close before sprinting away with tail low and tense. Ahraia felt the cool shadows of the woods.

All right! Let it go.

Losna jeered at the bull, then jogged towards Ahraia. Just as Ahraia had hoped, the keress charged after them, unwilling to give up. But it moved like the wind. Losna had to break into a sprint and Ahraia just reached the woods before her shadow and the keress were upon her.

She waved her arms and shouted, drawing the bull's attention. She darted through the narrowest trees she could find, hoping its antlers might catch and hinder it. Instead, the beast trampled through the thicket, nearly crushing her. It kicked, and its front hooves grazed her shoulder, knocking her to the ground. She gasped, the air suddenly ripped from her lungs.

Losna leapt to her defense, but the keress kicked again, casting her to the bushes. Their link suddenly erupted with pain. The keress plowed through the underbrush, swinging its antlers violently back and forth, tearing shoots and fronds from the trees. Losna was howling in pain, calling out to the night in mindless fury.

"Ahooo!"

The keress's antlers tore great gashes in the ground, unhindered by the vines and boughs clinging amongst the points. Losna snarled, cornered and injured.

Hey! Ahraia conveyed to the keress, enchanting it firmly to grab its attention. *Come and get me!*

Her taunting drove it berserk. The bull turned and she took off running. Leaves and limbs whipped past her. She sprinted, not needing to look to know the keress was just at her heels. Trees and boughs whined as they passed. The ground beneath her rumbled; the keress ran like a thunderstorm, and she like the wind on its front.

You won't catch me, she jeered. She dimly noticed the Bright Moon had nearly set. The night was failing.

"Ahooo," Losna called. It sounded gravelly and different. Their link was dimmed by distance.

"Ahooo," Ahraia heard again, behind her.

The keress was almost upon her. She burst through two elm trees and heard a tremendous crash. She didn't turn to see where the beast was, but just kept running.

Another howl echoed from beside her. She looked, wondering how Losna could have covered so much ground. Then another howl came from ahead of her. *Impossible.* She saw dark fur dashing next to her. Black fur. Another howl. White fur. Her heart sang with bindings.

"Ahooo!" A whole pack of wolves ran with her—hunting with her. They were bound to her, just as she was bound to Losna.

Gray fur and streaming tails streaked on all sides of the keress, and fear belied its bellows now. The wolves surrounded it. The keress slowed and stopped. The pack moved endlessly tighter around the beast, circling with bared teeth. They yipped and called. The keress swung its antlers wildly, trumpeting into the night. Familiar fur flashed in front of Ahraia: Losna running with the pack, a seamless part of their collective. The eyes of the keress darted around wildly. Its movement grew more erratic, trapped by the forest.

I need to make a clean kill, she thought to Losna. *Make them understand.*

The wolves, however, already seemed to grasp what she needed. None made any move to attack—they nipped, but never bit, lunged but never clawed.

Ahraia scanned the woods and found two trees standing nearby, about the span of the keress's antlers. She bound them, her will forcing them to spread ever so slightly. The binding strained at her mind.

Bring it to me, she thought. The wolves circled about the keress, herding it about until it faced her.

Ahraia? Losna thought. Her worry surged through their link.

Ahraia pulled the drain from her cloak. The keress's eyes settled on her.

Come on. Come and get me.

The blacks of its eyes gleamed in the last light of the Bright Moon. The Dae-Mon was coming. Ahraia knew the bull wouldn't allow itself to be enchanted, but she didn't need to enchant it now, she needed it enraged.

Come on. Kill me and you might get away. But if you don't, we'll go hunting all of your kin. Every calf and cow.

It stomped and snorted in response.

"Come on!" Ahraia yelled.

It charged.

It galloped towards her, knocking aside brush and limbs. *Thirty strides away*. The wolves howled on either side.

Ahraia bared her teeth, her tiny knife held at the ready. *Ten strides*. The keress lowered its head, ready to skewer her. *Five strides*. Its antlers were so wide. *Two strides*. Too wide.

She unbound the trees. They sprang back.

Boom!

The whole forest shook. The antlers of the keress slammed into the trees, lodging deep within the heartwood. The bull bucked. Leaves cascaded and rustled in the tempest of shaking, but neither the trees nor the antlers budged.

The keress was trapped.

The wolves slowed, circling to watch. They willed Ahraia to make the kill, eager, with tails high and snouts panting. Ahraia's heart hammered in her chest. She walked forward, relief roiling through her and her bond.

The eyes of the great bull widened in panic. The keress bellowed, getting more and more pitiful as she approached, snorting and huffing.

"Shhh." *Shhhh*, Ahraia bid it. The keress's breathing became more regular. Its struggle lessened.

The Bright Moon dipped beneath the horizon. She needed to make the kill. In the west, gray was giving way to pale yellow, the first sign of the Dae-Mon. The beast continued to struggle, albeit less than before.

"You fought well," she said, reaching up with a hand to comfort it, its beard hanging to the ground at her feet. She felt its snout; it was wet. It flared its nostrils at her, but each breath came slower than the previous, already resigned to its fate. Its hooves had stopped stomping.

Kill, the wolves thought. Losna circled, her emotions twining with the pack.

The yellow was growing brighter in the west. Ahraia could feel the Keress' breath hot upon her face, its chin still above her head.

"I'm sorry." Ahraia said. *I'm sorry.*

She plunged the drain into its throat. The keress groaned, but hardly twitched.

The keress met her eyes. It let out a shuddering breath and Ahraia felt its life expunge.

It was dead.

And then the loss struck her, heavy and agonizing. She had bound the keress, however briefly—trying to stop it, taunting it, trying to bring it after her—and she had killed it. The wracking pain roiled within her, and tears welled in her eyes. She choked, searching for breath, then collapsed to her knees and howled in anguish.

17

BENEATH THE DAE-MON

The keress's blood seared Ahraia's nostrils, stinking of death. Her stomach turned. She was going to be sick.

We need to go. You need an underdae, Losna thought worriedly.

Ahraia wiped the tears from her cheeks, inadvertently dragging the sticky blood across her face. She was exhausted. And the part of her that had been bound pulsed with a deathly ache.

"Darkness," she said, dimly aware of the brightening sky. She stared into the lifeless eyes of the keress. The beast was still standing, locked in place by its antlers.

We need darkness, a shelter from the day, Losna thought to the wolves.

The pack shuffled and a wolf with a pure white coat came forward, its fur painfully bright, terrifying to Ahraia.

Shelter, the wolf thought vaguely while the rest of the pack watched on. It bounded off through the woods, leaping easily through the underbrush before stopping and turning, looking back to Ahraia to follow.

Losna's tail hung low. Though they had survived, she seemed distant. . . or angry. *She'll take you to safety. Follow her.* She avoided Ahraia's eye.

"What about the keress?" Ahraia asked, distracted by her shadow, but aware that an unprotected kill would draw a slew of predators to it.

We will keep it, Losna thought. *I'll stay with them.*

The wolves spread out around the keress and Ahraia had the vague feeling of assuredness from the pack, though it was soured by something else, something she couldn't place, festering in the air. Golden eyes watched her, noses turned towards her, all with tails low. In her state of mind, she couldn't place the emotion.

You need to go, Losna thought.

The sky was turning a thousand shades of yellow in the east, colors Ahraia had never seen. Without other choice, she followed the white wolf, who turned and bounded off through the woods.

The rush of the hunt was wearing off. Every step sent sharp pain pulsating through her side, throbbing up through her shoulder. Making it worse, she was suddenly aware of how light the woods were becoming. They were no longer dim or dark—they were bright, perfused by gray, the sky morphing into a color she had no name for. She took Hayvon's veil from her cloak, wrapping it haphazardly about her face. The reckoning of the Dae-Mon was coming. Her skin burned hot and the markings on her wrists were seared into her.

How much farther? she conveyed to the wolf, who bounded through the woods so quickly that Ahraia risked losing her. Her shoulder was splitting with pain.

Close.

Beyond the deep of the forest, the bright fire shone in the uppermost treetops. The Dae-Mon had risen. Her eyes burned.

How close?

Here.

The wolf stopped before a small opening in the ground, just beneath the roots of a massive tree. Her den. The closure wasn't much bigger than Ahraia's body.

The Dae-Mon's light crept swiftly down the tree tops. Ahraia paused, startled by the colors in the sky. But time had run out. She stooped and backed into the den, legs first, unsure what she would do if she didn't fit.

She slid down the hole, her last view a glimpse of the brilliant light against distant tree trunks. Loose dirt crumbled between her fingers and the smell of dried earth pressed all about her, masking the blood. She shimmied deeper, feeling a space behind her feet. The den opened up, and her whole body squeezed underground. A little further and her feet ran against the hard earth. The hole above hid the sky, though the tunnel burned with light.

She immediately wanted out.

The white wolf came halfway down and sniffed.

Safe, it thought. But Ahraia sensed the same sentiment that had drifted through the pack.

Ahraia met the white wolf's eyes, and in that moment, she understood the pack's emotion.

Wariness.

It was the bond. The link that she had used to kill was the same bond she had to the wolves—the same bond she had to Losna.

It's not the way, the white wolf thought vaguely. Then it turned and slipped away, leaving her in silence. Alone.

She wanted her shadow.

The den was strangely muted, with only the sound of her heavy breathing and the scrape of dirt beneath her, as though the world beyond didn't exist. How far she had run, she wasn't sure, but she couldn't feel Losna anymore, and the white wolf's last thought left a pit in her heart.

Ahraia took a deep, unsettled breath.

Losna?

Her skin tingled, singed by the light she had suffered. The blood of the keress felt hot on her hands and haunting to her thoughts. She wanted to run. The threatening light at the entrance pinned her in the space, cramped and close, dangerously bright. She wanted to flee. Hayvon's light veil pressed too tightly on her chin. She ripped it off, nearly mad from the closeness of it. She needed to escape: the den, her test, the horrible despair she felt, and, most of all, the disappointment she had felt in Losna. She felt sick. She felt like she was going to burst. It was bubbling up within her, until it couldn't be contained any longer.

Ahraia screamed in helplessness, the sound driving her mad even as the ground swallowed it. She beat at the earth in fury, overwhelmed as she thumped her fists inconsequentially against the walls of the den. She clawed at the ground, grabbing handfuls of loose dirt. When she stilled, she lay panting, crying and unable to flee, trapped in her own mind.

She lay curled away from the light for what seemed like an eternity, longer than any day she had ever lay awake, consumed by thoughts of her test and what would happen if she couldn't manage the next task. The worry threatened to suffocate her, and the ache inside her pulsed with every heartbeat. Eventually, her thoughts passed into sleep, but her dreams were no better than her waking thoughts: filled with antlers and lifeless eyes, but the eyes were Losna's eyes, and her shadow lay dead, held by the Ahraia's own enchantment. She wished for death . . . for anything other than living without her shadow.

When she awoke, the den was dark, or at least dark enough that she was safe. But the closure was still brilliant, and there was no telling what time of day it was. She sensed something blocking the entrance, a comforting presence. She reached out and discovered that it was Losna, keeping watch.

Are you all right? Losna thought. *Are you safe?*

Yes, Ahraia answered. Having Losna close was soothing, like a cool stream passing over her light-scars. The quietness and emptiness that had lingered all morning were gone, and instead, Ahraia felt the first measure of peace. But Losna was anxious, and a sense of disappointment lay at the front of her mind.

Ahraia rolled over, risking exposure to the dim light that streamed in. *What's wrong?*

Losna turned about in the entrance, trying to block as much of the brightness as she could. Then she put her head on her paws, and peered down at Ahraia, her sharp ears forming a soft silhouette against the bright fire beyond.

"What's wrong?" Ahraia asked again, terrified to know the answer. The fur above Losna's nose furrowed.

This test. I don't want to go through with it. She huffed loudly, as though it was Ahraia's fault.

"Neither do I," Ahraia said, raising up on her elbows. "I never did."

Losna shifted to block the light better, but glared at her. Her nose flared, and dust rose as she huffed again.

I don't want you making bindings anymore. Not when you're hunting, she thought. The conviction of her emotions shone in her golden eyes.

"I don't either—it's not like I wanted to bind the Keress. We didn't have a choice," she said. "We agreed to that plan."

You're not listening to me. Losna raised her head off her paws. *You can't keep doing this. It changes you, every time. I can feel it! The second you killed that keress, it was agony, like a part of you was ripped away. And you didn't even have it bound tightly.*

"I know," Ahraia said, startled by how angry her shadow was, "but—"

You don't know! Losna growled. *The rest of this test is only going to get worse. It's like you can't see what becomes of shades who go through with this. Look at Kren. She was our sister, our pack—now she doesn't even recognize her own nit. Or if she does, she doesn't care. She's dead inside. That's what this test does. It kills that lingering part of you that is alive. Wherever Flit is, I hope she never sees what her shade has become. It would break her if she did. And honestly, if that's what becomes of you, I won't want to see it either.*

Ahraia fell silent, feeling even more helpless than before. Losna stood up again, putting her back to Ahraia and closing her thoughts. Ahraia opened her mouth, but knew there was no point arguing—there was no argument to be had.

She turned back over, wishing she could run, wishing she could hide from her shame. The weight of the test was too much. Becoming a sprite was the only choice for her—it was that or die. But what did living matter, if she lived without the truest part of herself? What did it matter if she had to ravage herself to belong? She pressed her eyes closed, her ears tucking back so tightly that they ached. She took a shuddering breath, feeling as though she was suffocating. The earthen tomb seemed to steal any calm she could grasp and she sobbed silently. A terrible thought rose in her, knowing she was too weak to finish the test: Could she ask Losna to go back to her pack? Would her shadow spare her seeing the test to the end?

Losna lifted her head, sensing the blackening of her mind.

What? she thought, still angry.

Ahraia shook her head, unwilling to voice such a hideous thought. She curled tighter, hiding herself, feeling guilty for being so weak, guilty for being so frightened. Guilty for even thinking of separating herself from Losna.

She lay with the ache of the binding pulsing at her mind. Losna didn't press her, and Ahraia let her mind drift into nothingness.

She slept again, a feverish sleep, and when she woke, the haunting fear remained. Her heart was tormented by what Losna wanted of her. To run. To flee. To leave Daispar and the darkness forever.

"It would mean I'd have to walk in the light," she said aloud, not sure if Losna would even care. She heard her shadow shift in the entrance, still blocking Ahraia's conveyance.

"We'd have no choice but to leave the Gelesh. We'd have to find a way to get the spritelings and Kyah, and convince them it's for the best." Her jaw clenched. The prospect was daunting. Getting the spritelings and Kyah would be difficult. And getting away from Daispar would be even harder. *Impossible.* They would have to run beyond the edges of where any of them had ever run, in to the unknown—into the light.

Losna turned in the tunnel, her muzzle pressed against Ahraia's back. Her warm tongue ran roughly against her neck, not forgiving, but comforting.

"And we would be hunted." Ahraia stared blankly at the wall

before her. The Astra would send wards. And what would she and Losna do if they were caught, or if the spritelings couldn't keep up? What would Losna do?

Ahraia lay paralyzed by fear, turning over every horror they would face: light, wards, lightwalkers, the edge of the forest, the end of the Endless Plains. At some point, her daze of worry must have turned once more to sleep, and when she awoke, she was alone.

The Dae-Mon had drifted and her shadow was gone. Panic rose in her heart, an emptiness that brought tears brimming to her eyes.

"Losna?"

A scratching sound penetrated from outside, then the dim thoughts of her shadow followed.

"There you are." Ahraia exhaled, relief easing the tightness in her chest. The clammy sweat on her brow was coarse with dust and dirt.

It's getting too bright. Losna dragged a great branch across the opening, scooting her hindquarters half way down the tunnel into the den. She looked over her shoulder in the tight quarters to make sure no light sifted past her. Then she fixed her golden eyes on Ahraia.

What were you thinking earlier? When you were thinking of the pack?

The den felt hot and close, and Ahraia had the urge to feel fresh air on her face.

"What time is it? Is it almost dusk?"

Losna's eyes shifted and an ear turned about, but otherwise she didn't move. She stubbornly ignored Ahraia, waiting for an answer to her question. Ahraia took a shuddering breath, feeling as though she were about to plunge into a frigid pool.

"Those wolves?" she started, "Are they your pack?"

Losna's eyes were fierce. *You are my pack.*

"You know what I mean. Are they your family?"

Yes.

Ahraia's words felt sour on her tongue and a great fear clutched her heart. She swallowed. "Do you miss them ever?"

Losna didn't answer at first. Ahraia wondered if it was a thought her shadow didn't understand, or worse, that she understood perfectly well. But Losna breathed out and settled her chin on her paws.

At times, she thought.

Ahraia's next words caught in her throat, not wanting to come out. "Would you go back to them?"

My place is with you. You are my shade.

"What if it meant living? What if something happened to me?"

Losna furrowed her brow, not bothering to answer.

Ahraia nodded understanding, glad that Losna felt that way. She raised an eyebrow. "What if I made you?"

Losna's throat rumbled challengingly. *You couldn't.*

Ahraia smiled, and turned back away from the light. But her eyes were open now. Her shadow's feelings had confirmed something that she had been wrestling with all morning, even in sleep. Killing the keress had taken another piece of herself—and Losna was right, more bindings would only make it worse.

Her shadow let out a huff, her own anxiety resting at the tip of her thoughts. Ahraia was terrified for what she was about to say. Her whole life had been pointed towards this moment, from the day she had bound Losna. She thought of her mother, of the words she had left Ahraia with even as she was condemned.

"Breaking the bond is what makes us sprites. If, when the time comes, you cannot live with that void . . . then it will be you walking across this bridge."

Ahraia let out a shuddering breath. And she knew in her heart the fate she was choosing. She had always known, like the first time she had ever stepped on the Endless Plains.

She couldn't become a sprite.

Her breath felt too shallow. The den felt like it was constricting. The realization was paralyzing. But it was the truth.

"I can't do it. I can't become a sprite. I can't go on with this test."

Relief like Ahraia had never known flowed across their link, and she sensed Losna turn towards her. Ahraia stared at the earthen wall in front of her, realizing her life would never be as she had imagined it. No darkening. No shade tree. No nit or spritelings. She would be forced to forge darkness on her own. And it wouldn't be easy: they would be outcasts. And she would have to look after Thelon, and Alua, and Kyah as well. She swallowed guiltily. She was making the choice for her siblings as well, one that they had no say in. It wasn't fair, but it was the only way. She couldn't go on destroying herself in order to become a sprite.

She exhaled, actually feeling relief pass through her. Admitting it lifted a weight that had been laying on her mind for half of her life, and for the first time in years, she realized the strain it had been.

She felt the brush of Losna's tongue across the back of her hair, roughly dragging across half of her head in her excitement.

"Stop that," Ahraia laughed, turning about. She wrestled her shadow off. Losna nipped and embraced her, easily overpowering her. Ahraia tried to cuff her ears, but Losna pinned her to the ground heavily, twisting her sideways into the dirt.

"You know I'd win if we weren't in this accursed den."

Losna was panting, a smile spread across her face. *This den is all that is keeping you alive. Where will we go? Plain Dark?*

"No, they'll expect us there. We'll have to go farther. Much farther."

Ahraia was thinking about Kyah and the spritelings. They wouldn't be able to run like Ahraia and Losna—and the Astra would likely set both sprites and dae-wards to hunt them.

Across the Endless Plains?

Ahraia doubted even the unhindered Dae-Mon would stop the Astra's wards, but she nodded.

"Maybe. I would ask if we could go to your pack, but they are creatures of the light . . ."

They will help us, Losna thought eagerly. *I will make them dig dens if they must.*

The thought seemed horrid, but it was better than going through with the test. She nodded, her mind made up.

"Tonight, we'll go back to Daispar. We'll find a way to get the spritelings and make a run for it."

~

"An impressive kill," the Masai said, gazing at the antlers of the mighty keress. They spread before her, thick as her arms, sharp as her drain, the blood still coating the burr where they had been cut from the beast's head. The Astra stood smugly to the side, her lips curled upward, apparently pleased with Ahraia's feat.

Ahraia stood blankly in front of them both, trying not to look at the gruesome reminders of her act. Her eyes saw but she was far away, wondering how soon she and Losna could reach the southern mountains and whether they might find shelter beneath them. It would be a difficult journey. And it wouldn't be easy persuading the spritelings to leave Daispar.

"A keress? I've never seen such a kill," the Astra said. She ran her hands from one tine to the next, a crazed gleam in her eyes, as though she already held the darkening seeds.

Night unfolded around them, but Ahraia's markings throbbed painfully, and though her decision to flee brought overwhelming relief, the rest of her day had not been pleasant. Late afternoon had brought the Dae-Mon streaming through the entrance of the burrow, scorching her directly where she had lain. It had been hot, and entirely too bright. She had curled up in the deepest corner of the den, using Hayvon's light-veil to cover her face. Losna had gathered loose branches to screen the entrance, until Ahraia had been forced to stop her for fear of suffocating.

The keress had still been standing when they had returned from the den, held rigid by its antlers, kept upright by the trees. An enormous pool of blood had drained down its beard to its hooves, and its eyes stared forward like black pits, haunting Ahraia. When the sprites had finally arrived, Losna's pack was long gone. The sprites had stood about in awe, whispering in disbelief and moving warily about the kill.

Now, Ahraia's scars showed under the moonlight like beacons of her tribulations. Her shoulder pulsed with every heartbeat, so tender that each breath sent shivers of pain through her entire side. A cut stung at her cheek, probably from a stray branch, and Losna's fur was stained with blood where she had been caught by an antler in the chaos of the fight.

"A truly impressive kill," the Astra said, echoing the Masai.

The bony nubs of the antlers were stained with blood. Ahraia could still smell that same blood on her hands, shuddering when she remembered the way the great beast had resigned itself to death. She hated the Astra for forcing her into this. She despised the Masai for her part as well. Ahraia couldn't bear to even find out what the second task entailed. If everything went as planned, she would never have to.

The Masai was watching her intently, and for a moment, Ahraia worried that she could sense her thoughts.

"It is a magnificent kill. And yet, it makes me wonder . . . In the quiet hours before dawn, there were many voices on the wind—the voices of wolves."

Ahraia's breath caught. She looked at the Masai with as little emotion as she could muster, trying to keep her mind blank. She kept her ears straight, hoping the strain didn't show.

"How did you enchant the beast?" the Masai asked. Her tone was unassuming, but Ahraia could sense the trap being set. Sure enough, the Masai flickered her ears for conveyance.

Ahraia set her mind upon the most appealing version of what had happened.

I bound it from its herd, at the edge of the plain, she conveyed truthfully, remembering her binding of the bull before it had charged. *Then I—*

The Masai cut through her thoughts, holding up a hand.

"On the plain? Walking unabashed under the moonlight?" She frowned, her eyes brushing over Ahraia's angry scars. The Astra glared at Ahraia. Light filtered through the forest was one thing, but admitting to walking openly beneath the Bright Moon was just short of proclaiming allegiance to the Dae-Mon. It wasn't condemnable, but it was close.

Ahraia shook her head, keenly aware that her markings betrayed the truth: They held the color of the Bright Moon, the stars, and the Dae-Mon.

I bound it from the safety of the woods. But the herd was on the plains.

"Then what?" the Masai pressed.

Losna scared the rest of the herd away from it. It was her howls you likely heard.

There were many more than one—there was a pack, the Masai conveyed loosely.

Ahraia kept her mind as blank as she could. The sprites about her tensed. The accusation was clear and dangerous. The Astra's ears stiffened, unfurling to their full length.

"What are you accusing her of?"

"Nothing, sister. I simply want the story," the Masai said evenly, holding idly at an antler of the keress. She turned to Ahraia, fixing her with a piercing stare. "Do you deny there were more voices than one?"

There were . . . Ahraia conveyed, her mind racing to twist the conveyance into truth. *But that was later, near dawn. They called in answer when Losna howled. It was a call of triumph and Losna's kind celebrated with us.*

The Masai turned to Losna as though she could hear the thoughts running through her mind.

Meat, Losna thought, sniffing towards the keress.

"I see," the Masai said at last. "I wonder then, how did you enchant the keress as you did? How did you trap it here?"

The Astra and her father watched on intently. *I lulled it into the forest, and when I found this place, I enchanted it to be angry at me,* Ahraia answered, searching for the half-truths of the binding. It certainly wasn't what the Masai had intended.

"There is a path of ruin stretching all the way back to the plains. And this was the place you chose? Was it still enchanted when you killed it?" the Masai asked. The other sprites listened intently, ears twitching, arms folded across. The Masai's eyes narrowed. "Was it ever enchanted?"

Of course it was, Ahraia conveyed, trying to muster all her truth into thought. She had been comforting it when she killed it, and that was far worse than just holding it still.

The Masai shook her head. She frowned and looked to the Astra.

"This isn't how the test was supposed to go,"

The sprites butchering the great beast stopped and listened, ears turning and twisting towards the group. The Astra nodded towards the antlers.

"I think no shade as ever come close to killing something like this. No sprite has, either. I think she's marked by the Masah, for all to see." She nodded towards the Bright Moon. *I doubt even you or I could have managed this as shades.*

I agree, Ahraia's father conveyed quickly.

A muscle in the Masai's cheek twitched. "I'll tell you what I think," she said, staring right at Ahraia, her eyes nearly golden. "I think she's lying."

Ahraia's ears twitched. Losna tensed next to her, ready to leap to her aid.

"Lying? What do you think happened?" the Astra asked, her brow furrowing sharply. "You can't tell me she managed to kill a keress with a drain and think she didn't enchant it."

The Masai's face was rigid. "I can," she said, her voice deadly quiet. "I think Losna's pack helped corral the keress, driving it into the tree. I think it was their doing, not Ahraia's."

Ahraia's breath caught in her throat. She looked from the Astra to the Masai.

Is she condemning us? Losna thought, growling low.

To the Shad-Mon, a sprite conveyed across the group. Every hair on Ahraia's body stood on end. She was vaguely aware of the burning sets of eyes all about her. A welling excitement was growing among the sprites.

"That is absurd," the Astra said, snapping the tension like a howl would split the night. "How could she manipulate a whole pack of wolves?"

"And if she *did*, wouldn't that be an even greater feat," her father said. "The enchantment of an entire pack of wolves?"

The Masai turned to them, her ears stiff and aggressive.

"Beran is right," the Astra said, her ears flickering belatedly for him to speak aloud. "If she didn't manage to kill it by enchantment, how did she guide and direct an entire pack of wolves?"

"Indeed," the Masai said.

"It would be a powerful enchantment. More powerful than any binding enchantment of a keress."

"Is that what happened, Shade Ahraia?" her father asked quickly.

Ahraia remembered all too well what the truth could bear; she recalled what the Astra had done to Tev and knew that the Masai would do the same to her, if not worse. But perhaps if she conceded a small part of that truth, the Masai would find her story more believable. She nodded.

I did enchant the keress . . . but I also bound the wolves, she admitted. The conveyance carried true.

The Masai shook her head and seemed to resign her opposition. Her ears dropped slightly and the tension passed. Her demeanor shifted, her ears turned back just a hair. In disappointment? In defeat? Ahraia couldn't tell. She spoke before Ahraia could discern her thoughts.

"What you did was foolish. Whether you did it by misjudgment or misfortune, you should have failed. And you *should* be given to the Shad-Mon for such absurd exploits." She paused and Ahraia held her breath, her spine tingling at the implied edge they were poised upon. The Masai went on. "In a way, however, I *am* more impressed than if you would have done as you were asked."

The Astra's smug look returned and her father let out a visible sigh.

A few of the sprites fidgeted in disappointment. Ahraia shifted nervously, wondering what punishment was still to come.

"As it is, you've succeeded. You killed a keress by enchantment. You have passed your first task, but only just."

Ahraia let out sigh. It was as though a great tightness had burst around her chest and she could suddenly breathe. She smiled, but the Masai did not return the look.

Well done, Ahraia, the Astra conveyed, but the Masai held up a hand.

"Your second task, however, will not be so easy."

The Astra's eyes narrowed. Ahraia let out an easy breath. She didn't care what the Masai had to say about her second task. It didn't matter. She and Losna would be under the shadow of the mountains by the time the Bright Moon was full again. The Masai's sprites could chase her under the bright fire if they wished, but she would never know the depravities of her second task.

But the Masai hadn't finished. Her sprites moved closer to Losna. Ahraia hesitated, wondering what was happening.

"Tonight, I am returning for Angolor," the Masai said. The Astra and her father looked up, obviously surprised. The Masai stared dangerously at Ahraia.

"And your shadow is coming with me."

18

SEPARATION

Ahraia felt as though a spring branch had suddenly splintered in her hands—plunging her downward with no ground beneath her—plummeting her towards a fate she had never imagined and one she couldn't accept. She grabbed Losna defensively.

"You can't take my shadow!" she said, her hands wrapping tightly in Losna's fur.

"This is her shadow test," the Astra said. "You can't do that—" The Astra faltered as the Masai's ears turned back dangerously.

"I don't care if this is her shadow test. I'm the Masai, am I not?" Her eyes glinted dangerously, ears tucking back even lower. "*Unless you wish to challenge that.*"

Sprites recoiled, and the Astra grimaced at the implication. It was an invitation for a Posturant.

The Astra, however, lowered her eyes and ears in a bow of deference.

The Masai's voice reverberated with finality. "Her shadow is coming with me."

What does she mean? Losna thought, her ears twitching about and her body suddenly stiff.

Why? Ahraia conveyed desperately. "Kren didn't lose her shadow," she said, unable to keep her voice in. It was true; Kren had stalked gloomily through Daispar for three full turnings before her final test, followed every night by Flit, swooping behind her like some brooding cloud, right until the end.

"Your sister likely followed instructions," the Masai said. "And Kren was not in position to be the next Masai."

I followed instructions, Ahraia conveyed. *I passed, didn't I?* The Astra and her father were signaling silently for her to stand down.

"You may have passed your test but not in the manner it was meant to be," the Masai answered.

She enchanted an entire pack of wolves, her father conveyed, his tone careful and measured.

Ahraia looked on helplessly. Losna couldn't be taken from her, not now, not when they were going to flee. She looked about for someone to help her, but the Astra was silent, and her father's face was just as helpless. Losna's eyes were wide with fear, begging Ahraia to do something.

"Did she?" the Masai asked. "Did you enchant the pack? Or did your shadow?"

Ahraia opened her mouth to speak, but no words came out.

"If you mean to become a sprite, Ahraia, then you'll pass your second test without your shadow."

Ahraia bit down on her desire to reject the test then and there. "You can't take her from me," she pleaded.

"One more word aloud and you're both dead!" the Masai said. Her ears flickered three times. "Not only can I, but your shadish insistence forces me to. This isn't some game, Ahraia. This is life and death." A shared bonding took shape, and the Masai's threats flashed before her eyes: Losna dead, the Shadow Woods, a ghastly monster with a bloody mouth.

Ahraia dropped her gaze to the ground, knowing that she had crossed the line.

What's happening? Losna asked. *I'm not going with her.* She whined loudly, drawing the ire of the sprites around them.

The Masai's eyes narrowed. They were true golden now.

"I am leaving for Angolor tonight. Your second task begins when the Bright Moon is new, and must be complete by the time the Bright Moon and Blood Moon are full together. If you wish to see your shadow again, then you will arrive in Angolor before that turning is complete. And your second task better be finished as intended."

The Masai glowered at them, and with a wave of her hand, she dismissed Ahraia and the other sprites. Losna stood with her tail between her legs and her ears down, twitching all about. Her eyes shifted nervously.

What's happening? she asked again. *You can't do your second task without me. Ahraia, don't let them do this.*

One of the Masai's sprites stepped towards Losna, producing a thorn-covered rope. He fixed it in a hasty loop.

Losna bared her teeth and raised her hackles. The Masai turned towards Ahraia.

"Tell your shadow to cooperate or she'll be shown the light."

Ahraia's face flushed, suddenly wanting to attack the Masai. She barely stilled the urge. Every sprite watched on.

The Masai stared at her. *Do it. Now.*

An icy enchantment billowed over her, a second warning of what awaited if she didn't cooperate. She saw haunting details: the bridging tree springing back, leaving her on the far bank, the roar of the Shad-Mon, hauntingly close, Losna's eyes staring forward, dead. Ahraia's resistance folded.

"Losna. Let them," she heard herself say with wretched guilt. *I'll come for you,* she conveyed, crumbling under the Masai's threats. Losna whimpered as the sprite tied the rope around her neck.

Where are they taking me? she thought, with the same desperation flooding her mind as was in Ahraia's. The sprite tugged at her leash and wrenched it tight around her neck. Losna resisted, trying to keep her eyes on Ahraia. The sprite pulled harder on the rope, jerking Losna after him.

"It's okay, Losna," Ahraia said. *I'll come for you. I'll find you.* An ache hollowed out her chest, stripping out her insides and numbing her lungs until she thought she would never breathe again. "Go with them." *I'll be there soon.*

Losna let out a deep woof. *No!* She jerked against her leash but it only earned her a sharp tug and a handful of insults. Ahraia flinched as Losna was cuffed over her head and pulled through the woods, whining.

Don't let them do this. Please. Don't let them take me. You can't let this happen, Ahraia. The second task—don't make a binding. You can't make a binding—

The sprite jerked Losna hard, causing her to yelp. The barbs of the rope pinched into her neck, and the more she struggled, the sharper they gouged her.

Losna's barks soon turned to howls that ripped at Ahraia's heart. They were slow to fade, and even when they eventually did, Ahraia still felt them pulling at her.

And with that, she was shadowless.

~

AHRAIA'S WRIST was still drenched in the sallow blood of the keress. It had run and dried right to her elbow, red and sticky—a mark of her feat.

A mark of becoming a sprite.

Her other wrist was etched with light-scars, startling bright, to the point of permanence. She looked at them both, leaning over a quiet creek she was standing next to. The water stilled, showing her unsettled face. Her tears had smeared with blood on her cheek, mixing with the light streaks and markings, giving her a wild and frightening look.

Blood and light.

She turned her hands, taking a shuddering breath.

To flee or fight?

She lowered her arm to the water, rubbing and scraping the blood from herself. It spread in the eddy, circling with the slow currents and defiling the cool stream. It stuck to her, holding on as a reminder, clinging to the space beneath her nails, filling her nose with the lingering odor of death.

She pulled her tarry-vine from her hair and dipped her head. The biting water shocked her, flushing all the way to her fingers and toes. She scrubbed her neck and pulled out, breathing sharply. She was free of the blood.

But not the light-scars; she didn't try to wash those away. They were hers. Earned and true. And they would be brighter again.

Soon enough, they'll show like beacons, she promised herself.

Ahraia stood up, looking down at her reflection: silver-white hair and yellow-bright eyes, just like Losna.

I'll come for you, she promised to the night, turning back towards Daispar. She could still feel the faded echoes of Losna's howls tugging at her heart, and though she was surrounded by sprites, she was alone.

The hollow in her chest deepened when she stepped into the darkening. It was the first time in years she had returned without Losna. Her heart felt like it was tearing from her chest. The rest of the sprites were celebrating her kill, making a feast of the keress. Ahraia retreated to her nit, feeling a void so deep that it threatened to suffocate her. She sat in the pitch black, too sick to even move and wishing beyond reason that they had run when Losna had first wanted to.

The nit was empty. Hayvon, Altah, and Kaval were dead. Kren had become a sprite. Kyah and the spritelings had been taken by the Astra. And now Losna had been taken from Ahraia. The tree felt like a cage—a bare and bitter cage.

She missed the steady presence of her brothers: the shuffle and shift of fox paws and owl wings, the air thick with conveyance and fiendish laughter. She missed Kaval's trickery, and Altah's screeching laugh. She missed Hayvon lumbering about, so impossibly different from Vesta. She missed Kren, remembering bitterly when her sister had been herself, ordering them about, counting off who was meant to do what—arguing with them all as they negotiated for the easiest and laziest tasks.

Most of all, Ahraia ached for the comforting presence of Losna.

She missed everything about her shadow: her quiet padding feet and constantly rumbling belly; her ears perking up with any mention of food; her long, silly tail streaming behind her as she chased Ahraia farther and farther onto the plains. But more than anything, Ahraia missed the touch of her mind: that steadying presence that guided and protected Ahraia, that part of her which was not her, and yet, was the best of her.

The shade tree made the pit in her stomach tighten even further, sour bile spreading into the corners of her mouth. The ground where Losna usually slept was worn into a painful reminder of what had been taken from her. Sleep wouldn't come, so instead, she sat in the endless dark, hugging her knees and wondering how she was going to get her shadow back.

Day came and passed in a fog, and when night fell again, she still didn't bother getting up. It would still be a half a turning before she could go after Losna.

Eventually, she did fall asleep but her dreams were worse than her waking thoughts. An endless howling drifted across a plain that she couldn't cross. She saw the Dae-Mon rising over her, and it had the eyes of the great Shad-Mon. She dreamed of death and daemons and awoke to helpless separation and paralyzing loneliness. She lay in a mindless stupor.

Ahraia? Are you in there?

At first, she thought she had imagined the thought.

"I know you can hear me."

It took her a moment to realize that she hadn't been dreaming, and that the voice was her father's. He stood just outside of her shade tree.

She didn't answer. She hadn't spoken to him alone in half a turning: not since before seeing Shim in the chasms, not since she had discovered the truth in her suspicions. His role in her current plight blinded her of any coherent thought or reason. She wanted to cast light upon him for laying the roots of this evil; she wanted to watch him writhe beneath the Dae-Mon. His voice was entirely too fatherly.

"You need to come out. Your second task is approaching and there are things that you must do in the meantime. You're going to have to make the journey to Angolor and you need to be ready."

Ahraia heard him step forward. She made a quick binding of her shade tree, flexing it rigidly to make sure that it wouldn't move. She heard him push against the branches, and saw the boughs rustle, but no opening formed.

Go away.

"Ahraia." His reproval bled from his voice. She felt his mind trying to pry open the branches, but she stubbornly held them closed.

"I said, *go away.*" She mustered every ounce of anger and hatred as she spoke, hoping that he would know the pain that she had suffered. He wouldn't, of course. He didn't have the capacity to feel.

"The Astra has called for you."

"Wonderful."

"She's still your Astra," he said with a note of impatience. "If you don't come out right now—"

"You're going to what? Going to give me to the Shad-Mon?" Ahraia kept her mind focused on keeping the closure tight. "Your threats can't touch me anymore."

"What about Kyah and the spritelings?" he said, holding the Astra's promise in his mind, holding their lives in his thoughts.

Before she knew what she was doing, Ahraia leapt up, the closure bursting open before her. Her drain was in her hand, and she formed a stifling enchantment of her father, catching him off guard and holding him paralyzed. In an instant, she had the drain pressed to his throat, his blood pulsing right beneath the point of her blade. She shook, hardly able to contain her anger.

"I should end you right here," she whispered with teeth bared. "And believe me, I would love to. What would your Astra do? What *could* she do? Nothing. She needs me more than anyone. Without me, there are no seeds—no new darkenings—her plans go bursting into the light. But without you . . . none of this happens."

Her father took a deep breath. He struggled against her enchantment but she held him all the firmer. Her heart hammered in her chest. She felt his hammering in unison through the bond, but a smile spread across his face.

"Maybe you will become a sprite after all . . ."

Ahraia stared at him, every muscle in her cheek clenched, quivering. She wanted so desperately to push the blade into his neck—for her brothers' and mother's sake, for her own sake, but most of all for her siblings' sake. It was one thing for the Astra, wraith that she was, to threaten Ahraia and the nit, but it was something far worse for him to make those threats.

Ahraia lowered the blade.

"Get out of my sight."

Her knuckles were white from squeezing the drain's handle. Her father stepped back, holding her eye. After a long moment's gaze, he turned, and walked from the nit without another word.

"I don't want to be a sprite," she said, casting the drain down.

She stepped back into the shade tree and sat. The silence bore down on her with the weight of the entire darkening, as though the darkness itself was her tomb. She lay down and felt something press against her hip. She pulled the broken orb from her pocket, feeling the creases that were drying shut. She needed to protect the spritelings once she was gone. And she needed her shadow back.

You can't have both, a voice inside her said.

She rolled over, her shoulder hanging uncomfortably over the hollow where Losna would have normally been curled. Maybe Kren would come around. Maybe she would be persuaded to look after the spritelings once Ahraia left the darkening.

She lay in the bitter dark, a plan slowly taking form in her head.

Ahraia awoke with hunger gnawing at her stomach and the absence of Losna gnawing at her mind. She rolled over and groaned with dread. She couldn't make the ache of missing Losna go away, but the turning of her stomach was sharp. It had been three full days since she had eaten anything of consequence. She sat up and pulled aside the branches of her shade tree. It was the late afternoon beyond the darkening and rain rattled off the shell above.

The putrid odor of the keress meat infected the air, bringing bile to the back of Ahraia's throat and the memory of the kill to her mind. She plugged her nose and bent double, trying not to be sick. For a moment, her hunger dissipated. She pulled her cloak close and headed out into the darkening past the central hollow and the cook fires, past the chasms and the cores, instead looking for and eventually finding a small nit tree tucked away towards the far edges of the darkening. It was no larger than a shade tree, nascent, with lustrous gray leaves speckled in silver. Ahraia approached cautiously, reaching out with her mind rather than her voice.

Kren?

There was no answer. Ahraia gathered her will about her, keeping her emotion from tarnishing her conveyance.

I need to talk to you about the spritelings . . . I need to know you'll look after them if I can't . . . if I don't become a sprite. Ahraia waited. She probed out, searching for the brush of Kren's mind. The nit felt empty. Ahraia bound the tree, forcing it to form a closure. The inside was barren.

"What are you doing up?" a voice said from nearby. Ahraia turned, and found herself facing Leran, one of the nitesses.

I'm looking for Kren, Ahraia conveyed.

The nitesse eyed her reproachfully, her gaze lingering on the ward-like markings at Ahraia's wrists. "She's gone with the Masai. The Astra uprooted her after all. Now get back to your shade tree, you shouldn't be out at this hour."

Ahraia frowned, unable to hide her disappointment. Kren had been the spritelings' last hope for guidance. Her ears batted downward, upset even further to think that her sister had been willing to go, wanting to be uprooted—never once considering their nit. Fuming, Ahraia stalked back to her shade tree under the leering eye of the nitesse. She slumped down, still starving, and waited for night.

The moment dusk settled, she headed for the darkening wall.

The branches she had previously softened rustled at her mind's touch, ready to move to her will.

Open, she commanded, in no mood to be disobeyed. The branches burst before her and she slipped out into the night. The rest of the wall quivered, sending boughs and shoots down to grab her but she flitted out of reach. The darkening shook in disapproval but she didn't stop—tonight was a scavenging night.

She found a suckle pine and climbed to the top, using springs and shifts to get her to the ripe cones. She sat in the high branches and messily drank the sap of as many cones as she could reach. It was still dusk, but the evening was so gloomy that she hardly noticed the blazing colors of the Dae-Mon behind a layer of clouds in the west. The mountains to the south were just visible over the forest, marking the lands towards Angolor, where Losna would be. The thought made her heart ache.

The suckle sap was too sweet for true sustenance, but it quelled the grumbling in her stomach, at least. She swung back down to the forest floor, wondering if the wall had alerted the Astra. As soon as it did, wards would be sent out after her.

Try and catch me, she thought grimly. She would run them ragged —run them right into the light if she was forced to.

She moved quickly as the forest grew darker, still wet from the fresh rain. No matter what the second test entailed, she needed to find a bowstring if she was going to pass and she knew just the place. The wind rose, sending leaves spinning all about her with spurts of scattered drips. Without Losna's company, the woods seemed entirely different. They felt alive—and dangerous. Watchful eyes chased her, some even preying after her, stalking behind the dark layers of the forest.

The clouds broke and the stars emerged as she ran, her shoulder aching and her stomach twisting tighter than ever. Slivers of the Dark Moon and Blood Moon watched her on the western horizon. She drank from a deep pool, her hands slick upon the wet rocks, the icy water sending shivers inside and out. She ate a pair of yellow-stem mushrooms, careful to pick away the poisoned frills. She painstakingly gathered and ate several handfuls of small midnight berries, mixed among a bloom of charberries whose ashen fruits were worth an empty stomach and a drink from the Daemon's Creek. When nothing else made itself available, she chewed on bitterroot, gnawing at it just as Losna's absence gnawed at her mind.

When she finally reached the meadow of the Stone Tree, the Bright Moon was climbing in the eastern sky, rising over the treetops as the clouds drifted overhead. The Dark Moon had disappeared, and the Blood Moon chased it over the horizon. The meadow was laid bare in pale light—empty and cold and quiet, with only a gentle brush of wind across it.

No menace remained.

Ahraia didn't bother with her hood as she picked her way towards the remains of the wagons, hoping the fire hadn't consumed what she sought. A single twisted piece of metal and a few ashen timbers were all that revealed where two of the wagons had stood, and the wheels and the white covering of the lone unburned wagon were missing, leaving it sitting like a skeletal duck on a wind-rippled pond.

Ahraia approached and eyed the Stone Tree warily, wishing for the comforting warnings of Losna.

Please be here, she thought, clambering up the ribs of the wagon. Her nose stung with must and mirk of things neglected. She covered her face and peeked inside.

Dae-Mon above, she cursed, staring down.

Her bowstring was missing.

She swung her leg into the deserted belly. The place she had seen the dead child was bare, but the stain of dark blood lingered in the wood. Ahraia rustled about amongst the wagon's contents. She pushed a heavy sack out of her way and grains slumped out with a hiss, wet with rot. She sniffed at another sack and wrinkled her nose. It smelled of sheep and damp.

"Where is it?" she muttered, standing straight. At the front of the wagon, she noticed a perfectly flat wooden slat that stretched across the front of the wagon. An odd, straight crease of darkness lay just beneath it. Slipping past the upturned sacks, she ran her fingers over the polished board. She tried to lift it and was surprised to feel the heavy-looking wood shift, creaking as it did. She inched it upward, trying to peek beneath it. Suddenly, it slipped and slammed back heavily.

Crack!

The loud smack of wood against wood filled the meadow like a tree breaking.

Light and fire, Ahraia cursed, ducking down. She looked nervously about; nothing moved except the rustling grasses. The night seemed all the quieter.

With her heart still racing, she lifted it again, seeing that the wood was fixed by strange metal roots that somehow kept it from falling away. More human magic, but the insides were just filled with human nonsense.

"Where is it?" she said in frustration, having half a mind to drop the wood again. It whined as she lowered it carefully. She let out a loud sigh and looked about. Something seemed off about the wagon. Something was missing—besides her bowstring, of course.

"Where are the dead?" she murmured, leaping down from the wagon.

Something had moved the bodies. Sprites would never touch a dead human; it was terrible luck. She wondered if more humans had passed through the meadow since the massacre and burned their dead. She looked about for a pyre, shuddering at the thought of being consumed by light and fire. Or perhaps the alps had meddled with them? Ahraia thought of the flaxen haired alp who the Astra had colluded with—Ahraia was sure she would have no qualms dealing with the dead.

Ahraia moved to the other wagons, already knowing that she wouldn't find her bowstring. *Charred wood and bare ash.* She looked up to the night sky, where Seti, the great bowman seemed to taunt her from his perch in the south. She didn't have time to grow a string . . .

She lowered her head and sighed. Her eyes settled on several strange mounds of dirt near the first wagon. They were almost like spritish graves, covered by the everdark of the earth, hidden from the Dae-Mon.

They can't be . . .

She wondered if her father had buried Kaval and Altah right out in the open. But there were too many . . .

With a flutter of hope, she realized that they *were* graves. The mounds rose from freshly turned dirt, all aligned in a neat, unnatural row. Did the humans bury their dead as well? It was a strange thought, lightwalkers laying hidden from the Dae-Mon for eternity. But they were strange people . . .

At the foot of one mound, she noticed a small sack and hurried towards it. As she approached, she could see that it had been opened, probably by some day-walking creature, but its contents remained.

The sack was leather, smooth and worn. She opened it and reached inside, pulling out the first thing she touched. It was an unnatural object, obviously some kind of human tool, made by magic. It had a wooden handle and was flat, about the size of her hand, with dozens of narrow metal tines, all in a tight line. They weren't sharp, but they seemed odd and wondrous. Ahraia ran it over her palm and delighted in the tingling scratch across her palm, her heart aching to imagine how Losna would love to feel it scratching behind her ears, something to comb through her fur.

Ahraia set the metal comb carefully to the side.

Next she picked up a small, round wooden piece. It was smooth as the smoothest water-worn stone. She turned it over—

"Aghh!" She panicked, reflexively throwing the piece to the grasses and scrambling away.

She had seen the eyes of a dae-ward in the object, yellow-bright and light-seared. She snapped her head about, turning one way and then the other, her drain clutched in her hand. She was breathing hard, still twisting in search of the ward. But the meadow was empty. She was alone. Her heart felt like it was going to burst.

She crept back cautiously. The wooden side of the object faced upward. She reached out with her drain and flicked it onto its back.

She looked down on it in amazement as it reflected the stars in the sky, like a solid, perfectly dark pool just as wide as her hand.

She leaned over it and saw herself in a flawless reflection, clearer than any pool of water, even on the stillest nights at the darkest ponds of the Endless Plains. Her skin was as scarred as it had ever been. Her hair looked darker, gray and silver, like the color of starlight and fog mixed. She leaned closer, staring at her eyes. They were brilliant yellow, like the radiant sky before a lightrise.

She stared a moment longer, marveling at the magic of the humans. It was a perfect mirror.

A looking mirror, she thought. A deep ache swelled in her chest, wishing she could share it with Losna. Losna loved her reflection; she stomped and ran about wildly whenever she saw herself. Ahraia let out a heavy sigh and pocketed the mirror and the comb in her cloak.

The other mounds were mostly barren, but the last had another small leather satchel upon it. She moved closer to it, careful not to step on the graves. She squatted down and flicked it open.

Her chest loosened in relief.

"There you are . . ." she said as she reached into the bag. She grabbed hold of the human figurine that the boy had held in his dead hand. She pulled it into the night and held it up.

It dangled from her hands with four perfect lengths of string.

Just the right length.

She checked the tension, wondering how humans came about such string; it didn't look grown, but it was strong and tightly woven, and already oiled, it seemed.

"I'll just take one," she whispered as she trimmed the string with her knife.

She smiled, for the first time in days. Then she lay the figurine back in the satchel and put it back where she had found it.

With her bowstring in hand, she headed away from the Stone Tree.

~

AHRAIA RAN for an underdae at the fringes of the Gelesh. She couldn't bring herself to stay in the Stone Tree, and Plain Dark would be the first place the Astra would expect her to go. Instead, she headed for a cave that few sprites or shades ever used.

Along the way, she found a squirrel hidden in a small hollow of a tree. It didn't feel right making a bond with any creature other than Losna, but she coaxed it out of its hole.

I need food, she thought, lowering herself to the most basic emotion of hunger. Luckily, it wasn't hard as her stomach was a tight knot. The squirrel understood.

It scrambled down its tree and led her to a patch of ground where it started digging. The moment she saw the first husk of a hazelnut, she let go of her bonding and brushed the squirrel aside. It chittered away angrily as she dug the nuts from their hiding. Fingers muddy and clinging to a handful of her treasure, she plopped down on the still-wet ground and used her drain to work the soft tops from the nuts, popping the bitter insides guiltily into her mouth.

"Sorry," she said when she had finished. The squirrel fussed his whiskers and glowered at her.

Feeling both better and worse, she continued on. She kept her eyes out as she ran, looking for a young yew or ash to make her bow. Eventually, she came across a grove of dorn trees.

Sturdy enough, she thought as she pushed against a thin trunk, avoiding the sharp thorns. She stooped to the ground and sawed at it with the drain. The knife was meant for letting blood, not trimming trees, and the night was turning towards dawn.

Come on . . . Her knuckles scraped against the ground and the lowest thorn. Eventually, she cut through it, sloppy in her eagerness to break it loose. It toppled over her when she least expected, the thorns scratching painfully over her arms and neck.

"Getoffame!"

She pushed it aside, standing and brushing the dirt away. She quickly stripped the remaining branches, then she cut the top half away, leaving what she didn't need.

She jogged towards her underdae, dragging the staff along after her. She slipped into the cavern just as the first gray hues of dawn gave way to yellow in the east.

Ahraia slipped to the back of the narrow cave and through a small fissure into a hidden inner chamber. She settled down in the perfect dark, remembering a time that she and Hayvon had hunted with Altah here. Between the three of them and their shadows, the cave had seemed cramped and overcrowded; she had hated the way Altah's shadow cawed out, grating at the dark and alerting the whole woods to their presence. Now, the cavern felt empty and overlarge. She put her back to one of the walls, thinking darkly of the company she missed.

It's the Astra's fault.

She rested the dorn stave across her knees and began to strip the bark away, working around the thorns.

And father's.

The bark was ashen, just like her skin, flecked with gray-speckled markings and scars.

And the Masai.

The shavings piled up at her feet.

I'll get my shadow back. And when I do, none of them will get what they want.

Outside, the Dae-Mon started to cast its light over the world, and the narrow fissure glowed with deadly light.

She set to her task in a haze of determination. For the first time in days, she let her mind focus on something other than her shadow test. She whittled at the wood, stripping it of its outer husk, leaving the thorns except at the handle. She worked towards the ends, taking down the back of the bow first before fine-tuning the belly. The day was full bright outside, and she stood occasionally to check the bend and the balance of the bow. Slowly, the bow emerged from the wood. Her hands were tired and worn and her eyes burned, but Ahraia kept working through the afternoon. She made nocks on either end and smoothed the handles. Eventually, it was ready to be strung. She looped the string into two careful knots, measuring it over and again to make sure the length was right. She nocked the first end and then stood, stepping over the bow, putting her weight into the shaft to draw the string to the second nock.

She drew the bow. *Too stiff.* She unstrung it and stripped away more wood, until it felt just right. The light was changing in the entry, going from the steady bright to a golden veil. She lay down in the lonely dark of the cavern and slept.

19

WANING

The nights of the Bright Moon's waning were the longest Ahraia had ever known. The Blood Moon and Dark Moon set early, and the Bright Moon rose late, leaving only the stars for company. As expected, the Astra sent out nit- and dae-wards for her, but Ahraia had underdaes they had never seen before—the forest about Daispar was laced with her creations. At night, she avoided the Astra's scouts easily; they almost never searched the trees with their eyes and only scratched at finding her with their minds. Like the golden-haired alp that had avoided being discovered at the Stone Tree, Ahraia cultivated an emptiness in thought to avoid being found, and she formed an airtight barrier to keep any errant bindings from taking her. Even a few nitesses passed by without the barest hint that she was there.

Fools, she thought.

When she wasn't evading capture, she spent her nights gathering what she could to eat. Hunting with a bow was easy enough, but she had no means of making or keeping fire. So instead she foraged, gathering berries and roots and other bits the forest provided. She guiltily stole more nuts, but only from the fattest squirrels. She searched out sweet pines, suckle pines, and midnight berries. She dug for tubers with grimy, light-scarred fingers.

She folded darkness as well. She returned to Plain Dark, fortifying its weave until it was darker than it had ever been: a good starting place for Kyah and the spritelings if they needed a place to run. She journeyed deeper onto the plains to another island of trees, and formed a shelter there too, just in case.

But most of all, she worked on her bindings. Not to kill—Losna didn't want that and neither did she—but to control. To move without conscience. To command and dominate.

For as long as she remembered, Ahraia was the strongest shade in her nit—likely in the whole darkening. She was stronger by far than her brothers, stronger even than Kren. Losna was her evidence—no one else's shadow was half as powerful—not the imps or owls, bobcats or foxes. And no one else ran without fear, out beneath the moons and stars, as far as they wished. No one else was as adept with the forest: folding darkness with the grace and ease of a nitesse, forming springs and lifts that no one else would dare. But if she was going to get Losna back, she needed mastery of her enchantments.

Her blundering inability of late had been her ruin: the human she let slip away had cost Hayvon his life and her nit their orb, her weakness with the keress nearly ended with her trampled and Losna skewered. The alp at the Stone Tree, her father and Hayvon, Gavea . . . they had all overpowered her when it mattered most. She had let her perception of her bindings surpass the reality of her strength: sprites were stronger than her, and alps too. Her bow would help her pass her second task, but she needed to be able to save herself when an arrow wouldn't.

And so, she formed bindings with everything she could: she bound the forest, moved by springs and shifts, faster and higher than she ever had before. Branches broke and trunks bent; she fell more times than she could fathom—and she had fallen fathoms as well—but with each night, she moved more easily. Holds came naturally, choosing branches instinctively. She bound everything: saplings for give, old trees for strength, hemlock and maple for soft landings, fir and cedar for height, long limbs for swings, short limbs for climbs, vines for hanging, trunks for casting, leaves for cover.

And she bound animals as well. She enchanted squirrels and raccoons, bullying them for their food—she considered sharing afterwards, but only if they could behave. She bound deer and otters, delighting in how she could make them prance and swim; she ensnared a pair of fiendish foxes, following them halfway down the Narrow Canyon before she sensed the Jontun that lived there and turned back. She even bound a forest bear, as large as the keress—it was lumbering and uncaring about the enchantment; she could have made it dance in a meadow around a human fire and it wouldn't have noticed. She bound an imp, though she let it go because it was damned, through and through. She even tried to bind a mara, but instead, found only thin air and her mind filled with bitter and sour faults. She hardly slept that night, dreaming of enchantment killings and Losna dead at her feet, with her snout bloodied and a drain sticking from her neck. When Ahraia looked closer, it was her own drain. She tried to awake, sensing but unable to see the mara sitting on her chest. It took a full night and another day to shake the memory, and after that, she stuck to more corporeal bindings.

She bound wards. Warily at first, only to keep herself safe, but more daringly as the nights went on. She haunted one, walking just behind him from the North Vales all the way back to the Daemon's Creek. She forced another to dip his veil in a stream before donning it. The icy water caused his mind to buck against her hold, but Ahraia held him until he calmed, and then forced him to wade into the middle of the creek. She let her binding go once he was waist deep, unable to contain her laughter at the wild and preposterous thoughts of the ward. He cursed in ways that made her blush, and she blundered away as carelessly as the bear, leaving the ward splashing franticly to get out.

Ahraia moved everything she could, right to the edge of night and to the precipice of her test. She was exhausted, but her mind felt pliable and strong, with bindings forming almost without thinking. She guessed she could even make a kill now, though she didn't plan on it. The mere possibility brought a spate of imagined warnings and threats from Losna, each one more absurd than the next. Her heart ached with the thoughts.

On the eve of her test, she slipped across the plains into Plain Dark just before the lightrise. She had already carefully hidden her bow and arrows well away from the darkening, and she had left the few tokens she had taken from the humans along with them, the mirror and the comb for Losna, as well as enough of her foraged food to last the journey to Angolor.

She slept briefly but awoke around midday. Just as she hoped, birds sang beyond the underdae, filling the warm, windless air with their strange daytime songs. She listened for a time, marveling at their shrill voices. Eventually, she bound the one with the clearest voice and coaxed it into the underdae. It was a tiny thing, a sparrow, but it was boisterous and proud.

I need your help, she conveyed, letting it sense her raw emotions.

It bobbed its head, hopping closer.

I need you to pass a message for me. Can you do that?

It chirped and zipped closer, landing on her hand.

She spent the rest of the day awakening it to the most basic conveyances. It was so used to singing that conveyance wasn't difficult, just different, like a song it hadn't yet sung. Ahraia gave it the message piece by piece, ingraining each part deeper into the sparrow with each repetition. When she finished, the Dae-Mon was getting low in the west.

Okay. Let's go over it one more time.

She held the sparrow on her hand.

When you see Kyah . . . Ahraia forced herself to imagine her sister's face in every detail: from the way she let her hair fall across a small light-scar on her cheek to the way her left ear curled back slightly more than the other.

You let her hold you, like this. You let her bind you, like I am now. She let the sparrow feel itself on Kyah's palm, seeing itself waiting calmly.

Once she binds you, you tell her that if she hears that I didn't pass my test, she has to take the spritelings and run. This part was more difficult, as Kyah would have to draw out most of the meaning from the little bird's limited, albeit proud, conveyance. Ahraia imagined a runner from Angolor meeting the Astra. She felt her heart beating faster, imagining Losna dead and herself walking the bridging tree across the river to the Shadow Woods. It was all too easy to imagine.

They have to leave the darkening and never return. They have to find safety far away from here. Ahraia imagined the spritelings, imagined Kyah taking them and fleeing to Plain Dark. Fleeing while being chased. *If she doesn't, the Astra will kill her and the others.* Tears welled at the corner of Ahraia's eyes as she pictured the Astra coming into the nit. She imagined Kyah's shadow dead, then the bodies of the spritelings. A bitter, fearful part of Ahraia worried that it would come to pass no matter what. She wondered if the mara was still following her.

Night had settled about them when she finished. It was a complex bit of enchantment, full of nuanced memories and projective thoughts. It could go wrong in so many ways, but she had no other way of warning Kyah. She hoped desperately that her sister would understand.

Do you have it?

The sparrow chirped and bobbed in her hand. Ahraia nodded then tucked it carefully into her cloak and headed for the darkening, the tightness in her chest growing with every step, wondering about Losna and her second task.

When she reached Daispar, the wall seemed loath to let her in. Ahraia could feel its hesitancy. A closure did form, but it had been overlaid with thick branches and new vines, which were slower to respond.

I'm going back in—in! Where I'm supposed to be.

Hesitantly, the closure enlarged. A few branches reached out to forcefully pull her back, as though it was their choice and not hers.

Thank you, Ahraia said in irritation. They let her go and closed tightly behind her.

She hurried towards her nit on silent feet and slipped in unnoticed. She was just heading to Kyah's shade tree to hide the sparrow when she froze. Someone was lurking in the dark. A sprite, sitting just beyond her shade tree, toying idly with its drain. *The Astra.*

"What are you doing here?" Ahraia asked, startled by her ghostly presence.

The Astra stood up, her eyes gleaming malevolently as the blade disappeared into the folds of her cloak.

"Where have you been?" she asked, sweeping across the nit. "You knew you weren't supposed to leave the darkening."

"I wasn't?" Ahraia said, carefully forcing silence over the sparrow. It stilled next to her heart, puffing out its chest nervously.

The Astra's ears flickered, twitching downward with the sound of Ahraia's voice, more in annoyance than in admonishment. But Ahraia could tell her calm was forced. Her anger lurked just beneath the untouched surface of her face like a snap perch lying in wait beneath a tranquil river pool. Ahraia's heart was beginning to beat faster. Almost instinctively, she reached out to bind the Astra, before realizing what that would mean.

She stopped.

"You knew perfectly well you weren't to leave," the Astra said, seemingly unaware of the brief brush of Ahraia's mind. "Where have you been?" she asked again.

"Roaming . . ." *Were your wards looking for me?* she added. A sudden absurd desire to carry through with her binding tingled across her mind, to hold the Astra, to bind her firmly in place, just to see if she could. Ahraia hardly noticed that her thoughts had tumbled out unchecked. But the Astra had. Her ears turned down in truth now.

"You forget yourself, Ahraia . . ." She bristled at Ahraia's contempt. Her lips pursed dangerously.

Ahraia met her eye, feeling nervous but defiant, refusing to bow or apologize.

"Do I?" she said.

"*Silence*," the Astra ordered, forcing Ahraia's mouth closed with a binding. But Ahraia let the next words escape by sheer intention, undiminished by the enchantment.

"You aren't welcome here."

The Astra froze. Ahraia's spine tingled, first with accomplishment —followed swiftly by fear. She knew the fear was unreasonable: what more could the Astra do? What had her hand not already taken? The darkening beyond the nit rippled.

The Astra stepped forward and grabbed Ahraia by the arm, casting a heavy-handed enchantment at the same time.

But Ahraia was ready; she had been expecting it. The filaments of the enchantment were palpable, like the faintest hanging threads of an unseen web draped across a forest path. But instead of sticking to her face, they fell over her neck, right down to her spine. The first was the bonding, the *link*. Next was *stillness*, the Astra's intention. Beyond that there was *fear*, sown by the Astra's thought.

She fought the urge to submit, stepping backward and pulling her arm free, as the Astra tried to keep her enchanted. They stood eye to eye, both surprised.

"You don't control me. Not anymore," she said. Ahraia had never been so bold or rebellious with anyone, not even Gavea or her father. The surge of control was intoxicating.

"I'm your Astra," the Astra said, obviously stunned by Ahraia's resistance, tightening her binding.

Ahraia felt her mouth forced closed by enchantment. She choked, feeling as though her tongue was being shoved back down her throat.

The Astra's face was inches from her own, her voice tempered by forced calm. "This is my darkening. You answer to me." She drew her drain from her cloak.

It's your darkening. But this is my nit. Ahraia bound the nit above, the branches swinging easily to her mind. Ahraia brushed the Astra's head with the bough, as though she had flicked her with her own fingers.

The whole darkening shuddered, threatening to rip the nit tree apart if it touched the Astra again.

"*Let go of your tree,*" the Astra commanded.

Ahraia managed the barest smile. "It doesn't answer to you, does it?" She flicked the branch just behind the Astra again. The darkening creaked and shuddered.

"Don't forget, your sisters and brother are under my watch . . ." the Astra said.

"And those seeds you want are under mine," Ahraia answered, unflinching.

The Astra stepped back and the binding dissipated.

"If it were any sprite but me, you'd be dead." She slipped the drain back into the folds of her dress. "The Bright Moon is waning. Your task is almost upon you."

Ahraia remained silent, with nothing to say.

"Tomorrow night, your second task begins. Come to the central hollow for your instruction, once the Dae-Mon is down." The Astra turned, giving her one final glance before departing the nit.

Ahraia had half a mind to smack her across the head with the nit tree, but resisted. The moment the Astra disappeared, she imagined a thousand different insults she could have said. She wished she could have let the nit tree grab the Astra and drag her unwilling into the air. Still, Ahraia reveled for a moment in the sensation of surprise that had flowed from the Astra when the branch had brushed her head.

It made her ears quiver right to the tips.

She felt a flutter at her breast but it wasn't her heart. She heard a small chirp and remembered the sparrow.

You weren't supposed to hear that. She took the sparrow from her cloak. It burst into flight, zipping all about her head, hopping mad and ready to fight, chirping and puffing its chest exuberantly.

"*Quiet,*" Ahraia urged, laughing at its diminutive courage. Eventually, she got the little bird to calm, by which time she had settled as well. She turned back to Kyah's shade tree.

You'll have to stay here for a couple of days, she thought to the sparrow, taking it inside the tree. She persuaded the tree to form a small nook, filling it with seeds for the sparrow. Once she finished, she left the little bird in the fold and hurried back to her own shade tree.

She looked about in search of a marker that Kyah couldn't miss. Only one thing was unmistakably hers.

Her moon flower.

She took a deep breath and made a binding, running her thoughts from the tip of its roots to the edge of its curled petals. It had taken her a full three seasons of coaxing until it had agreed to bloom. Now, she needed to persuade it to let go of its hold. It was a testament of its trust that it slowly loosened its tendrils, letting the roots detach until she held the whole flower in her hands. Its senses were fogged and unformed; it was naked, vulnerable and frightened. She soothed it, promising good earth and fresh darkness as she carried it carefully to Kyah's shade tree. Inside, the little sparrow watched curiously as Ahraia convinced the flower to send its roots into the earth and its stalk along the trunk, until it rested just beside the sparrow's nest. When she was finished, it looked as though it had never moved. Its petals hung like the Bright Moon, but outside, that moon wouldn't be hanging at all, it would be turned, facing off with the Dae-Mon just as Ahraia would be facing her own daemons. She leaned back, finally ready to leave. Kyah couldn't possibly miss the signal now.

Ahraia bound the sparrow, holding out her hand.

Now repeat it back to me, like I am Kyah.

The sparrow twittered out of its perch and landed on her hand. It wanted to sing the message, but Ahraia had stressed that there were no songbirds in the dark. She bound it and listened as it relayed the message. The intention was fairly clear. She hoped Kyah saw it the same as she did.

"Good. Now, just remember, Kyah has a fox—don't let him eat you."

The sparrow zipped into its nook, peering out fiercely, with only its eyes and beak showing next to the moon flower.

As the evening of her test approached, Ahraia lay half-awake and bitterly alone, waiting for the Dae-Mon to drop from the sky for the last time. The crackling air of afternoon buzzed outside, but inside, the darkness was absolute, pressing inward.

It was the first time in weeks Ahraia had sat idle, and now the absence of Losna struck like a thunderstorm from an already black sky. The weight of the second task loomed before her, unknown, unwanted.

Unwilling.

She worried over Kyah and the spritelings, and the message the sparrow bore. But more than anything, she worried for Losna. Half a turning had passed, and yet, another whole turning would come and go before she saw her again. She wondered if Losna was fed. She wondered where she slept. Was she still hurt from the keress? Was anyone looking after her? The day turned to dusk, and the light turned from gray, to dim, to dark. She rose from her shade tree, knowing it would be the last time she ever set foot inside.

I'll miss you.

The tree shuddered. Its leaves hung downturned, spent. It was an empty farewell.

A closure formed without her asking. She looked about one last time, searching for any belongings she might miss. Hayvon's light-veil was already stowed away in her pocket. The drain she had carried since the first task was at her hip. A blanket of winter-weave lay tucked in the corner, along with a few keepsakes and tokens from the woods. She took a step and stopped. Something was off.

Something was missing.

She turned about.

The blade from the Stone Tree. Ahraia frowned. The alp's blade was gone. She had left the handle sticking from the branches, *just so*. The Astra had been sitting at the edge of her tree, playing with a drain. Ahraia hadn't taken notice of the blade, but she would bet her shadow's life it was the one.

Her ears batted angrily, her markings flushing.

She stepped from her shade tree. Part of her wanted nothing more than to accuse the Astra in front of the whole darkening for her brothers' murders. She wanted to see the guilt in the pale of the

Astra's eyes; the rest of the darkening deserved to know their Astra was a coward, who had used an alp to kill Daispar's shades, all for darkness she couldn't fold herself.

Cursing, Ahraia left the shade tree.

The nit tree above rustled in farewell. She stepped light-footed and heavy-hearted into the central hollow, letting the closure form behind her for the last time. Every sprite in the darkening was gathered, without any of the shades or spritelings. Her father stood at the center of the gathering, near the springs.

"Shade Ahraia . . ." He nodded in greeting.

She didn't acknowledge him. Instead, she looked about, noticing how empty the hollow seemed. Several sprites and wards were missing. One absence in particular was more apparent than the rest.

"Where's the Astra?" Ahraia asked aloud.

Sprites flinched and ears flickered all about the hollow. Ahraia ignored their disapproval, looking towards the Astra's nit tree, expecting her to come swooping out at any moment: she never missed the chance to glower over Ahraia, especially considering the lengths she had gone to bring the test about. The silence grew but she didn't emerge. Ahraia bristled, shaking from the compulsion to confront the Astra. She clenched her jaw, until comprehension dawned on her.

"She's gone to collect her seeds, hasn't she?"

Her father frowned deeply, ears curving down just enough to belie his calm.

"She left for Angolor last night, to oversee the completion of your task," he said. His ears flickered, permitting her to speak aloud. From the twitch in his cheek, she could tell it came only to lessen the edge of her voice. "You're to meet her there before the Bright Moon is turned again."

"And how am I supposed to know where Angolor is?"

"Golan will show you." Her father gestured to one of the Astra's dae-wards. The ward's veil was woven of the Astra's own eaves-web, a sign of her favor. He was young; his scars were lighter than Ahraia's, and his eyes were still pale, not having suffered enough light to turn true golden. Ahraia hesitated, unsure what her father meant for the ward.

"He's not coming with me," she said.

"No. He'll show you the way." *By memory.*

Golan smiled at her, his eyes lingering on her entirely too long.

Why him?

Her father furrowed his brow.

Because he knows the way. And he's not one of the Masai's. Now sit down.

Ahraia hesitantly lowered herself in front of Golan, who was already sitting. The ward scooted closer, until their knees almost touched. Instinctively, she fortified her mind to keep him out.

"I'm going to need to bond you," he said. She felt the coarse brush of his mind and resisted. His teeth showed in what he surely thought was a reassuring smile.

For a moment, Ahraia feared what he might see if she let herself be bound. Would he see the bow? Or know about the sparrow? She pushed the thoughts down deep, remembering he was just a ward. She leaned forward. Golan did the same, until their foreheads pressed together. Ahraia smelled the lingering stink of milde-weed and needles of an unfamiliar nit tree, and felt the warm press of his head. Slowly, she let him bind her.

She saw the darkening, where they sat, and then suddenly his thoughts burst into her mind.

A thousand miles of night-strewn forests unfurled before her, through foreign woods and past shadow-clad mountains to endless valleys beyond. Narrow spritish paths peeled back before her eyes along with human paths, wide enough for ten sprites to walk abreast. She saw fallen trees spanning perilous creeks and chasms, and great stone bridges that stretched impossibly over churning rivers. Finally, she saw deep, dark vales rippling one after another out of sight.

In an instant, she knew the path to Angolor, towards the rising Dae-Mon and to the south, around the human realm and the great snowcapped mountains.

Golan pulled away, opening his eyes.

That is the way to Angolor.

"The Astra is making that journey?" Ahraia swallowed nervously. She closed her mind, detesting the sensation of being bound.

Her father nodded.

"I'm supposed to travel there in one turning?" Ahraia said. "*And* I'm supposed to complete my second task?"

He nodded again.

She stood up, brushing the dirt from her knees.

"What must I do?"

"Bring the provisions." Her father beckoned another ward forward.

A sprite brought forward a travel sack, stinking with the dried keress meat. Ahraia's stomach turned dangerously. She shook her head.

No.

"You have to eat along the way," her father said.

Grudgingly, she took the travel sack. She felt sickness rising in her throat.

Next, her father drew something from his cloak and extended it to her. It was another drain, far more elegant than the one she carried at her side. It was the opposite of the stolen blade: white to the other blade's black, and stout to the other blade's frailty.

"I already have a drain," she said, not reaching out to take it. It looked to be solid bone, with a handle wrapped in tight, soft leather. It was intricately carved along the flat of the blade. Her father pushed it towards her, forcing her to take it. The instant she touched the handle, she knew it came from the antlers and hide of the keress. She barely stilled the urge to cast it away from her.

"It's custom to make your drain from your first kill, taken by force from the innocent," he said. *Since you weren't here, I did it for you.* He glared at her, then went on. "With it, you must make a sacrifice of an enemy. That is your second task."

Dread seeped into Ahraia's heart. "An enemy? What kind of enemy?"

Her father's eyes shone as cold and pale as they ever had.

"A lightwalker."

Ahraia's ears turned down, ringing in the silence. "A lightwalker?" She let out a shallow breath, trying to force her ears upright.

"And once I do, what then? Am I supposed to drag it all the way to Angolor?"

"Just its head," her father said matter-of-factly.

Wonderful, Ahraia thought. *What a lovely journey.* When it was apparent that no other instruction was forthcoming, she turned and walked from the central hollow. Her father's face was measured, and no farewell followed after her, though his voice rang out one more time.

"Remember what is at stake, Ahraia—not just yourself—but the very darkness around us. The whole darkening is counting on you . . . most of all, your nit."

20

LIGHTENING

Ahraia ripped back the branches of the Astra's shade tree and tossed the travel sack inside. It landed with a lifeless thump, the top tearing open, exposing the keress meat within. She hoped it reeked like a jontun by the time the Astra returned; she hoped the smell ruined the tree forever, a permanent reminder of the death and decay the Astra spread.

She hurriedly withdrew from the nit, hating to be under it, and departed from Daispar without another word to her father or the other sprites. A few had conveyed goodbyes. A few had even wished her luck. But the threat towards Kyah and the spritelings had been aired openly, aloud, and no one so much as looked twice at her father. They were all guilty, with their fiendish insistence on enchantment killings and their ruthless acceptance of condemnations—their willingness to kill and let kill. It burned in her ears and her heart.

She slipped from the darkening into a silent night, lit only by the stars and the Blood Moon overhead. Not a sound stirred the woods.

A good night for shades and shadows, she thought bitterly, remembering Havon.

"Speak for yourself," she whispered, slipping the new drain into her cloak next to her metal drain. She retrieved her bow and arrows, gathered up the food she had scavenged and the small human tokens and tucked them all close. Stomach grumbling, she ate a handful of berries when suddenly ash spread through her mouth, coating her throat and ruining the taste. A charberry had gotten mixed up with the rest. She spit it out, scraping her tongue across her teeth, wondering if it was a sign of her luck. She spat again, and stood up.

Then, with an ashen taste in her mouth, she began to run south towards the human's realm.

It felt surreal, leaving Daispar for the last time, but in truth, the peril of her second task was far more unsettling. Killing a lightwalker wouldn't be easy. The thought sent crawlers up her spine, as though tendrils of a leech fern were creeping towards her neck to paralyze her.

I don't have a choice, she thought, determined to see the task through. Losna's life depended on it. And if she did it with an arrow, without a binding, then she could live with the guilt.

It was just a matter of finding one alone, and at night.

THE FIRST SEVERAL nights passed easily—if easily meant dread with every step and only her brooding thoughts to keep her company. For some reason, she felt ill at ease—not just with her task, but with the very woods. The trees creaked ominously. Maple spinners whirled down amongst the leaves in a steady crackle. She sensed padding feet and watchful eyes, but every time she turned about, she was alone. She imagined bushes rustling and her ears twitched to the sound of leaves crunching underfoot. Twice she hid in trees, even circling back, but eventually she decided she had just been without her shadow for too long.

Her mind was fraying. She needed Losna back.

Before dawn of the third day, she passed beyond where she and Losna had ever run. She was getting closer to the human realm and the woods were changing. The trees felt different: quieter and slower, asleep even, with light sewn right to the tips of their leaves and needles. The creatures felt different too: timid and skittish. They darted away from her, leaving the woods as empty as the night she had bound Losna. It made her nervous. And yet the watchfulness remained.

On the fourth night, the clouds broke and the mountains of the south emerged in earnest. They were far grander than they looked from the Endless Plains, and even in the night they were radiant, capped in white snow. She wondered if there were deep hollows beneath them for a shade and a shadow to hide. It was hard to imagine there wouldn't be.

The next day came swiftly. She spent it huddled in a hollowed log, wishing for the thousandth time that she and Losna had fled when they had the chance. She bound a pair of scanty pines and brought them down over the entrance, creating darkness, cramped and incomplete. She slept fitfully, awaking hungry and stiff, her mind strained from holding the trees all day, and her stomach clenched from eating nothing but acorns and berries for the last turning.

The thinnest crescents of the Dark and Bright Moons waxed in the west when she crawled from her underdae. The Blood Moon was high overhead already. She had hardly taken two steps when she stopped and sniffed the night air. It was fresh, crisp with dry leaves and the first cold of autumn. And with it hid the faintest hint of...

Woodsmoke.

The wind came out of the south and she sniffed again.

Humans.

She took the bow from her shoulder, her eagerness to be done with her task heaving against her rising dread.

What an impossibly light-wrecked tree, Ahraia thought, staring in disbelief at the shade tree before her. Or was it a nit? She wasn't sure. The scent of humans had led her to where she stood, cowering in the woods, staring at the strange tree. She ran her thumb over her own nit's broken orb in her pocket, the rough touch of it reassuring.

The human's tree grew as an unnaturally neat gathering of wood, harnessed together in the most preposterous of shapes: a perfect square—with light streaming from square closures in the sides, even though night already engulfed the world.

Hesitantly, she searched out with her mind, not for life within—she had no intention of bonding anything inside—but to the structure itself, to see if it was alive.

It wasn't. It felt as dead as a rock.

She had heard of their stone darkenings, and had expected something like the Stone Tree. But this was something else entirely. The light made her stomach turn.

Her nostrils flared. Iron and horses and woodsmoke scented the air. But something else smelled rich and simmering. *Food.* It also made her stomach turn—though in a much different way.

The light formed a steady, yellow glow, without the flickering of their angry fires, shining like light stolen from the Dae-Mon. It lacked the gelded quality of a nit orb, but she wondered in terror if there were some other form of orb, a day orb of sorts, like a miniature Dae-Mon that they kept inside their walls.

It's not a shade or a nit tree . . . it's more like a light tree, she decided from the safety of the woods. *A lightening.*

She watched the lightening, wondering how the humans got in and out through the closures. They were small, and too high to be of any use—almost above her head. She wondered how they opened and closed. If the wood was dead, how could they? Or did the humans crawl in and out like some wild, overlarge insects? The lightening was rather like a nest of sorts, she supposed.

From the far side, she heard something whine, almost like a tree creaking in a high wind, but loud and sharp and—

Bang!

Wood clattered against wood, slapping out after the whine. Startled, Ahraia ducked behind the cover of the trees.

"Damnit, Yewl . . . I told you to bring more wood about today," a human voice said from out of sight. It was gruff and deep. A man, likely.

"Sorry, Da. I can get it," came a softer voice. The whine rose again and then another bang echoed out. Ahraia flinched.

There was more than one human.

"I'll manage. Get back inside the house and get your sister another blanket, her fever will break yet."

House. The word passed through Ahraia's thoughts and formed into the strange structure. *A house*, a human lightening.

Suddenly, something brilliant burned around the house's side, somehow getting brighter, bouncing towards her and sending great flares under the eaves of the woods.

Ahraia ducked lower. A radiant light emerged around the corner of the house. Panicked, she stumbled at the sight, staggering away through the underbrush. Leaves shook and branches broke.

She scrambled into a dark shadow and stopped, chest heaving, well aware of the obvious racket she had just made. She was crouched behind a large, unnatural stack of broken wood.

The bouncing light stilled.

She held her breath.

The night was suddenly silent. She peered over the stack of wood and saw a man standing perfectly still, raising a dazzling *something* in his hand and staring right at her. Ahraia's skin and eyes burned, her heart racing. She squinted from behind the wall, not daring to move.

The *something* spit light across the space between them, spreading dangerously over the woods about her.

Holding light in its hand . . . his dae-mon. Ahraia couldn't imagine the horror of the human's magic, or the pain of holding it. It took all her self-restraint not to bind him, to make sure that he couldn't see or sense her.

"Oi! Bear! Get out of here!" the man called, unflinching.

Ahraia stared back, wondering if his senses were so blunted that he really thought she might have been a bear.

Maybe they are as blind as trees, she thought. She didn't move.

The man grunted and kept walking, hardly seeming concerned. He was tall, at least two heads taller than the tallest sprite, with a beard thick beneath his chin, like a keress. His breath rattled out loudly as he wrestled something from beside the house: a miniature wagon that he pushed by hand. It rumbled across the ground before him.

Ahraia watched, rooted where she hid. She couldn't have run if she wanted; the forest was overflowing with searing-hot light. The maples about her shimmered in fiery colors: angry red and burnt yellow. The night burned with an unfamiliar scent, like pine oil spilling into the cook fires. She wrinkled her nose, peering through a tiny gap in the wall of broken wood. The human was hardly a dozen paces from her.

There won't be a better chance, she realized belatedly. She hadn't bound him yet, not beyond just mirroring his words. Hastily, she slid the bow from her shoulder and placed an arrow to the string. She readied herself, closing her eyes briefly and steadying her breaths. The string whined quietly, drawing tight.

She hesitated. There was still the damned light. It was everywhere. Once she shot him, his body would fall, still surrounded and protected by the dae-mon.

A scratching came from the other side of the human lightening, breaking off her thoughts. A moment later, she heard the same whine and crack of wood that had proceeded the man. Expecting another human, she peered towards the lightening. But what came around the corner scared her far more than any human or light would. Ahraia drew a sharp breath.

A shadow.

It was slightly larger than a fox, with long drooping ears and a strange coat of broken black and gray.

Humans aren't supposed to have shadows, she thought, letting out the tension in the string.

"Come on, boy," the man said to it.

It didn't look like a "boy" to her. It looked like Losna and Reyn mixed—but all out of sorts. It was too small by half, with short legs, and broken ears that fell down next to its jaw.

None of the other humans she had seen had shadows. To make the kill now would be impossible; she wasn't about to kill a shadow.

She watched numbly, paralyzed by fear, unsure if the humans could, in fact, make bindings.

The human placed his dae-mon inside the wagon, then turned and pushed it right towards Ahraia. The shadow jogged next to him, sniffing at his heels. In a panic, Ahraia crouched deeper beneath the broken wall of stacked wood, drawing a small maple over her, desperately exposed and woefully hidden by the sparse undergrowth. She couldn't see the man, but his footsteps grew louder. His breathing grew closer.

And then stillness.

Ahraia hardly dared to breathe. The shadow sniffed the ground nearby, growling.

"Quiet, boy. That bear's up the hill by now," the man said.

A terrifying scraping sounded directly above Ahraia's head. She flinched, and a great booming noise of wood knocking against wood filled the air. Startled, she nearly split from her cover. Did the human know she was there? Was he trying to get her to run, like a rabbit from its hiding?

Another scraping noise and she saw a piece of wood taken from atop the wall, followed by another boom.

Ahraia held her breath, too scared to act, shuddering with every scrape and thud.

The noises came again and again. The smell of the man pressed into her nose, all musk and sweat and sour cloth. She huddled low, waiting for the end to come, but eventually she heard a heavy grunt and a great rumble, and his footsteps faded.

She peeked around the wall and saw the human pushing the cart filled with broken wood towards his house, followed by his shadow. Ahraia let out a relieved breath, still hardly daring to move.

The kill was out of the question.

I'm a coward, she thought, filled with guilt. Her ears batted, knowing she might not get another chance. The human rounded the side of the house, his unceremonious light gratefully disappearing.

Ahraia gathered her courage. She stalked after him through the woods, reminding herself that one way or another, she needed a head.

The house creaked and a stiff closure formed, twice as wide as the man. Light streamed outward. A smaller human emerged, a boy, who took the wood the man handed him and disappeared inside. All the while, the shadow sniffed about their feet, so distinctly similar to Losna.

Without thinking, Ahraia reached out and bound it.

Food, it thought, snuffling across the ground, giving Ahraia a sharp pain of memory. She let the binding dissolve, desperate for Losna.

The man and the child worked in silence, if anything humans did could be called quiet. When they finished, the man wheeled the push-wagon back against the wall and disappeared into the cover of the house. The closure slapped closed behind him.

How in the light can I kill one of these?

An arrow would do the trick, but then what? Would she take the head and leave the body for the rest of its nit to find? The man had a small one, maybe more . . . and a shadow too.

This is madness, Ahraia thought, swallowing painfully. There was no sense in this task at all. Killing a human wouldn't make her a sprite, it would make her a wraith.

Her link to the shadow must have lingered, because she heard its thoughts from inside, *food . . . food . . . food.*

She needed Losna back. A mix of guilt and fear rose; her best opportunity to make the kill had likely just slipped away.

"I'm going to have to do this," she whispered, cursing her own cowardice.

The wind stirred up from the south, rattling dried leaves against the house. She was going to have to approach the house. Maybe even bait the human out somehow. She thought about making a racket, trying to draw them into the night, but that might bring them all out, and she didn't know how many there might be.

She watched and waited, but the closure stayed closed. The

humans' voices carried out from inside from time to time. A horse brayed off in the distance. Ahraia's ears twisted forward.

Ahraia lifted her nose to the air. A smell wafted from the house towards her. She sniffed, unexpectedly salivating.

Meat, she thought, reminded of the cook fires in Daispar. Her stomach grumbled. She hadn't had meat in half a turning, and roots and berries had twisted her stomach in a knot. She couldn't believe she was hungry at a time like this. Only Losna would think of food.

Her chest tightened. There was no choice but to get on with it. She adjusted the arrows at her hip, her decision made. She needed to look into the house, to see what she was up against.

Steeling herself, she stepped out from the woods.

Her skin was afire with nerves and dim light. She flitted across the barren earth to the pall of the house. She crept around the corner, away from the swinging closure.

The horses snickered and stomped away in the meadows. Ahraia moved silently, each step hushed, until she was just below the yellow-laced closure, spitting light outward. Thin wooden vines crisscrossed the opening, perfectly straight. She paused and listened, hearing the dim murmur of the humans inside. She set her bow and clutch of arrows quietly against the wall, and slowly raised her eyes to the closure. Blinding light spilled outward. Ahraia squinted tightly and peered inside.

The humans huddled close to a bright, angry fire, sitting in silence, strangely muted.

Ahraia's ears quivered, pointing straight up. She couldn't imagine the torture of sitting before a fire.

The man's dae-mon was hidden and she was glad; she didn't want to see how they kept the night at bay. Her eyes were already burning from the brightness.

Nearer at hand, some sort of cooked bird sat just inside the closure. A pheasant she guessed, though it had already been dressed and cooked. A small one.

Ahraia sniffed. It was strange, she couldn't smell it as strongly as before, though it was right before her eyes. Still, her mouth watered. She thought about just reaching through the closure and grabbing the meat. The humans wouldn't notice; they were all looking towards the fire. But maybe they *would* notice. Maybe they would think it was a fox or a bear. Or maybe they would think it was something more devilish. Maybe they would come looking for the thief.

Her stomach growled.

It was a brilliant plan. When they noticed it missing, they would come looking for her. Maybe just the big one, the man. She could make her kill in the safety of the dark woods and be done with it without a binding. His head would be hers.

Ahraia made her mind up in a split second.

Impressed with her ingenuity, she raised onto her tiptoes and made to quickly reach through the closure to grab the bird—

Thunk!

Her hand smacked against some unseen barrier and a loud slap echoed out. She ducked down, flushing in panic as the humans all turned toward her. The human shadow began to howl inside the light tree, its voice muted by the invisible barrier.

"Ahooo. Ahoo."

Ahraia scrambled for cover, knocking her clutch over and breaking the tie. Her arrows spilled on to the ground.

Light take me, she thought, her heart racing.

"What was that?" one of the humans asked. His voice was muffled and Ahraia realized some devilry kept the closure closed, even while she could see through it. She ducked into the deeper shadows along the wall, just as a grizzly silhouette stood before the light. Her arrows were hidden, but they were scattered everywhere.

"Was that an owl? Sounded like it might have hit the window," a human said.

Ahraia held her breath. She resisted the urge to bind him.

"Can't see anything," one of them said. Ahraia's ears strained.

The shadow was still howling incessantly.

"That didn't sound like an owl to me. Yewl, get the axe."

Ahraia struck out with her mind and softly linked the shadow. At first touch, she flinched, but then she soothed it. She heard the humans talking but couldn't hear their words anymore.

It's okay. It's okay. Shhhh, Ahraia thought, stilling the shadow. It quieted, but a moment later, she heard the strange creaking closure and then the bang of it closing.

Cold sweat broke out across her neck, and she saw light tumbling towards her. Instinctively, she reached out to bond the human, forgetting all intention to avoid enchantments. She sensed it coming around the house, and darted in the opposite direction, having no choice but to leave her arrows. She would just have to come back for them—

Shouting erupted inside the house.

"Da, I see it! I see it!" one of the humans called.

Light jumbled around the outside of the house. She gave up any pretense of enchantment and scurried for the woods.

"What the hell is that? Da, get back in the house!" one of them shouted.

"Ealor get in the house," a woman's voice called out.

Ahraia sprinted for the woods. The night around her was thrown into light. She turned and saw the brilliant dae-mon being held by the human as he emerged around the corner. Ahraia stumbled back, blinded by the brightness of the light. She raised her hand to her eyes, unable to discern shade from the shadows.

But the man was staring right at her. She turned and fled as his voice called after her.

"Raise the town!" he shouted at the top of his lungs. "It's a demon."

21

BROKEN DARK

The true Dae-Mon had almost risen when Ahraia finally stopped. Miles lay behind her, and she was sure the humans had given up the chase. Even with their shadows, they couldn't possibly keep up with her, not if they followed her all day and all night.

Her mind had gone blank. The frayed edges of her fears strained against the dull, haunting pulse of reason. She was going to have to go back; she had to make a kill.

And she was going to have to be ruthless about it.

Her stomach tightened in a knot.

I'm going to have to make a binding, she thought darkly, *at the very least to get them alone without light.*

A memory of the keress swelled up, filling her mouth with ropy saliva. She felt dizzy. Losna had begged her not to, but trusting luck had nearly ended in ruin. She spit, trying to rid herself of the chalky taste. The humans were too dangerous, too clouded in light . . .

"I'm going to have to, this once . . ." she said. She swore she could hear Losna's thoughts in reply.

It will destroy you . . .

Her ears batted in shame.

You won't recover . . .

Her palms were sweating. She pushed her worries aside. The gray of dawn was coming and if she didn't find shelter soon, nothing else would matter. She turned her mind to finding darkness.

The woods about her felt strange, and awake. She knew she was still on the borders of the human realm, just a night's run away, but the woods felt familiar now. She smelled wickers and pines, and the faintest lingering of eaves-web growing wild.

I'm going to have to go back, she thought again, her ears twitching at the familiar caw of a moon raven.

The human road would likely be the place to make the kill. An arrow from the woods and maybe she wouldn't need a binding. Or maybe if she folded a corner of darkness just at the fringe, she could coax one off the path during the day. *A light binding.* Maybe even just a noise to draw them in.

Her heart eased with the thought. If she took it with an arrow, and they fell unseen, she could wait for darkness and claim her prize. She grimaced. She would need new arrows . . .

I'm no better than the wraith in the Stone Tree, she realized darkly.

She walked for a time, looking about for any deep shade to underdae beneath. With each step, the forest felt more and more like Daispar, and she soon realized that her feet were leading her by a path, forgotten and overgrown, but folding back willingly, even eagerly, out of her way.

She saw the Dae-Mon's faint glow and began to jog again, but she didn't have to follow the track long before a hulking mass loomed before her.

A darkening. Abandoned, but unmistakable. Dimdale or Holcrek . . . one of the first of the Gelesh to fall.

The once tight shell had disintegrated without the support of enchantment, sagging inward, and the nit trees looked burnt from too much light. The central hollow lay between them, broken open to the graying skies above. The forest had crept back in over the years, sending tendrils and crawlers over everything. A gnarled pine grew through a half-formed shade tree. A nit collapsed under the weight of a fallen darkening core.

She found a shade tree that was largely still intact, overgrown with thick brambles. She pushed a hole through the edge, and wheedled the shade tree into opening. It rustled, as though roused from a long and deep sleep, and she crawled inside, brushing aside the dried leaves and broken branches that had accumulated over the years. The shade tree was old, almost older than it could remember, with only the faintest memory of its shade. It felt strange. *Foreign*.

Ahraia lay in the semi-dark, brooding over her task as the Dae-Mon climbed in the sky. She knew, deep in her heart, what she was going to have to do.

I'm going to have to make a binding. She felt a lump in her throat. The pain would be excruciating—and knowing how deep the human abyss of emotions went, the aftermath would be unescapable. The severed part of her would rot and die. The guilt and grief would coalesce within her, forming a solid hollow, a permanent void—an emptiness that would either make her more spritish or destroy her.

Losna would be furious.

Maybe she won't know. But it was a feeble thought. The emptiness always showed.

Ahraia had seen it in other shades in the midst of their shadow test. Their moods worsened as they progressed, growing darker and more deathly, until they became sprites: wraiths, empty and wain. Like Kren. Like her father and the Astra.

That was the purpose of the test: to solidify that part of her who could be ruthless, that part of her that could kill without thought or care. She felt sick knowing every shade before her had faced the same act. The realization took the breath from her. The roots of the shade tree could be holding her to the ground for all she knew.

But what other choice did she have? She would kill a hundred humans if it meant Losna returned safely to her side. She would walk in the light. She would make a binding and kill a lightwalker.

I should have done it already. She cursed herself for being so childish with her first attempt. But she had only wasted a night. And she could make more arrows.

When darkness came again, she wouldn't bother imping about without the will to kill. The human realm was large, and she refused to let the task be the end of her.

I have to enchant to kill. Just this once, she thought as she drifted off to sleep.

AHRAIA AWOKE, sensing dusk and movement. Her ears twitched, and she thought she heard the swish of branches being pushed aside.

She sat up.

A moon raven cawed close by. She held her breath as the last echoes faded. Silence settled across the darkening, but it was short lived as a branch dragged distantly over fallen leaves.

Ahraia crawled to the thick skirt of branches, hardly stirring any noise as her mind teased apart a small closure. Outside lay a broken kind of dark. Late afternoon had given way to the long shadows of dusk, but shafts of light cut dangerously across the darkening, stabbing down like spears of death.

Ahraia squinted, scanning the woods. Something moved distantly through the darker shadows.

A deer?

She held her breath. It moved strangely. And stealthily.

Suddenly, she saw a hooded figure walking between the trunks. A veil hung across its face. A veil made of eaves-web.

A dae-ward.

Ahraia lowered the branches, just enough to see. She could sense a rippling tension in the nit and shade trees; the ward wasn't from the darkening. The raven cawed again. The ward looked about. He moved carefully, avoiding the rays of light where he could.

The transient flicker of a mind searched past Ahraia. Not expecting it, she didn't deflect it quickly enough. She flinched when his voice suddenly cracked the silence.

"Shade Ahraia?" the ward called. He turned about slowly, seeking her. "I know you're here."

The hairs on the back of her neck stood on end. For a moment, she wondered how he knew her, but then she recognized him. It was Golan, the same ward who had given her direction—one of the Astra's dae-wards. He turned about again, hunting for her.

"I don't want to start shaking shade trees," he called out. His voice was boisterous. She felt the brush of his mind and he turned in her direction. Realizing he somehow already knew she was nearby, she parted the closure of the shade tree.

"What are you doing here?"

The tension in the ward eased visibly. He let out a sigh.

"Finally. I've been looking for you for days and nights on end. Haven't hardly slept . . ."

He hurried towards her. She scuttled backwards as the closure enlarged against her will, letting in more of the diffuse light. He stooped at the edge, peering in.

"It's me, Golan."

"I know," Ahraia said. She was so surprised by his presence that she didn't think to convey. His ears didn't flicker. His eyes glinted with excitement. He waited.

"You're letting in the light."

"Oh . . . right." He stepped inside, letting the closure re-form. The dark swelled around them. "Dae-Mon above, I hate these veils, haven't figured out how to grow it any thinner . . ." He pulled the web below his chin, pushing back his hood to reveal fresh scars. They were still red, rising from his neck to just below his jaw.

"What are you doing here?" she asked again. He stunk of milde-weed.

"I . . ." he stopped. A lie wreathed itself on the edges of his thoughts. Ahraia's eyes narrowed and she formed a light bonding, trying to sense his mind. He seemed to know it too, as his shoulders loosened.

"The Astra sent me after you," he admitted, his ears downturned, "she wanted me to look after you . . ."

"Look after me? This is my shadow test."

Golan looked guilty. He shrugged. "I do as I am told. I'm just supposed to see that you finish your task." His eyes flickered to her bow, which she had laid next to her. *By any means necessary,* he conveyed.

Ahraia hesitated. The Astra *would* put a ward to the task. With how badly she wanted darkness, there was no doubt she would try to tip the balance.

"That's an awful risk. If the Masai finds out . . ."

Golan smiled. Ahraia strengthened her binding, trying to discern his emotions. They were blank. Empty. *Spritish.*

"That's the trick, isn't it?" Golan said. "But the Astra didn't think your shadow should be taken." *And she didn't think you*—He stopped, looking as though he had swallowed his words.

Ahraia waited and then finished the thought. "She didn't think I could do it without Losna."

He grimaced and nodded.

"How did you find me?" His presence made her uncomfortable. She was sure it had been his padding footsteps tracking her the last several days.

"Well, it wasn't easy," he said, not noticing how Ahraia leaned away from him. *The Masai has spies everywhere . . .* He met her eye conspiratorially, his ears flickering nervously. His allegiance didn't surprise her. Though he had come from the eastern woods, maybe even Angolor, he was bound to the Astra. She had taken him in, and likely would make him a nit-ward for a task such as this. He would be a young one, without even scars to show for it. He went on, oblivious to her thoughts.

"I headed for the human realm, by the same route I showed you. Here and there a tree had memory of you, but I'm not great at bindings. Just had to track you by ear and eye and mind, as they say."

Ahraia didn't say anything when he paused.

His smile faded slightly, seeing her doubt.

"Then I got to the first human settlement around dawn—they

were all gathered, dozens of them, with torches blazing and bright swords. I only just got away. I've been running ever since . . ."

"You ran through the day?" Ahraia shook her head, imagining the horror of it. She wondered if she could survive the same. If she could, maybe she could make a kill in the light. She frowned, ashamed that she would rather face the light than make a binding.

"The Dae-Mon's not really deadly, not if you ease yourself into it," Golan said, mistaking her frown. "Just a little light sickness here and there. Burns a bit at first. And the veil helps. Not with your eyes, but you get used to all the light eventually—"

"Never mind that," Ahraia said. "I don't need your help. I need my shadow back."

He fell silent, looking startled by her admission. "Right . . ." he said, as though he didn't know what else to say.

"Listen, I don't want—" she stopped short as a branch broke away in the woods. Golan's ears twitched. Ahraia scrambled across the shade tree and re-formed her closure, peering out into the dusky darkening. Her ears turned down, seeing more movement, and another hooded figure. She turned to Golan.

"Are you alone? Were you followed?"

"I—followed? By what?" Golan widened her closure, tugging at it roughly, staring out beside her.

For a moment, Ahraia feared it would be another ward, sent along with Golan, or a spy of the Masai's possibly, who would condemn her for conspiring with the ward. But the figure moved loudly, brutishly —not at all like a sprite. Leaves crackled underfoot, and he pushed branches roughly aside. Through the tree trunks, she saw he was without a veil, and his skin was dark beyond just light-scars.

A lightwalker.

The figure paused, looking about. The silence of the woods was suddenly shattered as his voice sounded out.

"Hello?"

She couldn't believe her ears. *A human.*

Golan looked out through the crease, his brow furrowing.

"There's no way they followed me—"

Shhh.

Through the gaps in the darkening wall, Ahraia could see the rough spin of his clothes and the ungainly way that he moved. Had he hunted her? Or Golan? Breathlessly, she looked about for others, for more trailing him. None appeared. He was alone. She looked for a torch, a shadow, or a dae-mon, but saw none. She smiled, a feeling of undue elation coursing through her.

"This is my chance," she whispered.

22

KILL

What's a human doing in a darkening? Golan conveyed, looking perturbed.

And he's without any abhorrent dae-mon, Ahraia thought. Her smile spread, her nerves prickling.

"You're going to try and make a kill? At this time of day?" he whispered.

"You're not my shadow. Stay out of this."

"I could help."

"I don't want your help. I don't even know why you're here. Whatever you do, just don't interfere."

The ward's eyes wrinkled into a smile. Ahraia ignored him, wishing she had salvaged at least a single arrow.

She pulled out the longer of her two drains. The bone felt brittle in her hand, tainted. The only part of her that didn't recoil at the touch was that which had been severed with the keress. She quickly put it back, choosing instead the small metal drain that she had used in her first task. An echo of the last time she had used the drain pulsed through her.

You're going to hurt yourself, the deep part of her thought.

"Quiet," Ahraia said, forcing that part of her into silence.

Golan looked over at her as though she was mad. His ears batted for silence, but she ignored him, intent on the human.

The stray light stabbed lethally through the darkening. The day ward's smile faded briefly as Ahraia removed Hayvon's veil and wrapped it around her face.

"Any means necessary, right?" she said.

Golan smiled wide again, nodding.

Soundlessly, she enlarged the closure and then shifted into the darkening on all fours, staying hidden behind the jumble of nit trees. She stalked towards the human, not yet daring to make a true bonding. A crease in the shade tree was all she could see when she glanced back.

The human had stopped, examining a portion of the unkempt wall. He reached out, running his hand down one of the cover vines.

Ahraia edged closer.

"Hello?" the human called loudly.

She ducked down, wondering if he had sensed or seen her. Or maybe he expected others to be about. She smelled the faint hint of human clothes . . . and something else. Maybe it was Golan. She wiped her palms on her cloak, sweat forming even though the evening was cool.

The human turned about, his eyes searching the darkening. She saw a gleam of something bright at his hip, and saw a clutch of arrows at his other side. *A sword,* she realized, having seen them in memories before. How humans grew such weapons was a mystery, and in all her roaming, Ahraia had never seen stone or tree or dirt like that.

Her drain felt like a twig in her hand. She looked longingly at the black-feathered arrows at his hip. Maybe it would be better to wait for the night. If he was asleep, she could avoid enchanting him. She could creep forward without a noise and kill him quick and quiet.

Ahraia blew out a slow breath.

The dark wouldn't come quickly enough, and other humans could be about.

Do it already, Golan conveyed behind her. The crease in the shade tree was hardly more than a dark line. She wanted nothing to do with the ward, particularly one whose will bent to the Astra—but having him there provided a layer of reassurance. If things went to the light, perhaps he could help . . .

She frowned and turned back to the human, letting out a long breath.

She cast the first threads of an enchantment, melding the human's mind. The bond took hold, like tendrils of a vine wrapping up the trunk of a sturdy tree, encasing it.

A thin web of wariness lay across the human's thoughts, but it nearly burst with underlying emotion. *Excitement. Longing.* A deep ache that reminded Ahraia of how she longed for Losna. The reflection, vague as it was, made her yearn for Losna all the more. She swallowed down the feeling, uncomfortable with the breadth of human emotions, uncomfortable with how similar he seemed to her.

The human moved along the outside of the wall, his footfalls tumbling out in haste. She could tell at once his mind was different from the girl she had bound. He was searching for something. And he seemed to search with eyes and ears and mind as well. He felt aware. *Awake.* Like a sprite. He knew what he was walking into. He knew it wasn't like the rest of the forest. And he was excited. He knew it was . . .

A darkening.

Ahraia shivered. She was well aware she had put the word to the human's thoughts, but he understood the place—which meant he was all the more dangerous. He wasn't stumbling blindly through the woods as she had hoped. The handle of his bow was worn, the wood smooth from use. And the sword at his hip was no drain. It was long and lethal and razor bright.

What would she do? Would she walk forward and kill him quickly? What if she jumped him? Surprised him? Could she avoid a deeper connection? If he got his sword out, she was dead. She had to disarm him before making her move—

The human put his hand to the handle of his sword. Dim as the bond was, he was tensing. She had let her thoughts cloud the enchantment.

It's okay. It's safe. It was just a feeling. A silly feeling, really, she thought. This lightwalker was a gift from the night, alone and without light. She *had* to make a kill. She couldn't let her fears ruin it. She let out a breath, letting her mind go blank, forcing her fears to retreat. The human mimicked her, exhaling slowly. The tension bled out of his shoulders. His excitement returned, the gleam in his eye shining with the day's last light.

It's safe, she encouraged, feeling the tendrils of thought creeping through his mind. Her legs quivered; her whole body was alight with anticipation of what was to come.

Come. It is safe here . . . set your bow and sword aside, they look heavy.

The human surveyed the darkening, his caution still outweighing his excitement.

"Hello?" he called again.

Ahraia flinched, shushing him to silence. *Set aside your things and rest. This is home for tonight.* She reached inside herself and drew out the most comforting memory she could find: she thought of her shade tree, with Losna curled close on a brittle winter day. She imagined the smell of fresh winter-weave and fallen leaves and dry dusty fur. This was home. This was where she belonged. *This is safe.*

The human set down his bow, seduced. He was fully under her spell—the kill was going to be excruciating.

You are weary, set down that heavy sword and rest a while.

The human drew his sword and set it against a tree.

Now, come. Come inside, there is shelter here.

The last daggers of light crept up the trees, slanting dangerously across the decaying darkening. But dusk was deepening.

Come, the woods are getting darker, it's not safe out there. Come away from the wild things, the wicked things. There are no evils here, no mara or imps . . . no daemons or darklings to haunt these lands. I will keep you. You are safe now.

Ahraia ducked closer, forcing the human to look away as she moved behind the trunk of a withered nit tree. Each movement she commanded, each time she glazed his eyes, or softened his ears brought them closer.

Ahraia leaned out from behind the trunk, her face hidden by a screen of eaves-web. *Deeper now, come and find shelter here.* Her ears twitched. A leaf crackled loudly away through the woods. She glanced back towards Golan but didn't see him. The human didn't seem to have noticed. He stepped through the old woven wall.

Ahraia let out a slow breath. He was tall, and not nearly as ungainly or graceless as the other humans she had seen, and though his face was half-hidden by his hood, he looked almost striking, without the roundness of eye and ear and face she had previously seen. For a moment, she forgot herself, staring at the strange creature. It was oddly satisfying having him spellbound at the tip of her fingers.

What are you waiting for? Golan's thoughts invaded her mind. She bristled, perturbed by the infiltration of thought and suddenly remembering her purpose.

Stay out of this, she conveyed, only having a loose idea where the ward was.

The human stopped, suddenly tense once again. A barrage of distrust reverberated across the binding. His eyes scanned over nit and shade tree until they came to Ahraia. They hesitated for the barest moment, lingering on the eaves-web, before slipping past. Her ears twitched nervously, startled by the brief and unexpected touch of his gaze.

It's safe, she conveyed unconvincingly.

The human reached for his hip and suddenly realized his sword was missing. His fear burst across the binding. The sensation was familiar, like when Ahraia had suddenly sensed the menace of the Stone Tree, overwhelming and repulsive.

Except this time, she was the wraith.

The urge to let the binding drop surged within her, but she resisted, closing her eyes, clinging to the enchantment. She forced stillness into her mind, drawing forth the first memories she could find: anything to calm herself.

They started simple: A pair of turning ears, the press of a wet black nose and the brush of fur against her leg. She heard the sound of laughter across a forgotten winter pool. She saw eyes, golden bright and brilliant. They were Losna's eyes, moving in absolute laziness, the only part of her shadow willing to move after running across the Endless Plains on a moonless night.

I'm being watched, the human thought.

It's just a feeling. Ahraia reassured him. She closed her eyes, forming a pool of stillness in her mind. She stayed that way a long time, trying to think of nothing at all. She took deep settling breaths and when she finally opened her eyes, the tranquility remained. The human's fear was subsiding.

Do it already, Golan urged.

She shut out his thoughts, blocking him from her mind. Her attention was fixed on her prey. She tightened her binding, holding him still.

The human's back was to her. She stepped from behind the eaves-web, drawing her drain. She took the first step, not thinking of what she was doing, not daring to bring fear into the human's mind. She danced closer, letting him look about as she slid from one tree to the next.

She was twenty paces from him, hiding behind a large nit tree. A ray of sunlight lay dangerously overhead. *I'm going to see my shadow.* Ten paces, behind a narrow alder. *This accursed task will be done.* Five paces. *What was that noise?* Two paces. *This is it.* One pace. She stopped, the drain poised but her will quavering.

She was right behind him. The smell of his clothes pressed against her nose, his musk stinging at her nostrils. Her knuckles were blanched, white around the drain. He *knew* she was there. He could feel her, and though his fear was true, it was nothing compared to hers. She held the blade forward, ready to strike.

Ready, but not willing.

Her fears and doubts slithered up her spine, rooting her to the spot. She couldn't move. A force within her—that part of herself who knew what would come, that part that had heard Losna—held her firmly.

You bound him, tightly. That means he's a part of you, it said. *You can't kill a part of yourself.*

Ahraia grimaced, fixing her grip, ready to push the blade forward.

There isn't a choice. I need my shadow. She braced herself. Knowing the pain that was about to come. *I'm going to be okay. I'm going to be a—*

A ray of light shifted. She drew her hand back, nearly exposed to it. It settled, directly between herself and the human. She waited, holding the enchantment. Once it passed, she would finish—

Snap!

A branch broke nearby. Ahraia flinched, startled to see movement off through the woods. A second human was stalking towards the darkening, still mostly hidden from view but coming closer. Ahraia's concentration broke, and the human in front of her swept back his hood, apparently just as startled by the noise as she was. He reached for his sword, then remembered it wasn't at his hip. A redoubled sense of fear echoed across the bond. Ahraia stood transfixed, paralyzed by the sudden fear, unable to push the drain forward.

The underbrush rustled with movement. The human's ears twitched and turned.

His ears . . . Ahraia stepped backwards, her task forgotten as she realized he wasn't at all what she had thought—he wasn't even human.

His ears were sharp and pointed, and they moved, almost like hers.

Alp! She broke the binding, recalling at once how dangerous the alp in the Stone Tree had been. The alp was suddenly moving, scrambling away from her, sensing her menace without even looking back to see her.

In that moment, she heard a leaf crackle right behind her, but there was no wind to turn it. She spun about.

Golan stood just a pace away, with his drain drawn and veil pulled close. His eyes glimmered madly. Startled, Ahraia's conveyance bubbled out.

What are you—

A haphazard enchantment suddenly bound her, strong, like the fingers of a bog mara, sharp and bony and meant for one thing. Golan lunged at her with the drain swinging towards her chest.

She reacted on instinct; her mind flexed, snapping the connection. She spun to the side, slowed by the tendrils of enchantment. Golan's drain tore across the side of her ribs. Searing pain burned across her side and it took all her power not to scream aloud.

Lightening quick, Golan swung again, violently. She formed her own binding, slowing his arm and ducking his swipe. She stabbed outward, and then sliced back as he dodged away. Her blade caught and tore across his shoulder.

He bared his teeth.

Ahraia scrambled towards the cover of the nit, her task forgotten, unsure where the lightwalkers were or if they had even seen her yet. Through her fleeting link to Golan, she sensed a maddening urge for death. She fled deeper into the darkening but he sprinted after her, tackling her to the ground. He rolled on top of her.

Ahraia wrestled and squirmed, but Golan's fingers were like vices, bruising her wrist and pinning her to the ground. He pounded her hand against a root, knocking her drain away.

His blade rose to strike and then plunged towards her. Ahraia bound him, flicking his hand aside. The drain slammed into the ground, an inch from her throat. Golan punched his elbow down, hammering into her face. Her teeth clacked together painfully, and she saw a darkness far beyond the coming night. Still loosely bound, she sensed him swinging towards her again. She rolled away, realizing the binding was her only escape. She took him, firmly in her mind.

Be still.

Golan went rigid. He struggled and she tightened the binding.

Her hold was absolute. Suddenly in control, she spun him onto his back. In an instant, she was on top of him, pressing her elbow to his neck, drawing the bone drain from her cloak.

His body went slack, yielding. He dropped his drain. His veil was pushed back, the scars on his neck running red to his chin.

He grinned manically.

Ahraia tasted blood in her mouth. Her lip was throbbing. She glanced in the direction of the alp and saw he was with the second figure, with his sword drawn. But it didn't appear they had heard the scuffle, and it appeared the alp hadn't seen her as he scrambled away. Golan and she had come to rest almost out of sight, hidden by the remnants of a fallen nit tree, but she could hear voices. She looked back to Golan.

"What in day's light are you doing? Why did you do this?" she hissed, too flustered for conveyance.

Golan laughed. It was a gurgled laugh cut short by the press of her wrist on his throat.

"I came to finish what she started. But it doesn't matter, she'll finish you in the end."

"All this for darkness?"

He struggled against the binding.

"Darkness? She doesn't care about darkness. She just wants you dead. To think you worry her . . ."

Ahraia pressed the knife down. "What good am I dead?"

He laughed again, maddened. The link flooded with writhing disbelief. "What good are you alive?"

"Then why not do it herself . . ."

"Killing a wolf-binder . . . it would be enough to start a war."

Ahraia let the pressure up slightly, her mind roiling like a raging river. If the Astra wanted her dead, maybe it made sense, to force her into her shadow test before she was ready. Yet, it seemed a stretch . . .

As she was thinking, a sudden urge rose in the ward to alert the lightwalkers, to ruin her test at the least. His mouth opened, a scream poised on his tongue.

Without thinking, Ahraia slashed the drain across his throat, silencing him instantly. His eyes widened. The linked surged with disbelief. He gasped, gargling on his own blood, but she grabbed his jaw, pressing it closed and keeping him silent. The vile mess streamed through her fingers, and then the binding severed.

Golan was still. And he was silent.

Ahraia looked towards the lightwalkers, but they remained where they were, not having noticed anything.

She looked down at the blood on her hands, waiting for the pain to crash over her.

Her heart pounded violently. Her hands dripped with blood. Any moment now, the breath would be squeezed from her; the void within would be ripped open. She would crumple into a ball and lay upon the forest floor until the light forced her to move.

Ahraia exhaled.

Nothing happened.

Golan's jaw was still in her hands, and the only pain she felt was where his elbow had slammed into her face. But she was livid. She had half a mind to cut his head off and drag it to the Astra, to show her what became of treachery.

She stood up, looking back to where the alp and the second figure were. They were still talking quietly, unaware of the fight that had just taken place. Ahraia stepped over the dae ward's body. She had a task to finish. She turned her attention to the lightwalkers with blood still dripping from her drain.

It's time I get my shadow back.

23

WRAITH

Ahraia crept towards the lightwalkers, her heart still hammering in her chest. Her thoughts were sharp, yet strangely detached. The kill felt surreal—unwanted—but not debilitating. It had been far more physical than visceral, but a cloud of awareness descended about her, as though she watched herself from afar. The sounds of the forest seemed muted, her feet numb and slow. Her cheeks burned with tingling blood.

I just killed a dae-ward, she thought, wondering why it wasn't affecting her worse. *I killed a sprite.* The hot coating of his blood covered her fingers, the stench hanging right beneath her nose.

She paused, her thoughts cut off as the lightwalkers moved towards her. The alp's ears turned left and right, scanning the woods almost like a sprite's would. His sword glimmered in the last vestiges of day.

She was surprised to see the second figure was a human, a girl, who moved unafraid at the alp's side.

"Come on, Den," she said. "You've been waiting all summer for this. Don't you want to explore, at least?" Her gaze traveled over the nits and shade trees as though she too knew what they were.

The alp hesitated to follow.

"Something is out here," he said in the common tongue, not bothering to mirror his own language.

Ahraia's mind felt blurred after the jarring fight with Golan. Her lip felt fat and blood congealed between her teeth.

A human and an alp. Lightwalkers roaming alone in the woods, as night fell. They made an odd pair. But she had her choice of marks, and that protective part of her, the part who echoed Losna's worries, lay in a pool of still-hot blood beneath the fallen ward.

The human stepped past the wall, peering through the darkening. The alp followed, his eye's lingered when they passed Ahraia. She didn't have to bind him to know his initial eagerness was spent; he was wary, doubly so with how close she had come to the kill.

Wariness won't protect you from me, she thought.

The alp's ears twitched. He grabbed the human, pulling her back.

"It's getting dark, Merra. And we still need to make camp. Come on."

"Where's your sense of adventure gone? There's nothing out here," the girl said, a hint of play twining with her words. But she let herself be pulled away, taking one last glance of the central hollow.

Ahraia moved stealthily after them. She wondered if she should act before they conjured up angry light from nothing. She hesitated, wanting the full cloak of night.

If I'm going to make a kill, I should at least act like a sprite.

The deep part of her growled, but she ignored it, setting off after the lightwalkers, her plans well ahead of her feet. *Camp* sounded vaguely similar to an underdae, but to keep the night at bay instead of the light. Whatever it was, they would undoubtedly settle in for the night, absurd as that seemed and once asleep, Ahraia could finish what she started. A slight chill ran through her. Her thoughts felt clearer.

It won't hurt me, not with what I've just done, she thought, her nerves still alight from the tussle with Golan.

Except he deserved it, the deep part of her reasoned, *just like Gavea did.*

Ahraia pushed down the thoughts. She had already made a kill.

This wouldn't be any different. And she had been so close to finishing the task already. She could still feel the bond: the way the alp had stood perfectly still in her mind, enraptured by her spell. In a way, it was intoxicating. A part of her wanted to bind him again.

With a final glance about the woods, the alp and the human turned away from the darkening. Ahraia followed them at a distance, stalking after them, her intentions solidifying with every step. She *had* to make a kill.

When the humans settled, Ahraia tucked herself nearby, hiding in the darkest corners of the forest, forced to wait while she planned her journey to Angolor. If she was quick enough with the task, she could set out tonight. The thought burned like a fire in her chest, blazing bright and hot. She settled back, watching. Waiting.

Willing now, she thought.

She could still hear the soft murmur of the lightwalkers' voices. Her initial shock of discovering the alp had been forgotten with Golan's ambush, but it was returning now. The more she watched him, the stranger he seemed, though not in a frightening way. He moved and talked like a human, and though his words were muffled, she could hear the human tongue in the rough intonations of his voice. His ears turned at all the small noises of the forest. But they also turned towards the human when she wasn't looking. Ahraia had the sense that he was trying to impress the girl, like a ward trying to impress a newly made sprite. He carefully placed his cloak around the girl and she drew it close against the cold.

He doesn't seem a wraith, Ahraia thought, surprised how different he seemed from the alp in the Stone Tree. The deep part of her rumbled.

She watched nervously as he went about gathering dry wood into a neat pile. Perplexingly, he carefully took the string from his bow and replaced it with a second string, looking too long and too loose to be of any use. Curiosity getting the best of her, Ahraia crept forward to a better vantage, encouraged by the settling dark. She formed a light binding, trying to gain a sense of what he was doing.

Fire, his thoughts said. The flame in his mind made Ahraia's hair stand on end, but she watched, unable to take her eyes away and wondering how he could make fire and light from sticks.

The alp started with a straight stick, sharpening it to a blunt point. Once he finished, he took the loosely strung bow and twisted it about the stick, so that the string wrapped tightly about the middle. He carefully arranged a bit of dry moss on the ground, then placed the stick on a small, flat plank which he had carefully removed from his quiver. He sawed the bow back and forth, the bowstring turning the stick, the point whittling against the board. Wood grated against wood. The soft noise sawed out in a steady rhythm, running against the erratic sounds of the forest awakening for the night.

The girl watched too now, and Ahraia sensed contentment in the alp's emotions. She wondered if making fire was some strange ritual for lightwalkers, like when wards sometimes tried folding darkness for sprites. The alp pushed the bow backward and forward, backward and forward.

Nothing happened.

Ahraia shifted, wondering if she wasted a binding in vain, when suddenly smoke began to curl upward. She froze.

The alp kept working, his concentration wrinkled across his brow. Smoke rose more quickly. He stopped, stooped and then somehow breathed flame into the moss. If Ahraia hadn't been bound to him, she would have been sure it was some alpish magic, but all he had done was breathe. And suddenly the small bit of the moss ignited, a miniature flame flickering to life. The alp carefully added more moss, and then the fire formed in earnest, burning outwards. The light touched Ahraia's skin, but she didn't flinch.

Instead, she settled in and waited. Waited for the cover of true dark. Waited for the lightwalkers to grow complacent. Waited for the moment to coax one away and finish her task.

Above, the clouds were breaking and a few stars were beginning to emerge. Her anticipation grew, watching the flame fighting feebly to keep the dark at bay. It wouldn't last forever. She sat, trying to decide which one she would kill.

The alp was certainly the more dangerous of the pair—with a

sword and bow and a searching mind. The girl was just a pixie of a thing, nearly as small as she was. It seemed almost unfair to kill her, without any virtue in the least. The growl inside her was quieter than before. At this point, Ahraia just needed the kill. The alps ears twitched at the call of an owl through the woods. His wariness fortified her decision. Ahraia buried her guilt.

The human it is, she thought.

~

MIDNIGHT CAME and went and still the lightwalkers hadn't slept. If they didn't soon, they were both dead. Ahraia wouldn't have a choice.

The flame of the fire—once wicked and gleaming—waned, hardly more than a flicker. And while the fire waned, the Dark and Bright moons waxed; both coming towards full though the Dark Moon would be far slower than her sister. The journey to Angolor would be long and perilous. Ahraia needed to be on the move, back to her shadow.

The barest cold brushed against her nerves. *Autumn's first chill*, she thought, missing the warm comfort of Losna. Deep down, she knew it was more than the cold that chilled her. It was the coming kill.

The stars turned about the world. The Dark Moon slipped downward in the west. Soon enough, the Bright Moon would follow, leaving only the Blood Moon. *Fitting*, Ahraia thought. The fire settled and the forest grew darker. A few stray leaves drifted down amongst the underbrush. Eventually, the girl lay down and slept. The alp stayed up, sitting late into the night, watching. He stoked the fire again and his sword glimmered in the new flames, but it was just a flicker in a world full of night. Eventually, he too, lay down to sleep.

Ahraia's gaze settled on the girl. She lay next to the alp, sleeping with her arm stretched above her head, towards his, but never touching.

Such a simple mistake.

Ahraia knew to keep Losna within touch. If one was roused, the other would be too. The Bright Moon dropped beyond the trees in the west.

Good. Ahraia didn't want the great hunter to know what she was about to do. Even as it did, the Blood Moon seemed to brighten, watching her like a single, red eye. The alp was deep in sleep, his chest hardly rising.

Time for this to be over. She was ready.

The link formed easily as she cast out her enchantment. The girl's mind was filled with simple dreams, unfettered by worry, and without any resistance to Ahraia's touch.

The girl had seemed curious about the darkening, so instead of rousing her outright, Ahraia made thoughts of Daispar drift across her mind, like the lazy clouds in the sky above. She closed her eyes, imagining rain streaming through the darkening's sieves and pools, the patter of water and incessant dripping that sang both night and day during a storm. She envisioned autumn leaves snagging on the wall. She could smell eaves-web being grown for cloaks and summer blankets, and hazelnuts being roasted in the hidden cook fires.

Wake up.

The girl stirred, her eyes coming open and her head rising off the ground.

Quiet, Ahraia insisted, brushing the girl's thoughts, careful not to arouse suspicion. *Aren't you curious about what's in there? Wake up.*

Ahraia formed a hazy image of the darkening wall, imagining a closure forming invitingly. Trying to make it more appealing to a lightwalker, she placed a tiny Dae-Mon sitting within, casting light all about the central hollow. It took all her cunning not to recoil from the vision.

Come here, Ahraia coaxed.

The girl rose to a knee. She stood and eagerly peered over the alp. Before Ahraia could stop her, she opened her mouth to speak.

"Denali—"

Shhh. Ahraia jumped as her voice leapt into the night like a lightning bolt. *Shhh,* she urged in panic. *Quiet. Don't wake him!*

The alp stirred slightly, but he slept on.

Ahraia let out a silent sigh. *Just you. He won't come, not tonight*, she thought, regaining her composure. *Come. Come, see what I have to show you.* She purveyed another thought of the darkening, this time at twilight, even more alluring.

The girl rose, wrapping her cloak tightly about herself. She stood a moment longer, looking towards the woods. Ahraia saw the alp's arrows lying close to him and hope stirred in her chest.

Bring his quiver. Carefully.

The girl leaned down and grabbed the clutch of arrows.

Good. Bring them with you, Ahraia conveyed, excited by the prospect of having arrows to do the task rather than her drain. The arrows were thick and straight, with silky-black feather fletchings.

The girl started towards the darkening, choosing each footstep on her way out of the firelight. The barest sense of fear crept into her thoughts.

It's okay. You're safe, Ahraia soothed. The keress had been hesitant to follow her, and every stag or rabbit she had bound was wary through and through. But the girl's fears seemed eager to fall to the point of absurdity. She followed Ahraia away from the firelight towards the darkening with the naivety of a spriteling.

Willing as she was, she stumbled as though she were blind. She stepped on branches and ran into tree limbs, moving so loudly that Ahraia was sure the alp would awake.

Quiet, Ahraia hissed, forcing the human to stop after her feet snagged an enormous fallen limb and dragged it across a bed of ferns. *That's too loud, even for a bear*, she chastised, *And you're not a bear, are you?*

Dim shame flowed off of the girl's mind. "I'm not a bear," she answered in a whisper. "There aren't bears out here, are there?"

No. Ahraia thought firmly, not about to let unnecessary fears creep into the girl's mind. Staying hidden, she folded back a branch for the girl.

Move slowly. Put your foot forward, keep it low so it doesn't catch, seeing as you're blind as a sheller pike.

"I'm not blind."

Yes, you are. Now slowly. Ahraia bent back ferns and limbs, pointing out roots and brambles, trying to clear a path for the girl to stumble forward by. Ahraia darted from one tree to the next, never allowing herself to be seen.

Finally, and with great difficulty, they reached the darkening. She guided the girl to the middle of what had been the central hollow. She lingered, half-hidden behind an old nit tree as she gathered her courage for the task.

The old shell trees were frayed and tattered, no more complete than a thick but unsewn forest. A hole was torn from the central hollow and the human stood bathed in untarnished starlight, casting about with dim eyes.

She looked as innocent as a fawn.

Sacrifice an enemy? Ahraia tried to suppress the rising guilt in her stomach. This girl was no enemy. If anything, she was more innocent than the keress, and the keress at least had an instinct to defend itself. This girl was simply uninhibited. *Curious.*

The girl stirred. She looked up, her gleamless eyes turning straight towards Ahraia. A shiver of awareness travelled through the bond. Ahraia held perfectly still. But the human's voice broke the night with the soft suddenness of the autumn wind.

"What are you?" she asked. "Are you a faerie?"

Ahraia ducked further behind the nit tree, heart hammering. The girl *knew* she was there.

"Don't be scared," the girl called.

No, no, no, Ahraia thought, trying to separate her worries from the binding. What was she supposed to do now? She had intended taking the arrows and then letting the girl loose. Would the girl call the alp? Could she make light like the other human had?

The girl stepped backwards, her knuckles tightening around the quiver.

Ahraia took a settling breath, forcing calm over herself. She couldn't let the chance slip. She peeked around the tree. *Innocent,* she thought, forcing the idea through the bond.

The human stared at her, mouth hanging open in a nervous smile.

"It's okay. I'm not going to hurt you . . . are you a faerie?" the girl asked again. Ahraia stepped cautiously out of the woods, keenly aware of the cool starlight against her skin.

A faerie?

"No . . ." the human said. "You're more like an elf, but your ears are longer. And your skin is so pale."

Not pale. Ashen, Ahraia thought, distracted.

"Pale's the wrong word," the girl said slowly. "More like ash—brushed in moonlight." From the girl's tone, Ahraia could tell she didn't expect to be understood.

Ahraia stepped timidly closer, feigning that she was afraid of the girl. And curious. It was easy enough, as she was both.

"I won't hurt you," the girl said again, completely still, as though worried Ahraia might startle. "Don't be shy, little elf."

"Elf?" Ahraia asked, her curiosity getting the best of her. Her ears batted nervously, and she mirrored her next words. "What is an elf?"

"You understand me?" the girl said in shock. Her eyes were as round as the moons. "Denali is an elf . . ." The girl gestured back through the wood.

An alp, Ahraia realized.

"But you're not an elf . . . your skin is too light . . . and your ears are too long. What are you? Are you a mare of sorts?" The girl was getting worried.

"I am a shade."

"A night elf?" The girl's worry solidified, manifesting in the turn of her shoulders and the short, rapid rise in her chest.

"A night elf?" *Is that what humans call us?*

The girl nodded. Her emotions were terrifying. Her curiosity and fear were deep wells, threatening to drown Ahraia. The side of Ahraia that feared the kill was rising to the surface, taking control of her mind.

"Is this your home?" the girl asked, gazing around them. "Are there others like you?"

"No," Ahraia said. "But it's like my home." The human was frighteningly familiar. Like a shade. Like herself. Like Losna. Ahraia shook her head, struggling to remember her purpose, struggling to remember she had already killed a dae-ward without harm. *I need to make this kill. I need to get this over with.*

The girl shifted uncomfortably, words coming to her mouth as a sort of defense.

"Denali thinks it might be an elvish village, but I didn't think there are elves in the North Woods. He's looking for them . . . he's always been looking for them . . . I didn't have the heart to tell him that I didn't think they were out here. But you're out here, so maybe there are elves too."

Ahraia shook her head, her enchantment slipping slightly. The girl's rambling was overwhelming. Her pitter-patter thoughts were like Losna's—rich and unchecked, tumbling out like an overflowing stream.

"My brother thinks elves are dangerous. That's why he doesn't think I should be friends with Denali. He thinks that we should keep to our own kind. Which isn't hard. Denali is the only elf in Holbrook. He might be the only elf in all of Astenith . . ."

Friends? The concept was like a light-burst of emotion within Ahraia. She had never heard the word, but she immediately thought of Hayvon and Kaval, and Losna. Or Kren before she had been condemned to her test. Only to this human, it meant something more, something beyond the nit, almost like a shadow. The thought of what Ahraia was about to do sickened her. The enchantment slipped even more.

"I'm Merra." The girl swallowed nervously. "Merra Avvington. If this isn't your home, then what . . ."

Shhhh, Ahraia conveyed, unable to take it anymore. She was so innocent—just a spriteling. Simple and naïve. Harmless. Hopeless.

"Shhhh," Ahraia said, recalling the word again. *Friend*. Her heart was going to burst. A noxious pain welled up inside her. She had to get it over quickly, before the girl's madness seeped into her, before her own instincts corrupted her. She didn't have time for the arrows. She pulled the drain from her waist.

I don't mean to hurt you, Ahraia conveyed, stepping forward.

"What are you doing?" Haunting fear reflected back through the link, showing in every crease and corner of the girl's face and body. "You're scaring me."

I'm sorry. Ahraia firmly took hold of the girl's mind, trying to focus on the fact that Losna would be saved, trying to remember that it was all for her shadow.

"Please. Don't hurt me."

Hold still. The less you fight, the less troubling it will be.

"Please," the girl managed to exhale, stricken with panic. "I have a brother. He's only eight. He won't understand."

"I don't want this, either," Ahraia whispered. She tried to tighten her will about the girl. *The innocent girl*. Tears welled in her eyes. She didn't want this burden. The girl's mind wasn't even scratching or clawing to break free.

Ahraia stepped forward, having no choice but to finish it. The girl went blank with fear, no longer seeing or feeling, just trapped by the paralysis Ahraia was inflicting.

Ahraia heard howling, not in the night, but inside. Some part of her, the part who knew Losna through and through, the part of her that had wanted to run, had wanted to be done with the test, was howling in anguish. It didn't want her to carry through with it.

I'm no better than the wraith . . .

The howling intensified, driving her mad.

"I can't do this. This isn't me," she whispered. She lowered the drain, unable to go through with the kill.

She felt tears brimming beneath her eyes, disgusted that she had even thought to do it, knowing how Losna would have hated her. The girl's lip quivered. Ahraia looked at the human and saw before her a scared and broken child. She peeled her mind away, ashamed and took a step back.

From the corner of her eye, she saw movement and she glanced toward the woods just as the alp emerged, his sword glinting in the light of the stars.

"Get away from her," he said in the human tongue. The blade moved easily in his hand.

Ahraia reached out to enchant him, to slow him, and found a raw and ragged courage brimming up in him. She sensed him on the verge of leaping at her. His ears turned downward, spritishly.

She seized the clutch of arrows, trying to wrest them free from the girl who mindlessly clung to them.

The alp lunged forward, his sword singing through the air. The girl let go and Ahraia stumbled back, the quiver rattling with arrows. The alp shouted. Ahraia leapt aside, tumbling across the overgrown green, no longer thinking of the kill, thinking only of escape.

She grabbed the quiver and ran.

24

SEVERED

The next several nights passed in a haze. Ahraia kept as close to the human realm as she dared, even walking down the center of their great flat roads. But at night, the roads were empty—as empty as spritish paths were by day.

She passed houses with golden lights, but she skirted far beyond them, not wanting any more trouble with humans and their nits. The mountains soared towards the stars, their white flanks reflecting light even in the dead of night. She came upon a whole darkening of lights, hundreds of bright points scattered across a great bowl of a valley. The sight made her stomach tighten in a hard knot. She heard bleating animals, and smelled the steady stench of humans mingling with wood smoke. She stayed well away from the light, and only ever saw humans from afar. In a way, she was glad. She had already resigned to the fact that running was her only hope. She had to find Losna and she would have to send a message to Kyah to flee. If the spritelings headed south, towards the mountains, and if she could free Losna, maybe they could all escape their fates . . .

Still, she hesitated sending her message to Kyah. Finding the right bird to carry the message would be difficult, and holding an enchantment over that distance . . . she wasn't even sure if it was possible.

It was with these thoughts that Ahraia found herself facing a monstrous stone bridge. Below, a river frothed in the moonlight, filling the night with an ever-churning roar. It was too wide and too angry for any spring branch, and swimming was out of the question. Golan's guidance had showed her this bridge, and she knew that her way forward lay across it.

And they say lightwalkers are graceless, she thought, staring at the unbreakable stone. How it came to be, or how it could stand unending, with the waters ripping at its feet below was beyond her.

She slunk back into the forest, too terrified to cross the bridge. The Bright Moon was low in the west, radiant beyond a thin veil of fog, bathing the stone in cloudy white. The Blood Moon was watching from above, slower than her bright sister. Ahraia searched far along the deep canyon for a place to cross but none showed itself. By the time she returned to the bridge, a storm was moving in.

First came the wind, setting the treetops swaying loudly. Next, a bank of great clouds moved in from the south, bringing with them a fitful darkness that came and went with unnatural suddenness. A bank of fog followed, crawling up the valley until it engulfed the bridge. Ahraia cursed herself for hesitating. She reached out with her mind for any humans who might be watching.

The night felt empty. She smelled human horses, but it was a stale smell, pressed into the stone, and without other choice, she moved out on to the stone column.

Look away. Nothing but night here, she projected. Her feet whispered against the stone, but a growing sense of dread came with each step. In no time at all, she was out over the river, the waters rushing below. The wind pulled at her hair. The trees on the far bank suddenly emerged ahead, like the Shad-Mon stepping from the fog. Ahraia, stopped, overwhelmed by fear.

She took refuge in a small nook made by a knot in the bridge from which the pillars extended downward. She was almost across, but couldn't bring herself to move.

Suddenly, the forest ahead erupted with noise. A terrible trumpeting rose, like the call of some enormous, unknown beast.

Ahraia threw herself to the ground, recoiling in panic. The moons were covered by black clouds, and in the darkness, she heard the shouts and screams of humans.

Wild, preposterous thoughts came to her. *Could they have been hunting me all this time? Did they alert the entire realm?* Trapped, she waited for humans to charge the bridge.

But nothing came.

The horns called again, and she heard distant noises. Metal clanged against metal, and the screams grew more wild and terrified.

Look away. Look away. Look away, she projected blindly, hoping she hadn't been seen.

Suddenly, she heard footsteps. A human sprinted onto the bridge, a sword in hand. Ahraia pulled the bow from her shoulder, reaching in panic for an arrow. A great clattering sounded, and she froze. Hooves echoed against stone, and she saw a beastly silhouette charging behind the human. Ahraia pressed herself into the small corner, her heart hammering. Before she got the arrow to her bowstring, the figure ran straight past her and a moment later, the beast charged past as well. It was a horse, and astride it rode a hooded human who didn't even glance at her.

The first human ran screaming into the fog. The rider stormed to the far side of the bridge and Ahraia heard a howl of fear suddenly cut short. It was difficult to see, but the rider stopped, and his horse turned, wreathed in fog. She heard the canter of hooves coming back towards her.

Ahraia didn't wait to see what had happened. She stood and sprinted off the bridge. She thought about the kill, about trying to bring a human down, but the woods were echoing with shouts and clashing metal. She had no idea how many of them there were, and no idea if a horse would attack—maybe it was like a shadow or a keress. Either way, she didn't want to find out. She couldn't imagine what could cause such a cacophony of noise, and wished only to be away from it.

She scrambled into the woods where the sounds were growing

more and more unpredictable and strange. The forest was a medley of noise and wind, of dark and light.

She found a dark patch of trees and slithered between them. Her breaths came rapidly. Scared and unsure, she bound a tree and let it spring her into the higher branches. She climbed higher and stopped only when she was sure no human could reach her.

She took a steadying breath, but held it as she heard movement below. The wind stilled, swelling away over ridges, distant and haunting. Leaves rustled and she heard grunts and crashing through the underbrush. She looked and saw a human tumble down a hillside. He rose over a log and collapse behind it.

Don't look. Don't look, Ahraia projected, scared that he might call more humans to him. He didn't, and instead lay on the ground panting hoarsely.

Slowly, he settled, as did the sounds in the forest. There were no more trumpeting calls. But the storm remained, passing through the trees in great swells and fits. Ahraia thought she smelled blood on the wind. She definitely smelled the reek of humans. There were more about in the woods, she was sure of it. But this one was alone. And she had the alp's arrows . . .

Her test, already abandoned, suddenly seemed possible. She hadn't bound him yet—she could hardly even see him—and if she got a clean shot, it wouldn't hurt her. She could claim his head and be gone.

Her heart thrummed with hope.

In an instant, Ahraia made her decision, pulling an arrow from her clutch. With the breeze and distance, the shot wouldn't be easy. Impossible, really. Thick tree trunks hid the human. She thought about moving, but just then the wind died, leaving her in total silence. The leaves trapped her where she stood.

But the human began to move. He crawled across the ground, his breaths coming in sobs. With all the noise he made, Ahraia wondered if his eyes were closed, but he was crawling closer.

Keep coming, she thought to herself, not daring to reach out with her mind.

She balanced on a slender branch, drawing an arrow to her bow. The alp's arrow was perfectly straight, heavily weighted by the sharp point and balanced by the feathers.

One more step. A clean shot was all she needed.

The branches swayed with a gust of wind, then settled. She bound them, holding them out of her way. The human stood just behind a tall pine. Ahraia's breaths were steady, one eye closed as she sighted down the shaft. If he so much as leaned forward, he would be her's.

Something grunted off through the woods. Something moved beneath her. Slowly. Quietly.

She froze.

The human—a boy—didn't move. He had heard it too. Hooves stepped quietly over dry leaves, like a keress stalking beneath her in the woods. Ahraia stepped silently closer to the tree, the moment for her shot having passed. She sniffed.

A horse.

The human slunk out of view, hiding in the underbrush.

Ahraia waited as the sounds that had burst through the forest earlier slowed and disappeared. The moons drifted between the clouds. Then she saw a figure away through the woods.

More humans.

The trunks were too thick to get any sense of them, but a moment later, she heard something rushing through the underbrush, running down the hillside.

A shout rose through the air. Ahraia flinched, instinctively shielding her mind, even from mirroring. She hugged the trunk of the tree, pressing her body against it so as not to be seen. There was more yelling—a tense voice. And then silence.

Don't see me. Don't look up. There is nothing in these woods. You are alone . . . she projected, hoping the open enchantment would keep prying eyes away. She couldn't afford a true binding. If there was any chance for a kill, she couldn't let that weak part of her rise up. She held perfectly still. Through the woods, she heard more humans, their voices muted, too dim to hear. The boy was cowering in the brush.

Ahraia nearly fell from the tree when a horn suddenly trumpeted through the night. She heard a horse snort and then hoof beats and the group of humans was moving off through the woods. A moment later, the boy was out of hiding and running after them. Ahraia thought she saw a glimmer of a sword.

Hardly thinking, she formed a shift and stepped in to the air, her bow still in hand. She swung down to a lower branch that delivered her to the ground in a single motion, dropping her the last two feet with her heart thudding heavily in her chest. She landed on the ground as the boy passed out of sight.

Tonight, I become a daemon, she thought, sprinting after him.

AHRAIA STARED through the dense trees, struggling to understand what she was seeing. An alp stood in the woods. Along with a sprite. And a human. And before them all, another human knelt on the ground, breathing shallowly, with three arrows sticking from his chest.

What made it stranger was that it was the same golden haired alp that had been conspiring with the Astra, the same one who had killed her brothers.

Ahraia's neck hairs stood on end, remembering how the alp had sensed her before, when she had been searching out her father. She quickly formed a barrier to any thoughts, dimming her mind in hopes of staying hidden.

No one's out here. You are alone. Nothing but night and woods, she thought repeatedly, until she almost believed it. But beneath those thoughts, she wondered what she was seeing. She had never seen anything like this. Sprites, hooded and pale, stood next to alps, tall and deadly, with humans among them too. Some were afoot and some on horse. Some were veiled and others not. The boy she had followed was hiding in the trees ahead of her, legs shaking as he watched on.

She watched the alp with the golden hair, still projecting her thoughts nervously. *Don't look. Don't see. Don't hear*, she thought, concentrating on being indistinguishable from the night.

The alp was speaking to the injured human in front of her. Ahraia couldn't hear their voices, but the human looked like he was on the brink of death. He was bleeding, laboring in his movement. The boy in front of Ahraia was quivering, almost leaning forward as though held back by invisible bindings.

The injured human stood, pressing himself up despite the arrows. The golden-haired alp calmly stepped forward, drawing a short dagger. In the moonlight, it looked dark, almost black. The alp said a quiet word and then punched the dagger into the human's chest.

Ahraia gasped.

The boy in front of her flinched, as though he had been stabbed himself. The human slid off of the blade, still rasping for life. Ahraia shuddered, wondering if it had been the same for Kaval and Altah. She wondered if the Astra had returned the blackened blade of the Stone Tree to the alp. The alp called out to the others, and the strange group gathered themselves and made off through the woods. As soon as they did, the menace lifted. The forest seemed empty where a moment before it was filled at every corner.

The boy she had followed suddenly started moving again. He stumbled forward as though unfrozen. Ahraia heard his voice, and watched as he curled over the body of the fallen human and cried. She crept closer, leaving her arrows in their quiver. She didn't intend to bind him —she had no interest in knowing how broken he was, but she mirrored his words, just as she saw the fallen human's hand go limp. *Dead.*

"Brother? Edwin?" the boy choked in the human tongue. She could hear him sobbing into the dead man's chest. She broke the bonding. The pain was too sharp, even just to mirror his words. The dead human and the boy were of the same nit, the same *house* as the human at the lightening had called it.

She slumped to the ground, hearing only the sobbing sounds of the boy.

Ahraia couldn't bear to even listen. She felt like she was losing her own brothers again, like she had just watched Kaval and Altah die, like she was re-living Hayvon disappearing into the fog. She hated herself for what she was supposed to do. She lay looking the other way for a long time.

You have to be ruthless, a voice within said.

Ahraia stood up, drawing her drain.

I will be.

25

LOST

The head swung back and forth in a makeshift sack, bumping Ahraia's leg with every other step forward, dragging over low ferns and swinging wildly as she leapt over logs. She couldn't bear the smell of dried blood and ruined flesh, but even worse was the guilt wracking through her for taking it. It hung like a weight on the back of her tongue, threatening to gag her at every breath. The dead weren't meant to be meddled with.

Not even by daemons, she thought, sickened by her own actions. Even with the razor-sharp bone knife, it hadn't been easy.

To top it off, she was lost—and she was out of time. The Bright Moon's turning was all but spent.

"Where in the light are you, Losna?" she muttered, seeing only the same rainswept woods she had seen for the last two nights. Droplets fell from dying autumn leaves and pine needles alike. With every step, water squelched up from the sodden ground. Her boots were soaked through, her feet within were heavy and wrinkled and numb. The Bright Moon had already passed the Blood Moon in her circuit. She wouldn't be rising except just before dawn.

If she isn't already turned, Ahraia thought darkly, unsure. The nights had melded together into one unidentifiable mess. She guessed a dozen nights had passed since she had taken the fallen human's head. The full alignment of the Blood Moon and Bright Moon had come and gone, and all she knew for sure was she hadn't seen anything recognizable for the last three nights. Her desperation had long ago passed to resignation.

I'm never going to find Angolor, she thought.

Thick fog swirled through the tree trunks.

Her hair was lank and dripping wet. She guessed she was close—close enough that she had hidden her bow and the alp's quiver in case she stumbled upon the darkening.

The fog shifted and Ahraia wondered where she had gone wrong. More than once it had occurred to her that Golan's directions could have misled her. But it had been an open enchantment, and surely someone would have spoken up—her father, at the very least. Unless he was in on it with the Astra.

She felt blood warming her cheeks.

If Losna's been shown the light, let these be the Shadow Woods. Let me be done with this, she thought. The dimmest light in the east began to show. A raven cawed nearby. She looked about and saw its brilliant, white feathers. A moon raven. The worst omen.

The time had come to send a message to Kyah.

Ahraia looked about the woods for any other birds. The spattering of rain swelled as though trying to drive all living things deeper into their shelter. She reached out with her mind, searching for life. She was alone. There were no other birds to be had.

Just my luck.

It seemed as soon as she had taken the human's head, she had been cursed.

The days and nights afterwards had been the worst Ahraia had ever known. She spent the first day tucked beneath the roots of a monstrous human bridge, just across the river from one of their stone darkenings. Under the bridge wasn't nearly as sheltered as she expected, and she listened in terror as the humans clanged bells and trumpeted horns all day long. She heard shouts and marshaled voices, and then an endless line of lightwalkers had emerged, shaking the bridge with their passing. Ahraia cowered in the darkest shadows, tucked in against the cold stone, sure that they would sense her or the head she carried: the stench of blood was nauseating. The next night, she had pushed on with all haste, putting as many miles between herself and the human realm as she could.

But the nights had not grown better.

The forests had become less familiar, with endless, deep valleys and ever-churning rivers. Strange creatures haunted the woods. A lone Hob had tried to surprise her, and a bear had nearly stolen the human head from her while she was trapped underdaeing. Her mind felt raw binding it, and she barely managed to send it lumbering back through the woods.

At night, there were plenty of maras to avoid. Like biting bugs that emerged in the summer, she couldn't fathom how they survived without flesh and thought to sustain themselves. She even saw a massive jontun wading in the river, and when it spotted her, it rushed towards her with earth-shaking strides. In the Gelesh, these creatures feared sprites and kept their distance. But here, they seemed wild and unafraid. One pair of imps had followed her for an entire night before she managed to scare them off with a well-placed arrow.

By the fifth day, the smell of dried blood and sweat beneath her nose burned her nostrils. Her underdaes hadn't afforded much protection from the Dae-Mon and her markings were seared-in by the constant light that she had suffered. She slept wedged beneath fallen logs one day and fought a fox for its undersized den the next. She had even tucked herself beneath a crowded clump of pines in the deepest corner of the forest when she couldn't find anything better. She rested fitfully, and when she slept, her dreams were filled with the sobbing voice of the human boy, calling "*Brother . . . brother.*"

And if the daytime dreams were bad, the waking nights were even worse.

She felt the head thump against her leg.

Brother.

Another step.

Brother.

She swallowed down her rising sickness. A weight, far greater than the contents alone, lay upon her. The human boy's anguish haunted her, gnawing at her conscience. The world seemed intent on condemning her, and the rain fell even harder. The Dae-Mon was coming.

Ahraia wondered if it was even worth finding an underdae. The forest around her was dark enough to sleep where she stood. At first, it had seemed a boon, a sign that she was close: the canopy was thick and healthy, and the understory thin and spritish. The only things growing were those plants that loved the dark: sap pines and leech ferns, willow root and spindle elms. But the Masai had spoken of walking for days beneath the dark, and now Ahraia understood why.

Losna! Just call out. I'll find you, she conveyed desperately.

But the bond was still stretched too thin.

The eaves-web of her cloak succumbed to the wet, seeping through as though she had jumped headfirst into the stream she was running alongside. She leapt over a fallen log and flitted down a mossy hillside. A valley wall loomed ahead. The pervasive gray of the coming dawn spread like fog through the rain-laden trees. Ahraia's time was up. There was no more night to run in. She passed through a low dell, with sparse grass and stopped dead in her tracks.

White wings of a moon raven fluttered across the shadows.

A figure stood at the edge of the glade. A sprite, standing before Ahraia in a black fur cloak.

A smile spread across Ahraia's face in recognition.

It was the Masai. Her eyes glowed out tenebrously.

Shade Ahraia. You're just in time.

THE TREES beyond the Masai rose in great, towering columns. Far within, the rough form of an enormous darkening wall melded with the forest, a shell so expansive that Ahraia had mistaken it for a valley wall. The rains were lessened where she stood, and stopped entirely a dozen feet away, funneled down by a series of spiraled spinners and leaf-turns. Hooded sprites and veiled wards materialized from the shadows, wings rustled distantly and ravens cawed in chorus. Ahraia's heart unclenched.

The tension collected across her mind broke for the first time since Losna had been taken from her and her lungs swelled with fresh air, as though she hadn't breathed properly in a full turning.

"This is Angolor?" she asked. *I'm going to see my shadow.* The thought escaped in a moment of unchecked elation.

But it only lasted a moment.

Her relief faltered as her gaze came to rest on the Masai and the black cloak that she wore. Ahraia's smile slid from her face.

The cloak, black as true dark and draped skin-like over the Masai's shoulders, was an enormous wolf hide. The hood was the wolf's head, and its bone white teeth hung above the Masai's stark yellow eyes.

The blood drained from Ahraia's face. Her stomach clenched and she felt lightheaded, her worry for Losna redoubling.

"At the last possible moment." The Masai shook her head.

More sprites were emerging from the shadow-clad trees. With a flutter in her chest, Ahraia saw Kren amongst them. Both relief and anger twined together, but at once, her attention was drawn away. The Astra hurried towards her, unimpeded by the dim glow of dawn. She was followed by a harrowed looking group of wards and sprites from Daispar.

"Shade Ahraia! Where have you been?" she said crossly. *Did you swim here?* She glanced towards Ahraia sodden hair.

Ahraia's tongue pushed against her thickened lip where Golan's elbow had slammed into her. She glared at the Astra.

Are you surprised to see me?

The Astra furrowed her brow. Her skin had the faintest light markings, and her eyes had just a tinge of gold at the edges.

You're late, she conveyed. She was tensed forward, like a tree grown against an ever-blowing gale.

"She *is* late," the Masai said flatly, drawing Ahraia's attention sharply back. Her ears flickered in an aggressive manner, indicating she didn't want any conveyance beneath the surface.

"Late?" Ahraia said, her voice weak from disuse. "I'm just in time. The Bright Moon is still turning."

The Masai pursed her lips. The sprites from Daispar were nodding. The Astra's eyes flickered towards the sack in hand.

"Have you done it? Have you killed an enemy?" The tension seemed to bleed from her and her voice quavered with excitement.

Feigned excitement, Ahraia thought, glowering at her as she remembered Golan's words. The Astra's act was convincing. The fact that she had sent a dae-ward to kill Ahraia didn't show on her face in the least. The Masai's eyes narrowed.

"Yes. What have you brought me? What enemy have you killed?"

Ahraia walked across the glade, looking for Losna.

Where is my shadow?

You'll see her soon enough, the Masai conveyed.

Ahraia handed the rain-soaked sack over with a breath of relief. The Masai opened it and tipped her head down to peer inside. The wolf's lidded eyes stared at Ahraia.

The Masai smiled a sickening, flat smile. The Astra peered over her shoulder, insincere relief spreading vacantly on her face. The sprites around the glade leaned forward, ears twitching and gazes shifting to get a better look.

The Astra reached into the sack and grabbed the human head, withdrawing it by its lank and blood matted hair.

"A man," she said with a wild look in her eyes. "And a healthy one, at that."

The Masai looked at the head, then at Ahraia.

"You should have been here nights ago."

Ahraia kept her eyes down. The Astra seemed ambivalent to the Masai's mood.

"Come. Let us get away from this accursed light and you may tell us all about the kill."

Ahraia couldn't look at the head. Her stomach turned. She swallowed, and found the Masai staring at her.

"Did you kill it in the day time?" *Get her a veil and make her a ward*, she conveyed loosely. Wicked smiles mixed with condemning muttering. The sprites from Daispar shifted uncomfortably.

Ahraia flushed with embarrassment, wishing she could cover her markings. When the Masai made her thoughts known again, they were just for Ahraia.

I hope you know how close it was, she conveyed.

The Astra swung the human head in her hand as though she had just learned the Dae-Mon was dead.

"Your task isn't finished yet," the Masai said. She nodded to one of her wards. "Give me the spire." A sprite stepped forward and gave her a long spear, bone-white and as tall as Ahraia was.

The Astra held out the human's head, but the Masai's ears batted back, and she pushed the spear into the Astra's hands.

"You show her."

The Astra took the spear and tossed the head casually onto the ground. It thudded and rolled onto its side, staring up at Ahraia with blank, horrible eyes. The Astra brought it about with a kick of her foot.

"The trick is to hold it steady with your feet." She demonstrated, positioning it so that the severed neck was pointing to the sky, muscle and ligaments and flesh all ragged and rotten. She lined up the spear. "You want to hit it slightly towards the back of the neck. Where it's softer. That way you won't hit bone, right about here." She pointed with the spear. "But if you're not careful, you'll skewer your foot. Here." She handed the spear to Ahraia.

Ahraia immediately recognized the bone by touch. It was from the keress, likely the long bone of the leg, sharpened into points on both ends.

"Innocent and enemy together," the Astra said, nodding.

The spear felt rotten to her hand, but Ahraia had seen enough staked heads to know its purpose. Revolted, she arranged the mangled mess so the neck faced upward, lining up the spear while clenching her stomach and holding her breath.

"Do it," the Astra urged her.

Excitement swelled from the sprites surrounding them. Ahraia's thoughts went to the human boy crying over his brother; she tried not to imagine what he would think if he ever knew what she had done.

I'm sorry, she thought. She held her breath and raised the spear. She plunged it downward. Hard bone and tissue crunched beneath the point.

"Good!" the Astra said. "Now, go and mark your territory. Put it away from the darkening, where any unexpected visitors will see it. This is your land now too, Ahraia." The Astra smiled at the Masai.

The Masai watched on silently.

Ahraia carried the spear back towards the dimly lit forest, holding the head away in disgust. Stringy saliva flooded her mouth.

I need my shadow, she thought, horrified at what she held. *Losna?* She reached out again with her mind, but felt no sense of her.

She found a place of soft earth and pushed the spear into the ground. It stood unbearably tall. She wished she could bury it. *Or burn it*, she thought, *if that's what the humans do.*

She hurried back towards the darkening.

"Well done, Shade Ahraia. Your second task is complete," the Masai said.

When do I get to see Losna? Ahraia conveyed, desperate to be reunited. She was ready to run, to flee and be done with the test. The Masai stared at her, with no light in her eyes.

"You don't," she said. "Not until your third task."

26

DARKNESS

Ahraia could feel each individual heart beat in her ears, pounding, one after another. Her vision narrowed to a dark point.

"Why not? Where is she?" She looked at Kren. "None of the other shades were taken from their shadows before their third task."

"You aren't one of the other shades, Ahraia. Stop groveling." The Masai turned back to the darkening, gesturing for her wards to follow.

Ahraia's despair threatened to suffocate her. For the whole turning, the only thought keeping her sane had been that Losna would be waiting for her.

I just want to see her. Just once, she conveyed, unable to contain her thoughts.

"Another half a turning isn't going to kill you," the Masai called back, with finality. "You are on the verge of becoming a sprite."

The eyes of the sprites in Angolor seemed whiter than those in the Gelesh, milky pale, and more indifferent than the stars on a winter night. Dozens of them stared cruelly at Ahraia from the deep dark of the woods. Kren stood amongst them, hooded and empty eyed.

"Half a turning?" Ahraia said breathlessly. She couldn't last that long. Another day or night without Losna would kill her.

"Come, Ahraia. You've passed your second task," the Astra said.

But Ahraia was unable to move as the Astra and Masai turned towards the darkening. *I want my shadow back.*

The wolf cloak trailed after the Masai, its legs and tail dragging lifelessly on the ground. The rest of the sprites followed. Kren's gaze lingered on Ahraia. An impassivity spread across her face, but her eyes burned with something else. *Fear? Hatred? Hope?* Ahraia couldn't say and Kren quickly turned about when Ahraia met her eye. Her sister hurried after the sprites, falling in amongst the nitesses of Angolor.

The sprites from Daispar followed the Astra, relieved, chattering quietly and filling the corners of the forest with conveyance. They obviously weren't aware that the Astra's intentions had failed.

Ahraia's gaze followed her sister. Her feet started to move.

Kren, she conveyed, keeping her thoughts subtle and hastening after the group.

Kren's eye twitched. Binding her sister's mind was like holding a stone after a dry freeze: cold through to its inner heart.

Have you seen Losna? Is she well? Ahraia conveyed.

Kren didn't answer, but walked briskly forward into the waiting wings of true dark.

Kren! Ahraia conveyed more forcibly. *Have you seen her?*

Several heads turned towards Ahraia, including the Masai. A sharp conveyance from the Astra told her to keep her thoughts to herself. Ahraia slowed. Kren glanced back but didn't answer, moving quickly towards the darkening. The bond grew dimmer, the cold stinging worse than the sodden cloak Ahraia wore. She let their bond dissolve.

Half a turning? she thought again. Her despair solidified with every step, anchoring her heart to the ground.

Deep shadows layered the forest even though they were still well beyond the wall. The ground was dry, the rain flowing down flutings and out of sight. The light back in the glade wasn't growing, it was murky gray though the day had certainly risen beyond.

And still outside the darkening, Ahraia realized dimly.

Finding Losna wouldn't be easy. Trunks towered upwards, sweeping out in sprawling webs of intricate darkness. It was excessive —and immersive. There was no understory, just hollowed vaults higher than Ahraia had ever seen, higher even than the central hollow of Daispar. This was an old forest, darker and deeper than the Gelesh. Proud, from root tips to branch tips. And this was only the outer edges of the grove, one small fragment of a greater swell. Ahraia's heart sunk.

Losna could be anywhere.

She wondered if there was a place like the chasms, or maybe even the Makers.

The ribs of the shell stood a dozen feet across and sweeping vines as thick as tree trunks were the smallest threads in the woven palisade. When the closure formed, it uncurled into a great, sweeping arch, tall enough and wide enough for a pair of the largest keress to pass beneath, with room to spare above and beside.

Ahraia stopped on the threshold, overwhelmed by the darkening.

A stream gurgled forth near at hand, spreading into a broad sheet before cascading over an arc of short hanging cliffs to a shallow pool below. Other rivulets chattered to life, either from underground or overhead, pouring over falls and catch-lips in a chorus of water.

If not for the empty pit in the depths of her belly, Ahraia would have been stunned by the sprawling dark before her. It was vast. Open. Held by columns wider than any trees Ahraia had ever seen, fading into the shadows.

Shadows . . . Ahraia thought, distracted by a moon raven flapping and cawing. A fox hopped after a shade over a series of broad, flat stones amidst the streams.

Losna? She searched out again, hardly noticing as a younger sprite joined them from the pools below. Ahraia's calm was unraveling. For a whole turning she had kept her desire contained, knowing there was nothing else she could do about getting to Losna without finding

Angolor. But now, knowing her shadow was close, she was desperate. She wondered if she could search during the height of day.

It must never get light here. Even on a midsummer's day. She guessed there were sprites and shades about at all hours.

"Ahraia," the Masai said, bringing her out of her reverie. "This is Sprite Shalih," *My youngest daughter.* "She will be a sister to you, should you pass your test."

Shalih's gaze was fixed on Ahraia, boring into her. Kren's was too.

Ahraia ignored them, distracted. *Dusk,* she thought. *It might get light at dusk.* The hill faced west. If it got light enough, maybe she could go looking at the lightest moment . . .

"Shade Ahraia," the Masai's daughter said without bowing.

Sprite Shalih. Ahraia nodded, hardly aware of herself, forgetting to tuck her ears. She wondered if Losna had been hunting. *Was she fed? Was she well?*

"While you are here in Angolor," the Masai said, "you will be a guest to Shalih until you have seen yourself through your shadow test."

Shalih didn't look much older than Ahraia, a couple of full turnings of the Dae-Mon at most. The night-gleam in her eyes was bright, but her face was pale and sunken. Like Kren's.

Lifeless, Ahraia thought to herself. *Lifeless and dead. Like I'm going to be if I don't see my shadow soon. I need to leave this place.* Her markings itched. They always did when she had been in too much light.

"You'll have her former nit. It's empty now that she's passed her own shadow test," the Masai said. "She'll be growing her own."

Congratulations . . . Ahraia nodded absentmindedly. *I need my shadow. I need to leave here.* Her eyes flashed up realizing that she had let all of her thoughts out to Shalih.

The sprite's ears twitched. She smiled but said nothing.

I'm sorry. I just want to see my shadow. Ahraia swallowed nervously, hoping the Astra or the Masai hadn't known her thoughts. *When will I know my test?* she conveyed loosely, hoping to distract them.

"Eager, aren't you?" The Masai smiled a flat, placating smile.

"You've only just arrived. We must make you welcome first." *Shalih, show Shade Ahraia the darkening.*

By your will. Shalih bowed, formally dropping her head, eyes, and ears before gesturing for Ahraia to walk beside her.

Ahraia realized belatedly they were dismissed and flickered her ears with a half-bow of her head. Her eyes never met the ground. She hurried after the Masai's daughter, feeling Kren's gaze burning after her. Shalih led her across the top of the falls by a pathway of precarious stone steps. Water flowed on all sides, shallow but swift, and surprisingly quiet, rolling over the edge and out of sight. Ahraia nearly slipped in carelessness, her eyes darting about, searching for Losna.

They crossed a stair, wound beneath a tunnel of massive roots and emerged below the falls. Out of earshot, Shalih dropped her stiff manner. Her eyes warmed and her ears drooped slightly as she turned to Ahraia.

"Your shadow is gorgeous," she said.

"You've seen her?" Ahraia blurted before she realized that she should have conveyed it.

Shalih smiled, pardoning Ahraia's voice with a casual flick of her left ear.

"Yes, quite beautiful."

Where is she? Ahraia flushed, feeling panicked and out of sorts. *I'm sorry. I just want to know that she is okay.*

Shalih laughed.

"It's all right. She's well. And she's fed. I've never seen a shadow eat like her. She could eat a deer a day, I swear."

A great weight lifted from Ahraia's heart.

Good, she conveyed from her deepest depths.

Shalih smiled again. "Did I say a deer a day? Maybe a keress." Her eyes gleamed conspiratorially. "I heard about it. About your first task. I heard the keress was magnificent." She eyed Ahraia's hip where the white drain rested. "My mother said she had never seen such an impressive kill. Her wards were talking about it for nights on end when they returned." *She said you enchanted a whole pack of wolves.*

Ahraia nodded, surprised the Masai had been impressed. *She seemed so angry when I arrived*, she conveyed, not knowing what else to say.

Shalih's smile faded somewhat.

"She was worried. We thought you'd arrive sooner. But what a kill! A human and a brute of one at that. I've never even seen one before," Shalih said in awe. She hesitated and then looked at Ahraia's drain again. *Is that it?* she conveyed sheepishly.

Ahraia nodded.

May I?

Ahraia took the drain from her belt and held it out to Shalih. She took it with reverence, as though it were the most delicate leaf.

"It's beautiful," she said. Her ears twitched permissively as she handed it back. "And please . . . speak. I'm only just a sprite. The Dark Moon hasn't even turned once—I'm not used to all this deference."

Ahraia slipped the drain back into her cloak, her discomfort allayed partly by Shalih's kindness. She was nothing like her mother.

"You've never seen a human?" Ahraia asked, wondering if her task was particularly difficult, like the keress. Her gaze travelled through the darkening, seeking any hint of Losna.

"We don't have lightwalkers near here. Well, there are alps in the mountains but they keep well away."

"Then what was your second task?"

"Just a goblin." Shalih looked disappointed and suddenly younger.

"Really? Where did you find one?" Ahraia said in surprise. Shalih brightened seeing Ahraia's curiosity. In a way, she reminded Ahraia of Kren before her sister had taken her shadow test. She was expressive and curious. More like a shade than a sprite.

"Ha. They swarm the woods south of here. We're constantly hunting them. I'm surprised you didn't see one on your way here. Nasty, vile creatures of the deep—but nothing as vile as a human. Come, I'll show you the darkening."

Ahraia stared about her as they passed through the closures.

You keep them open? Even in the daytime?

"Only on special occasions." Shalih smiled. *I think my mother wished to impress you and your Astra.*

The vaults of the central hollow were so high Ahraia couldn't separate the branches above from one tree or another. She followed Shalih along a stream, the support trunks growing larger and larger, older and older. But something was missing. The forest was *too* empty.

Where are the nits? she asked.

Shalih laughed.

"Around the central hollow, of course." She nodded for Ahraia to follow. "These are just the outer halls."

"The outer halls?" Ahraia said, staring upward.

The stream was growing louder. It chattered between two massive trunks, each with roots as thick as trees clawing at the earth in smooth, sinuous fingers. Shalih led her around the trunk on the near bank, following a dirt-matted path away from the stream. They circled the trunk and stopped. Ahraia felt like she had stepped onto the Endless Plains for the first time.

The stream cascaded away, but it hardly seemed to move or make a sound. The air before her was rigid. Fixed in place by dozens upon dozens of colossal trunks, rising one after another from the midst of the hollow, supporting the shell, which draped like impenetrable clouds over a dark sky. The columns were too big. Ahraia couldn't understand what she was seeing. A great owl glided silently behind one of the trunks; she counted to five before it sailed from the other side. Nit trees sprawled about, crowding the valley floor and fading into the woods. The noise of the rain was a distant rapping above, but not a single turn or run could be seen. It was eerily quiet.

"Is Daispar like this?" Shalih asked, watching her.

"Not in the least," Ahraia answered, completely in awe. Yellow tails hung between leech ferns, and bellow blossoms wrapped about the darkening cores, black as night and ringed with foxfells. Moon flowers grew at every level of the darkening, sprouting off trunks and branches as though they grew as easy as ferns.

"Come . . . I'll show you the rest."

Shalih led her into the bellies of the hollow, pointing out different sprites and the nits they governed. Ahraia quickly got tangled in all the names and relations and fell silent, listening and searching for any sense of Losna. They walked for what felt like miles, the very ground just as woven as the unbroken cover above. Sheets of eaves-web, grown and plated by whole teams of spinners, spread in intricate patterns. Paths twisted beneath archways of decorative shade maples, their blackened leaves hanging with perfect stillness, branches pointed outward from a breeze they never felt. Nit trees formed walls so thick and dark that Ahraia imagined even sprites had trouble seeing in the deep.

She continued to reach out for Losna but felt nothing. If Shalih noticed her probings, she didn't say anything. Eventually, the nits thinned, and the river flowed through a grove of wild trees and then passed beyond the darkening wall, through another set of open closures. An outer hall extended beyond, towards a faintly glowing fog, lit ghostly white by the morning light, like clouds in a moonlit sky.

Ahraia heard the rain again, and a river beyond the fog.

Shalih nodded towards the light-laced woods. "That is where the River Umbar lies. Beyond that, the Shad-Mon roam."

So close to the darkening? Ahraia conveyed in surprise. Shalih nodded with a gleam in her eyes, watching Ahraia with intense curiosity.

"Have you ever seen one?" she asked. *All gray and shadow?*

Ahraia nodded faintly, shuddering to remember the hand swinging out of the fog. Shalih's eyes glimmered faintly against the glowing fog. She blinked it away, turning back to Ahraia.

"Let's get away from here. It is no good looking at such things." She led Ahraia back through the darkening, back through the nits, almost to the head of the first falls. She stopped outside a nit tree, sunken in a low depression, almost like it was half-nit and half-den.

"This was my mother's first nit tree. Before she became the Masai . . ."

The tree was oddly spartan. No extra vines grew or flowers

bloomed. But it had a certain strength, a certain necessity to it. Shalih formed a closure and led Ahraia inside the protective dark. It was totally black. And silent. Ahraia could only make out the vague silhouettes of shade trees, and the pinpoint glimmer of Shalih's eyes, framed by her white hair.

"This can be your shade tree for now." She showed Ahraia to a shade tree that looked as though it hadn't been used in a number of full turnings. *It won't be for long. You'll be a sprite soon. A sister.*

Ahraia nodded, unable to answer.

"You miss your shadow, don't you?"

Ahraia swallowed, hardly able to see Shalih in the perfect dark. She didn't dare to speak, but nodded. Shalih's gaze dropped to the ground. She grimaced as though remembering something she didn't want to remember.

"I miss mine too," she whispered. She kicked at a small twig on the ground. "It's not fair that my mother keeps you two separated before you must part from each other permanently."

Ahraia couldn't speak. It felt as though her mouth was sealed shut. Shalih had put to words the deepest emotions in her heart. She nodded.

Shalih looked up, and Ahraia could see true loss in her eyes.

Shades and shadows shouldn't be separated.

Ahraia kept nodding, still not knowing what to say. Shalih was staring at her, a penetrating look that made Ahraia glance away. She felt a tenuous bond form. When she looked, Shalih's eyes were locked on hers. Her conveyance came through soft, whispered, like the faintest falling of rain on the shell above.

I can show you to her. Would you like that?

Ahraia's breath caught, unable to contain her desire. "More than anything!" she said desperately.

Shalih smiled, a true smile.

"When night falls, I'll take you to her."

~

Ahraia stole from the darkening just as dusk fell. She went by the southern closure, beneath an archway of rowan trees, just as Shalih had instructed. She brushed past two shades, both with pure black ravens for shadows. The birds cawed loudly, their calls swallowed easily by the vast dark. A few sprites were up and about, but none seemed to take notice of Ahraia as she slipped to the edges of the outer halls. She didn't have to wait long before Shalih joined her.

"Did any sprites see you?" she asked, her hood pulled close.

Just some shades.

"Good. Come on."

Shalih was nothing more than a sliver of a figure dashing beneath the outer halls. Ahraia followed at a run, the air cold against her still damp cloak. When they emerged, thick clouds lay overhead, and no signs of the Dae-Mon remained. The forest was still wet from the day before. It was deeper, darker and more alive than the forest of Daispar. Shalih led her by paths that rose and fell through deep ravines. teeming with shade maples and timber ferns. Even well beyond the darkening, trees and limbs linked to each other, like ice crystals spreading outward from the first freeze on a cold pond. Ahraia would have been amazed if she weren't so eager to see Losna.

Shalih moved in silence but Ahraia didn't mind. Her hands were shaking in eagerness. Her ears twitched at every noise, expecting it to be Losna. She felt like her heart was going to burst from her chest.

She wondered if tonight would be the best night to flee. If she found Losna, maybe they could run—maybe they could make for the mountains or the plains or even the human's realm, where no wards would follow. She could send messages to Kyah to flee, and if everything went perfectly, she could meet her siblings and take them beyond where any wards could reach them. The prospect was daunting. If the darkening was any indication, the Masai's realm would be teeming with wards.

Full night had fallen before Ahraia started to wonder where Shalih was taking her. She had imagined that Losna was being kept in the Makers, but Ahraia's senses told her they were in the deep woods. Alone.

Where is my shadow being kept? she conveyed finally.

Shalih didn't stop. *Your shadow? Not far*. She hurried forward.

Ahraia wondered if a world lay beyond the mountains. Would it be possible to cross under them in their deep shadows or did these woods stretch forever? Would she be chased all the way to Everdark, where the Dae-Mon was said to never rise?

Shalih came to a sudden halt, her ears twitching. She smiled. Ahraia stopped too, taking a cursory look around. She didn't see Losna and she didn't feel any sense of her shadow. But she sensed something else, something distinctively familiar.

A pair of ravens glided to a perch on the limbs of a small ash, causing the branch to sway precariously.

Shalih's eyes gleamed brighter than the stars ever had. It made the hairs on Ahraia's neck stand on end. One of the raven's cawed. Ahraia recognized the call.

"You're awfully bold, Shade Ahraia, coming here with me."

What do you mean? Ahraia conveyed, not liking Shalih's tone.

A smile uncurled on Shalih's cheeks, her eyes gleaming all the brighter.

"Where is my shadow?" Ahraia said aloud, her pretenses gone. A voice behind her caused her to jerk about.

"I told you she was as naïve as a spriteling."

Kren dropped down from the crook of a maple tree.

Ahraia turned to her sister, not daring to believe what was happening.

"This isn't about my shadow, is it?" Ahraia stepped back, but sensed movement behind her. Two shades emerged from behind the trees. The ravens cawed louder and louder.

Kren smirked, but it was not a smile. It was a pained, pitying look.

"It's always been about your shadow, Ahraia. You *never* deserved her." Without any flourish, she drew her drain.

27

SHADOW BOUND

"I can't believe she really followed me," Shalih said to Kren, shaking her head. "I thought you were the naïve one when you said she would." The shades each bore maddening smiles and their own drains. Their ravens' calls echoed off the steep hillside. Ahraia's heart was racing.

"She's always been a touch . . . soft," Kren said. Her eyes narrowed, directing her conveyance to Ahraia. *Trying to get me involved with the spritelings. They can fend for themselves. Unlike you, who never had to . . .*

Shalih looked about, taking in the forest in a single glance. Her eyes circled back to Ahraia.

"Here is as good a place as anywhere to settle this."

"I was particular in the choosing," Kren said, never taking her eyes from Ahraia.

A shiver ran ragged along Ahraia's spine. Her gaze flickered towards the forest: tall firs rose with broken branches crowding up their trunks, a few vine maples lay low over the ground. The shades were creeping forward up the hill, cutting off her escape.

"There's nothing for you to bind," Kren said, guessing her thoughts.

"I'm your sister—" Ahraia hardly had time to think before a

sloppy enchantment clapped her jaw shut. She bit her tongue, tasting blood. *What are you doing?* she conveyed to Shalih, sensing her mind as the source of the enchantment. She tried to raise her hand to her drain but she was paralyzed right down to her voice.

"How naïve could she be?" Shalih said, holding Ahraia as still as the forest.

You're letting her do this? Ahraia conveyed to Kren, feeling a mind numbing strength take hold of her. A second binding had formed. Kren's eyes were devoid of any emotion but Ahraia was sure it stemmed from her.

"It's no different from what happened to mother. The weak need to be culled. And it's only sparing you what is to come."

Shalih was still shaking her head. "You think you can come here? To my darkening? To be *my* sister and take *my* place beneath my mother? And you expected me to help you find your shadow?" Her face twisted in disgust. "Only shades have sisters, Ahraia. Surely even you must understand that. There are no allegiances once you're a sprite. The strong rule."

Then I submit, Ahraia conveyed quickly, knowing she was outmatched.

"You would," Kren said. She scoffed. "You're too weak for your shadow." The shades were creeping closer, with drains in hand. Shalih's tongue ran across the tips of her teeth.

Losna! Ahraia conveyed, hoping beyond hope that her shadow was close. Shalih stepped dangerously forward, drawing her drain from her side.

"Your shadow won't save you now."

Ahraia struggled to free her mind. Kren's jaw was set firmly, holding her.

"You don't deserve to be the Masai," Shalih said. "You don't even deserve to be in line for it."

Ahraia wrestled with the enchantment.

I don't want to be the Masai, she thought, clawing to get away. Shalih's binding was firm, but Ahraia knew Kren's binding. Even more, she knew her sister.

Do you not remember? she conveyed angrily. *You were my ward, my keeper. Have you lost all dignity?* Kren's grip tightened, trying to silence her. *Flit didn't. She would have never stood by this.* Ahraia's emotions crashed against her sister, and she felt the enchantment slip. *What happened to you? Did you lose all memory of the shadow you cast?*

The bonding loosened. Kren was shaking as though she had been touched by light.

Shalih didn't notice. She walked purposefully towards Ahraia. A deep part of Ahraia wondered if this is how Kaval and Altah had gone. A terrible anger rose in her heart. Kren was just going to watch.

Flit would be ashamed.

Kren's binding suddenly disintegrated. Ahraia felt as though her teeth were going to crack from clamping down. Shalih was two strides away.

Ahraia thought of Losna, alone and without her. She felt a flush across her face, angry. She thought of Kyah and the spritelings, under the knife of her father. She sensed the web of enchantment holding her. She understood it. She knew it.

Stay, Shalih's enchantment directed her. *Fixed.*

Ahraia resisted, prying back Shalih's hold. The Masai's daughter was strong, but Ahraia was a wolf. She bared her teeth, bringing to bear the full strength of her mind.

Shalih's drain was poised. She punched it forward.

Ahraia flexed against the binding. The enchantment strained and then shattered, like a shell of ice from a wind shaken limb. Shalih's eyes went wide as Ahraia spun aside.

She pulled her drain from her hip and sliced across Shalih's face. Blood spattered across black ferns and Ahraia tumbled backwards, down the hill. Shalih screamed.

Ahraia scrambled up and knocked into one of the shades, sending him plunging down the embankment. Black wings fluttered about her, thrashing at her face. The piercing beaks of the two ravens stabbed against her arms and neck. Instinctively, she bound the ravens. She stopped the wings of the first and it plummeted it towards the ground.

Thump!

The shade cried out in dismay as his bird crashed down. Ahraia sent the second bird screeching towards a tree. It crumpled against the trunk, falling in a limp mass of feathers. Ahraia leapt down the hillside, sliding wildly towards a ravine below.

"Get back here!" Shalih said.

A wave of enchantment tried to slow Ahraia, but her mind was firm and ready for it.

Fool, she thought, running headlong through the woods, angry that she trusted Shalih so blindly. And Kren . . . Kren was worse than a wraith. Ahraia fumed as she sprinted through the undergrowth, parting trees and ferns before her with her bindings. Shalih and Kren were in pursuit, shouting and cursing her. But they weren't as fast as Ahraia.

She leapt upon a fallen log and ran its length. She sprang from it to another. And another. She melded a tree ahead and used it to swing her effortlessly across a deep fold in the earth. She let the tension in the branch remain after she had let it go and released it a moment later.

Crack!

She heard Shalih gasp in pain as the branch crashed against her body.

Try and bind me . . . Ahraia thought remorselessly, running on.

"Ahraia! Get back here. We were just playing," Kren called after her.

Get away from me.

Ahraia didn't slow as she leapt across a creek, dancing over the rocks and scrambling up the far bank. A fresh wave of disgust roiled through her. *She tried to kill me,* she thought. It made her sick. Kren hadn't just stood and watched, she had even drawn her drain. Ahraia wanted to go back and pull her sister's ears from her. She was so distraught, she didn't notice the woods suddenly teeming with movement ahead.

"Ahraia?" A voice suddenly called.

She pulled up short, recognizing it. It was the Astra, with a retinue of sprites in tow behind her. She looked livid.

"What are you doing here? Where have you been?" she said.

Ahraia spit the blood from her mouth, wondering if the Astra had been behind the attack. *Just like Golan*, she thought darkly. She pulled the drain from her hip defensively, looking for a way out, a place to run.

The Masai slipped from behind a pair of broad trunks. "Did you find them?" she asked.

"She's here," the Astra said.

Ahraia's tension ebbed, reassured by the Masai's presence. But her relief was short lived. The Masai's gaze was sharp, her voice accusing as she spoke.

"Where is Shalih?"

Ahraia was sweating, still breathing hard. Bright red blood dripped from her bone-white blade.

"Where is my daughter?" The Masai's ears turned back aggressively.

She tried to kill me, Ahraia conveyed, realizing how terrible this must look. *She tried to bond me and kill me.*

The first hint of an enchantment clawed out from the Masai, and Ahraia braced herself, trying to form a barrier around her mind. Just then, Shalih sprinted from the woods. The cut across her right cheek was perfectly straight and dripping, smearing across her jaw, like the mark of a posturant. A welt rose on her other cheek where the branch had caught her. Kren burst from the woods a moment later. The Astra's eyes widened but she didn't say anything.

"What have you done?" the Masai asked, looking between Ahraia and Shalih.

I didn't do anything! Ahraia conveyed.

Shalih looked terrified. "I woke up. And Shade Ahraia was gone from her shade tree. I went to Kren first, to see if she was visiting her sister—"

"That isn't what happened—" Ahraia started.

"You can ask Uan and Periah," Shalih said louder, pointing to two shades with ravens for shadows. Both cradled their birds in their arms and glared at Ahraia. "They saw her leaving by the southern closures and came and warned me. That's why I went after her—I took her sister in case things turned nasty. Kren warned me she might try something like this."

"That isn't true." Ahraia said, in disbelief. The shades were nodding along with Shalih, and Kren was as well.

"—and when I caught her, she said she was looking for her shadow. She planned on fleeing. She bound me and cut me, then she ran off towards the Makers and we were trying to stop her."

Ahraia stared at Shalih in disbelief, her mouth agape.

You don't believe this? Do you? Ahraia conveyed, turning to the Masai and then the Astra. Her eyes flashed at Kren, a brief shared memory of Flit causing her sister to look sharply downward.

The Masai was considering her pointedly. The Astra remained quiet, looking back and forth between them.

"*Were* you looking for your shadow?" the Masai asked at last.

Ahraia stared at her, still in disbelief.

"Yes. I was," she said meeting the Masai's eye. "And *your* daughter had told me she could show me where she was."

"What?" Shalih exclaimed. "Why would I do that?"

The Astra's jaw flexed, the muscles tightening to hard knots. *If you managed to condemn yourself . . .*

Don't act like you didn't have a role in this, Ahraia conveyed quickly. *You set that ward after me. And you set these two as well.*

The Astra's eyes narrowed but the Masai's voice cut off her response.

"Shalih, Kren, go back to the darkening," she said.

But I didn't do anything, Shalih whined.

Go. The Masai's ears flickered for obedience. Then she turned to Ahraia, her eyes gleaming dangerously. "You—come with me."

"Where are you taking her?" the Astra asked.

"To see her shadow." *I'm not going to spend the next two weeks chasing after your shade.*

She stalked off through the woods, gesturing for Ahraia to follow and signaling for the others to stay.

Ahraia glared at Kren and Shalih, then walked warily after the Masai. The group remained, and all too soon they were alone in the woods. A pretense of calm settled about the Masai as they walked, far more disconcerting than if she had been angry. The silence between them stretched, until Ahraia couldn't help herself.

That isn't what happened, she conveyed, not wanting to break the silence. *What your daughter said—that wasn't what happened.*

The Masai pointedly ignored her. She kept walking, unhurried. Ahraia's dread swelled with every step. She thumbed the hilt of her drain, unsure what the Masai meant to do, remembering the way that her father had marched Hayvon back to the darkening before condemning him.

She offered to show me . . . what would you expect me to do?

The woods were changing. She thought she saw fog ahead. The hairs on her neck stood on end, but she realized it had been a trick of her eyes. She let out a worried breath and saw a wall of woven trees ahead of her. Except all of the closures were open.

Another darkening? she thought, knowing they couldn't have reached Angolor yet.

A hillside rose beyond the closures and the Masai led her past the palisade. Gloomy clouds drifted beyond gaps in the massive trees and Ahraia was surprised to see that the ceiling of trees overhead didn't form a true darkening.

Where are we? she asked.

"The Makers," the Masai conveyed.

Ahraia's scars flushed. *What are we doing here?* A thousand possibilities flashed into her head. Was she being forced into her third task early? Was the Masai taking her to Losna to show her shadow the light?

The Masai stopped.

Whoosh!

Ahraia flinched, spinning about as a hundred different closures shut with a resounding rustle of leaves. The wall was laced with serapin trees that continued to slither and move, seeking towards her.

The Masai stood calmly with her hands clasped behind her back.

"Understand this, Shade Ahraia. I won't tolerate being disobeyed."

I didn't disobey—

"I don't care what happened between my daughter and you. It's finished." Ahraia swallowed hard, holding back her conveyances. The Masai glared at her.

"I can't spend every night chasing you about as you seek your shadow." She waited until Ahraia nodded in agreement. The silence stretched. The Masai considered Ahraia a moment, then turned to the wall, running her fingers over the woven branches. A serapin tree snaked a branch caressingly over her shoulder, as though it was a shadow.

"Can you open this?"

Ahraia hesitated, wondering what she was getting at. The Masai raised her eyes questioningly.

"Your Astra tells me you're quite good at folding darkness. Show me."

Ahraia looked towards the wall. The Makers in Daispar had no wall at all. This one wasn't much different from a darkening wall, though it was laced with the sharp thorns of dorn trees and the slithering vines of serapins. She stepped away from the nearest serapin, having no interest in trying to wrestle with it.

She reached out with her mind, bonding the wall. She kneaded the branches with her enchantment and though she was adept, they were slow to respond—slow to trust and slow to act—which meant they were slow to move too. She gave herself the proper time, not wanting to rush things that didn't want to be rushed. This wall was reluctant, so she coaxed it until it agreed. She let it grow accustomed to her and its woven branches loosened, becoming willing. She waited, slowly turning her bonding to a binding, connection to control. Gradually, the wall's willingness transformed to eagerness. It was ready.

Open, she thought, sensing the branches ready to burst.

Thwack! A branch struck out before she could duck.

Suddenly, Ahraia was on the ground looking up at the clouds through a mess of white hair and trees, wondering what had happened as the Masai leaned over her.

"Let that be the first lesson. No one gets out of the Makers without my say. These woods answer to me and me alone. If you enter them against my will, don't expect to leave freely."

Ahraia was dazed. By the time she stood up, the Masai was already walking steadily up the hill. Ahraia followed, her head aching and her lip split anew. She tasted blood for the second time.

They climbed steeply through the woods. The clouds broke and starlight tingled faintly on Ahraia's neck. But something else touched at her heart as well; a deeper void started to fill.

It started as a trickle. She was breathing heavily, but when she noticed she paused, holding her breath to listen.

She brushed her hair from her face, her ears twitching in search of a noise that she couldn't hear. A silent howl that made no sound and never stopped. She took several more steps and the void filled with a rush, her heart rate quickening. She scrambled up the hillside. The feeling swelled. It was familiar and hungry, this strange and beautiful feeling. It was the feeling she had been seeking for the whole turning.

Losna?

She felt the bond suddenly come awake and alive.

Ahraia?

She scurried towards a break in the trees, seeing silver fur and sharp ears perked in the air.

"Losna!" she said. Overwhelmed, tears of joy streamed down Ahraia's face, and her heart felt as though it had burst in her chest. Her shadow stood atop the hill. She rushed towards her.

"*Stop*," the Masai commanded, binding Ahraia firmly at the edge of a stony hilltop ringed in tall trees.

Losna jerked wildly against a rope tying her where she stood.

Ahraia! You're here. Let me go. Let me go. My Shade! Let me go.

Ahraia tried to run to her, but couldn't; she was held unwillingly by the Masai's mind.

Losna pulled and fought against a vine that fixed her where she stood. But it glinted unnaturally, and rattled like human metal, holding her firmly and choking at her neck.

Ahraia! There you are! Where have you been? Are you all right? Losna twisted and leapt, trying to shake free from the thick shackles. Ahraia could see dried blood on her neck from where she had already strained against the bonds. The metal vine was attached some twenty feet away, disappearing beneath a twisted and skeletal tree, polished smooth by untold turnings beneath the rain and the wind.

Losna! Ahraia thought. A thousand emotions tumbled between her and her shadow—relief, fear, joy, worry.

Losna stopped struggling and stood at the very limit of her fetters, her front paws dancing off the ground. Ahraia leaned forward against the enchantment of the Masai. Her ears quivering at the sight of her shadow.

"That's close enough," the Masai said. Her binding stifled Ahraia, rooting her feet to the ground when her entire being wanted to run to her shadow. Seeing Losna again was the greatest relief Ahraia had ever known. It was like suddenly finding darkness after a whole turning cast in light. The Masai was speaking, but Ahraia only vaguely heard her.

"I brought you here to see your shadow, Ahraia . . . because I don't want any more trouble out of you."

Are you okay? Are you fed? Ahraia conveyed to Losna. *What is that holding you? Is it cord? Thorn-stem?*

I don't know, it's metal—a chain? Losna thought. *They snapped it on and it won't come off. I've tried everything.*

Metal? Like a drain? Ahraia conveyed. She had a vague sense of Losna tearing and biting at bright, heavy links of metal.

We need to leave here, Losna thought. *These woods are evil.* She was disturbed, all the way through to her bones. She was desperate to get away, to break the chain and run. *This place is evil.*

Ahraia could feel it as well. The very ground felt tainted. The Masai's gaze was fixed on her.

The Masai stepped in front of her, blocking her view. Ahraia tried to see past her, but was held firmly by the enchantment.

"Your shadow test is half a turning from now—" the Masai said loudly, drowning out their conveyance, "—and I don't want to spend the rest of the nights between now and then chasing you about while you try and find your shadow."

Can you get free? Ahraia conveyed subtly, so that only Losna could sense it.

"So let me be clear"—the Masai's voice rose slightly, grabbing Ahraia's attention— "your shadow isn't going anywhere."

The words were lethally clear. Ahraia looked guiltily towards the Masai, who went on, her voice hardly raised above a whisper.

"You're not coming back to these woods until your test, unless you both wish to end up dead. These walls are mine. They answer to me, and they'll alert me the instant you try and come back here, so no, she cannot get free. You are going to finish this test, Ahraia. And surely by now you've guessed what that means."

The air felt thin, and Ahraia's skin tingled at the coarseness of the Masai's words.

"What must I do?"

The Masai shook her head, as though she couldn't believe that Ahraia still didn't know.

"You must break the bond—you must cut your shadow from you."

Ahraia's lips were numb. Her face was hot. Losna stared at her, her golden eyes two points of night-gleam on the hilltop.

How? Ahraia asked.

The Masai frowned.

"You must kill your shadow."

28

DISCOVERY

Ahraia locked her knees, stopping herself from crumpling to the ground. Her breath didn't fill her lungs. Losna pulled right to the edge of her chain, her foreclaws dancing off the ground.

What did she say? What's happening? Ahraia hadn't mirrored the Masai's words, but Losna felt her shock.

Why? Ahraia conveyed in disbelief.

The Masai's voice was even as she spoke. "Between the shade and the shadow lies a bond that only death can sever. Both the shade and the shadow will die—and from that darkness, a sprite is born."

Losna had gone still. Her eyes shone nervously from the hilltop.

The Masai stood close to Ahraia. "A sprite must have the will to follow the Masai through harsh winter and bright summer, through bitter loss and better dark. This is the test that all shades must pass."

"And every sprite does this?" Ahraia whispered, the breath leaving her chest. *They all kill their shadows?*

It suddenly made sense why Kren was a ghost of herself, why half of the darkenings were filled with ghosts who floated aimlessly through the night.

The Masai held her eye. "It's what makes us sprites."

Ahraia understood how a sister could kill a sister, or how a nitward could betray his nitesse. If they could kill their shadow . . .

"We're leaving," the Masai said, jerking her head towards the woods.

Ahraia's feet lurched away from Losna as the Masai dragged her down the slope by the enchantment.

Losna! Ahraia thought, resisting the command to follow. With tremendous effort, she planted her feet in the ground, bracing a hand against a cedar trunk.

Where are you going? What's happening? Losna's whines turned to yips of distress.

The Masai stopped.

"If you don't come willingly, we will have this done with tonight."

Ahraia stared at her shadow, disheartened.

I have to go, Losna. I'll come back. Her heart felt like it was being ripped from her chest.

We have to flee. Don't leave me, Losna pleaded. Her yips turned to howls.

Ahraia was forced to follow the Masai, tripping and scratching herself, trying to keep sight of Losna, who howled louder and louder. With a last glimpse, Ahraia turned and stumbled blindly down the hillside, hopeless.

When they were outside the Makers, the Masai stopped. Losna's howls tormented Ahraia from above, but the Masai held her gaze.

"There are wards watching these woods day and night. If you return here before your test, I will know." She stepped closer, threateningly. "If you do, your shadow will be shown the light and you will be given to the Shad-Mon."

AHRAIA MOVED LIKE THE WIND, running freely from Angolor, checking behind her for wards. She stopped, panting. She scanned the forest.

Alone.

She craned her neck skyward.

The trees around Daispar were unreasonably tall, with hardly any understory covering the ground beneath. It made escaping the wards difficult—and getting into the canopy harrowing. To do it without being seen was even trickier. Ahraia used two different squirrels as scouts and had already doubled back twice. The woods were empty. The wards were lost.

She got a run and used an alder tree to vault her to the first branches of a fir. It swung inward, too weak to carry her outright, and she hit the trunk heavily. She latched on, scraping her knee. It stung as she scanned the woods below. *Still desolate. Empty.*

Turning her eyes upwards, she climbed the broken lower limbs, up and up, until she reached a second spring. It whipped her higher, to a third and then a fourth, until she came to rest upon a tree's broken top, large enough to lay flat upon and high enough so the ferns above looked like a carpet of fallen leaves. She squatted, once more surveying the forest floor. She saw movement below, and a ward traipsed hurriedly through the woods. He wasn't even following the path she had taken, and within moments he disappeared, in the wrong direction.

Ahraia let out a breath before carefully negotiating across the treetop. The splintered wood was slick with rain, and the ground was perilously far below. She used a double binding to swing herself to a monstrous fir, unreachable except by wings or claws.

Or springs, she thought, glad that no other sprites ever thought to use the forest.

She stood on a thick branch, at the yawning opening of an abandoned owl's nest. The night before, she had retrieved her bow and clutch and used an owl to find the hollow. It had taken half the night to find a way up. With the bow, she kept her remaining possessions: the mirror and the tined comb, both wrapped in Hayvon's veil, tucked inside the quiver beside the odd bits the alp had used for his fire. She reached in and checked them again. They were secure and dry, even with the days of incessant rain. Through the mist and the treetops, she could just make out the rise of Losna's hill.

Now I just need a way to break that chain, she thought.

Breaking wood was one thing, but breaking metal was entirely different. Scabs encrusted her knuckles from her attempts to break her metal drain—she had tried bindings and springs and rocks and anything else she could get her hands on. Nothing worked. It was as dead as stone and twice as hard.

Her plan, if she could break the chain, was simple: *run*. But without the ability to break Losna free, she wasn't going anywhere. And the Bright Moon was almost turned. The Dark Moon was at its apex. The night of her test was near.

She eyed the hill and felt something move at her breast. Distracted, she removed a miniature horned owl from her cloak. She had been working on the message to Kyah, and the owl, it seemed, was finally ready.

"You know what you have to do," Ahraia said.

The owl looked at her with enormous, gold-ringed eyes and gave her a reassuring *whoo*. Its tiny talons pinched against her skin as it leapt away, plummeting downward before spreading its wings and gliding silently away through the understory. It was the seventh bird she had enchanted, the third owl and undoubtedly the smartest of the lot. One of them, she hoped, had the strength to reach Daispar before the enchantment wore off. Kyah had to get the spritelings to safety: first to the plains, then onward, to the mountains of the south, where Ahraia could meet them.

If I can even break that fiendish chain, she thought. She wanted to bind a dozen more owls to send to Losna, but she knew the messages would be lost on her shadow: Losna couldn't bind them, and would be driven mad by their circling. If anything, she would end up trying to eat them.

At least Kyah will be warned, she thought, swinging back to the forest floor by a series of drop branches. She landed softly and turned for Angolor.

Besides the chain, there was still the wall of the Makers to contend with. It answered to the Masai, and only the Masai. If Ahraia couldn't manage to break the spell, she would be trapped as soon as she entered the woods, waiting for a death too easy to imagine.

Her lungs didn't seem to fill properly. Gray light swelled in the east; morning was coming and she had no choice but to return to the darkening.

Another fruitless night, she thought as she passed the outer halls. Leaves tumbled down, the life drawn from them as they passed to the forest floor, where the musty rot of them covered the deep hollows.

The Bright and Dark Moons were nearly full, setting together before the dawn.

She returned to the central hollow. Shalih stood across the streams, watching Ahraia with a heavy scowl. Her white hair was tucked behind her downturned ears. The scab on her cheek was bright and the welt dark. Kren stood next to her, like a nit-ward to a nitesse. Ahraia ignored them, blood suddenly ticking in her own ears, causing them to bat against her will.

Both had kept their distance after trying to kill her, but they watched her, like glowering vultures just waiting for her to show weakness. Angry as she was at Kren, in a way she was glad they had attacked her—it had at least given her warning of her test. Even so, the cloud of foreboding was growing.

There were three nights until she would be forced into the Shadow Woods. She couldn't sleep.

Then there were two. She couldn't eat.

Then one. She couldn't breathe.

The dawn was coming. In no time, the Dae-Mon would rise and her last day would arrive.

She took a shuddering breath.

She lay down under the foreign nit tree, knowing she needed rest, knowing that when night came again she would be forced onto the hill, without even the thinnest thread of hope. Losna was fixed to the very ground. The wall of Sprite Makers would give her no quarter. And the woods would be filled with every ward and sprite the Masai had.

She couldn't close her eyes. How many shades before her had known their fate? How many had tried to break the chain or escape the confines of the hilltop? And all of them failed—it was no wonder so many ended up condemned.

She lay in motionless agony, time neither passing nor staying. She wasn't even sure if day had broken yet when a voice came to her.

"Ahraia? Are you in there?"

A sprite, Ahraia realized, was standing just outside of the shade tree.

It was Kren. She sounded tense.

Go away, Ahraia conveyed, her blood surging through her suddenly tightened chest.

"The Masai is calling for you."

Don't you have something better—

Get out here!

Ahraia rose instinctively. Something about Kren's voice sent lightening through her skin. It carried a hint of concern, a touch of worry that had been hollowed out of Kren after her shadow test. Had the Masai found the bow? Or the clutch? Did she know Ahraia planned on trying to escape?

The shade tree moved by her mind's direction, and she stepped outside. Her hand went to her hip, but stopped. Kren looked gaunt, her hollow features twisted in what almost looked like regret.

"Come on," she said, without explanation.

Ahraia followed with a dozen questions springing to mind. But she bit her tongue, still furious with Kren.

A few sprites were still awake, moving between the stream and their nits. Small groups gathered in close whispers. They glanced at Ahraia, their faces narrow and wicked, dropping all but their barest conveyances. She followed Kren past the falls, back towards the outer hall where she had first entered.

"Do you know what the Masai wants?" Ahraia said at last, not wanting to touch Kren's mind.

Kren didn't answer. She kept walking.

Ahraia looked up and saw the Astra waiting for them, standing at the closure of the darkening, her ears turned down in irritation or fear, Ahraia couldn't tell which, but she felt her feet slowing.

"What is this about?"

"You tell me," the Astra said, glowering towards the forest.

Ahraia followed the Astra's gaze towards the outer halls. A group of sprites and wards had gathered at the edge of the darkness, towards the direction she had hidden her bow. Fear flushed through her.

The Astra's ears twitched for obedience and Ahraia followed nervously. Far away through the trunks she could see where the woods weren't light, but they weren't dark, either. She swallowed, hoping desperately her bow hadn't been discovered.

The Masai had her back turned, but in front of her, Ahraia caught sight of golden hair—golden hair and bright, green, alpish eyes. She stopped.

It was the alp: the same one she had seen in Daispar, the same one who had killed the human, the alp who had killed Kaval and Altah.

What is she doing here? Ahraia conveyed.

The Astra frowned but didn't answer.

The Masai's ear twitched beneath her repulsive black cloak and she turned, a placid look of contentment spreading across her face. Her eyes gleamed brighter, her brow turning inward like an imp. She leaned in and spoke to the alp, never letting her gaze leave Ahraia.

The alp's white teeth showed in a half smirk and she nodded with the Masai.

"Welcome, Shade Ahraia, Astra," the Masai said, nodding in greeting, the black fur wreathing her head.

The Astra gave a deferential bow to the Masai. Surprisingly enough, she did the same to the alp and said nothing, though her face was rigid and her ears back.

"What fortuitous circumstance smiles upon us. Do you know who this is, Shade Ahraia?" the Masai said, nodding towards the alp.

Ahraia hesitated, fearing why she had been summoned. She wondered if the alp had seen the head. Angry as she was that the Astra had used the alp to kill Kaval and Altah, she thought it better she played dumb. She shook her head.

I don't, she conveyed.

A smile spread across the Masai's face, one that mirrored the alp's and showed in bright, sinuous contrast to the grim lips of the Astra.

"Please speak—" The Masai's ears twitched. "We have an esteemed guest. She is Anasazi of the Cirice. Do you know that name?"

Ahraia shook her head again, this time not having to feign ignorance.

"You should. The name of the Cirice was once as important as the name of the Masah,"—she gestured to where the two moons had just set—"all sprites and shades knew it, and they will remember it soon enough. Anasazi has come to us for help in a matter of some importance; the same matter she came to your Astra for, I believe, some turnings ago." The Masai nodded to the Astra, who was still watching in rigid uncertainty.

"A war is coming in the world of light. The Cirice has been set to rid the world of humans and other graceless creatures since before Angolor even existed. Soon, they will finish it. It is a noble cause. And one that I mean to help her with."

Ahraia's eyes darted between the sharp-eared alp and the long-eared Masai. She said nothing, still hoping the alp hadn't seen the head. The Masai seemed too pleased. Was this important if she became a sprite? Did the Masai think she was beginning her tutelage now? Ahraia assumed she didn't. The alp was too smug. More sprites gathered, with word of the strange meeting having already spread through the darkening.

The Masai's eyes narrowed dangerously.

"And while her task is important, it is of no importance to you. She told me something tonight, however, that does concern you. Do you have any idea what that could be?"

Ahraia felt dread sweeping through her. *The head.* She had to act normal. She tried to clear her mind. She shook her head.

The Astra looked still looked confused. The alp's icy smile was like the winter-wind blowing from the north. Her teeth looked almost human, and the whites of her eyes shown unusually large, in an unnerving way.

"She told me the most extraordinary tale when she arrived," the Masai went on. "Something that she saw, that she didn't expect to see. Can you guess what?"

Ahraia's heart had taken root in her stomach; she fought to keep her ears from betraying her, though she was sure the flush of her scars would. The Masai nodded to the alp, who met and held Ahraia's gaze. She could see the Masai leering triumphantly from the corner of her eye.

"Where did you kill that human?" the alp asked with terrible calm. Her voice was soft and musical.

"What human?" Ahraia said, trying to stall, trying anything to find a way out.

The alp pointed through the hall to where the light dimmed and the head from her second task rested, still rotting without peace.

"The human from your second task," the Masai said.

Ahraia's mouth was bone dry. "I killed him. In the human realm —outside one of their stone darkenings," she said. She projected a memory of the stoned walls and great bridge, having no difficulty conjuring the thought. More sprites were gathering. The hall was almost full by now. A small contingent from Daispar stood crowded around the Astra.

"Is that so?" the Masai said.

"Yes. It is," Ahraia said, meeting the alp's eyes.

"Please," the alp said dismissively. "You didn't kill this human." Her voice, strange and demure as it was, hid an unflinching violence.

The Astra, who hadn't said a word, was nearly shaking with rage.

"What are you saying? What are you accusing my shade of doing?" She turned to the Masai with questioning eyes. "This is absurd. I won't stand for it. What is she being accused of?"

"I'm saying that your shade didn't kill this human," the alp said. "I did. This was the Prince of Astenith, heir to their throne."

The Astra's markings flashed from red to moon-white in a heartbeat. She rounded on Ahraia, her face twisted in anger.

"What have you done!"

A buzz of conveyance flooded the hall, mixing with murmured voices and the grating caws of a raven. The Masai flickered her ears for conveyance, stopping Ahraia's heart. She firmed her mind around the idea that she *had* killed the human, knowing condemnation was coming.

I killed him, she thought to the Astra, letting it drift far enough for other sprites to hear it too. *I killed him and I brought him here.*

The alp was shaking her head. Rough hands seized Ahraia's arms as the Masai's wards grabbed her.

Ahraia flushed. "You're trusting her? She killed my brothers! She killed them at the Stone Tree. And now for some reason, she's trying to condemn me—" Ahraia's jaw clamped down under a heavy enchantment. She wrestled free of the spites that held her, only to feel more hands upon her, and more enchantment weighing her down. *How could you trust her? She speaks through a light-laced tongue!*

The Masai stood passively, watching on with steady eyes.

"She killed Kaval and Altah!" Ahraia spat, managing to break through the enchantments to hiss out a few words. *How are you going to trust—*

"*Silence.*" The Masai's command snapped Ahraia's thought in two. "She didn't kill your brothers."

Ahraia stopped struggling. The Astra's eyes narrowed and her hand rested near her drain. Black fur wreathed the Masai. She stepped towards Ahraia wickedly.

"I did."

The lifeless black eyes of the wolf stared at Ahraia and she understood. A binding emanated from the Masai, the same menace and power from the Stone Tree. It hadn't been the alp. It had been the Masai all along. Ahraia would have screamed in fury, in wrath and outrage, but she couldn't. The binding was too absolute.

The Astra's ears batted once but remained straight. "I knew you did, I just never figured out how . . . or why. You couldn't have wanted Ahraia in Angolor that much." Her words surprised Ahraia almost as much as the Masai's admission.

"I didn't."

The Astra furrowed her brow. "Beran and Gavea said you were in the south."

The corners of the Masai's lips turned devilishly upwards

"Gavea . . . precious Gavea. My niece was always loyal. And your faithful nitmate, Beran? Of course he said I was in the south. He had already betrayed his first Astra. Were you so foolish to believe he wouldn't do the same to you?"

The Astra flushed. "At what price?" she asked, shaking.

"A place in my darkening . . ."

"And Gavea?"

"Daispar." The Masai beamed. "But she's dead now."

The Astra looked stricken. *Traitors.* An echo of her thoughts escaped her. Her voice shook as she spoke. "This was never about Ahraia's shadow test, was it? You were never going to give me the seeds."

The Masai scoffed, her eyes cold and uncaring. "Seeds of a darkening tree . . . as though I would give them to an Astra like you. Your forests are light strewn and your darkenings are failing. The Gelesh is lost."

"You made a deal." The Astra spit at her feet.

"And your shade failed that deal."

"This was never a fair test. You wanted her dead. First, you set her against that keress, and then you took her shadow. You don't even have any evidence that she didn't kill the human."

"Except for the word of Anasazi, Lord of the Cirice with nothing to gain . . . or your shade who's set to run from these woods this very evening."

Anasazi watched on easily. The Astra looked light-sick.

"Nothing to gain? I'm sure you have some arrangement. Some alliance to her *Cirice.* And my shade would never dare run." The Astra shot an angry glance at Ahraia.

Ahraia couldn't respond. The enchantments holding her were absolute.

The Masai smiled.

"Your shade *is* set to run. You can ask her. She has her *bow* tucked away in a nice fir tree. Quite a hiding place really—my sprites haven't managed to reach it. She's already sent half a dozen messages to a sister of hers. Kyah, I believe," the Masai said, her eyes glinting.

A wave of panic rippled through Ahraia's chest. She struggled against the binding.

"They're quite impressive really. Detailed, right down to the underdaes Ahraia made for them." An image of Plain Dark formed in Ahraia's mind.

Ahraia struggled against the enchantments, sensing what was to come.

"You're lying," the Astra said, but her voice trembled with doubt.

"I'll show you . . ." The Masai's gaze rose to the shadowy ceiling of the outer halls. *Come down here*, she conveyed for all to hear. A small robin, one of the first birds Ahraia had enchanted, flitted down from the understory of the hall. It had seemed so eager and honored to carry her message. The little bird landed on the Astra's hand, stoic and beady-eyed. Ahraia wished she had sent it to Losna instead.

"Bond it," the Masai instructed the Astra, her eyebrows raised.

The Astra hardly moved as she unraveled the message. Slowly, her eyes shifted from the Masai to Ahraia, her ears laying flatter and flatter, until they were tucked back tight against her head. When she finished, she tossed the bird into the air. It twittered angrily away and filled the darkening with beating wings.

"I have more if you would like," the Masai said. The air was suddenly full of Ahraia's other messengers: the common owl, the black-beaked owl, another sparrow. Ahraia's face flushed. The Masai's lips uncurled in a sneer.

"Your shade seemed to forget that these are my woods—and nothing goes on without my knowing."

The Astra walked to Ahraia, grabbing her by the face and squeezing her nails into her cheeks. She leaned in close, so that when she spoke, no one else could hear.

"I'll have you know that your sister and your precious little spritelings are already dead." The Astra's lips flared, showing her teeth. "I had your father kill them the second you left. Your nit has been nothing but trouble for me." She pushed Ahraia's face away, wrenching her neck back.

Rage and grief blinded Ahraia. The enchantments seemed to wither away from her, and she lunged forward, trying to get at the Astra with her bare hands.

"I'll kill you!" she managed before a fresh barrage of bindings swarmed her. She fell forward, writhing in the dirt, wishing nothing more than to have a chance to enchant the Astra, to bind her and end her.

"She's a fighter," the Masai said, sounding pleased.

The Astra turned back to the Masai, furious. Her ears batted and her voice quivered as she spoke.

"You were just waiting for her to run. This was what you wanted from the beginning; this was never about her shadow test—or the seeds."

"No, this was never about her shadow test." *This was about her being dead.* "A wolf-binder . . . in my realm?" The Masai shook her head. "My shades know better than to bind a wolf. When word of this spreads, so will the rest of the Silh. But I am impressed. I didn't expect her to get this far."

"I want what I came for," the Astra said. "I want my darkening seeds."

"You can't possibly expect me to give them to you."

"You got what you wanted. She's dead. I want what we traded for."

"Or else what?" The Masai let a devious smile run across her face.

The Astra's eyes glanced around the darkening. Her hand rested on her drain. Ahraia knew she was thinking of rebellion from the Gelesh.

The Masai sensed it too.

"The Gelesh is too small and too divided. Too many darkenings have already failed, and the rest are failing. Do you think they'll go to war when I've already offered each my protection?"

Ahraia could see the Astra's threat fizzling out. But a maddened gleam had taken her eyes, like a beast cornered and already knowing she would die.

"Then I want this darkening. I want the Silh."

Conveyance startled the air like a flock of angry birds taking flight. Ahraia heard echoes of a dozen conveyances.

A Posturant?

What a fool . . .

Impossible—

The smile fell from the Masai's face, and silence crashed over the hall.

"You wouldn't."

"I want what I came for," the Astra said heavily. "I'm not leaving without the seeds."

"Then you're leaving dead."

The Astra drew the drain from her hip and held it out straight, as far from herself as she could. Cold determination played at her eyes, and though the other sprites from Angolor murmured in dissent, she stood untarnished by fear. Held down by enchantment, Ahraia could hardly see, but she remembered the last time a challenge like this had been ushered—it had been the night her mother had been given to the Shad-Mon.

The Masai shook her head.

"You're making a mistake. I don't want this."

"Then you shouldn't have meddled with my dark."

The Masai's face was placid.

"All this for darkness? When you could fold it yourself?" she said.

"You think you're invincible." *You've crossed the wrong sprite.*

The Masai shrugged, pulling her drain from her hip without flourish. Ahraia recognized the black blade at once—it was the same blade she had taken from the Stone Tree. The Masai had stolen it back. She extended it easily, a wolfish grin playing at her lips.

"So be it."

Ahraia wasn't sure which sprite she wanted to win. She hoped they both died.

The Masai nodded to the sprites about her and they formed a

clean circle. The alp was watching with the keenest interest. Ahraia was dragged by her hair out of the way.

"Ready?" the Masai said.

The Astra nodded.

The enchantments took the air like a sudden wind. Neither sprite moved, but Ahraia knew they had bound each other and were trying to force the others' own knife against themselves. The Masai concentrated intensely, and the Astra's hand was shaking, her knuckles white around the handle of her drain.

Ahraia's mind was a haze. She knew what was happening, but it was distant, hidden beneath the layers of enchantment lying over her. The struggle went on, in absolute silence, undisturbed by even a breath of conveyance.

The Masai grimaced. The calm of her face clouded. Her ears turned down in effort. Her arm bent slightly.

The Astra's eyes gleamed triumphantly.

But then a smile spread across the Masai's face. The Astra's hand twitched. The knife moved. Her elbow bent and the drain turned back towards herself. Her arm shook violently, and still the drain came closer, until her arm was entirely bent and the blade pressed into her cheek. A drop of blood formed at the tip. The conflict writhed upon the Astra's face; the pain was overwhelming her, but she was unwilling to give in and had no control of her hand or body.

And then the knife started to cut, deep and steady, her face twisting in agony. Blood ran freely over the blade of the knife. Suddenly, the Astra screamed and the knife sliced across her cheek. She threw it to the ground as though it had burnt her.

Blood dripped down her face.

The Masai's smile spread.

"It seems you both have a meeting with the Shad-Mon."

29

HUNTED BY DARKNESS

Ahraia's mind was numb, blinded by anger and repressed by bindings. She only had the cloudiest sense of what was happening beneath the fog of enchantment.

Condemned, she thought dimly, trying to remember herself. *My sisters. My brothers. All murdered . . . by the Astra, by the Masai. All of them. I have no nit left.*

Then something stirred within her, a memory of connection. *Losna. My shadow!* Ahraia's heart surged and she rose faintly out of the haze.

Two wards grabbed her by her arms, jerking her towards a rapidly forming closure in the darkening wall. Her body was stilled, limp; her feet dragged over stone and root alike. Sprites all around her jeered and called as they passed towards the river.

"And the Dae-Mon's risen!" one of the wards said with particular delight.

The fog glowed dangerously and shafts of light pierced the woods above. But the outer halls held shadows right to the river's edge, where the eaves leaned out over the frothing water.

Dim as her thoughts were, her hatred of the Masai and the Astra kept her aware of what was happening. She tried to break free, to even squirm or wrestle, but too many sprites bound her. She couldn't speak or scream. She could hardly think.

Every one of her siblings was dead. And the Masai was going to kill Losna.

Let me go! she thought violently.

"Don't drink the water! Don't touch the trees! Don't break the silence!" sprites called from all around her.

An Astra and a wolf-binder! Another thought. The air bristled with the like. The Astra was ahead of Ahraia, hanging just as limp, blood dripping freely from her cheek. Ahraia wished it was from her throat.

You killed my sisters. You killed Thelon! she conveyed in fury, unsure if her thoughts escaped at all. The woods swelled with sprites, emerging from their shade trees and nits and pulling their hoods close, their collective thoughts rising into a swarm of excitement.

"Your shadow's going to the light," a ward jeered.

Spit foamed from Ahraia's mouth, but no words came. She conveyed a steady stream of curses at her captors, but they ignored her, gloating as the light grew and the roar swelled.

The river was close now. She could see the fog boiling over the water and felt the mist brush cold against her cheeks.

The Masai stepped in front of her, the black cloak of the wolf grinning horribly over her brow. An equally dreadful smile spread wide across the Masai's face.

"Bring down the tree," she called, her eyes locked on Ahraia.

The bridging tree's crooked trunk whined, unbending. The leaves rustled, shifting as though a gusting wind was suddenly running up the river.

"Bring it down!" the Masai shouted.

More sprites hurried forward, their focus turning from the Astra and Ahraia to the tree. The trunk's resistance folded. It groaned against dozens of enchantments, leaning out over the water with branches quivering and leaves coming to rest: first in fog, then in water, and finally on the far bank, in the Shadow Woods.

The enchantment on Ahraia grew lighter, enough so she could think again.

"Shade Ahraia." The Masai nodded to her path. "You're first."

Ahraia glared at her, a fire burning hot within her chest.

"My shadow's done nothing," she said, fighting through the oppressive layers of enchantment. "Give her back to the woods."

The Masai's eyes gleamed with white light. The black fur wreathed her gaunt eyes as she stepped closer to Ahraia, looking more lifeless than she ever had. "Tonight I'll be wearing your shadow as a cloak. Her blood will stain me like the light. And no shade will ever think of binding a wolf again."

A hundred eyes glowed beneath hoods and veils, beneath white hair, translucent like the fog. But not a single face showed disgust. The Masai's voice had carried to every turning ear, and none of them challenged her.

Ahraia shook with fury.

"I'll kill you. I swear it on the Bright Moon and the Dae-Mon both. Your nights are numbered. I promise you this."

The Masai smiled. "No one comes back from the Shadow Woods."

"I will," Ahraia said through gritted teeth.

Wicked laughter broke out all around her.

The enchantments redoubled around Ahraia, joined now by an unbreakable thread: the same thread of binding she had felt at Stone Tree. *The Masai's binding.* Ahraia recognized the taint of it, the impossible strength of it as it pushed her feet, one after another, towards her own death. She crossed stones to dirt, dirt to roots and roots to bark. The tree quivered beneath her toes, shaking against the raging river. For a brief moment, she wondered if she should leap, and let the river decide her fate. It would be certain death, one of dark water and monstrous stones, but it wouldn't be fair to Losna, chained and alone on the hilltop, waiting for night.

The enchantment loosened, until she was walking by her own will. Fog billowed all about her. The water churned below, raging and swift. She had never known hatred or hopelessness like she knew now. She tried to turn back, but a new wave of binding forced her forward, slipping past branches that jutted skyward like spears. She reached the far bank and leapt down, sinking into a cushion of soft moss.

The Shadow Woods.

It wasn't the mist that sent shivers down Ahraia's spine—it was the waking nightmare she had lived a thousand times. A moment later, the Astra leapt down beside her, holding a hand over her face, trying to stem the flow of blood and trying to shield herself from the fog-dimmed light.

"This is your fault," she hissed.

Whoosh!

The bridging tree soared suddenly skyward, spraying heavy drops of water across the bank. The wind pulled Ahraia's hood from her head, and the mist billowed after the tree, as though nothing could escape the Shadow Woods without chase.

Ahraia's mind was finally clear of enchantment. Their retreat was cut off.

The sprites on the far bank gathered, a collective yearning for death billowing across the river like the fog. The Masai leaned forward to drink, and every sprite mimicked her.

"What do you know about the Shadow Woods?" Ahraia said to the Astra, already moving along the bank.

"Don't drink the water. Don't touch the trees. Don't make a noise."

"What about the daemons? Don't you know anything more? You're the Astra!"

"They protect the heart of the forest, the seed. The *source* of the—where are you going?"

Ahraia began to run over unsteady stones and tilted trees, looking for the right break in the river or the right tree to spring her towards the other bank.

I'm going to get my shadow back.

"Your shadow? You're delusional. There's no escape from this. Not unless you can spring wings."

Spring wings. Ahraia wondered if any bird could carry her. *Not here.* Maybe a vulture of the plains or a jont owl of the west vales. *But nothing here*, she thought, looking to the dead woods.

And no spring would bear her more than a fraction of the way across the water. Unless she could find a place where the river narrowed, where maybe two trees leaned together from opposite banks. It wasn't likely, but it was better than waiting.

The Astra followed right behind her. "Ahraia, we need to stick together if we are going to have any chance."

"Stick together?" Ahraia scoffed. *I should stab you in the neck and leave you to rot.*

A roar trumpeted through the forest, filling the spaces between fog and trees and moss. It filled the space between Ahraia and the Astra. They looked at each other. Ahraia's ears twitched. The last echo was swallowed by the moss-carpeted forest. The Astra looked pale and stark, not ashen in the least. Her eyes were clouds of white, her pupils mere pinpoints in the bright fog.

"We'll have a better chance together," she said hoarsely, pinching her hood closed in front of her eyes.

Ahraia's skin was burning too. The forest ahead wasn't dark. It was day. And a steep, open hillside of rocks blocked her path. She looked towards the deeper-dark, towards the shadow-draped woods.

"I'll stick with you." *But only so the last thing I see is you in the Shad-Mon's claws*, Ahraia conveyed loosely. Farther upstream, she hoped there would be a place for her to cross. Maybe even the current would break, and she could swim. She saw sprites following her on the other bank, and she guessed their enchantments would drown her if she tried. Another roar rent the air. The moss swallowed the echoes reluctantly. She was going to have to go into the woods to get past the sunlit hillside.

Without another choice, Ahraia turned into the cool fog, towards the roar. She scrambled up the hillside, her hands sinking in deep, wet moss as she climbed. The slope plateaued in flat woods and almost at once, she was disoriented. Swirling gray mist danced devilishly amongst the dark trunks.

"Where are you going?" the Astra said, breathing heavily. "You're heading right towards it."

Ahraia opened her mouth to answer, but dove to the side as an enormous arm loomed out of the fog ahead. She drew her drain but looked up to find it was only the ghostly figure of a moss-laden tree. The Astra had lunged beside her, and lay in the soft-blanketed ground, white-faced and wide-eyed.

The river could still be heard, but its roaring was dimmed, dampened by the forest. Ahraia scrambled up and hurried upriver, above the rockfall that had blocked her way at the water's edge.

Where are you going? the Astra conveyed.

I'm getting across that river.

There's no use. The dae-wards patrol the other side. We'll never get away that way.

Ahraia spun about. "We?" she shouted.

Shhh, the Astra conveyed.

"*We* aren't doing anything," Ahraia said. "You can go and die wherever you like. Just get away from me." She turned back, but immediately felt something grabbing at her hip. The Astra, who had lost her drain in her fight against the Masai, had grabbed the bone-drain from Ahraia's waist.

"What in the light do you think you're doing?" Ahraia said just as an enchantment crashed over her.

The Astra's face was crazed. The cut on her cheek still ran with blood.

You're going to get me out of this, she conveyed. She held the drain before her, but was backing away with a maddened gleam in her eyes. *It's your fault I'm here. The Shad-Mon needs food. Maybe a sacrifice will appease it. Maybe it will let me be—if I hand you over.*

The enchantment held Ahraia's neck back, as though a firm hand grabbed her by a fistful of hair. It stilled her mind and her feet. The Astra stepped under the cover of a large fir tree.

But Ahraia hardly noticed the enchantment.

A menace was moving towards her through the forest, far beyond any hold the Astra was capable of casting. It came first as a stillness, a serenity belied by the ever-drifting fog. It settled next as a silence, a swallowing of footsteps and shifting trees, a muting of sounds too consequential to be dimmed. And lastly, it came as inevitability: a lurking shadow where no shadows were cast, a fate already decided. She could sense it in her bones.

The Astra hadn't noticed it yet. She was still staring at Ahraia, her conveyance touched with insanity.

A sacrifice will certainly do. Isn't that how we came to be? We emerged out of our bond to the daemons, from the need to keep them, and guard them . . . and to sacrifice to them. She clung to the trunk, as though it would keep her afloat in the sea of fog.

Ahraia struggled against the binding. She thought of Losna and Kyah. She thought of Alua and Thelon. She thought of Kaval, Altah and Hayvon. And her mind suddenly spit with fury, with a rage that far outweighing her fear. She couldn't break the binding, but she could form her own. She reached out to the Astra and made her bond. She forced the Astra from her hiding.

No! What are you doing? the Astra conveyed, suddenly aware of what Ahraia intended.

Ahraia moved her one step at a time into the clearing.

"Stop. Let me go!" the Astra said.

"We can both go down together," Ahraia said. It gave her a certain pleasure to know that the Astra was going to die. A tree trunk groaned and the Astra's head snapped about.

You'll kill us both. It's coming! the Astra conveyed desperately.

Ahraia grimaced. It was all she could do. Her nose suddenly stung with a foul scent of rotting flesh. Her own fear held her rooted to the ground.

"It's already here."

The Astra's struggle suddenly stopped and her thoughts went blank. Her eyes went wide and her ears curled back. Abysmal fear spread across their bindings.

A chill ran through Ahraia. While the Astra's reason fled like crows from a fox, Ahraia's senses sharpened. A branch moved that had no place moving. The ground trembled, muted by the moss. A fetid smell was smothered by the fog.

It's here, the Astra thought, more to herself than to Ahraia. Ahraia followed her gaze. All she saw were dark trunks. Dark trunks and shifting fingers of fog. *Fingers . . .*

A hand.

She saw it.

A monstrous, clawed hand gripped a tree trunk as wide as Ahraia was tall. It gripped a tree impossibly high—a spring length above the ground—but the body was hidden by a gnarled cluster of trees.

The fog shifted, making even the trees ghostly trunks shift with it. When it cleared, the hand was gone.

Ahraia stared in disbelief.

Where did it go?

The thick trees crowded together without any hint of the monster hiding behind them. Her heart pounded in her chest. She kept her gaze on the forest, searching high and low for any hint of the claw. Midway up, the trunks melded, rising skyward before stopping abruptly as a round, misshapen stump. And then Ahraia realized what she was looking at.

The Shad-Mon.

Standing on its hind legs, one arm formed what Ahraia had thought was a half-fallen tree, slanting across the wood to hold itself up. Its head stood taller than the tip of the tallest keress's horns, and its arms would have rested on the ground if they weren't suspending the monster, like some horrible, drawn-out imp. The daemon's hands were larger than Losna, ending in long fingers, tipped with razor-sharp claws. It drew itself forward, like an enormous spider, using the trees as its web.

I'm dead, the Astra thought. The enchantment holding Ahraia was wavering. The Shad-Mon's second hand crept forward, wrapping around a broad fir as though it was as small as an arrow shaft. Even the fog couldn't hide the daemon now.

Its eyes were black pits of the night. Its mouth stretched all the way across its broad head, with jagged teeth spanning the curve of it.

Ahraia wondered if her ears had stopped working; nothing that big could move in such silence. But she knew they hadn't; a tree creaked behind her.

Another, the Astra thought, looking past Ahraia's shoulder. Ahraia glanced back and felt her blood run cold. A second Shad-Mon was closing in behind her, eyes just as black, its feet curled about a fallen log like a second set of hands.

Even as she looked, however, Ahraia knew her mistake.

In the span of a breath, the binding holding her broke, and a moment later, she felt the brunt of the Astra's mind buck against her enchantment. The hold snapped and they were both suddenly free.

Ahraia spun back, but too late. The Astra stabbed out, the white bone slashing towards her heart. She deflected the blow, but the blade sliced across her shoulder. She cried out in pain, leaping back. She pulled her metal drain free. It glinted weakly in the half-dark. Her ears turned as a tree groaned behind her. The woods all about her were suddenly in motion, and she knew both Shad-Mon were closing in.

The Astra cast another enchantment, seizing Ahraia as she stabbed forward. The fear of the Shad-Mon sharpened Ahraia's mind. She overpowered the binding and fell backward as the blade passed just before her eye. A footstep shook the ground. Ahraia knew the hand of the Shad-Mon was coming.

In a single movement, she bound the Astra, ducked forward and stabbed down into her foot. The blade pierced through skin and tendon, past bone and muscle before embedding deeply in a root beneath.

The Astra screamed.

Ahraia jerked the blade free, rolling away. She came up ready to fight, but the Astra wasn't there.

The ground where she had stood was empty.

Ahraia froze and looked up. The Shad-mon had plucked the Astra into the air. She beat uselessly against the massive hand and a shrill scream escaped her lips. The gaping maw of the Shad-Mon opened and a horrible crunch cut her cry violently short.

Half the Astra's body disappeared in a single swallow. The Shad-Mon threw its head back. Her legs flopped lifelessly about before disappearing into the gaping void. Bones crackled. Tendons tore. The air was filled with crunching. Then silence.

Blood streamed between the Shad-Mon's teeth.

Ahraia didn't have to turn to know the second daemon was almost upon her. She leapt up and ran, linking the nearest branch she could find.

The bough swung down as a massive hand swept across the moss-strewn ground. Ahraia reached up blindly, letting the spring twist about her wrist. As soon as it touched her skin, she directed the binding upward. Mid-run, her feet jolted off the ground. Wind and hair swept across her face. Something passed terrifyingly beneath her, like a great bird of prey suddenly sprung from the shadows.

The Shad-Mon roared. The air shook with the closeness. Ahraia's ears were ringing as she landed along a thin branch.

Too thin. It bent under her weight and she leapt away at once, swinging back into the air just as the Shad-Mon crashed into the tree.

Ahraia let go of the branch, tumbling to the soft moss. She formed her next spring and it carried her up again, a dozen feet off the ground.

Next spring. For a moment, she was airborne, waiting for the branch to reach her. She grabbed hold, feeling the perilous pull of the ground before it carried her higher still.

Every corner of the woods shook with violent roars. Both Shad-Mon were chasing her, no longer creeping through the woods, but careening through trees, snapping branches and trunks alike. Ahraia formed spring after spring. The fog made every direction seem the same, and soon enough she lost any sense of the river.

Get me out of here, she thought desperately, unsure which direction she was heading. She formed a shift between two maples as one of the daemons crashed against the trunk. Ahraia slipped; the branch cracked, and she tumbled into the air. Suddenly, she was falling. And the hand was waiting beneath.

Instinctively, she bound the daemon, stilling the monster's hand, keeping its fingers splayed wide. In an instant, she plummeted past stony skin and slipped through its claws before crashing to the mossy ground below. She tumbled down a short hill, saved by the slope and the deep moss. The binding remained and she tried to hold the Shad-Mon, fighting to still it with her mind. The daemon roared and the binding frayed, too insignificant to contain a thousand years of instinct. In that moment, she sensed that it was protecting something, and she had no interest in finding out what.

She pushed herself up and ran towards the next spring she could find.

Where is this dark-forsaken river? she thought, sprinting over a fallen log. She heard something through the woods. Something distinctly familiar that wrenched at her heart and legs.

A long, drawn out call to counter the roar of the daemons.

It drifted, fighting through fog and mist to reach her. Ahraia turned, running the length of another log to try and hear it. A monstrous hand smashed down behind her, sending the log spinning like a twig; splinters and debris fell all about her. She landed on all fours and was up and running. Then she heard the call again. Louder this time. It stirred her heart. A howl.

"Ahooo!"

"Losna!" She turned towards her call, springing through the woods, and feeling her heart soar with hope. She found herself slipping down a hillside, sprinting towards the rising roar of the river. A thousand nights spent running unfolded in one smooth motion between her mind and feet: *Over that log. Fold back the brush. Slick moss. Sliding.* It happened without thinking. Running so fast she was past obstacles before she had time to worry if they would stop her.

A narrow maple leaned from the hillside. She ran the length of the trunk, feeling it bounce and bend even more, so it was almost flat. She was out ten feet, twenty feet from the hillside. She formed a binding and lunged off the tree, grabbing an already-swinging branch in midair. The spring plunged down. Down and down, slowing just before she landed on soft moss. The bellows of the Shad-Mon echoed after her. But Ahraia knew the way now. The forest passed in a blur.

Ahead, light was spreading radiantly in front of her. The fog glowed, bright and luminous. She had never been so excited for light in all her life.

She heard the deadly roar of the river. From the sound of it, she guessed it couldn't be swam. She needed a bridging tree. But such an enchantment—especially alone, without proper time or care—would never work. Behind her, a tree crashed to the ground, shaking the forest.

Several cottonwoods towered at the edge of the fog, their yellow leaves tipped in light. A fir tree amongst them stood dead, a pillar, stripped of bark and branches.

Boom.

Another tree crashed to the ground.

Suddenly, Ahraia knew how to form her bridge. No living tree would bend across the river, but maybe the dead tree would.

Losna's howling was growing louder.

I'm coming, Ahraia thought, binding the two cottonwoods beside and beyond the dead tree. Her mind strained for the connection, the binding on a scale beyond anything she had ever done.

Bend for me, she thought, ignoring the swell of noise behind her. *Move!*

The tops of the cottonwoods turned inward, blowing in a windless gale towards the dead fir.

Behind her, the Shad-Mon pulled themselves through the forest by clawed hands and feet. The air whirled through her hair. Something had fallen, close. *A branch,* she hoped. *Not a hand.*

The cottonwoods leaned. Their tops were nearly touching.

Farther, she urged, pouring her will into the enchantment. The first branch touched the smooth bark. It strained—wrapping about the dead tree. More branches seized hold, pulling the trees into a forced embrace.

Now back to center! Towards the river, she commanded, releasing the trees back to where they wanted to be. They heaved, leaning all their weight back towards the river, pulling the dead tree with them.

Ahraia stumbled to the soft moss, exhausted. The fir leaned but didn't break. It was too deeply rooted. The daemons were right behind her. The ground buckled at their weight.

At any moment, stony hands would lift her bodily into the air, and that would be it. She would know nothing but blood and teeth.

"Ahooo!"

She scrambled up, willed on by Losna, darting sideways as the daemon's claw slammed to the ground. Losna's calls were louder now.

"Ahooo!"

The daemons extended to their full height, driven mad by the noise. Both paused, looking towards the river, towards the sound of the howling.

Ahraia used the distraction to gather her strength. She made for the dead tree. She could see frothing water through the forest. She reached out and bonded a third tree. It was smaller, but it leaned in eagerly and grabbed the dead fir, joining the other two in their task. Together they pulled, branches straining, trunks leaning.

"*Farther!*" she screamed.

A massive whine filled the air and the dead tree tipped as its roots began to give way. A slow groan reverberated from the deep, then grew, crackling through the earth.

Snap!

The roots ripped away.

Rock and dirt and debris spit violently into the air. Ahraia covered her face as she ran, the light spinning all about her. The dead tree tottered and then fell. Roots emerged from the ground, rising upward.

Ahraia formed a spring, leaping into the air just as the fog behind her stirred by a clawed hand.

The dead tree toppled across the river, crashing down over the water half a moment before her feet landed.

Boom!

It exploded with tremendous force. Freezing water sprayed upward. The fog billowed away and the massive trunk split right in half in the middle of the river.

Ahraia's feet were churning—she was running into the light, out from under the eaves of the forest and over the raging water. The river poured over the break in the tree. She leapt over the channel, landing on the other side just as the first half broke away and settled deeper. She ran the length of the log, pulling her hood close. She didn't stop until she leapt onto the banks of Angolor.

The Shad-Mon roared and shook the trees. They gnashed the teeth and bellowed in anger.

Ahraia turned back to the forest nearer at hand and slipped into the merciful shade. The Dae-Mon rose so bright that she was sure it would seer her in place if it touched her. Terrible and radiant. Round as the Bright Moon, but bigger, brighter, resplendent and frightening all at once. It stung her eyes and burned her skin all over again, and yet, she was alive.

Movement through the woods caught her eyes. A hooded figure was running towards her.

A dae-ward.

Given all the racket streaming out from the Shadow Woods, she couldn't tell if he was running towards her or away from the Shad-Mon. She didn't wait to find out. Shouts filled the woods. Light streamed into the upper canopy. She started towards Losna's howling.

Her feet carried her like the wind, and she didn't know how long she ran when she finally saw the Sprite Maker's wall ahead. The closures were still open. She ran headlong, dodging shafts of light as she went.

I'm coming, she thought.

She slipped through a closure. A rush of leaves and swishing branches filled the air. The wall snapped together, forming a tight barrier with a resounding rustle, like a trap ensnaring its prey. An owl screeched nearby and took flight, its wings beating heavily against the air. Ahraia ducked, covering her head as the great owl thundered into the canopy. She turned towards the hill, unconcerned with the wall. As fast as her legs would carry her, she clawed up the hillside, feeling a familiar tug at her mind.

The howling stopped.

Ahraia?

She sprinted through the woods, scrambling towards the dazzling morning sky. The Makers were mercifully shaded and the exposed hilltop still rested in shadow, blocked by the towering eastern firs.

Losna! She saw day-lit fur and sharp ears. Ahraia pulled her hood close and sprinted out beneath the light for the second time.

Ahraia! Losna whined and pulled at her chain, jumping, choking herself in her excitement. Ahraia crashed into her shadow, throwing her arms around Losna's neck.

My Shadow.

30

UNBROKEN BOND

Losna's coarse tongue lapped wildly across Ahraia's face. Ahraia ignored the burning light, her arms wrapped tightly in thick fur, her hands clenched about the folds of her shadow's neck. Her heart, weighed down by so many hopeless nights, unclasped, and tears streamed down her face.

Ahraia. My Shade! Losna thought. *What are you doing here? It's full day.* She tried to cover Ahraia's face, wrestling her to her knees.

"I've missed you," Ahraia said, flooded with relief. But worry tarnished their bond; Losna was beyond nervous.

You can't be here. It's too light, she thought. Her tail was stiff and her ears pointed.

Ahraia held her, uncaring. Her shadow pulled away.

I've heard things . . . the Shad-Mon has been roaring.

"Dae-Mon and daemons," Ahraia shuddered. "I've seen them both."

You saw it? What happened! Losna pressed in closer, trying to shield Ahraia from the light that hung everywhere in the air.

"Daemons," she said, sharing a memory of the Shad-Mon. "There are two of them."

Losna fur bristled like it never had before. *You saw them?*

Ahraia wrapped Hayvon's veil beneath her eyes and drew her hood tight as she told Losna all that had happened. Losna's eyes glowed golden and she bared her teeth as Ahraia recounted the Astra's words. She let out a growl when she heard what the third and final task would have been.

I knew this place was evil. It's soaked in the blood of a thousand shadows. I can feel it beneath my paws. I can smell it with every breath. It lingers on me, even in sleep.

Ahraia could feel it too. The hilltop was a place for killing. Even the day light couldn't burn away the touch of it.

Our siblings are dead? Losna asked.

Ahraia nodded.

Losna butted her forehead into Ahraia's chest. Her low whine turned to a growl. *And the Astra too? Good.* Her brow furrowed with grim satisfaction. Ahraia released the clump of fur she held.

"But the Masai's still out there," she said, leaning back, "and she wants us both dead. We need to get you loose before it gets much lighter." Her eyes burned. Even with all that had already happened, the Dae-Mon had only just risen. Soon enough it would scorch directly down on them with its fiery eye.

She fumbled at the tight collar choking Losna's neck. *We need to get you to darkness,* Losna thought.

"How does this confounded thing work?" Ahraia asked.

The outside of the collar was perfectly smooth, but sharp metal thorns ringed the inside, cutting into Losna if she tried to pull free. Ahraia grasped the chain; the metal clinked together as she tested it. It was cold as though wet, flexible, and yet, solid.

"We only have until nightfall to get away from here," Ahraia said. *If not sooner.*

Losna's gaze turned to the sky then dropped to the woods. *Do you think the dae-wards will come for us?* she asked, sensing Ahraia's concern.

"I don't know."

Ahraia wasn't even sure if the wards had seen her, but the wall would have alerted the Masai by now. Would she wait for nightfall? It wasn't as though Ahraia and Losna had any means of escaping: they were trapped in the Makers, in the beating heart of the Silh, surrounded on every side by woods teeming with wards. And Losna was rooted to the very ground.

Ahraia ran her fingers over the unnatural metal, feeling the links one at a time. She tried to bond them, but they were lifeless, just like the smooth tree the chain was affixed to. She searched for springs to rip at the chain but nothing of any substance would reach Losna.

Light pervaded the hilltop. A disturbing, pale color spread across the sky. The top of the skeletal tree was glowing in the first rays of the Dae-Mon. She kept her eyes down.

"How did they fit this on you?" she asked, her hood pulled close and a sheen of sweat sticking the veil to her cheeks.

Losna watched her, worry furrowed across her brow. *Ahraia, you need darkness.*

"How did they even get it around your neck?" *Was it all one piece?* Ahraia conveyed, shaking the chain. The collar was too perfect to have been placed at once, and yet, she saw no seam or flaw in it. Sweat beaded beneath her nose. The collar was magic.

They had me enchanted, Losna thought nervously. *It folded. From two pieces. The Masai somehow fixed them together once they had it on me. She slipped something beneath my chin, on my throat. I couldn't see. It made a noise.*

"A noise?"

Ahraia remembered the metal fittings of the wagon, the strange magic of the humans that had held the dead wooden piece together. She recalled them snapping shut.

"Show me," she said.

Losna focused on the memory, and Ahraia formed a deeper binding. She closed her eyes, drifting into the thoughts of her shadow. She heard the wind growing, and felt starlight on her skin.

When she opened her eyes, it was night. A sliver of Blood Moon hung above her, silhouetting a sprite. *The Masai.*

Losna lay pinned to the ground, immobilized by a dozen enchantments. Only her eyes could move. Fetid, blood-soaked ground lay beneath her, stinging her nostrils, reeking of rot and decay and odious betrayal. The Masai craned over her, a smile spreading across her face. *The cloak.* It smelled even fouler than the ground.

Something metallic rattled nearby. She heard a voice—it was the Masai's voice.

"Bring the chain."

The clinking came closer. Something heavy draped across her back, but she couldn't even lift her head to see it. The Masai stooped, her hand resting in Losna's fur. When she spoke, her voice was soft and calm.

"The beauty of a lock is it is not a spritish thing. It is a type of human devilry. Incorruptible, to its very core."

Losna felt the heavy thing draped over her back.

"It cannot be bent, or bound, or broken, though your shade—should she ever show up—will undoubtably try. It's the nature of shades to try. For a lock, you must have a key. Of which, there is only one."

A cold *something* slid around Losna's neck. She whined as barbs dug into her skin.

"Tighter . . ." the Masai said. "Until she bleeds."

Losna yelped. Stabbing pain bit into her from every angle. She yelped louder as the sprite cinched it down, knives piercing through her fur.

Slowly, the stars came into focus and the pain receded to a sharp ache.

The Masai grabbed her firmly by the muzzle. "You see, the lock is dead," she said calmly, as though they were strolling through the woods at midnight. "Should it be of wood or living thing, then your shade's mind could bond it or bind it to trick or coerce it. But this is a lifeless thing. Which is fitting, considering where you lie."

Losna lay in a daze. The Masai fidgeted with something at her throat. She heard a small click beneath her chin.

Tick.

And somehow, she knew it wouldn't move again. The Masai let

her head fall just as she slid something into her cloak. Then she used Losna to push herself up, sinking long claw-like fingers into her ribs.

With the sharp pain, Ahraia withdrew from the memory and the night faded.

She blinked, squinting her eyes against the stark brightness of the day.

"What in the name of light is a lock?" Ahraia said, rubbing her sides where the Masai's fingers hadn't truly been. The fur of Losna's neck was matted with blood. Ahraia followed the stains to where the Masai had meddled with the collar. A narrow opening formed in the metal, a fissure that she hadn't seen before. Her shadow held perfectly still while she examined the small hole.

It was precisely shaped, too small for even a finger. *A hole for a key.* Ahraia had never heard the word "key" before, but the Masai had inflected enough meaning that she could guess what it was. Taking her drain, she aligned the tip against the opening. The blade was too wide, and butted uselessly to a stop. Ahraia didn't dare press harder —not with Losna's throat beneath.

The thick chain looked even tougher than the collar.

I've already broken two teeth on it, Losna said, sensing Ahraia's thoughts. Nonetheless, Ahraia slunk across the hilltop in search of a large stone. Finding one, she hurried back, raised it high above her head and slammed it down.

It clattered away uselessly.

She hefted the stone again and again, each time the chain wriggled and jerked, unaffected. She bloodied her hands in the process, flinging the stone aside in frustration. The Dae-Mon's rays were halfway down the skeletal trunk.

Next, she went to the forest, dragging back a large branch, almost so big she couldn't carry it. She dropped it on the chain. It bounced harmlessly. The Dae-Mon crept higher in the sky, almost clearing the eastern trees.

Losna huffed in frustration and dismay. Ahraia was sweating worse. Her knuckles were scraped raw from pulling and twisting at the metal but it hadn't even been marked.

You've got to find shelter, Losna thought.

Ahraia examined the connection where the chain met the collar. That joint was thinner, but still far too strong to break. *Maybe with an arrow*, she thought, wishing she had her bow. Even if she did, it would be a risky shot so close to Losna's neck.

Do all sprites really kill their shadows? Losna wondered. *Did Kren?*

Ahraia knelt, her options exhausted. She nodded. Light-scars etched across her fingers and hands in gray permanence. She squinted and pressed her palms to her eyelids. Her eyes stung in the morning light. Losna's yellow eyes flared, bursting with gold and wreathed in white. Ahraia had never seen her like this. Full day had come.

That's what this place is, Losna thought. *A place to kill shadows.* She held Ahraia with a penetrating stare. *You're going to have to leave me.*

"I'm not going to leave you," Ahraia said firmly. "We've just got to find a way to break the chain. I need something stronger. I need my bow."

She startled as the air snapped with a raven's call.

Caw!

Losna flinched, then turned her gaze skyward. A moon raven, whiter than the brightest snow, circled. It landed, its red, beady eyes staring at the pair of them. It hopped closer, cawing again at Ahraia.

That's a spy of the Masai . . . I've seen it before. Losna poised herself to leap.

The raven stayed beyond the reach of the chain. It hopped closer to Ahraia.

"A messenger."

I'll give it a message. Losna pulled right to the end of the chain. The raven cawed mockingly.

Ahraia walked towards the bird, eyeing it before she bound it. The message lay at the tip of its thoughts.

Ahraia closed her eyes. As soon as she had, murky dark surrounded her, and she was in the deep of the forest. The Masai's black cloak glared at her. Ahraia tried to reach for her drain, before she remembered herself, though her heart beat hard against her chest. The Masai was surrounded by a host of wards, both day and night. She spoke directly to the raven, but her words were made for Ahraia.

"My wards tell me you are alive. How? I cannot fathom. I would call them liars, but I've heard the Shad-Mon roaring and my walls tell me they've been breached." A twisted sneer spread across the Masai's face, beneath the black maw of the wolf's mouth. "And to think, you could have run." She shook her head, and then went on.

"Once night falls, I'm coming for you, Ahraia. And when I bind you, I won't put you back in the Shadow Woods. I'll make you suffer as you never thought possible. You were a threat to me. But now you're going to be an example."

Visions began to flow through Ahraia's mind; threats from the Masai. Ahraia saw Losna laying in total darkness, whimpering in pain. Her eyes were glazed, but she was alive. The Masai stood before her with a knife, and a cloak: it was gray and silver, dripping in blood. It was Losna's fur.

"You'll watch as I skin your shadow alive," the Masai said.

Ahraia broke the bond, unable to suffer the sight or sound. The raven hopped closer, the message unfinished.

"Get away from me!" Ahraia said. She scampered towards the bird, hands raised. It took flight, squawking and cawing at her.

What did it say? Losna thought.

Tears of rage stung at Ahraia's eyes. Losna leaned in closer, pressing her to answer, but she couldn't.

"It said we need to break that chain before nightfall." Ahraia set her jaw. She glared after the raven, who took a perch in the highest fir.

Ahraia looked to the dead tree, its weather-smoothed roots snaking over rock and barren dirt, making small shadows. The Dae-Mon's light was moving across the ground. It was only feet away from where she stood.

"Can you make me darkness?" she asked. "Can you dig me a den? Somewhere to hide from the light?"

To what end?

"I'm going to get my bow. We need something stronger to break the chain, and I don't know how much more light I can suffer."

Losna's fur was brilliant in the morning light. Her tail hung between her legs.

Where is your bow?

"Outside."

Losna didn't move.

Ahraia reassured her through the bond. "I'll be back. Just make sure I have somewhere dark to hide." She ruffled her shadow's ears and headed for the woods.

Losna growled but turned and began to claw beneath the deadened roots of the withered tree.

Ahraia retreated from the hilltop, stumbling into blissfully dark shade. Her feet crunched over fallen charberries, her eyes feeling a stinging relief while her bond with Losna faded with every step.

The alp's arrows were metal tipped, and if she was going to have any hope breaking the chain, it came from that. Her hiding spot wasn't far from the Makers she could move through the canopy, recover her things, and slip back to the hill before the Masai could even cross the central hollow. Losna's thoughts carried down through the woods before her mind became too distant.

Be careful . . .

The link faded to a thin connection, buzzing from both ends with anxiety. The dark became truer with every step—a murky sort of daytime dark. She heard an owl call loudly, the same one she had startled before.

A solid wall of leaves waited for her at the base of the hillside. Branches, tied together by centuries of enchantment, frowned down at her menacingly. Ahraia let out a slow sigh. She pulled the veil down to her chin. The scars felt crisp and hot, and the skin at her wrists was charred gray. She wished for a cool pond. *That and a key . . . or at least a way through this fiendish wall.*

All hope of breaking the chain lay outside, and the Masai's enchantment lay before her. But foldings were her province.

She sat down, arranging herself carefully—close, but not too close—before closing her eyes. The binding came naturally, though with resistance, of course. She hesitated a moment, choosing her tack. *Honesty*, she decided. Trees were proud things, and anything else would end up getting her thumped again.

I'm not going to coerce you . . . I need you to listen to me. I am a daughter of the forest. And I come to you in need.

The enchantment sang with her soul. Branch by branch, tree by tree she bent them to her will. One by one, they relented, surrendering to her pleas, spreading her desire to those about them. The Dae-Mon, hidden by the canopy, crept skyward and still she worked. The morning stretched on. Birds sang with her, their calls forming a harmony with her enchantments. The wind settled to listen. The whole wood turned inward on itself.

Soon, a sheet of the wall as wide as she was tall and twice that again was hers. It itched to move.

"Here we go," she said, standing up, ready to spring into the canopy once she was outside. "*Open.*"

The branches peeled back, forming an escape from the Makers. In places beyond her control, the wall coiled and lunged at her, but a wide swath of it lay motionless, held still at the tip of her mind. The woods of Angolor spread beyond, dark and deep and undoubtably guarded.

Ahraia took a step, her mind full of worries. Would the closure hold? Would the wall let her back in? Were wards hiding in the forest beyond? She took another step into the wall's shadow. The binding felt firm. She hesitated and then scampered forward. Half-way beneath, however, the enchantment soured. The branches, overly eager, sang her praise too easily.

A step too late, she stopped.

The closure snapped shut. Vines shot down like arrows from above. Branches swung inward like the arms of the Shad-Mon and a large serapin root slithered towards her. Ahraia leapt back but not before a thick branch crashed over her, jarring her to the ground. She scrambled up and darted towards the hillside as a tendril of the wall snaked around her ankle, jerking her to a stop.

In an instant, her drain was out, slashing downward, cutting deeply across the vine. It withdrew angrily, but a dozen more struck forward, slamming her to the ground. She covered her face as the wall battered her, striking painfully over her chest and shoulders and head. She rolled away with blood in her mouth and her arms stinging from the bruising blows.

A sinuous root seized her—the serapin tree. The branch constricted about her leg, dragging her effortlessly towards the awaiting trunk. She clawed at the dirt, her nails scraping across leaves and mud and stone. A smaller branch from the same tree slithered forward. Its stinger emerged from a narrow tip. Desperate, Ahraia sliced across the root holding her. The tree writhed in pain; black sap oozed like blood to the ground. The serapin's grip loosened and she fell back, but the stinger darted towards her. It landed across her chest, the tip inches from her face. She sliced at it in a panic, rolling away while trying to disentangle herself from the still wiggling branch. Suddenly, a searing pain shot through her hand.

"Aghh!" she screamed. She flung the branch away, looking to her palm where a long red sliver stuck outward. Her fingers immediately tingled with fiery pain; her hand shook violently. She used her teeth to pull the stinger out, spitting it away. At once, her lips started to burn with numbness.

Not that deep. It's not going to hurt me. I need my bow. She sucked the blood from the palm of her hand, spitting it out. The taste was foul—blood mixed with sour sickness.

The venom was spreading, as though the tree's roots slithered inside her. She felt a stabbing pain in her elbow. Then beneath her shoulder. She needed bitter root. *Or Charberries.* She glanced about for either. She blinked, her vision blurred. Her breaths were growing faster. She stood up and nearly stumbled.

The whole woods seemed to be caught in a windstorm she couldn't hear or feel. Trunks bent in ways no binding could manage. Leaves tumbled about her without falling. Her breath wasn't enough to feed her.

She started back up the hill, panic suddenly settling like a knife inside her heart. A stabbing ache pulsed from her elbow through her whole body. She staggered, scraping her leg heavily against some log she hadn't seen.

"Losna," she said, well aware her wits were unravelling.

She crawled towards what felt like upwards, though she tipped onto her face, smelling dirt and moss, and dried branches. She searched across the roots. Bitter root was everywhere. So were charberries. *Why couldn't she find them?* They were as common as maple and fir.

Her face was suddenly resting on the ground. She didn't remember falling. Before her, she saw gray bark speckled with black. *Is it bitter root?*

She looked up at the tree in a daze. Looking up was a mistake. Her head spun. The trees above her turned, their branches like a falling maple seed, spinning in a steady circle.

She fumbled with the knife. Her hands shook violently. She cut through the thin root, roughly pulling the dirt and mud from it. She peeled a thin piece of bark with her teeth. She shoved it in her mouth, unable to taste it.

Bitter. It's supposed to be bitter.

She shaved another piece away, larger than the last. She worked her jaw but her teeth wouldn't seem to meet. Her mouth and face were tingling with numbness. Nothing changed. Her vision was blurring. She crawled away.

Losna, she thought hopelessly. She thought she heard howling, but she wasn't sure. It could have been inside her head. The forest blurred. She felt something squish beneath her hands. *Berries.* She couldn't see their shape. It might have been blue. It might have been black.

She swept a handful into her mouth, unsure if they even made it in. Everything was fading. The Masai was going to skin Losna. The light would consume her. Ahraia tried to crawl, but fell and couldn't get up.

Her breaths came shorter. And night, deeper than any she had ever known, settled about her.

~

A HOWL, lonely and harrowing, echoed through the woods.

Light pierced the forest, stabbing down at Ahraia, stabbing right through her cloak and burning at her side. She rolled over, eyes still closed and skin stretched dry. Her mouth overflowed with a bitter and sour *something*. Bark was stuck beside her teeth and she spit out dark ashen mush. Berries. *Charberries.* She opened her eyes, feeling as though she had been beaten.

The memory of the serapin tree came back to her. She *had* been beaten. She lay under a char bush. Black juice stained Hayvon's veil and crusted about her lips. Sleep tingled through her left arm and when she moved, stabbing pains followed her nerves right to her fingertips.

The light lay dangerously close and fog wove between her thoughts. She looked up, trying to determine the time of day.

It was still day. That was all she could tell.

Losna. The chain. My bow . . .

Her failure spread over her as though she had been doused in true light. The night hadn't come yet, but she had no way of breaking the chain. She thrust herself to her knees. Her head spun and pain seared through her arm. Trampled berries and bushes showed the aftermath of her sting.

She took another handful of charberries and put them in her mouth. Ashen juice stilled the little saliva she had, but her vision seemed to sharpen. She spit them out and pulled herself to her feet.

She climbed towards the hilltop, startled to see it was late afternoon. Her lungs burned but she pulled herself onward, knowing she couldn't break the chain. She wondered if somehow—some way—she could jam something small enough to unhook the lock. She doubted it. The Masai's voice had been devious in her delight with the lock, as though nothing more perfect could exist to hold a shadow.

When Ahraia reached the top of the hill, sweat dripped along the line of her jaw and her side burned. Losna stood at the very edge of her chain, already in shadow.

Where have you been? It's almost dusk. Her ears stood on end. Her tail lay low and stiff. *Where's your bow?*

Ahraia stumbled from the woods, the inevitability of what was coming suddenly striking her like the serapin tree had. Tears welled in her eyes and she wanted to scream with helplessness. She staggered to Losna's side.

"I couldn't do it . . . I didn't even get beyond the wall. I got stung by a serapin."

A serapin tree? Losna whined. *Was it a big one? Are you hurt?* Losna froze, staring at Ahraia's side. *What's that light?* Losna sniffed at Ahraia's cloak, where a burning pain lingered. Ahraia hadn't noticed, but a dim shining emerged from beneath her cloak. She flinched.

"What is that?" She shook her cloak, and the orb tumbled out, burning hot. "Get it off of me." She kicked it across the ground, cowering away. Losna quickly took it and hid it in the den she had dug, where its white light glowed outward.

"It must not have been broken," Ahraia said, brushing at her side, feeling burnt skin where light hardly ever shone. She looked up, and found Losna staring at her.

We can't do anything about the chain, can we?

Guilt, heavier than any emotion Ahraia had ever known, crashed down on her. She felt tears welling up in her eyes. "I thought . . . I can't . . ."

Losna lowered her head, resigned to her fate. Her tail tucked below her. Ahraia rushed to her, embracing her. The touch was painful. Ahraia's failure burnt into her worse than any light ever could. She broke down—angry at herself for failing, angry that she had come so far only to be defeated by a vine of metal.

"I thought maybe something—maybe we could find something small enough to trick the lock." Her words tumbled out. She searched the ground, but tears flooded her eyes, blinding her. Her hand shook violently as she tried to bring a twig to the keyhole. It broke halfway in and only managed to clog the fissure. Panicked, she blew at it, terrified that she had just sealed their fate.

She's going to kill us at sundown. Losna's whole body quivered. Ahraia knelt in the dirt, weeping freely. She saw the image in her mind of the Masai wearing a blood-drenched coat of fur. She would rather die than live to see her shadow suffer that.

Losna was looking at her. She nuzzled under Ahraia's chin, bringing her eyes up.

You're going to have to do it, she thought. *There is no breaking this chain. And when they come, I'd rather be dead than skinned alive.*

Tears of frustration streamed down Ahraia's face. Losna knew what would happen if night fell and they hadn't broken the chain. She knew how gruesome and terrible it would be. Ahraia held onto her shadow, burying her face in her fur.

This is your shadow test, Losna thought. *You'll become a sprite. It's the way it's supposed to be. You can still flee, Ahraia.*

Ahraia sat with bloody knuckles and light-burnt eyes. She held her shadow for a long time, knowing that neither of them could suffer the fate that was coming. Losna didn't have a choice. She was trapped. But Ahraia did. She could spare her shadow. She could spare herself having to watch the Masai torture Losna. It was the only choice. The alternative would be unbearable.

She held on to Losna, not daring to let go. How much time passed, she didn't know, but when Losna licked at her face, nuzzling her again, the Dae-Mon was sinking in the west. The shadows stretched to the foot of the eastern trees, slowly climbing onto their trunks. Dusk was coming. Losna butted her forehead against Ahraia, the hard bone nearly pushing Ahraia's hood back.

There is no more time. You'll be a sprite.

"I won't," Ahraia said.

Losna nipped at her. *That is what this place is. A place where shadows pass and sprites emerge.*

Ahraia shook her head, her teeth digging into her lip. Losna nuzzled her.

My shade . . . there's no other choice. You have to finish this.

The late afternoon had passed and the Masai would come on the heels of dusk.

Losna was resigned. Ahraia couldn't believe it had come to this. She was going to have to put Losna down—for her shadow's sake. She cried bitterly, her whole body shaking with sobs she couldn't control. She buried her face in Losna's coat, wanting to die rather than go through with what Losna was asking her to do.

Ahraia, I don't want to be skinned.

Ahraia pulled herself away, still sobbing. Her eyes burned with light and tears. She would do it, but she wouldn't flee. She wasn't going on without Losna. When it was finished, she would wait for the Masai and if the Masai wanted to kill her, so be it. Her breaths were hollow. She didn't care that her skin and eyes burned.

"How has it come to this? How can shades cut their shadows from themselves?" she said, staring at the glowing sky. The wind set the trees swaying and the cold light of the Dae-Mon danced about her. It was a lifeless dance. A hopeless one.

They were dead.

The night was coming.

Ahraia reached into her cloak and pulled forth the metal drain. Losna lay her head down and readied herself.

Do it.

The drain felt poisonous and wretched in Ahraia's hand. Tears came harder and faster than before. Her jaw was quivering and she couldn't stop it. She couldn't believe that it had come to this, after everything they had been through. A thousand nights spent running together melded with a thousand nights of laughter and joy. She couldn't do this. She felt a howling inside her heart.

But it was her only choice for Losna.

She raised the drain over her head. The warmth of Losna radiated up, through the air and through the bond. They were one and the same. She was killing herself. Ahraia sobbed. Tears filled her eyes so thick that she couldn't see. Losna lay with her head down.

Do it. Now. Please, Ahraia. I don't want to be skinned...

Ahraia steeled herself. Losna's breaths rattled in her chest. A single golden eye stared up at Ahraia.

Become a sprite, my shade.

I'll avenge you. I swear it. Ahraia gritted her teeth together furiously. "I swear it. To the Moons and the Stars."

Losna's eyes closed.

She took her last breath.

Ahraia's whole being cried out in terror as her hands plunged downward. Her mind recoiled, and a howl erupted from her mouth. She slammed the drain down, screaming as she did.

31

DIGGING GRAVES

The drain plunged into the shadow-drenched earth, an inch from Losna's throat. An inch from her own.

"I can't! I can't do it," Ahraia screamed. She pulled the knife from the ground and flung it away, disgusted she had even raised her hand.

Losna opened her eye hesitantly.

Ahraia, you have to. She'll torture us both.

"I can't," Ahraia sobbed. "I'd rather scorch beneath the Dae-Mon. I'd rather face the Shad-Mon again. I'd rather bond another shadow and burn by fire . . ." she trailed off, her thoughts crashing together like a radiant burst of light.

Losna lifted her head, feeling hope in the bond. *What is it?*

Ahraia leapt up, realizing what she should have done right away.

That's it. "Losna. That's it!"

The sky burned with a thousand colors, bursting like Ahraia's hope. But night was almost upon them—they were out of time.

Losna was looking up at her, expectant.

"We need a hiding place," Ahraia said. "One where the Masai can't find us. Can you make that den big enough for both of us by nightfall?"

I can. But what about the chain?

"You worry about the den, I'll worry about the chain." Ahraia stood up, her body tingling with every thin hope she had ever felt. Their minds melded, and Ahraia showed her shadow exactly what she was thinking.

"Keep the opening small, we're going to have to keep it hidden," she said. "And find a place to hide that orb!"

Losna turned back to the den and began to dig with her fore-claws, spinning loose dirt onto the ground about her. Ahraia sprinted from the hillside. She leapt over logs wreathed in moss and dusk, her feet crunching over molten-yellow and orange leaves. She dashed between trunks that were crossed dangerously by tapering shadows; the treetops blossomed in fiery red, burning hot like her heart.

"Where are you?" she said, seeking out with her mind for one particular shadow—one she had already seen. Worry simmered within her. What if every subject of the woods was as loyal to the Masai as the wall had been?

"Some creatures have more honor than that," she said aloud, hoping her voice carried.

Her mind scanned all about, but the woods were empty. She felt three smaller sparrows, and a single squirrel, but nothing that would be adequate to retrieve her bow. The Dae-Mon was sinking too quickly. Ahraia never thought a day would come that she needed more light.

"Come on, where did you get to?" She reached the wall of the Makers where she had first entered. The malice of the palisade hung in the air and she felt the brush of a dae-ward's mind beyond. She slowed, walking about the hill, following the wall, conveying loosely all the while.

Help me. Please, she conveyed outwardly. *I know you're out there.*

Something flitted through the canopy. She sensed watchful eyes, familiar and yet wary.

Is that you? she conveyed again.

Movement swept behind her. Ahraia spun about, the hairs on her neck standing on end. A single leaf fell to the ground, crackling against the silence.

"Will you help me?"

She held her breath, hoping—hoping that at least one fragment of these woods had honor.

She sensed a branch move. She turned and flinched. Noiselessly, an enormous owl leapt from the shadows, spreading its wings wide. It hurtled through the dusky canopy and in the span of a breath, its talons uncurled, sharp and broad, and its wings billowed out, slowing it. It landed just before her, on a branch as big as her thigh. The branch bowed under its weight.

The owl watched her with perfectly indifferent eyes. It was the same owl she had startled when she had entered that morning. It seemed a lifetime had passed since then.

Ahraia swallowed. *I need your help. I need you to retrieve something for me.* Her desperation bled through her thoughts. Owls were a proud type. the type that didn't like to be controlled, not even as shadows. And this was an eagle owl, like Flit had been. The proudest of all.

The owl shuffled its feet with its arms tucked behind its back. It twisted its neck, looking first left and then right.

You're one of them. The thoughts were half-formed, but Ahraia knew it was thinking of sprites.

"I don't want to be. I want to run from this place."

I don't like the howling. I want it to stop.

"I can make it stop. If you just help me . . ." *I came to you, because you're the only one who can help me—the only one strong enough. And honorable enough.* Ahraia's earnestness melded with every word. The owl puffed out its chest, its breast feathers ruffling proudly. It turned its neck about again, then ducked forward in acceptance.

"Whoo," it called softly. *Where?*

Ahraia breathed a sigh of relief. She focused her mind and shared the memory of her hiding spot, the specific tree and specific nook where the bow rested. She imagined how the owl could retrieve it and carry it, careful to emphasize keeping the clutch upright. She finished and the owl blinked in understanding. It seemed to trust Ahraia even more upon seeing her choice of hiding spots.

"You have to be back here by nightfall."

"Whoo," it reassured her. With a blink of its great, round eyes, it leapt into flight. The branch shook, leaves all swishing once, and then heavy wings beat the air. The owl soared across the forest and then up, and out of sight.

Ahraia exhaled. The arrows were her only chance. She only hoped the owl didn't tip them out.

She climbed the hill to Losna, fearfully aware how dim the Dae-Mon looked behind a distant wall of clouds. She hoped that she had been clear enough with the owl. It was the shortest bonding she had ever tried and her and Losna's lives depended on it. She found Losna with her haunches sticking out of a half-dug hole.

Losna scrambled and scraped and then wiggled back out of the den. Ahraia helped her pull the loose dirt away from the area. She set about stirring the ground with a fallen branch to hide the evidence of her digging.

"Where's the orb?" she asked, wondering where the brilliant light had gotten to.

I buried it. Losna kept digging, clawing at the ground frantically, burrowing beneath a large tree root. *What are we going to do about this chain?*

"I'll have my bow any time now."

You think you'll be able to break it? Losna asked. She continued to dig, spinning loose dirt onto the ground, her whole body disappearing into the den.

"I think so." *They're alpish arrows—with metal tips.*

Losna dug, worrying and working. The Dae-Mon dropped lower.

Ahraia turned her eyes to the sky, growing more and more nervous with the lengthening shadows.

"It shouldn't be taking this long," she said finally. Too much time had already passed; the owl should have retrieved the bow and returned already. Dark thoughts began to creep back into Ahraia's heart; the burst of hope that had blanketed her despair now drew back, poisoned with dread. What if the owl couldn't find the bow? What if he couldn't carry it? What if he was another spy of the Masai?

Losna peeked out, looking towards the sky. The first sliver of the Bright Moon slipped into the sky in the east, yellow like a wolf's eye, watching as the west burned in red light. The Dark Moon followed minutes later, a smaller grey eye joining the first.

Ahraia, are you sure . . .

The owl was nowhere to be seen.

Even with your bow, can you really break this? Losna lurched her head, causing the metal links to clink together.

The Dae-Mon sank behind the mountains. Dusk had come, and the first star twinkled in the east. Red. *Bloody.* The Masai would be coming at any time. Losna's digging was done.

Where is that drain? Losna thought sniffing in the direction Ahraia had cast the blade.

Ahraia couldn't believe the owl hadn't returned. She had been so sure that it would work. She heard a sharp, loud rustle down the hillside, towards Angolor. The wall had opened.

The Masai was coming.

A wet nose pressed at her elbow. Losna was holding the blade in her mouth.

You have to end this. I'm not going to be skinned. You can still hide.

Ahraia refused the blade. She looked to where the moons were rising in lockstep over the silhouettes of the fir trees. Losna butted her head against her.

Please.

How long would it take the sprites to climb the hill?

Losna whined, pleading with her. Ahraia looked to the sky in desperation.

A dark shape drifted across the Bright Moon, then the Dark Moon. The breath in Ahraia's chest caught.

Broad wings stretched wide, sailing swiftly and silently downward with something misshapen beneath it. Her bow and quiver. Ahraia's skin was aflame with hope.

What is that? Losna thought.

"That's our only hope. Get to the end of your chain and pull it tight—as tight as you can."

The owl's talons hung heavily, ladened by the quiver and bow. Inky feathers stuck from the quiver. It circled low, and dropped the clutch of arrows at Ahraia's feet, just as the Masai's voice rang through the woods.

"Ahraia, *come forth*." The harsh command carried up the hillside like the cracking of branches under ice. The owl's wings beat at the air, startled by the voice.

Ahraia could feel the words tugging at her, but she resisted. She picked up the bow, fitted an arrow to the string and took aim. Losna pulled the chain as tight as she could.

"Hold still," Ahraia said.

The arrow snapped off the bowstring and skipped off the chain.

Losna pulled tighter.

Ahraia took a step closer, holding a second arrow just a foot away. She let loose and it hit the chain dead on. It ricocheted back and sliced across her hand.

"Light take me!" she cursed.

Blood streamed off her fingers and ran down the shaft of the bow. She drew another arrow. She could *feel* the sprites coming closer; their minds reached out like feelers from a wicker spider. The sky was growing darker. Once close enough, the wards would weave their web of enchantment around her and Losna.

We're running out of time. I can hear them, Losna thought. *I can smell them.*

Ahraia let the third arrow loose.

Crack!

The arrowhead snapped. The metal tip spun away uselessly. "Dae-mon above!" Ahraia said, accidentally kicking the quiver over in her panic. The remaining arrows spilled to the ground. The human's things tumbled out from the clutch—the mirror and the metal comb.

The comb! She lurched to the dirt, scrabbling for the fine piece. She bent a tine aside, a narrow finger of metal, almost as long as her drain but thin as a pine needle. She scrambled back to Losna, who stretched her neck skyward. Ahraia stuck the tine into the hole, quickly digging out the bark clogged the inside. She stabbed at the inside of the lock, unsure that it would work. She twisted and prodded, and suddenly—

Click.

Something had disjointed inside the lock.

"That's it!" Ahraia pulled and the collar fell open. Losna lunged backward, letting out a yelp of mixed pain and elation as the points came out of her skin.

Ahraia thought she saw movement away through the woods.

Quick. Into the den. She hurriedly gathered her bow, the loose arrows, and the human's things, and ran to the hole that Losna had dug. Crouching into the opening, Ahraia nearly retched. The den, steeped in the blood of a thousand shadows, reeked of death. The ground was so deeply saturated that it choked the life of the tree above it.

How did you stand it? Ahraia gasped.

Losna slipped in after her.

What choice did I have?

Ahraia swallowed down the bile in her throat and tucked her bow and the arrows underneath her. She reached out and pulled a lone broken branch over the top. Then, from within, she pushed death-riddled loose dirt towards the opening so that only a small closure remained, just enough to breathe through.

"Losna," she whispered. "They're going to try and enchant us—to bring us out."

Won't they think we've run?

"They'll know we haven't passed the wall. Whatever you hear, you can't follow. No matter what twisted thoughts or threats are given, no matter how sweet her lies sound." *And they will sound sweet, sweet as the ever-running plains and herds of deer and rabbits as far as you can see. But no matter what they say, you must remember that you are my shadow.* Ahraia held Losna by the ears, pulling her close so their foreheads touched and their noses pressed together. *You are my shadow.*

And you are my shade, Losna thought stoically.

Ahraia projected warding thoughts all about her, sending them out to any spritish mind she touched. *They aren't here. There is nothing here. They've gone. They made for the mountains.* She simultaneously readied herself to ward off the Masai's enchantments as she peered through the branches and saw sprites coming through the woods.

"Where are they?" one of them called.

They're gone. Ahraia projected in answer, keeping her mind and Losna's concealed.

"They're gone," a dae-ward echoed. "Get the Masai."

Broken chain . . . broken arrow. They've run. Ahraia continued, manipulating the clouds of thought passing over the hillside as sprites emerged on the hilltop. *They've escaped. Probably from your side of the woods. They're already in the forest.*

The faces Ahraia could see twisted in affront. Eyes narrowed beneath veils and hoods, as wards and sprites alike thought they had been accused of failing.

"She didn't escape our side," voices called defensively.

She must have, Ahraia conveyed, continuing to weave distrust and hoping in the confusion she could lead them astray. *She runs like a wolf. How did she escape the Shad-Mon? How did she open the collar? She must be strong—and dangerous.* Losna's chest rumbled in contentment at the seeds she was sowing.

Conveyance brimmed through the air from the wards, echoing Ahraia's suggestions: *How did she open the collar? How did she escape the Shad Mon?*

No wonder the Masai wants her dead. She's destined to be the Masai—Ahraia cast the last thought, treasonous and poisonous, like a serpent gliding openly between the wards' minds, the mere risk of its bite enough to incite panic. Confusion spread to disbelief, and disbelief to fear. They were looking at the chain and looking at each other, wondering who would dare think such a thought, seeing the arrows, the empty patch of ground and wondering: *Is she more powerful?*

A silence moved up the hillside: first as stamped out voices, next as extinguished conveyance. Even the wind squeezed from the night, leaving it thin and still.

She's going to be the next Masai, Ahraia projected, knowing it would be the last echo heard across the hilltop.

"Enough!" The Masai's voice split the air like lightning from a clear sky. "She'll no more be the Masai than the Dae-Mon will rise dark and shadowed." Her words intertwined with threats: light for sprites, exile for wards, and death for any whose thoughts tarried towards treason. Images of torture, too vivid to be anything but memories, danced before Ahraia's eyes even though her mind was closed: she saw faceless sprites writhing beneath the day in shadowless glades, without veil or hood or even cloak to guard them; she saw wards pinned with drains to the ground of the Shadow Woods, waiting for the Shad-Mon. Light, brighter than any she had seen, shimmered in her mind, searingly bright, so that her scars itched from within and she squinted her eyes that were already closed.

Ahraia lifted her head, just enough to peer through the thin gap in the earth. Through the pine bough, she could see the Masai standing over the opened collar. The ears of her terrible wolf-cloak rose above her, as though listening lifelessly for Ahraia.

The Masai picked up the abandoned chain, then the broken arrow.

"Check with the walls. See if they've managed to escape," she said, her voice terrifyingly calm.

Ahraia considered inciting her further, but swallowed back her thoughts at risk of exposing herself. Instead, she buried her face within Losna's fur, grounding her thoughts in the deep, coarse coat, smothering her mind from the hilltop, from the Masai—from the fate they hadn't yet escaped. Losna's heart thumped against her ribs, loud enough that, without the muted earth to bind it, Ahraia was sure it would give them away.

Her shadow smelled of dust and dried blood. The Masai's mind ferreted through the air, sniffing, feeling blindly for them. *Dust and blood. Dirt and death. That is all that is here.* Ahraia focused on being unidentifiable from the long-dead roots, well aware that if they were found, they would be no different.

"To the one who finds them, I'll make you Astra or nit-ward of your own darkening," the Masai called. The conviction of the Masai's words spread like unfurling darkness to sprites whose minds were flooded with unbearable light. Immediately, Ahraia sensed the brush of a dozen different seekers.

Where are you? Wolf? Shade? Where are you?

Ahraia overtook Losna's mind, making sure her shadow wasn't seduced by any spritish trick. She made them invisible, emptying their minds of all worry or fear, making them indistinguishable from the earthen tomb around her. Hiding from enchantment was different than hiding from eyes or ears or touch. It was a matter of not being—indistinct from dirt or den. Ahraia lowered herself into a trance. *Root and rock. Gray rock. Silver rock. Veins of roots. Intertwined and entangled.* She thought of anything to do with earth or the tree above her, the roots around her, the muted deep of the dirt.

A voice broke through her thoughts. "The wall says the shade tried to leave, but that was near midday. A serapin was able to sting her, but she escaped back to the hillside."

"Then she's bound to be here, possibly laying poisoned. But her shadow must be with her. I want them found."

Ahraia pushed a thought to a single ward. *If they escaped the Shad-Mon, they might be able to escape the wall unnoticed.* He opened his mouth without thinking and repeated it aloud, just as she had intended.

The Masai stepped in front of the ward, ears twitching. Ahraia didn't see the blade, but when the Masai stepped away, the ward's body crumpled onto the dirt.

Feeling the barest guilt, Ahraia made another conveyance. *But how did she escape the daemons?* She let the thought pass through another ward.

"I don't care!" the Masai snapped, spinning to see who had conveyed the thought. Her voice was sharp and violent now. "I want them *found*. Search the woods. Bring every tree and creature to bear if you must. Send them crawling beneath roots and climbing amongst leaves. I want them found and I want her brought to me. *Tonight!*"

The last word caused Losna to flinch, a shrill bark that sent the wards scattering from the hillside. Ahraia calmed her, stilling her mind through the bond. Soon enough, the Masai stood alone, a black wolf, corrupted by a thousand kills, the worst of which she wore draped over her shoulders. She prowled off the hillside, her wards fleeing before her.

The clouds broke and moonlight filtered down on the hilltop, protecting them. Ahraia let out a relieved breath, knowing the Bright Moon alone would keep all but the dae-wards away. Now, it was just a matter of waiting for morning. Once the Dae-Mon rose, all but the dae-wards would be forced back into the deeper forest. Losna felt her thoughts and grew worried.

But the morning? Won't it burn you?

No more than it already has. The scars on her arm ran like rivulets from a hillside, joining in a branching pattern that grew larger and larger from her wrist to her elbow, flooding together in darker and darker lines. Her neck burned all the way around her ears, and along the line of her jaw. She guessed they would be just as dark. *It doesn't kill.*

Losna licked at her scars.

The night never truly settled. The sprites kept to the forest, seeking her in the safety of the deep woods. Dae-wards crossed the hilltop on occasion, but mostly to pass from one side to the other, not figuring that Ahraia would have hidden so close. Slowly, the night passed, with Ahraia and Losna never daring to sleep.

Sniffing creatures shuffled out along the roots of the deadened tree. The hilltop was drenched in the smell of shadows, and of Losna, so they never truly sensed her. A few got close, but Ahraia simply bound them and reminded them they were searching for a wolf. The threat was enough to send them scurrying for the forest, eager to forget.

Midnight came and went. Ahraia had never hoped for the morning like she did now. Soon enough, the light would purge all but the lowliest of wards to the shadows. No sprite, and certainly not the Masai, would linger into the dawn.

They lay in the quiet dark, breathing in their slow, steady pattern, while the earth pressed around them. Their ears turned at any noise.

Their eyes came open at any call. The night moved agonizingly slowly, the stars revolving towards dawn.

It was nearing morning when Ahraia sensed most of the sprites gathering near the base of the hillside, in the direction she had tried to escape from during the day. She heard rising voices and some kind of disturbance.

Losna's ears turned towards them. The den pointed eastward, the narrow slit showing the faintest navy above the black-tipped firs. Losna's thoughts brought Ahraia out of her slow reverie.

What if we ran now?

With all these wards about? No.

But the Makers. The wall is open . . . the closures are still formed. They're off to the north. If we slipped away now . . .

Losna raised her muzzle, sniffing. Ahraia searched about the hilltop with her mind. She did it subtly, so that no sprite would notice if they felt her enchantments.

But they're gone. They're down the hillside. We could slip into the woods unnoticed . . . Losna thought.

Ahraia could sense the sprites, distantly. They were all gathered below, and the Masai with them. She could still hear their voices rising up the hillside. The blood in the dirt seemed to press inward. Ahraia wanted to be free of the den; she wanted to be running. Maybe Losna was right. Maybe if they went now, the closures would still be formed—they could slip away. They could run, beneath the moonlit woods of Angolor, out to the snow-capped mountains and their overbearing shadows, or to the plains stretching on and on, beyond forest and hill out into nothingness, where the Masai and no sprite would ever dare run. Now was their chance. The day would be burning bright. *Dangerous. Too dangerous.*

We can leave now, Losna thought, ready to be out of the cramp of the den. *While they don't suspect it. It's now or never.*

Ahraia nodded, slowly coming around to her shadow's thoughts. *Okay.*

Come on, Losna urged. Ahraia made her decision. Her knees

scraped against the dirt, and her back pressed against the top of the den as she readied herself to run.

Losna whined, unmoving. The noise was thankfully swallowed by the dirt.

Shhh, Ahraia hissed, crouching back down. *Didn't you just tell me to hurry?*

Losna's brow pressed down about her yellow eyes. *No.*

Ahraia shook her head, expecting Losna to already be out of the den. *But the closures, they're open. Didn't you just*—Ahraia stopped short. Sweat broke out all over her skin. The tendrils of a binding were already embedded in her mind, grown like roots through the bitter ground into the den, gnarled and creeping.

We're being enchanted.

Ahraia pressed herself closer to her shadow. She reached out to feel if a sprite was upon the hilltop. It felt *empty*. Empty like the Stone Tree had felt. She shivered.

The den seemed suddenly hot, the air too thick to breathe. An intense need to flee took her, and she only just overcame it. Ahraia was sure of it now. An enchantress was near—the Masai undoubtedly. Her spells came like the clouds, thick and pure, drifting over the full moon, allaying the light it cast, allaying Ahraia's fears.

It's safe. Come out. The sprites have gone.

The Masai was close—and clever—so subtle as to know the exact tone and tenor of Ahraia's thoughts. Like fog drifting through trees, it morphed before her, disorienting her as she tried to grasp it.

Let's go, it said, tugging at Ahraia. And though Ahraia knew it was contrived, she pushed off her knee again nonetheless. Losna grabbed her with her jaw, sharp teeth gently stilling her as though she was a cub. Losna's black-tipped nose flared. She sniffed at the air.

Something's out there. The Masai. I can smell her cloak . . .

Ahraia dug her hands into the loose dirt, the grainy pebbles grounding her and helping her renew her defense of them.

She reformed her protections, focusing on removing the lattice of roots that had already propagated through her mind. She joined

Losna's thoughts, reducing them together to the nothingness of the dirt and den about them.

Nothing's here, Ahraia thought, projecting outward faintly.

Above her, a voice suddenly called out, causing her to flinch.

"Find them! They're *here*. I know it!"

The hilltop came alive with sprites. A wave of stronger enchantment lashed out, grabbing Ahraia's wrists and legs, willing her forward. She gave up the pretense of pretending not to be there, instead focusing on Losna. *My shadow. I'm not giving up my shadow.*

She closed her eyes, seeing the Endless Plains stretch before her, their feet running together. The stars were calling them onward, farther and farther onto the plain. Losna's mind was racing with her, eager to be free of the den and unperturbed by the binding.

Where are you? The Masai's conveyance whipped against her mind. "Ahraia. *Come forth!*" The last was a command, so strong that only Losna's bite kept Ahraia from crawling out in compliance. The pungent odor of the cloak kept Losna from succumbing to the Masai, her distrust echoing through Ahraia's link. She held Ahraia firmly, biting sense back into her. Eventually, the enchantments flickered and went out, one after another.

Silence spread across the hilltop. The glow in the east was growing.

Finally, the Masai's voice roiled out into the last vestiges of the night, undoubtedly heard across all the Makers.

"I don't know what you think will come of this. Do you think you'll become a sprite? Do you mean to challenge me?"

The silence rang out. Ahraia had never wanted to be the Masai, or even an Astra. But she heard the ragged edges of fear playing at the Masai's words, being driven wild by the sheer threat of her escaping. She felt the collective confusion in the sprites too, wondering if a new Masai hid within their presence. It drove all reason from the Masai's voice.

"You can't win, Ahraia. And if you run, I'll hunt you, to the edges of the world. What hollow haunts of the day do you think will shelter you? The shadows under the mountains? What place is that for you?

A place where goblins and imps drivel in caves dug by red-bearded devils, where daemons prowl long-fingered beneath tombs with no light at all? Or would you seek the forests, light-strewn and leafless, cursed by the bright, to spend your days tarrying between lay-beasts and lightwalkers?"

The Masai's voice rose, like the light growing in the east.

"Do you think your shadow will protect you? To what end? When you wither beneath the burning Dae-Mon on the Endless Plains, do you think the wolves won't pick the meat from your bones as they do their own? Come forth, and have this over with. Come forth and fight like a sprite!"

Ahraia felt the rush of hope. The thought of defeating the Masai in a posturant, to hold her and turn her drain inward on itself, gave her a way out. But she knew the thought was projected onto her, the Masai seeking any way to draw her forth.

Ahraia closed her eyes, trying hard to remember herself. She shifted, and something sharp poked her ribs. She reached for it, feeling the tines of the comb. Something smooth and heavy came to rest in her hand. She pulled it in front of her. *The mirror.*

She stared at herself.

Her hair, marked by the moons and singed by the day, fell rag-tumble across her face. The light markings across her jaw were dark, brilliant—stronger now than they had ever been. Her eyes were bright too: incandescent and yellow. All of it inappropriate for a sprite.

And I am not a sprite, she thought defiantly. *Nor will I be.*

"Come forth!" the Masai screamed. The voice filled with enchantment, but it was losing its pull.

Ahraia stared at Losna, resisting the domineering urge that had pulled one foot after another towards the dark of the Stone Tree. Her shadow lay before her, a breathing reminder of who she was. Looking in the mirror and looking at Losna was no different: eyes wreathed in the same yellow rays, fur seared by the same yellow light, mind marked by the same need to run.

They were made to run.

Together.

And when the light came, they would. With yellow eyes and skin burnt by wind and light, they would run until they were beyond the reach of any judgment.

The gray in the east gave way to the pre-dawn gold. A line, crisp as the edge of the alp's sword, spread radiantly, dulling into diffuse blue.

"Come forth, you conniving little shade!"

The Masai, master of the night, had lost her pull on Ahraia.

The Dae-Mon is coming, Ahraia conveyed to the sprites, keeping her thoughts as subtle as she could. Ahraia stared out, willing the Dae-Mon up. It hadn't risen yet, but the east continued to brighten, spreading as an imperceivable fog of light through the woods.

Higher, Ahraia thought desperately. *Higher.*

"They are here. I can feel her! I can tell she is here. Find them!" the Masai shouted violently. The Masai's thoughts echoed long after her words had died. *Where are you?* "Where are you? I will find you!"

The Dae-Mon is coming, Ahraia projected.

A sprite's voice followed, quivering.

"Masai? We have to leave. The Dae-Mon is coming."

"I want these woods sealed. I want every dae-ward in Angolor watching this hill."

A narrow slice of brilliant sky in the east burned, with the intensity of a fire so hot it, could push the night from the world.

"Shade Ahraia!" the Masai called for all the woods to hear. "I will hunt you until the ends of the worlds. There will be no peace for you. The Dae-Mon will come for you, and when it has, I will be there to find your scorched body wherever it lies. If night comes again, I promise I will feast on your shadow before I give your body to the Shad-Mon!"

32

FIRE AND LIGHT

The Dae-Mon rose, lethal and swift. In moments, it chased the dark from the mountain peaks, hunted the shadows from valleys and spurned the night from the hilltop, leaving the forest red-branched and shimmering.

The sprites retreated to the deeper dark and the collective swell of enchantment receded, like winds dissipating on the tail of a storm. Only the dae-wards remained, and even they withdrew to the woods. The Masai's menace trailed away, chased by the light back to its dark.

Ahraia itched to crawl from their hiding spot, but she waited as the light swelled protectively.

The dae-wards are still out there, Losna thought, sniffing at the small opening.

Ahraia rearranged herself, pushing the quiver forward. "Half the wards think I'm the next coming of the Masai. They shouldn't give us too much trouble."

And the other half?

"I've got arrows . . . and you still have teeth."

Where will we go? Losna thought.

"Where they won't dare chase us," Ahraia said.

The Endless Plains? Losna's thoughts wavered in both hope and worry. *The Masai's spies will flood the woods between here and there.* She eyed a pale raven circling the hilltop.

"Not by the path we're taking," Ahraia said.

Losna let out a low, quiet growl. *What do you mean?*

"We need to get away from this accursed hilltop first," Ahraia whispered, "then I'll show you." She fumbled in the cramped space to find Hayvon's veil. She lowered her hood and carefully wrapped her face, running it just beneath her eyes and around her head twice. It smelled of Hayvon, and of Vesta. She returned her hood over the top so that only her eyes shown out. The few clouds glowed blood red in the sky. Ahraia could feel the worry radiating from Losna.

Arrows and teeth aren't going to dissuade the dae-wards.

"A few well-placed thoughts should do the trick. Are you ready?"

Losna quivered in answer.

Ahraia pushed the loose dirt outward, widening the closure, letting cold air and burning light stream in. Losna surged past her, scrabbling at the dirt and hurrying into the day, with tail low and ears turning about. Ahraia followed close behind. She squinted against the burn of the Dae-Mon and quickly scanned about for any wards. The moon raven cawed, a shrill shriek that set other ravens calling throughout the woods, spreading like a billowing cloud of noise that rippled and faded but didn't die.

Caw! Caw!

Ahraia knew it was the same messenger who had delivered the Masai's threats. She took an arrow to her bow and let it loose. It whistled and struck with a thunk, sending the raven crashing to the ground, wing over arrow. The calls faded through the woods.

You're not going to be able to hunt every bird, Losna thought, jogging towards the darker side of the hilltop.

"That one had it coming."

Ahraia spread a sparse web of enchantment over the forest, using it to sense any movement sifting through the woods. Branches were being pushed aside and creeping vines of tentative enchantment crawled up from the deeper shadows.

Here they come. She darted towards where she sensed a void in their movements with an arrow nocked to the string. Losna was right at her hip.

She saw the first emerge from the woods, crouching low and hurrying across the open hilltop. Others were skulking closer, like spiders moving swiftly across a shaking web. Ahraia reached out with her mind, making connections openly, unable to count how many wards were approaching.

Do you really mean to kill me? she conveyed sharply, putting an inflection on her thoughts, an echo of sorts meant to disorient and confuse them. Losna stiffened, her ears twitched.

The dae-wards stopped. One spun about as though Ahraia's thoughts had come from behind him.

Do you? Ahraia asked, sending her voice spinning like a leaf turning on the wind. *Me? Your future Masai? Me, who has returned from the Shad-Mon unharmed? Me, who walks beneath the Dae-Mon unafraid?*

Ahraia stepped out from the woods and pulled her hood back. It was still shadowy and dark where she stood and she squinted against the light. But she was unharmed. Dae-wards stepped out of the shadows, staring at her openly. She felt a surge of enchantment, but it was hesitant; they were young, hardly more than shades themselves. She shed their attempts aside, having suffered far stronger bindings.

"Go back to your shadows. Leave me be and you will be granted the Night. But should you test me . . ." She envisioned arrows slamming into necks, metal tipped and barbed. She forced the thought of the drain slicing across Golan's throat, the blood filling his mouth. And she showed them the memory of Losna tearing the throat from Gavea, the nitesse's crumpled body falling lifeless to the ground.

Sensing her intention, Losna stepped forward and let out a snarl that carried the weight of Ahraia's enchantments to the wards. Her hackles were raised and she bared her teeth viciously.

Through the enchantment, the ward's fear rippled inward, propagating from one to the next. Power and command radiated through Ahraia's thoughts: the projection became easier, the threats deeper, their feeble bindings simpler to turn away. The dae-wards cringed as though Losna's growl had been a physical blow.

It will be, Ahraia reminded them. A ward turned and slunk back into the forest. And then another. And then they all turned, their collective fear swelling across the hilltop. They disappeared, back to the woods.

Ahraia let out a wary breath.

"That will buy us time, but they'll remember their true Masai soon enough. Now, go and get that orb."

Losna jogged back to the den, scrambled in, and emerged a moment later with the orb in her teeth. It radiated out, even in the day. Ahraia shuddered, having Losna nuzzle it into her pocket. She felt a hot burn against her side—sharp but not ruinous.

She retrieved the arrow from the moon raven and slipped into the forest, dodging shafts of light and pulling her hood back up.

What's your plan? Losna was tense, ears turning, eyes turning, tail out and balanced.

"First, we have to get out of these woods." Ahraia hurried towards the wall, keeping a mind out for the wards but searching for the segment where she had been stung. "And then we will have to make a run for it—where they can't possibly follow us."

But the plains are half a turning away, Losna worried.

"Somewhere closer. Somewhere no sprite dares walk."

Losna stopped, asking a question to which she already guessed the answer. *Where*?

"Back to the Shadow Woods."

THE WALL of the Makers loomed menacingly before Ahraia, impossibly tight. Its facade writhed like serpents: limbs reaching to catch, branches seeking to strangle, vines and tendrils coiling to strike.

"Yesterday, I tried to make it easy for you," Ahraia said to the wall, dropping her clutch of arrows. The serapin tree that had stung her was twisted tight, hiding the branch that she cut away and rustling threateningly at the sight of her. She dropped to a knee and dug to the bottom of the alp's clutch, beneath her remaining arrows.

The older trees leaned over her, proud and unyielding; the younger trees stretched naively, wild and violent. Ahraia kept her distance while Losna prowled the hillside, guarding for wards. The Masai, luckily, didn't have the power to enchant the whole forest with the same loyalty and enmity as the wall; otherwise, every step would be treacherous.

Still digging in the quiver, her fingers came across the alp's spare string. She pulled it free and unstrung her bow. Then she gathered the driest bits of the forest: loose moss, dead twigs, and fallen pine needles.

What are you doing? Losna asked.

"Getting past this wall." Ahraia deliberately let the words pass to the palisade, watching as it tightened mockingly.

With twigs? Losna asked doubtfully.

"With tinder."

Losna cocked her head. Ahraia smiled, and formed a larger gathering of wood nearby. Losna looked even more worried.

"The wall won't listen to me," Ahraia said. She picked up more dried leaves and branches. "It won't let me bind it."

And how will this help?

"If it won't bend to my will, I expect it will burn to it," Ahraia said with a smile, letting images of flame take shape in her mind: a hungry flicker, leaping higher and hotter, crawling up vines and trunks and turning leaf to ash and trees to blackened bones. The wall either doubted her ability to create such havoc, or didn't understand the nature of fire. Its arms slowed warily, but it didn't quiver or fit as she expected it to.

How are you going to do that? With the orb?

Ahraia shook her head.

Losna watched her with big, fire-bright eyes. *Won't it burn you?*

"I'll live," Ahraia said. She took the alp's tools that had been in the quiver and laid them out carefully, just as the alp had. She took a moment, trying to remember how he had gone about making the fire. It seemed so long ago, and she had been so intent, so foolishly insistent on making the kill rather than watching his actions. "Killing just for killing . . ." she muttered, shaking her head. She cleared her mind, remembering the alp's process: *String on bow. Wrapped around the stick. Flat, board beneath.*

Ahraia restrung the bow with the longer thread, twisting it about the stick just as the alp had.

Where did you learn this? Losna thought over crooked-down eyebrows.

From an alp. For a moment, Ahraia absurdly wished he was there to make fire for her, as he had for the human. Losna let out a low growl. It made Ahraia smile all the more.

She carefully aligned the pointed stick on the alp's flat carved board beneath. She lay it on the ground and anchored it with her foot. She sawed the bow once, the fire-stick spinning roughly against her hand—painfully. Something was missing.

She leaned back on her knees, thinking.

Board. Stick. Bow. She checked them off in her mind. She dumped the quiver out, scattering the arrows on the ground, unsure what she would be looking for. But there was nothing more within.

She stopped, sensing wards nearby.

Outside the wall, Losna thought.

Ahraia put the arrows back in the quiver.

Losna watched with fur raised stiffly. *You don't know what you're doing, do you?*

"Of course not," Ahraia muttered. "I just saw an alp do it."

What were you doing near an alp?

Ahraia ignored her shadow. She closed her eyes, envisioning the alp as he peacocked for the human. But she remembered his subtle looks and twitching ears better than she remembered his fire. The spindle-stick had spun freely. He had palmed something . . . something to let it spin without cutting his hand, a wooden bit. She looked towards the quiver. The piece was missing.

"Can you find a yellow pine? Bring me a cone." *And don't go far!*

Losna dodged away and returned a moment later with one of the round cones. Ahraia used her drain to cut away all but its inner core, so that it was half-round and half-hollow. She coated the inside with mud and then palmed it, using it to hold the stick against the board.

She took a breath and began to saw the bow back and forth. The stick spun freely in the cone, back and forth, her palm spared the gouging point. The sawing noise was the only sound in the forest. She worked steadily as sweat formed on her brow.

Nothing happened. Her arms began to tire.

This isn't going to work, Losna thought, not understanding.

Ahraia didn't answer. She sawed the bow: the spindle turned into the notch of the board, the rough noise of it nosing into the wood, back and forth. She sawed the bow until her muscles burned and her ribs ached.

A moment later, she noticed a scent of heat. A small wisp rose from the blackened wood.

Smoke! Losna slapped her forepaws against the ground in surprise.

But nothing more happened. No flame leapt forth. Ahraia stopped and Losna froze.

Where's the fire? she thought.

Next to the branch was a scattered bit of loose shavings, warm to the touch, still smoking. Ahraia arranged her gathering of dry leaves around her stick. She picked up the bow and began to work again. Soon enough, the smoke returned.

Come on.

It curled and disappeared. Ahraia sawed harder, gritting her teeth. A wind stirred through the trees and the smoke rose and then spread. Ahraia dropped the bow and pressed her face to the ground, breathing gently, as the alp had. At first, the smoke disappeared. She stopped blowing, worried. But then it spread. She puffed again and it grew stronger. She blew again, and suddenly—

Fire! Losna leapt forward in excitement.

"Ha!" Ahraia shouted triumphantly. A single flickering flame rose, radiant and dancing with life. It devoured leaves and moss, the tinder curling away faster than Ahraia could imagine. She quickly added more leaves, slowing down when the flame disappeared momentarily, but then it rebounded, and grew, terrifyingly. A fire, as resplendent and terrible as any human or alp had ever made, now grew before her. The wall churned, apparently sensing the monster she had created. Her skin tingled with the flame. She pulled her veil up.

A ripple of fear tore a loose and ragged opening through the nearest portion of the wall. The serapin tree struck out defensively, falling short. It drew back, dragging its uncoiled branch back over fallen, dried leaves.

More tinder, Ahraia thought vindictively, letting the wall know she meant to burn it to the ground. The closure widened, large enough now that Ahraia and Losna could fit through side by side.

Let's go! Losna thought. Ahraia stopped her shadow dead in her tracks.

"Not yet." She eyed the opening. "I'm not going to fall for that again. Not today." Her arm still felt numb where the serapin had stung her. Her eyes burned from the flame and the smoke. Her face was alight with the heat, but she continued to add twigs and stems, and then sticks and branches, all the while watching in delighted terror as the flames grew to a roar, so that the whole forest seemed to draw back. A part of her wondered what the alp would think of it. She took absurd pride knowing that she had stolen his magic. The flames grew, like some monstrous creature that she no longer had any control of and of which she couldn't take her light-seared eyes away from. Ahraia smiled to herself as she restrung her bow.

Ahraia thought she sensed panic coming from a ward nearby, maybe one sent to watch her, to make sure they didn't escape; soon enough it faded, chased away by the mirthful fire.

Now what? Losna asked, flinching back. Her ears flattened as a bushel of pine branches smoked and popped.

"Now we have fires to set." Ahraia took a dead pine bough from the ground. Branches spread off its stalk like feathers from a wing, their needles still clinging to them dryly, even in death. She took a moment, tightening Hayvon's veil. Losna watched with gleaming eyes.

What about the sprites?

"They won't be about—just wards. It's still day out there." Ahraia had no doubt she could handle the dae-wards. Their minds were weak and malleable, and their bindings feeble and shadish. "Are you ready to run as we never have?"

Her shadow's eyes gleamed in answer, shining golden with the risen Dae-Mon. Her lean muscles rippled beneath silver-gray fur, fluid and yet stopped, like water stilled on the top of an endless falls.

Ahraia had never truly looked at Losna in the light. The day before, she had been too worried about the chain. Now she saw her in truth. She was beautiful. And fierce. Ahraia couldn't have hoped for a better shadow to follow her in the light.

"Head for the river, towards the Shadow Woods. When we get there, there is a log that crosses most of the river. We may have to swim a bit."

But you can't swim. Not well enough to cross a river. Is it like the Winnowlin, back home?

"It's worse." *Wilder. Angrier.* "I'm counting on you for that."

Losna's chest swelled as she took a worried breath. *And if we make it across?*

Ahraia snorted at the audacity of it. "Then it's simple. Just a matter of dealing with the Shad-Mon," she said, trying to make light of a fate she had run from her whole life. "We'll do what we always have—run."

She was thinking of her bow and their small beady eyes though, and she was thinking of the way Losna's howls had driven them mad. The daemons preyed on the defenseless, on sprites who walked despairingly into their grasp; at the very least, they would give them a fight they had never faced before. But she was also thinking of what she had sensed upon her brief binding of the Shad-Mon: the pervasive instinct of protection, the deep bulwark in their mind. Something was in the heart of the forest, and whatever lay there, the daemons lived to protect it, more than anything. If Ahraia and Losna could threaten that, perhaps the daemons would let them pass through the woods rather than fight. All she and Losna needed was a head start, a way to get to the plains or mountains without being chased. Then they would be free to seek darkness of their own making, without the violent expectations of the sprites or the wicked aspirations of the Masai. Ahraia could run forever with Losna, and she would be glad to.

The fire cracked and popped. Ahraia sensed wards on the hillside drawing nearer.

"It's time," she said to Losna. The needles ignited as she touched the pine branch to the fire, spreading swiftly from tip to stem. The scars on her wrist glowed, and she shielded her face, heading for the dried leaves beneath the serapin tree. They lit and shriveled, spreading like a flaming flood towards the wall, catching branches, pine needles, and dried moss in their flames as they went. The serapin tree thrashed, the wall flailed in surprise. Both drew back from the flames.

Ahraia bound the trees, showing the full force of her intentions to the wall.

"You are going to open," she said, spreading her binding farther and higher, jabbing the flame towards the wall. "Or I am going to burn you to the ground."

The wall writhed with a mixture of anger and alarm. The branches closer to the closure drew away, enlarging the opening, but others still grew stubbornly downward, blocking her path. An overwhelming sense of defiance swelled from the older pillars, and they seemed to rally the wall. Creeping tendrils folded over the closure while branches swung towards Ahraia as a unified front of resistance.

"Very well."

She pushed the flaming branch against the most aggressive vines. A branch swung down, forcing her back, but she swept inward, dodging the swaying limbs, setting flame to any bough or leaf that didn't withdraw. Realizing her single flame wouldn't be enough, she returned to the fire and lit a second branch. Her veil was sticky with sweat. Losna danced at her heels, ready to pull her back if the wall managed to grab her.

"*Open!*" Ahraia commanded.

The resistance felt more haphazard. The flames around the

serapin tree had settled to embers, leaving the trunk blackened and charred. She swept the fire closer and the wall pulled away, quicker than before. Fallen leaves were aflame, licking at its base; a trunk started to blacken and a wave passed through the palisade—fear was taking root. Another branch swung out at her and she held the flame towards it, gritting her teeth at all the light and warmth.

"Open." *Open!*

The branch pulled back, too slowly.

"Not good enough!" She torched the branch, seeing flames spread to the wall finally. The boughs flailed as though in a tempest—true panic spread through the wall and an opening formed, a full closure. Ahraia swept a wide arc and the wall peeled back, all semblance of resistance gone. Its will to fight her had burned away.

"Losna, you first," Ahraia said, keeping the flame steadily upon the edges of the gap and forcing it wider and wider. Beyond, she could see the forest was equally lit by the Dae-Mon, with slanting rays stabbing down to the understory. Shielded as the woods of Angolor were, light still penetrated in places.

Losna darted through the wall and Ahraia followed with flame held above. In a matter of steps, she was through to the other side, but the palisade collapsed around her. She dropped the flame and dove to the ground as a branch whipped down and lashed around her ankle, dragging her back. Losna lunged at it, snapping clean through the branch in a single bite. The wall groaned, thrashing in pain. Losna grabbed Ahraia by the shoulders and pulled her away as the branches lashed out at her.

Are you all right? Losna said in surprise.

"Yes . . . I'm fine," Ahraia said, glad to be free. She heard shouting away through the woods.

More wards.

Ravens cawed harshly, and the whole forest erupted in their terrible squawks. Both white and black wings filled the canopy. She heard the shouts of wards, and sensed waves of conveyance sweeping across the woods.

"To the river."

The days chained to the ground hadn't slowed Losna. She lunged forwards, tail streaming behind her and ears tucked back low. Ahraia sprinted after her, paring back branches before her every footfall. She used small springs and darted across logs while the ravens cawed and called overhead.

The woods were alive with movement and light. She sensed a weak binding descend on her. She saw hoods, some with veils, some without.

Dae wards and—

Sprites! Losna thought. A stronger enchantment swept through the woods, slowing Ahraia. A branch reached out and tripped her. She stumbled to the ground, then shoved herself back to her feet, but more sprites streamed through the woods. The whole darkening looked as if it had emptied. Makeshift veils covered their faces and they moved through the light with a madness that could only be driven by the Masai.

Look out ahead, Losna thought, darting to the side. Ahraia looked up and saw a swarm of sprites and wards. She turned to follow Losna, but saw more sprites closing in. They were shouting and calling to one another. Strings of conveyance billowed through the air, too convoluted and fragmented to understand. Ahraia ducked behind a fallen log with Losna next to her.

How are we going to get out of this? Losna thought worriedly.

By using as much light as possible. Come on. Ahraia stood up and headed towards true sunlight. It wasn't midday yet but the forest ahead was luminous and brilliant.

You're going to have to be my eyes if it gets much lighter, she conveyed. She squinted. The Dae-Mon was so bright. *Too bright for sprites,* she thought to herself.

This way, Losna thought, directing her away from the darkness and towards a seam of lighter woods. The sprites seemed slow and ungainly, like humans in the middle of the night, but the dae-wards moved quickly, accustomed to the light. Ahraia's skin was hot and angry.

Through here, Losna guided her, turning back almost the way they had come and sprinting up a ravine cutting through the hillside towards more light. The ravens cawed a raucous chorus overhead.

Ahraia's eyes were so close to shut that she had hardly any idea where they were headed, but Losna directed her as she ran, and she followed with only the vaguest awareness of obstacles: *Log. Root. This way. Sprite ahead. Low branch.*

Ahraia ducked but her hood caught and pulled off her face. For a fearful moment, she thought she would be burnt to ash, but gasped to find that she was still breathing. Still alive. She opened her eyes a hair wider and she saw the brightest forest she had ever seen: a vivid, day-colored wood that spread before her like a different world. Ahraia and Losna ran like the wind, remembering what it felt like to run under the moons for the first time. This was the same but wilder.

This way, Losna thought, but even as she did, a sprite's enchantment snagged Ahraia's feet.

"Stop!" it yelled.

Others didn't bother with voices. *Stop!* They commanded. Ahraia's feet faltered and she tumbled to the ground. Losna stumbled as well, but managed to stay up. A dae-ward leapt out from behind a tree, his eyes smiling behind his veil. Losna wasn't fully subdued, and she leapt at the ward, attacking him with brutal ferocity and emerging from the fight with a bloodied snout.

But more sprites poured through the woods, heavily cloaked and casting their enchantments like a web over Ahraia's mind. Her legs gave out, no longer answering to her. She tried to form a spring, but she was suddenly face first in the dirt, the earthen smell filling her nose.

Ahraia looked up and saw Losna clawing at the ground, already taken by enchantment. A sprite rushed out of the woods and tackled her, holding a drain to her throat. A dozen others circled closer and more were coming. Angry, light-bitten eyes stared at Ahraia. She pushed down the panic threatening to freeze her. She reached out and bonded the sprite holding Losna, barely managing to keep the drain from sinking into her shadow's neck even as her own body went limp. The other sprites advanced on her.

Desperate and unable to fight the overpowering enchantments, she bound every sprite in her mind's reach, forming a loose and commanding enchantment. The casting was weak because of the sheer number of sprites, but she didn't need it to be strong, she simply needed it to be sudden.

"*Hoods off!*" she said. None of the sprites expected it. Hoods and veils were ripped away without thought, and screams echoed through the woods, filling the world like the brightness that permeated everything. The enchantments holding Ahraia suddenly shriveled away in shock and anguish. Free, Ahraia reached in her pocket and grabbed the searing orb and tossed it high in the air above her. Light spit out in brilliant fullness. The sprites and wards cowered away.

Losna wrenched free as her captor screamed into his hands, covering his face. A moment later, his scream was silenced as her jaws wrapped around his neck. Losna turned and surged at the other sprites, attacking with the desperation of a cornered beast—growling and snarling, clawing and biting. Ahraia was right next to her, drain out, screaming into the fray. She slashed, the blade glimmering under the dae-mon's light. She cut the arm of a nearby sprite, and then shattered a brief binding as she plunged it into the neck of another. Two hooded figures were crouched, ready to leap on Losna. Ahraia formed a lightning quick binding and forced their hoods off. It was Shalih and Kren. They fell screaming to the ground.

"Run, Losna. Now!"

Losna broke away from the sprites and Ahraia followed, suddenly running free, back into darker woods, back through a stretch of Angolor's outer halls. The light of the orb burned behind them, and the woods ahead were smoky dark. Every sprite and ward from the darkening lay behind her.

She heard jeers echoing after her.

There's nothing but the river! Cut her off! She's pinned.

Ahraia ignored them, sprinting towards the river and the Shadow Woods beyond. She and Losna were going to reach the river before the sprites could catch them. She heard the waters rushing through dark trunks. She saw the fog billowing against the light of the Dae-Mon.

"It's just ahead—"

She skidded to a halt. An enchantment seized her, like jaws wrapping around her neck, the most devastating enchantment she had ever felt. Like at the Stone Tree, it settled about her: *paralyzing, absolute, unbreakable.*

"*Stop,*" a voice ordered.

Losna stumbled to a halt. Ahraia felt the darkness descend around her as the Masai stepped from the forest with a smile spreading across her face.

Almost there . . . but not quite.

33

BOUND

"And here I thought your shadow cast you."

The Masai stood wreathed in her wolf's cloak, shaking her head. Her jet-black drain slipped from her sleeve into her hand, and though the Dae-Mon had risen, she wore no veil. They were in her realm—under her spell now. The deathly grip of the Masai's mind crushed tighter and tighter.

"You've surprised me, Shade Ahraia, in every way," the Masai said. She stalked forward, a curious frown drawn across her face. "You didn't manage to enchant the keress. You didn't kill the human . . . and yet somehow you manage all this?"

Ahraia gave no answer.

"You managed to escape Golan and Shalih too?"

"It was you who sent the ward?" Ahraia felt blood surge to her ears. She remembered blood pouring from Golan's mouth, and forced the image to the Masai, whose frown deepened.

"I should have known you were stronger than your Astra made you out to be. You're a wolf-binder, of course you're strong. And that makes you wolf-like in every way: stubborn and dangerous, just like your shadow."

Losna bared her teeth. The Masai tilted her head slightly, her ears twitching.

"You've escaped the Shad-Mon. Come back from the dead?" She shook her head in disbelief. "You've managed to break your shadow free and hide from me. And somehow, someway, you've managed to free yourself from the sprite-wood. No shade, not once since the hearts of the forest were first laid, has managed to unlock their shadow or break through the palisade."

Ahraia glared at her, wondering if somehow she could challenge the Masai's binding. She tried to form her own enchantment, but the Masai flicked it away, as a nitesse would brush away the slapping hand of a spriteling.

"You use the very forest to move as though it is woven into your blood," the Masai said. "Tell me, how do you do it?"

Ahraia grappled with the enchantment. It bore the weight of all the enchantments she had ever suffered, like the Stone tree, but without the barest hope of resisting. Her right hand rested on the black-feathered arrow, poised, but paralyzed. The bow in her left hand hung pointlessly.

The Masai cocked her head.

"And your bow? I hardly even noticed. How did you retrieve it?" she marveled as though she had been privy to Ahraia's thoughts. The Masai's ears batted and Ahraia's jaws were suddenly slack with permission to speak.

"Did one of my wards help you . . . your sister?" The Masai's eyes narrowed.

Ahraia didn't answer. Her teeth were unbared, but she struggled against the mind-numbing force of the Masai's will, trying desperately to move her hand to the arrow. Her bond to Losna was muted, but it was clear her shadow was panicked, trying to escape;. Losna's eyes quivered with fear and high-pitched whines slipped out as whimpers.

"If you aren't going to speak, then it's your shadow that suffers." The Masai dropped to a knee next to Losna. The drain flashed in the dim light, stopping just short of Losna's rib cage. Losna let out a strangled whine.

"Let her go," Ahraia said desperately. All defiance fled from her, and she dropped any pretense of being able to undo the Masai's enchantment.

"Let her go? No, no, no, my shade. Neither of you are going anywhere. You're the most dangerous kind of trouble. Different . . . on a plain entirely changed. You would lead sprites away from me, but not into your own darkness, instead to whatever madness you see fit. No, this is it. I want my answers and then I'll be done with you. Now tell me, how did you retrieve your bow? Did Kren help you?" *Did she betray me?*

Ahraia remembered seeing Kren beneath the hood and had the sudden urge to condemn her sister—but she couldn't. The Masai pressed the blade against Losna. Fear wrapped around Ahraia's mind and drove her nearly insane.

"No. *No!* I used an owl. Kren wouldn't help me. She wants me dead."

"An owl . . . like a shadow. And how did you break the chain? With an arrow?"

"No. With a pick. I don't know what it is. I took it from a human." An image of the tines clicking into the lock formed in her mind, passing to the Masai.

"Pure luck," the Masai whispered. Her eyes were glazed. "And the Shad-Mon? How did you escape them?"

Losna's whines suffocated Ahraia's ability to think.

Tell me! the Masai commanded, pressing the tip of the drain deeper into Losna's fur. Excruciating pain formed in the bond and blood trickled over the blade.

Stop. Stop, Ahraia thought desperately trying to break through the enchantment. She couldn't. "I used the trees . . ." she said, her gaze flickering upward to the forest. She sought any living thing to bind; the firs were too tall, hemlock too distant. *I used springs*, she conveyed. She saw a maple, standing beyond the first ring of trees. It was the only tree within a stone's throw that would possibly reach the Masai, but it would require the whole tree lean downward, an enchantment Ahraia wasn't sure that a team of sprites could manage.

"The trees?" the Masai asked. "How?"

"I bend them to my will," Ahraia said, binding the maple, knowing it was her last hope. "I fold them, like darkness. But I do it instantly, without the permanence or repetition of folding dark." She turned the whole upper trunk down on itself, the tree straining to reach the Masai. It creaked perilously, a quiet noise that went unnoticed against the roar of the river. The Masai was standing over a tangle of roots. Ahraia formed a second binding, a deeper binding, through to the roots and the fir they connected to.

The Masai moved the drain from the Losna's ribs to the tip of her ear.

"You got away from the Daemons using trees? Using springs? Like an imp?" She stopped, and actually laughed. It was a terrible noise, letting the air out of the woods.

"And here I thought you had some mastery over the world—some grace that I did not have. I was actually scared for a moment."

"Don't hurt her." *Please.* Ahraia begged, stalling for time. The roots weren't awake yet. The maple hadn't reached the Masai.

The Masai locked eyes with Ahraia, the smile still spread wide across her face. She pulled Losna's ear tight. Ahraia sensed the roots slowly rousing. She focused her binding, setting her will into the enchantment.

"Hurt her?" the Masai said. "Do you not understand? You're going to watch her die. And then you're going to die as well."

"Why?"

Without warning, the Masai sliced through the tip of Losna's ear.

Losna yelped in terror and pain. It shocked Ahraia, a violent pain that coursed through her, right to the end of her enchantment, to the roots of the trees. They roused.

"I rule the night, Ahraia. I'm not about to let a shade spin chaos out of darkness." She moved the drain above Losna, both hands on the handle. Losna's eyes widened with fear. Her breaths were ragged. Ahraia bared her teeth at the Masai.

"The night may be yours. But that shadow is mine," she said, making her bindings work at once.

The roots slithered out of the ground and around the Masai's legs like serpents out of water. They coiled about her ankles and knees, fixing her where she stood. The sinuous branches of the maple above then swung the rest of the way to the ground, twisting around the Masai's wrist even as she slashed downwards. The leaves shuddered, pulling the Masai's arm to a stop, the blade brushing Losna's fur.

The Masai was shaking from effort. Ahraia felt her mind reaching out to the tree, trying to pry it from Ahraia's will. The Masai's hand inched towards Losna, pressing into her fur. Losna whimpered. Ahraia felt blinding rage and pain. She refused to let go, refused to let her shadow be hurt any more.

Ahraia gritted her teeth as a second limb snaked down and wrapped around the Masai's neck. Her eyes went wide as she realized what Ahraia meant to do.

You can't—

Ahraia released the first spring, keeping the Masai's feet rooted to the ground. The branch ripped skyward. Wood tested against bone and muscle. The Masai gave a long, agonizing scream before her arm was ripped from her shoulder.

The resistance to the bonding frayed. Ahraia had full control of the maple. It slithered tighter around the Masai's neck, choking off her scream. She spit and foamed at the mouth, her eyes going wide and staring at Ahraia with true fear.

Ahraia didn't hesitate. She directed the second binding just as she had the first. The second limb wrenched upward with the full strength of the tree. The Masai's head tore from her body, the maple slinging it into the canopy above.

The enchantment holding Ahraia snapped. Losna struggled up, teeth bared.

"Are you all right?" Ahraia said, dashing to her shadow. She knelt and checked her ear, still feeling the pulse of pain through their bond.

I'm fine, Losna thought. *It was only the tip of my ear.*

The Masai's body remained standing where the roots held her—exactly as the keress had been—fixed, even in death.

Ahraia's mind was suddenly free, and she sensed sprites swelling through the forest.

"We're not out of this yet. Let's go," Ahraia said.

A dae-ward lurched to a halt. He looked at Ahraia, then at the standing body of the Masai. It took him a moment to understand what had taken place, and his yellow eyes spread wide with fear.

"She killed the Masai!" he shouted. The alarm rippled through sprites, spreading like a windless wave through the trees. Wards were streaming towards them. Ahraia leapt past the headless body of the Masai, with Losna right on her heel.

The river wasn't far. The roar of it was growing. Anger and vengeance spread behind her, and light spread before her. Ahraia looked for the toppled tree to cross the river but a glance told her it was nowhere near.

"We're going to have to swim," she called to Losna.

A hail of enchantments fell at her heels. They were running at a full sprint, dodging trees and branches as they dashed towards the river and the break in the darkness ahead. She saw churning water and great spears of sunlight. Fog unfurled over the cold water.

"Capture them!" A sprite called. Ahraia recognized Shalih's voice. *Get them!*

Ahraia ran the length of a mist-slickened log, lunging to the rocks at the water's edge. The river lay before her: swift and wide, unshielded from light. The woods overflowed with wards and the air reverberated with enchantment. Losna was running next to her in great loping strides. Ahraia didn't hesitate. She leapt to the last rock at the water's edge and plunged headfirst into the raging river.

34

THE HEART OF THE WOODS

Freezing water pressed inward, stealing Ahraia's breath and shocking all fear and reason from her mind as the river's current engulfed her. She surfaced and saw Losna, her golden eyes wide with fear, before she disappeared. Ahraia cascaded over in a boil of spitting water. The river sucked her downward, ripping her away from her shadow. Water swirled. The torrent roared. Their bond thrummed in panic. Ahraia came up and gasped, and then she was dragged back beneath.

I can't breathe, she thought.

Light swelled above. Bright, brilliant, tumbling white. A gasp of air. Then back beneath. Rushing water and roaring noise.

She came up disoriented and swept past a massive boulder. She kicked and scraped at it, her nails sliding over hard, water-smoothed stone. The river churned into a yawning hole, sucking her beneath again, this time pinning her, holding her in a merciless current.

She couldn't breathe. The noise of rushing water was all she knew. Her lungs burned. Her elbow hit something hard and then something sharp grabbed hold of her, biting her.

Panic rose, and she seized, trying to pull away in terror, imagining what kind of monster could live in such a place.

Losna's thoughts suddenly came through the panic.

It's me, her shadow thought. *I've got you.* Losna dragged her upward.

Together, they kicked and clawed for the bank. They broke through the current and the river's roar lessened. Ahraia's skin and lungs were burning. Her arms ached when she finally felt hard stones beneath her. She slipped, legs numb, feet numb, hands shaking and hardly hers. She stumbled out of the river, weighed down heavily by her cloak and boots. Losna surged from the water next to her, fur streaming with droplets.

The Dae-Mon was covered by fog so thick it was hardly more than the Bright Moon.

Ahraia rose, shivering and triumphant. Their bond reverberated between them. Losna shook herself and looked up at Ahraia.

We made it! Losna thought.

Ahraia turned back to the river, staring across the waters. It churned and swirled, screaming that it hadn't taken them. The sprites and dae-wards of Angolor stood along the banks, hooded and sunlit. She knew the anger that festered in them. She could feel it, even spanning the river.

Ahraia shook her cloak loose, the eaves-web dripping heavily. She was too angry to be cold or light-burned. Her skin was aflame, but she wasn't about to die from it.

The sprites jeered and shouted, all stooping to drink. Ahraia bared her teeth at them. Every one of them had killed their shadows. Every one of them had found it in their hearts to cut the best part from themselves.

Kren stood at the water's edge. Her eyes were the only things that showed beneath a makeshift veil, but Ahraia could sense her disbelief. A faint bonding formed, and Kren's conveyance came through sharp, filled with disgust.

You fool. You've killed yourself. You would have been the Masai. Though her words were clear, Ahraia sensed something tugging at her sister beneath the enchantment: *yearning.* A deep jealousy flowed through Kren as she watched Losna standing at Ahraia's side.

Flit deserved better. Ahraia shook her head, not bothering to convey her thoughts. Kren was the last among the sprites to stoop and drink, summoning the Shad-Mon, but she pulled her veil aside and drank deeply. When she stood, her eyes gleamed with hatred.

Unveiled and unafraid, Ahraia stooped and drank as well, meeting her sister's eye.

What are you doing? Losna asked. Ahraia smiled darkly.

"They think I'm afraid. But while they stand in the safety of their darkening, I'm the one with a shadow."

Losna smiled back. It faded though, with a distant roar, carrying through the woods.

Ahraia pulled an arrow from the clutch, fitting it to the bow. Without another glance, she flitted into the underbrush with Losna close at her heel. She closed her mind to all but her shadow and the woods.

"If we're going to survive, we need to get across these woods. Then we can make whatever darkness we see fit. But we're going to have to get to the other side."

What are we doing about the daemons? Losna worried.

"There are rules here," Ahraia said as she ran. The woods were dark, the fog so thick and the forest so deep that it was night within. Losna loped after her, eyes turning with the drifting fog, her fear carrying through the bond.

"First off, no drinking the water." Ahraia stopped at a narrow stream that cut a swift path through a moss-covered glade. She stooped and drank. Losna quivered with worry, but Ahraia smiled and then hurried off.

"Secondly, don't disturb anything." Mushrooms spilled from a fallen tree. She kicked them, spraying their stems and heads across the forest. The woods teemed with life. She pulled fox tails from their stems, yanked ferns from their roots and shook every tree she passed, her heart racing. She formed bindings, the whole forest moving and shuddering at her will.

Losna looked about worriedly, then Ahraia stopped, breathing hard.

"The third rule," she said, panting, "is stay quiet." She threw back her head and let out a primal yell. Losna hesitated. Then, feeling Ahraia's urge, she threw her head back and let out a howl. Though the fog was thick, muting even the daylight, it seemed to carry their voices. They grew, louder and longer and stronger, until they were in chorus, howling into the woods. When they were done, Losna's fear was lessened. The blood was pounding in Ahraia's head.

She laughed. The Shad-Mon's roar echoed back, but it lacked the bite it had carried before. Their howls still echoed about them. Her madness bled through the bond, and Losna laughed with her, the roar a distant thought.

What are we doing?

Ahraia kept running. The woods were laced with channels and creeks. Water flowed and dripped everywhere.

She stopped and looked at her shadow. Her lungs and legs burned. Her skin and eyes burned too. But most of all, her heart was burning. She was alive. And she had her shadow. She looked in Losna's eyes, having no trouble at conveying her thoughts with her words.

"The last rule is no one survives."

She stooped and drank again. Losna followed her lead, leaning over and lapping at the stream, eyes gleaming.

We're hunting it, Losna realized. *Drawing it in.*

Drawing them in, Ahraia replied, checking the tension in her bowstring. It was damp, but it would do.

Losna's eyes widened, but then sharpened.

Good. I like a good hunt. She threw back her head and let out another powerful howl. It raised the hairs on Ahraia's neck. She grinned, a fierce grin. The roar echoed back, closer now.

They ran, as only they could. The deeper they went, the more the air reverberated, an ominous pressure building. At each channel, they knelt down and drank. At each passing of the forest, they moved it. And each time they stopped, they shouted and filled the air with their voices.

The roars grew closer and closer, until they didn't answer.

Ahraia stopped running. Losna pulled up short.

An emptiness beyond her thoughts filled the air. An all-encompassing darkness settled in her heart. A fear descended about her without her permission.

"They're here," Ahraia said. Losna scanned the woods, her nose to the air.

Ahraia reached out with her mind. The nothingness spread, surrounding her, enveloping and embracing her. She ducked behind a tree, nervously looking up for claws above her. Losna watched behind her, sniffing at the air and growling. Ahraia dashed to the next tree, her bow at the ready.

Creak.

Her ears twitched. A bird called shrilly. She smelled damp cedar and tallow mushrooms.

Where are they? Losna thought.

"Keep your eyes behind me." Ahraia turned about. Then she reached out to the forest in a massive enchantment, not of a single branch or single tree, but instead a bond to everything, melding every branch and stem, root and leaf. She felt the tall trunks, awake and watching, low ferns untrampled, leaves hanging, unshaken.

She could feel the forest moving. Her nights spent bonding every tree and branch gave her a web of clarity. She felt the hands moving across trunks as though they were sticks. She felt the moss pressed downward by clawed feet large enough to pin a bear.

One tree was swaying softly. So softly it might not have moved at all. But the rest of the wood was still.

Too still. Ahraia's eyes narrowed—and then she saw it.

Gray skin. Claws like oversized talons. Shoulders too broad to be hidden by any tree, no matter how large the tree.

The Shad-Mon was wrapped about a fir, watching her with lifeless, black eyes, skin the same color as ash blended with the fog, claws, each as long as Losna, wrapped easily around the tree. Vicious teeth ran one over another in all directions.

There's the second one, Losna thought with hackles raised. Ahraia glanced back and saw the second daemon midway between the trees, creeping closer.

Losna growled, a harrowing growl.

The type of growl a shadow made.

Ahraia smiled.

She raised her bow, taking aim. "Here we go . . ."

EPILOGUE

Ahraia dropped to the ground, never breaking stride. Losna bound a half a pace behind her. The roars were fading, swallowed by the fog, but still she kept her bow in her hand, her last arrow at the ready.

We lost them, Losna thought.

Ahraia laughed. Getting away the second time had been far easier than when she was condemned. Losna's howls had driven the deamons mad, and Ahraia's arrows had found their mark. Her blood surged through her chest as she sprang over the moss-covered ground. With every step that she ran, she felt the horrors of her people fading behind her. The choking grip of fear loosened for the first time in her life, and she kept laughing.

What do we do now? Losna thought.

Let's start by getting out of these woods.

They moved easily, leaping over slick logs and along narrow embankments between motionless pools. The pools were growing more frequent, one crowding next to another, separated by thin strips of woods with trees growing upward anywhere they wouldn't drown.

They moved in silence, and Ahraia reached out with her mind, searching for the deamons. They were far behind her, but she stopped, sensing something else.

Losna sniffed at the air, and her hackles raised.

The fog shifted and Ahraia saw a figure on the far side of a pool. A sprite-like figure—hidden in the mist. It's ears twitched as it stooped to drink. A sharp sword hung at its side.

An alp, Losna thought.

The alp lowered his lips to the water.

"Stop," Ahraia said instinctively. "Don't touch the water."

The alp leapt up, startled by their silent appearance. He drew his sword in a swift motion, holding it between them. They stood across the pool from each other standing perfectly still. A ripple moved away from where his lips had just touched the pool, disrupting the reflection on the perfect surface.

What is an alp doing in the shadow woods? Losna thought.

Neither the alp nor Ahraia spoke, but then she realized with a jolt that she recognized him. She had seen him before. He was the same alp she had hunted in the broken darkening, the same one whose arrow she had stolen.

I know him.

His brow furrowed as though he heard her thoughts.

"That's my arrow," he said in the human tongue, pointing his sword.

Ahraia raised the bow, the arrow coming to the string. She tried to remember what the human girl had called him. "What are you doing here?" she asked across the pool, mirroring her words. Losna growled nervously.

The alp was frowning. Something like hatred crossed his face. "Hiding from the Cirice."

Ahraia cocked her head, unsure what he meant. "With who?"

"The Cirice. With the one they call Anasazi." His mouth curled into a snarl. He paused, as though he realized he shouldn't have spoken. "You're with them aren't you? You were there that night—in the woods of Holbrook—looking for me."

The golden-haired alp. Ahraia shook her head. "*Anasazi.*" The name felt foul in Ahraia's mouth. Then she thought how satisfying it would be to bind her with a tree as she had the Masai. "I'm not with—"

A distant roar reverberated through the woods, reminding her just where they were. The alp's ears twitched fearfully.

"We have to get away from here," Ahraia said, more to Losna than to him.

Just then there was movement behind the alp, and to Ahraia's surprise, two humans—a boy and a girl—stepped from the woods. When they saw her, they froze. She recognized both of them.

That's the human girl, Losna thought, *the one we saved on the plains. The night we killed Gavea.*

Ahraia couldn't believe her eyes. The fiery-haired girl who had made flame from words was next to the alp. And following her was the same boy whose brother Ahraia had butchered for her second task. They all stood staring at her in the semi-dark of the deep fog.

Before Ahraia could think, the girl spoke.

"You're the sprite who saved me," she said in disbelief.

Ahraia ignored her. "You'd be wise not to linger here any longer. The Shad-Mon are coming."

"The who?" the alp said, obviously not understanding. Another roar echoed through the forest, drawing closer. The humans and the alp huddled together, their eyes searching the woods. Terror clouded their faces.

"You need to get out of these woods," Ahraia said. "The daemons will be here soon enough." She began to move. She pushed past several low firs and Losna followed.

"Hey! Where are you going?" the fiery-haired girl said. To Ahraia's surprise, she began to follow on the other side of the water's edge.

"We're headed to the mountains," Ahraia said, firming her mind around the decision.

"Will you show us the way?" the girl asked. The alp sounded as though he wanted to protest, but another roar drifted through the woods, cutting off his words. The human girl leapt across a constriction in the pond, coming to rest just behind Losna. Ahraia stopped, looking at the ragged group. She eyed the boy, who looked the weakest of the bunch.

"Can you keep up with wolves?"

The fiery hair girl nodded. "We sure as hell can try."

A great splintering noise rose, and it sounded like a tree had crashed to the ground.

"Don't drink the water. Don't touch the trees. Don't make a sound. And whatever you do, don't go looking for the heart of the forest."

A roar echoed after her.

She broke into a run. She glanced behind to see the human girl was following, with the alp and the boy trailing after her.

What are we doing? Losna thought, unsure why their pack had suddenly grown.

A grin broke across Ahraia's face. "We're running. Just like we were made to. If they want to run with us, so be it."

AUTHOR'S NOTE

This story began as so little and turned into something entirely different—more complex and enlightening than I could have ever hoped. If you've read this far, all I can say is, thank you. If you want to help me gain traction as an author, writing a review or sharing this with friends and family is the greatest compliment.

I can't tell you how much I appreciate it.

To tell you about the story, I should first explain that I've been writing in Ahraia's world—the world that I hope will one day be better known as *The Realmless*—for almost fifteen years. I brushed against the end of her story some ten years back while writing my first book. That first book (which will someday soon see the light of day) was a total disaster, a twelve-hundred page epic too big and too complex for me to finish, a twelve year project that was a horrific muddle of junk. The writing wasn't good. The characters were confused. The story was a jumble of yarn tied in a thousand knots.

I threw it in the recycle bin. I wasn't ready to write an epic yet.

I was down. And I was tired. I couldn't imagine sitting down at the computer any more because it simply wasn't going anywhere, so I stepped away.

But it didn't last long. The story was still inside of me and clawing to get out. I still dreamed of the world of the Realmless. I still kept working on it in my head. And slowly it came back into focus.

And so I found the thread of Ahraia's story—wondering about her origins. It was never intended to be the first tale to escape but it just so happened that she was insistent and I was intrigued. And in truth, it was the story I needed to tell.

As you've likely guessed, Ahraia's story continues, but not as a sequel or series. She is being swept into something much greater. This is the first novel in the world of the Realmless and the next won't necessarily be recognizable in the characters it follows or the corner of the world it explores, but it will be related, in a sense. These stories are all part of a greater story, and one that I hope to tell in full. There will be small stories and large stories, some connected, and some which stand apart. But all them, I hope are an adventure—a chance to step away from our world, to visit somewhere different, with characters and places that you come to love as I have.

My Best,

Coleman Alexander — March 18th, 2018

Made in the USA
Lexington, KY
01 August 2018